Hermeneutics, Intertextuality and the Contemporary Meaning of Scripture

Edited by

Ross Cole and Paul Petersen

Hermeneutics, Intertextuality and the Contemporary Meaning of Scripture

Edited by

Ross Cole and Paul Petersen

Adelaide
2014

Text copyright © 2014 remains with the authors.

All rights reserved. Except for any fair dealing permitted under the Copyright Act, no part of this book may be reproduced by any means without prior permission. Inquiries should be made to the publisher.

National Library of Australia Cataloguing-in-Publication entry (pbk)

Title:	Hermeneutics : intertextuality and the contemporary meaning of scripture / edited by Henry Ross Cole and Paul Birch Petersen.
ISBN:	9781921817977 (pbk.)
Series:	Avondale press series ; 1
Notes:	Includes index.
Subjects:	Seventh-Day Adventists--Doctrines. Bible--Hermeneutics. Intertextuality in the Bible.
Dewey Number:	220.6

An imprint of the ATF Ltd
PO Box 504
Hindmarsh, SA 5007
ABN 90 116 359 963
www.atfpress.com

Avondale Academic Press
PO Box 19
Cooranbong
NSW 2265

Table of Contents

Introduction
    Paul Petersen vii

PART ONE
Intertextuality: Foundations and Principles 1

The Pros and Cons of Intertextuality
    H Ross Cole..3
The Bible as Text
    Ray CW Roennfeldt...17

PART TWO
The Relationship between the Testaments 27

New Testament Use of the Old Testament
    Jon Paulien 29
Did Matthew 'Twist' the Scriptures? A Case Study in the New Testament
    Use of the Old Testament
    Richard M Davidson...51
Paul and Moses in 2 Corinthians 3: Hermeneutics from the
Top Down 74
    David H Thiele..67

PART THREE
Bringing Our Text to the Text...79

Our Story as Text
    Ray CW Roennfeldt...81
The Use of Scripture in Cross Cultural Context
    Matupit Darius 89

My Reading? Your Reading? Author(ity) and Postmodern Hermeneutics
    Grenville JR Kent..95

PART FOUR
Issues in the Interpretation of Ellen G White...................................115

Learning from Ellen White's Perception and Use Of Scripture: Toward An Adventist Hermeneutic For The Twenty-First Century
    Arthur Patrick..117
Hermeneutics of Parable Interpretation in Ellen White Compared to Those of Archbishop Trench
    Robert K McIver..141
Lifestyle And Hermeneutics: A Hermeneutic for the Writings of Ellen White and Contemporary Adventist Lifestyle Issues
    Barry D Oliver...153
Ellen White's Use of Scripture
    Jon Paulien..171
The Influence of Ellen White Towards an Adventist Understanding of Inspiration
    Graeme S Bradford 197

PART FIVE
Other Studies 225

A Feast of Reason—The Legacy of William Miller on Seventh-day Adventist Hermeneutics
    Jeff Crocombe...227
Where Did Satan Come From?
    Andrew Skeggs...239
Historicism in the 21st Century
    Donna Worley..255
The Fatherhood of God
    David Tasker 275

Subject Index 293
Author Index 295
Scriptural Index 303

Introduction

Paul Petersen

More than 110 scholars, ministers, and administrators convened at Avondale College in Cooranbong, Australia, in the summer of 2003 for the first Bible Conference of its kind for a long time. They were there at the invitation of the South Pacific Division of the Seventh-day Adventist Church, and for many of the participants this was the first such conference ever. A word of gratitude is to be extended to the leadership of the Division, in particular Pastor Laurie Evans and Dr Barry Oliver, who had the vision and provided the funding for this and subsequent conferences.

The focus was on hermeneutics, on intertextual readings of the Bible, and on the relevance of the biblical texts for our personal existence and the mission of the Church today. Invitations to contribute went out widely, and the responses in regard to topics and areas of study varied greatly.

You now hold the published result of the conference in your hands. The volume contains many of the presentations and papers read at the conference. It has been long underway, and thanks goes to Pastor David Edgar, Dr Ross Cole, and Eliezer Gonzalez for the difficult task of working with the copy editing of the very different types of papers and articles received. Some articles are intended to reach an academic audience; others rather reflect the writers' experience with the Bible as the Word of God for service and for personal existence.

All of these papers, however, illustrate an attitude that permeated this conference as well as those that the South Pacific Division arranged in subsequent years, namely the joy of reading the Bible with an open mind within the framework of faith. Discussions were flowing freely in an atmosphere of courtesy and kindness and mutual trust and respect. The conference was a gathering for exploration of the Bible and scholarly interchange of observations, and for reflections on God's revelation to us through His Word.

As you read, I hope you will enjoy the reading as much as we enjoyed the fellowship around the Bible, and that you will appreciate the variety. Even more, I hope that the papers in this book will inspire you to study and reflect on the

Word of God and with an open-minded dialogue with other believers and students of the Word, as we as Christians and Adventists journey together.

Dr Paul B Petersen,
Field Secretary and Director
of Biblical Research in the South Pacific
Division of the Seventh-day Adventist Church,
2000–2009

PART ONE

Intertextuality: Foundations And Principles

The Pros and Cons of Intertextuality
H Ross Cole

Introduction

The Pros of Intertextuality

The last few decades have witnessed a growing scholarly recognition of the contributions that the application of contemporary literary perspectives and conventions can make to biblical studies.[1] In particular, there has been a growing awareness of the value of intertextual study. For many scholars, the emphasis on intertextuality comes as a breath of fresh air. It is as though source criticism had done a cut and paste job on the Bible, subordinating the authority of some parts to others, denying the possibility of effectively interrelating even adjacent passages of Scripture. Now we have the whole Bible back again:

> For at least 150 years we have been accustomed to denying and pointing out the fallacies of a greater and greater atomisation of the Biblical text.
> We have insisted that the present form of the text is the very word of God and have demanded that any interpretation with pretensions of validity take into account that present form.[2]

What a validation it is, then, to hear scholars of unquestioned stature make bold assertions like the following:

> It is my objective not to study parts of texts but to study texts as wholes ... By understanding biblical texts as structures or wholes, I am approaching them as systems with an internal logic ... To analyse the text into bits and pieces and to read it in parts is to destroy the

---

1. For a summary of the some of the ways that modern literary criticism has impacted Old Testament studies in particular, see Paul R. House, 'The Rise and Current Status of Literary Criticism of the Old Testament', in *Beyond Form Criticism: Essays in Old Testament Literary Criticism*, Sources for Biblical and Theological Study 26, edited by PR House (Winona Lake, IN: Eisenbrauns, 1992), 3–22.
2. John N Oswalt, 'Canonical Criticism: A Review from a Conservative Viewpoint', in *Journal of the Evangelical Theological Society* 30 (1987): 319.

system. It is to impose on the text an alien and an anachronistic set of literary conventions.³

Receiving back a whole Bible is one of the pros of the contemporary emphasis on intertextuality, but not the only one. This emphasis reinforces the importance of the contemporary application of Scripture, reminding us that no reader ever reads the text in a vacuum, but always comes to the text with his or her own baggage of questions and prejudices.⁴ It can contribute significantly to homiletics:

> The preacher is called on not merely to expound its 'meaning', but to enter into its rhetorical dynamics, feel its emotional power, and then to give of her own imaginative resources in letting that dynamism generate a sermon that will be a means of encounter with God through the text.⁵

However, along with the pros there are also significant cons.

The Cons of intertextuality

Contemporary literary approaches to the text have tended to overshadow the historical-critical methodology that has been the dominant modern mode of discourse in academic dialogue, and even sometimes rejecting it outright.⁶ Given the largely negative impact of historical-critical discourse on the acceptance of conservative positions, this trend would hardly seem to be a loss to some conservatives. On the other hand, 'historical criticism generally pursues the authentication of the non-fictional text . . . Literary criticism, in contrast, focuses on fiction'.⁷ If we are concerned that historical critics have tended to minimise the historicity of Scripture, nothing would seem to be gained by supporting a method that reclassifies it as fictional rather than as non-fictional, for 'the commitment to historical validation' is not 'simply a fundamentalist aberration that we happen to share,

---

3. Edgar W Conrad, 'The Bible and the Reader', in *Colloquium* 23/2 (1991): 52.
4. John Riches, 'A Response to Walter Sundberg', in *Renewing Biblical Interpretation*, edited by Craig Bartholomew *et al* (Carlisle, Cumbria: Paternoster, 2000; Grand Rapids, MI: Zondervan, 2000), 89.
5. Stephen I Wright, 'An Experiment in Biblical Criticism', in *Renewing Biblical Interpretation*, edited by Craig Bartholomew *et al* (Carlisle, Cumbria: Paternoster, 2000; Grand Rapids, MI: Zondervan, 2000), 261.
6. So Conrad, 'The Bible and the Reader', *op cit*, 49–53. On the threat posed by contemporary literary method to historical criticism, see RN Whybray, 'Today and Tomorrow in Biblical Studies II: The Old Testament', in *Expository Times* 100 (1989): 364–368; John Reumann, 'After Historical Criticism, What? Trends in Biblical Interpretation and Ecumenical, Interfaith Dialogues', in *Journal of Ecumenical Studies* 29 (1992): 55–86.
7. Ronald C Tobey, 'Critical Historical Methods for Intellectual History: Historical Criticism in *Horus Gets in Gear: A Beginner's Guide to Research in the History of Science* (accessed on www.horuspublications.com/guide/tcl.html, January 2, 2002).

interestingly enough, with higher critics. We take this position, as the critics do, because the Bible takes it.'[8] The conservative scholar must thus always remain engaged with the historical issues raised by the text. In other words, such scholars must remain engaged with the sort of issues that historical critics have raised, even if rejecting many of their conclusions.

Another con to the contemporary emphasis on intertextuality is that final authority is often seen as lying with the reader rather than with the author.[9] This approach raises a serious challenge to the conservative position that the biblical writers were inspired rather than their receptor communities.[10] It also has the potential to introduce a dangerous subjectivity into the interpretation of the text.

The main body of this essay is divided into three parts. The first part addresses the issue of historical criticism and the Bible. The second part addresses the issue of the Bible and history. The third part addresses the issue of the way that an undue emphasis on response can introduce a dangerous subjectivity into the interpretation of the text.

Historical Criticism and the Bible

It is a commonplace assertion that Christianity and Judaism are historical religions in a way that other religions are not. Other religions have a history, but the truth of their fundamental teaching does not stand or fall on the historicity of that history, *per se*. Buddhism's central assertions would remain just as true or false whether Buddha ever lived or not. Not so with Christianity, at least as conceived by most Christians through the ages. It is not enough that Jesus taught fine moral teachings. It is pivotal that he died and rose again. So also Judaism traditionally presupposes the historicity of the central salvation event of the exodus.

Past attempts to dehistoricise Christianity's content have not fared well. Gnosticism tried to define Christianity in terms of the timeless platonic realm of the ideal, but Catholic Christianity strongly resisted the encroachments of Gnosticism. The Protestant Reformation's move away from allegorical interpretation to the natural historical reading of the text has further underscored the importance of history to Christian thinking.

Historical criticism is often viewed as minimising the historicity of Scripture. It is therefore not surprising that conservative Christians have usually reacted against it. For the layman the very term 'criticism' is often loaded with negative connotations of destruction and scepticism. However, in an academic setting critical thinking is not about 'criticising' in the popular sense, but is about thinking

---

8. Oswalt, 'Canonical Criticism', *op cit*, 320, 321.
9. For example, Conrad, 'The Bible and the Reader', *op cit*, 49–51.
10. Oswalt, 'Canonical Criticism', *op cit*, 322.

with all one's mental faculties in full gear. Textual criticism is not about criticising the text. It is about determining the original text and is a discipline in which evangelical scholarship has had a special role to play.[11] Historical criticism defined as establishing the original history behind a passage would seem to be innocuous enough. But the situation is more complicated than we might suppose.

The systematic application of historical criticism to the Bible is an Enlightenment project. Historical criticism of the Bible has developed as a full-scale discipline with various sub-disciplines of its own. Source criticism seeks to identify the original written literary sources behind the text. Form criticism seeks to identify the oral backgrounds and *Sitz im Leben* (life situation) behind the text. Tradition criticism seeks to trace the development over time of the oral and written traditions underlying the text. Redaction criticism focuses on the editor's adaptation of his sources. However, while historical criticism as a discipline may be a product of the Enlightenment, it has earlier roots.

Constantine's transfer of his capital from Rome to Constantinople left a vacuum in civil authority that, in time, was filled by the Bishop of Rome. Subsequently, the medieval partnership between church and state was more like a war than a marriage, with each side struggling for the upper hand. Long-term consequences must not be confused with initial intentions. Certainly Constantine did not willingly hand over anything when he shifted the seat of the Empire eastwards. However, it suited the pretensions of later popes to claim that this is exactly what Constantine had in mind. The Donation of Constantine appeared centuries later purporting to be a statement by Constantine donating Rome to the Pope in thanks for healing from leprosy. It became a major plank in the defense of the ever-growing scope of papal civil power. However, not even the most ardent supporter of papal civil power today would advance the Donation of Constantine as evidence of Constantine's intentions. The reason is that in 1440 the Catholic Lorenzo de Valla decisively exposed the Donation of Constantine for what it was: a pious (impious?) fraud.

De Valla's skilful use of linguistic, legal, historical, and political arguments earned him the later accolade of being one of the founders of historical criticism.[12] Any of us reading de Valla's work today would admire his courage in taking the stand he did at the time he did. None of us would question the validity of his findings. There is no doubt that his research was a factor in preparing the way for the

---

11. Gerald Bray even lists the universal recognition of the quality of evangelical biblical interpretation in textual criticism as the first of its main strengths. 'Thanks to the careful and patient work of generations of scholars, we now have biblical texts which are as close to the "autographs" as we are likely to get. Evangelicals have played an important part in bringing this about, and they continue to cultivate linguistic and textual skills to a degree scarcely paralleled elsewhere.' Gerald Bray, *Biblical Interpretation: Past and Present* (Downers Grove, IL: InterVarsity, 1996), 561.
12. Edgar Krentz, *The Historical-Critical Method* (Philadelphia, PA: Fortress, 1975), 8.

Reformation. However, it is one thing to suggest that the Donation of Constantine was a pious fraud. It is quite another to suggest that the Book of Deuteronomy was not just found in the time of Josiah, but also first written then. It is also quite another thing to claim that the Book of Daniel was a pious fraud, a *vaticinium ex eventu*, or history parading as prophecy in the times of Antiochus Epiphanes IV.

Given our respect for de Valla's work, we need to ask whether the problem is with historical-critical methods as such, or with the particular way in which certain historical critics have applied them to the Bible. Arguably, Scripture should not be treated in the same way as other writings. However, would we accept that the scriptures of other religions should be exempted from any and all historical-critical investigation? If not, how would we propose that claims of Divine inspiration be objectively tested? Certainly we cannot expect every question and objection to be answered this side of eternity. However, we would expect Scripture as the inspired Word of God to stand up to tests that a pious fraud could not bear. If faith is not blind, but based on the weight of evidence, we will surely expect to find historical evidence favoring Scripture.

It is significant that when historical critics challenge the historicity of Scripture, conservatives often respond by using the criteria of the critics themselves against them. Conservatives have used the criterion of dissimilarity to good effect to defend traditional dating of biblical material.[13] Niels-Erik Andreasen uses critical methodologies to establish that the Old Testament teaching concerning the Sabbath does not develop over time but appears full blown in its final form from the outset.[14] Gerhard Hasel uses critical methodologies to establish the authenticity of the passages he examines from Isaiah 1 – 39 in his dissertation.[15] Some Australian evangelists, as has been common for example, within the Adventist

---

13. For example, in defence of Mosaic authorship, Gleason Archer effectively points to the dissimilarities between the cultural customs, language, and historical and geographical details found in Genesis and Exodus on the one hand, and those applicable to the settings proposed for the traditional sources of Wellhausen's documentary hypothesis on the other. See Gleason L Archer, Jr, *A Survey of Old Testament Introduction* (Chicago, IL: Moody, 1964), 101–107.
14. Niels-Erik Andreasen, *The Old Testament Sabbath: A Tradition-Historical Investigation*, SBLDS 7 (Missoula, MT: Society of Biblical Literature, 1972). Andreasen accepts the traditional Yahwist, Elohist, Deuteronomist, and Priestly sources of the documentary hypothesis for the sake of argument. However, the more it can be demonstrated that various biblical themes appear full-blown in their final theme in even the earliest of the supposed sources, the more fragile the whole documentary hypothesis becomes.
15. Gerhard F Hasel, *The Remnant: The History and Theology of the Remnant Idea from Genesis to Isaiah*, Andrews University Monograph Series, volume 5 (Berrien Springs, MI: Andrews University Press, 1972). Jerry Gladson asserts that 'Hasel's dissertation, in fact, is really a tradition critical study of the word "remnant"'. Jerry Gladson, 'Taming Historical Criticism: Adventist Biblical Scholarship in the land of the Giants', in *Spectrum* 18, No 4 (April 1988): 24, 25. Gladson not only sees the irony of classifying Adventism's foremost opponent of historical criticism as a practitioner of that criticism, he positively revels in it.

tradition, have long used archaeology and the findings of history to foster confidence in the reliability of Scripture.

The major problem with historical criticism has been the prevailing assumption that history is a closed continuum. God, if he exists at all, does not actively intervene in history. Any miracle or revelation must therefore be explained in purely naturalistic terms. On the other hand, conservatives have long proposed criteria by which prophecy and miracles can be evaluated.[16] What if such criteria were accepted, or at the very least the possibility of periodic divine intervention were conceded? Could such a purified form of historical criticism not only be harmless to the cause of conservative Christianity, but actually be a positive tool in its defense? Or is talk of a purified form of historical criticism oxymoronic? Can one be no more slightly historical critical than be slightly pregnant?

The appropriateness or otherwise of the title 'historical critical method' for what is being described here is a matter of debate, for example, in Seventh-day Adventist scholarship.[17] The discussion may soon be moot. Changes in the use of language are not subject to individually preferred canons of reasoning. One of the problems with creeds is that language changes meaning. Many conservative evangelicals have long believed that a modified form of historical criticism is not only possible; it is also necessary.[18] Liberals are beginning to abandon historical

---

16. For example Bernard Ramm, *Protestant Christian Evidences: A Textbook of the Evidences of the Truthfulness of the Christian Faith for Conservative Protestants* (Chicago, IL: Moody, 1953); Daniel P Fuller, 'The Resurrection of Jesus and the Historical Method', in *Journal of Bible and Religion* 34 (1966): 18–24.
17. It has been argued that there was some formal denominational acceptance of the validity of certain historical-critical methodologies in the early 1980s. See Alden Thompson, 'Theological Consultation II', in *Spectrum* 12, no. 2 (December 1981): 40–52. On the other hand, any compromise with such methodologies is apparently rejected in the General Conference, 'Methods of Bible Study Committee Report', in *1986 Annual Council Booklet*, 7–23. That the issue is far from settled in everyone's minds has been recently demonstrated by Bert Haloviak, 'The Perennial Quest for the Word of Life: Seventh-day Adventists and the Synoptic Problem', in *Spectrum* 30, No. 4 (Autumn 2002): 5–10. Cf Robert K McIver, 'The Historical-Critical Method: The Adventist Debate', in *Ministry* 69, No. 3 (March 1996): 14–17.
18. As far back as 1895, the undisputedly conservative James Denney rejects 'a criticism which denies the supernatural on principle, and refuses to recognise a unique work of God as in process along this line'. James Denney, *Studies in Theology: Lectures Delivered in Chicago Theological Seminary by the Rev. James Denney, D. D.* (NP: Hodder & Stoughton, 1895; reprint, Grand Rapids, MI: Baker, 1976), 212. However, he immediately adds, 'within these limits criticism has its own work to do', *ibid*. George Eldon Ladd speaks of 'the necessity of historical criticism' and 'the basic validity of the prevailing scientific method', while insisting on 'its limitations at the point of redemptive history where God has entered history in self-revelation and redemption'. George Eldon Ladd, *The New Testament and Criticism* (Grand Rapids, MI: Eerdmans, 1967), 181, 191. 'We have argued that since revelation has occurred in historical events, the student of the Bible must employ historical criticism to understand these events in terms of their historical setting'. *ibid*, 189. 'To be non-critical means simply to ignore altogether the historical dimension

criticism for alternate literary methods and evangelicals often still want to engage in something they call by that name. Something called historical criticism may therefore become the domain of conservatives sooner than we would think, whether we like it or not.[19] What is critical is not the name for what we are proposing, but its practice. It is essential for conservatives to remain engaged with the historical issues the text present, and to seek to establish the history behind the text as well as within it. The reason is that history remains an essential category for Christian thinking. However, the relationship between the text and its underlying history is not always as straightforward as it might seem.

The Bible and History

That Scripture itself takes the category of history seriously is beyond dispute. We have already noted that Christianity with its emphasis on the death and resurrection of Christ and Judaism with its emphasis on the exodus are uniquely historical religions. Jesus falls out of focus if his historical context is ignored.[20] If Christ has

---

of the Bible and to view it as a magical book', *ibid*, 38. Richard Coleman states, 'It is now only a common misconception that liberals accept the [historical-critical] method and its conclusions without reservations and that evangelicals do not recognise the validity of critical analysis. Even the hardened sceptic has come to depend upon the dictionaries, atlases, grammars, critical texts of the Old and New Testaments, and general introductions, all of which are products of historical criticism.' Richard J Coleman, *Issues of Theological Conflict: Evangelicals and Liberals* (Grand Rapids, MI: Eerdmans, 1972), 144. Duane Garrett is the author of a major work opposing Wellhausen's documentary hypothesis of the writing of the Pentateuch, entitled *Rethinking Genesis: The Sources and Authorship of the First Book of the Pentateuch* (Grand Rapids, MI: Baker, 1991). He states, 'Historical criticism is a neutral term. That is, it does not imply that the document under scrutiny is either true or false. . . . Historical criticism is necessary and indeed universally practiced.' Duane A Garrett, 'Historical Criticism of the Old Testament', in *Foundations for Biblical Interpretation: A Complete Library of Tools and Resources*, edited by DS Dockery (Nashville, TN: Broadman & Holman, 1994), 187. Note also the recent comments of Grant R Osbourne, 'Historical Criticism and the Evangelical', in *Journal of the Evangelical Theological Society* 42 (1999): 193–210.

19. It is easy to dismiss Gladson's identification above of Hasel as a practitioner of historical criticism as an example of internal denominational politics. It is even easier to dismiss it since Gladson is no longer an Adventist. However, it is more difficult to dismiss the statement that Edgar Conrad made a couple of years ago to my Pacific Adventist University colleague, David Thiele. Conrad is an Old Testament scholar at the University of Queensland who identifies himself with the 'new literary criticism'. He was the external examiner for David Thiele's unpublished 1998 Avondale College Master of Theology thesis, 'The Identity of the "I" in the "Confessions" of Jeremiah'. David Thiele's conclusions on Jeremiah are no more radical than Hasel's on Isaiah. However, his research is just as historically oriented. Conrad stated to Thiele that the major problem with the thesis was that it was too conservative, that is, it is historical-critical in approach when historical criticism is now passé.

20. Cyril E Blackman, 'Is History Irrelevant for the Christian Kerygma', in *Interpretation* 21 (1967): 435–446.

not been raised from the dead, we are still dead in our sins. We are left with hope only in this life and Christian self-sacrifice and struggle are in vain (1 Cor 15:13-19, 29-32). The Biblical stress on history is the natural corollary of its strong emphasis on the theme of the covenant. An important component of Ancient Near Eastern treaties and Biblical covenants is the inclusion of an historical prologue, outlining all that the superior partner in the agreement had done for the inferior. When covenants are made and renewed, the historical prologue often takes pride of place, and when they are broken, the recital of the history is often used to underscore the heinous nature of the rebellion. Loyalty and obedience are simply the only appropriate responses to the display of such grace. Blessings and curses are also a frequent feature of Ancient Near Eastern treaties and Biblical covenants. These blessings and curses are first of all fulfilled in the context of history.[21]

History will clearly remain an essential category of thinking for the Christian who wants to take the Bible's own internal perspectives seriously. However, historical thinking is not the only type of thinking that the Bible countenances; nor is the relationship between the text, and the history underlying it, always as straightforward as it seems. It is the tension created by this paradox that makes it important for conservative Christians exegete to read with eyes that are sensitive to the role of history in Scripture and to ally themselves in some ways more closely with the historical critics of the past than with some of the literary critics of the present. The crucial issue is to discern when historicity is fundamental to a biblical faith claim and when it is not.

Biblical historiography does not always work in ways that we would anticipate. The past is not recounted in full nor is it repeated for its own sake. It is told selectively in order that we might believe (John 20:31; 21:25). However, sometimes it is almost as though the past is reconstructed for one reason or another. At the beginning of his Gospel, Matthew goes to great lengths to stress that there were fourteen generations from Abraham to David, fourteen from David to the Babylonian Captivity, and fourteen from the Babylonian Captivity to the birth of Jesus (Matt 1:1-17). History is being schematised here and the point is clear. It took fourteen generations for the Davidic king to appear, then fourteen generations for the Davidic king to be taken off the throne. Now that another fourteen generations had gone by, it was time for the Davidic kingship to be restored in the Christ. However, the 'artificiality of the arrangement is indicated by the fact that in the second series the writer omits the names of three kings between Joram and Uzziah; viz. Ahaziah, Joash, and Axaziah, descendants of the infamous Athalia who attempted to destroy the Davidic Royal Line (2 Kgs 11)'.[22] There are thirteen generations in the

---

21. The classic work on parallels between Ancient Near Eastern Treaties and biblical covenants is Meredith G Kline, *The Treaty of the Great King* (Grand Rapids, MI: Eerdmans, 1963).
22. David Hill, *The Gospel of Matthew*, softback edition, New Century Bible Commentary (Grand

second and third series, but 'Matthew's observation here is statistical rather than theological.'[23] Attempts to rectify this situation by double counting of names between series[24] only serve to illustrate how much the facts are being made to fit the point.

The problem is that Matthew skips a number of generations to keep the number at fourteen per division. Is his argument fraudulent? Hardly. His Jewish readers had access to the same Scriptures Matthew. He is making a statement rather than trying to prove a point. But what a circuitous route to follow! Matthew's logic here is quite different to any that I would use myself. But that is the point. If the Bible writers do things with history in ways that I find hard to understand, I should be wary of facile statements as to how they work. We need to read with eyes that are discerning of the facts, but deeply critical of our own assumptions about how things should and do work.

Two quite different statements of the Ten Commandments occur in Exodus 20 and Deuteronomy 5. One of the major differences is in the reason given for Sabbath-keeping. Another is in the specifications of what is not to be coveted at the end of each list. It is interesting to see how different interpreters emphasise one passage or the other for different reasons. For example, Adventists generally cite Exodus while non-sabbatarians generally cite Deuteronomy. The reason is that Adventists want to emphasise the universal dimensions of the Sabbath, something that is easy to do when the reason for Sabbath-keeping is tied to creation itself, as in Exodus 20:11. On the other hand, non-sabbatarians generally want to portray the Sabbath as simply being for Jews, so they emphasise the deliverance from Egypt as the reason for keeping it, as in Deuteronomy 5:15. However, there is no doubt that Exodus 20 has the more universalistic ring!

At the end of the day the differences can be readily explained. In Exodus 20 we have something akin to the original statement of the Ten Commandments on Mount Sinai, whereas in Deuteronomy 5 we have an editorialised, summarised, then expanded account of the same, specifically tailored to fit the context of Moses' sermon in Deuteronomy.[25] We can reconcile the two accounts. However, in

---

Rapids, MI: Eerdmans, 1981; London: Marshall, Morgan, & Scott, 1981), 76.
23. RT France, *The Gospel According to Matthew: An Introduction and Commentary* (Leicester: Inter-Varsity, 1985; Grand Rapids, MI: Eerdmans, 1985), 75.
24. For example, Barclay M. Newman, 'Matthew 1:1–18: Some Comments and a Suggested Restructuring,' *Bible Translator* 2 (1976): 209–212.
25. It has long been noted that the philanthropic motive assigned for sabbath-keeping in Deuteronomy 5:15 is in harmony with passages such as Deuteronomy 12:18; 14:26; 16:11. The recollection of servitude as a motive for showing kindness to others is reflected in a similar way in Deuteronomy 15:15; 16:12; 24:18–22, with remembrance of deliverance being specifically mentioned in Deuteronomy 15:15; 24:18. SR Driver, *A Critical and Exegetical Commentary on Deuteronomy*, International Critical Commentary, third edition (Edinburgh: T&T Clark, 1902), 85. In Exodus 20:17, the prohibition against coveting of the neighbour's house precedes that prohibition against coveting the neighbour's wife (Exod 20:17). In Deuteronomy 5:21, the order

the process we find evidence of direct quotations from God's own mouth being updated to fit a changing later situation. Nothing could demonstrate more clearly the need to read the history reported in Scripture in terms of the historical context of a writer, as well as in terms of the original context of the events themselves.

The difficulty in distinguishing between original statement and commentary particularly comes to the fore when we look at the parallel reports of Jesus' ministry contained in the synoptic gospels. Did Jairus's daughter die before the woman who had bled for twelve years touched Jesus (Matt 9:18), or afterwards (Mark 5:22, 23, 35; Luke 8:40–42, 49)? Well did Ellen White comment that not everything is in perfect chronological order in the gospel accounts.[26] Given the similarities of the synoptic accounts, it is hard to believe that such differences are coincidental. We would do well to study the differences in their context, and to attempt to understand the reasons for them.[27]

Adventist scholar John Brunt has suggested that a modified form of historical criticism be adopted. He argues from the three accounts of Jesus' parable of the wicked tenants of the vineyard that no writer was creating material out of a vacuum. However, he also argues that there was a discernable process of modification going on to meet the needs of each of the writer's communities.[28] Whether or not

---

is reversed. In Exodus 'house' is probably used metaphorically for 'household,' with the rest of the commandment listing what the household consists of. In Deuteronomy the word 'house' probably simply denotes a building. ADH Mayes, *Deuteronomy*, New Century Bible Commentary (Grand Rapids, MI: Eerdmans, 1979; London: Marshall, Morgan & Scott, 1979), 171. The literal rather than the metaphoric meaning would assume special importance on the border of the Promised Land after a long period of wandering in the wilderness. The shift from nomadic to settled conditions would also explain the adding of the neighbour's land to the list of items not to be coveted.

26. Ellen G White, *Selected Messages* (Washington, DC: Review and Herald, 1958), 1:20.
27. Matthew's reports of Jesus' teaching tend to be more expansive than Mark's. His narrative of actions tends to be more contracted. Matthew accordingly appears to have concluded that the messengers coming to Jairus is extraneous to his message. Mark and Luke's accounts would therefore be the more historically accurate in the technical sense. See DA Carson, *Expositor's Bible Commentary*, edited by FE Gabelein (Grand Rapids, MI: Zondervan, 1984), 8:230.
28. John C Brunt, 'A Parable of Jesus as a Clue to Biblical Interpretation', in *Spectrum* 20 (December 1982): 35–43. Compare how Robert Stein elaborates on the value of distinguishing whenever possible between the *ipsissima verba* (very words) of Jesus and the divine word of the evangelist, as if doing so enables us to hear the text in stereo:

In trying to discover the present-day significance of the text (which is, after all, the ultimate goal of interpretation), how much better off are we if we are able to arrive at both the meaning in the original *Sitz im Leben* as well as that of the Evangelists! . . . If we are successful, we then possess both the original message and its divinely inspired interpretation, which is in turn a divine message as well. Robert H. Stein, *The Synoptic Problem: An Introduction* (Leicester: Inter-Varsity, 1988), 157.

For a sustained discussion on the value of making such distinctions from an Adventist perspective, see George E Rice, *Luke, a Plagiarist?* (Mountain View, CA: Pacific, 1983).

we like Brunt's use of the appellation 'historical criticism' to define what he was doing, we can only benefit from a sensitivity to such differences.

How the Loss of the Historical Dimension Can Introduce a Dangerous Subjectivity into the Reading of the Text

In reader-response approaches to the text, authority ultimately lies with the reader rather than with the author.[29] Literary criticism offers a timely reminder that nobody approaches the text free of bias or questions. Anyone who has ministered in an intercultural context over an extended period understands how much individual cultural context can impact interpretation. However, for anyone who would jettison historical criticism in favor of literary criticism, the question naturally arises, 'Can the biblical text mean anything a reader wishes it to mean? Is meaning indeterminate?'[30] Edgar Conrad answers, 'No'. and turns the implicit critique back on the questioner:

> The tendency has been for readers of the Bible . . . to approach the Bible as if it were familiar, a text to be easily domesticated.
> This is easy to see in fundamentalist readings of the Bible. The Bible is clothed in twentieth century garb. It is read in such a way that creation becomes science and prophecy headline news. Fundamentalist readers of the Bible construct the Bible in their reading so that the strange and alien character of the Bible becomes comfortably familiar. It ceases to be foreign and, therefore, ceases to communicate from its origins in the remote past. It ceases to be 'other'.
> What is so difficult for many historical-critical readers of the Bible to recognise is that the reading strategies they bring to the Bible have the same taming effect. Historical-critical reading strategies literally re-shape [sic] the text in the reading process. The Pentateuch is not read as a single piece of literature bus as the Yahwist, 'Elohist, Deuteronomic and Priestly documents. Isaiah is not read as a book but as three books, which require even finer adjustments in the construction. In short, what historical-critics [sic] understand as reconstruction is, from the point of view of reader response analysis, construction. This construction also clothes the text in modern garb so that it ceases to display the alien dress of the 'other' . . . Extinguishing the perceived problems destroys the

---

29. So Conrad, 'The Bible and the Reader', *op cit,* 49–51.
30. *Ibid,* 51.

text as 'other'. When reading strategies recreate the text to conform to contemporary reading conventions, the text ceases to be alien.[31]

It is true that the historical critic can end up taming the text too readily. However, the solution lies not in the abandonment of an historical emphasis, but in the marriage of an historical emphasis to a literary approach. A dialogical approach to the text offers the best protection against an unlimited subjectivity.

It is true that it is the present text that holds authority over us, but it would be dangerous . . . to abandon the attempt to understand the text's meaning in its first historical setting. Between them, literary and historical contexts provide the channel for us to determine the meaning of any passage for our lives. To destroy one bank of any channel is to move from the river to the swamp.[32]

An extreme reader-response approach to the text can be as subjective as any other. In responding to Conrad, Majella Franzmann decries the danger of denying the initial text's power over the contemporary reader.[33] There is now the possibility,

> of rejecting/resisting what might be perceived as unacceptable introduction of ideologies. One is free, for example, to reject chauvinist or anti-Semitic tendencies or interpretive dependence upon the various mythological world-views [sic]. This has far-reaching political and theological implications, especially for believers within the mainstream Christian traditions.
>
> For the latter, a whole new definition of the word of God, or what it means to experience God in the reading of Scripture, have [sic] become necessary. Even in the rejection of the Scriptural text as perceived by the reader, the revelation of God may be experienced.[34]

Teresa J Hornsby provides an example of the sort of interpretation that Franzmann fears.[35] For conservative expositors of the Book of Hosea, the story of the

---

31. *Ibid*, 51, 52.
32. Oswalt, 'Canonical Criticism', *op cit*, 322. See also Thorsten Moritz, 'Critical but Real: Reflecting on NT Wright's *Tools for the Task*', in *Renewing Biblical Interpretation*, edited by Craig Bartholomew *et al* (Carlisle, Cumbria: Paternoster, 2000; Grand Rapids, MI: Zondervan, 2000), 172–197
33. Majella Franzmann, 'Response to Edgar W Conrad, The Bible and the Reader', in *Colloquium* 23 (1991): 57.
34. *Ibid*.
35. Teresa J Hornsby, '"Israel has become a worthless thing": Re-Reading Gomer in Hosea 1–3', in *Journal for the Study of the Old Testament* 82 (1999): 115–128.

prophet's response to his wayward wife provides a beautiful picture of what God himself suffers when his own people stray. It is surprising, then, to discover that Hornsby sees no marriage metaphor here, but only a picture of God as the 'jealous client of a prostitute who desires to possess an autonomous, strong woman'.[36] Yahweh is portrayed as a villain for using foreigners to bring the covenant curses on suffering autonomous Israel who finds ways to fight back.[37] Franzmann is correct. For this method, it is not only in 'the rejection of the Scriptural text as perceived by the reader' that 'the revelation of God may be experienced'.[38] It is even in the rejection of the revelation of God that God is allegedly seen. It is this sort of irrationality that leads Eric Osborn to denounce much of literary criticism as an enterprise beyond logic.[39] It is also such subjectivity that CS Lewis has in mind when he speaks of the danger of seeing 'only the reflection of our own silly faces' in allegorical reading.[40]

Conclusion

The contemporary emphasis on intertextual study opens up many new opportunities. We have a whole Bible back again that we can study in the broadest of literary contexts. However, we should not embrace the new trend as an unmitigated blessing. It is associated with a declining emphasis on the historical setting of Scripture, despite the Bible's own emphasis on the importance of history. An awareness of historical background affords some protection from the dangers of the extreme subjectivity that has enmeshed some practitioners of reader-response methods. While affirming a modified form of historical criticism, Clark Pinnock rejects 'the kind of negative criticism that . . . consists of theories that collide with the text and its intentions and discredit the force of its assertions.'[41] Whatever we call the approaches we use, this is a helpful guiding maxim. Our approaches need to be broad enough to accept a variety of methods that respect the text, but narrow enough to reject those that go against the grain of the text itself. It is the Word of God itself that must ultimately shape us rather than the latest winds of change, however strong their promise of a successful journey may seem to be.

---

36. *Ibid*, 124.
37. *Ibid*, 127, 128.
38. Franzmann, 'Response to Edgar W Conrad', *op cit,* 58.
39. Eric Osborn, 'Literature, History and Logic in the Formation of the Christian Bible', *Australian Biblical Review* 41 (1993): 49–63.
40. CS Lewis, *Reflections on the Psalms* (London: Fount, reprint 1977), 12.
41. Clark H Pinnock, *The Scripture Principle*, Regent College Bookstore Reprints (Vancouver: Regent College, reprint 1993), 145.

The Bible as Text
Ray CW Roennfeldt

Introduction

If nothing else, postmodernism has reminded us of the influence that our own experience has on how we interpret Scripture. We bring as our 'text' to the text, as it were. But if all of us bring our own 'texts' to the text of Scripture, how will we interpret it in a consistent, meaningful, and nourishing fashion? Such is the disparity among Bible-believing Christians regarding the 'plain meaning' of Scripture that some have given up the idea that Scripture is to be interpreted. Rather, they say it should be merely read or listened to, whereby the biblical worldview will automatically permeate the hearer.[1]

Several important factors necessitate the interpretation of Scripture. One of these is the fact that Christians of every ilk claim biblical support for their positions, no matter how unnatural. Although it may only be a very selective support, Mormons find their doctrine of baptism for the dead in the Bible, Jehovah's Witnesses base their Arianism in Scripture, charismatics offer biblical texts as the basis of their doctrine of health and wealth, and 'Bible Belt' snake handlers justify their practice by a clear word from the Scriptures.[2]

The other major factor is the nature of the Bible itself. In fact, the beliefs we hold in regard to what the Bible is, how it was written, and the manner of its transmission have an enormous impact on the way in which we will read it, interpret it, and apply it in our lives.

The Nature of Scripture: A Vital Key to Understanding

At the foundational level, conservative Christians attribute far greater authority and value to the Scriptures than they do to any other book. It is seen as God's

---

1. This option is mentioned by Gordon D Fee and Douglas Stuart, *How to Read the Bible for All Its Worth* (Grand Rapids, MI: Zondervan, 2003), 21. In the same place, Fee and Stuart argue that this is a 'false option'. 'The antidote to *bad* interpretation is not *no* interpretation, but *good* interpretation based on common-sense guidelines.'
2. These examples are mentioned in *ibid*, 20.

book, God's Word to humankind 'in every age and in every culture'[3] Thus, Christians do not just read the Bible. They listen to its words in order to obey.

However, while Scripture comes as God's Word to us, it does not appear in the form of a list of divine legislative decrees or propositions. Rather, its shape is very obviously human. It is characterised by human language and employs human modes of thought and expression. Differences of literary ability and style in its writers are clearly evident. Yet, in spite of the fact that the Bible does not 'answer to the great ideas of God'. God is satisfied that 'the utterances of the man are the word of God'[4]

Christians have stressed either the humanity or the divinity of the Bible. Focusing on its humanity involves one primarily in an historical and descriptive task. The meaning of Scripture, in this view, is to be found in what the words originally meant to the writer and his or her readers. On the other hand, an over-emphasis on the divinity of the Bible has resulted in its being read in an extremely literalistic fashion. The words of the Bible are considered to be God's words untainted by human culture.[5] This, of course raises the issue of the interaction of God with culture; both that of the writers of the Bible as well as our own.

God and Culture

At a cursory glance, the biblical writings do appear to make claims that put them above the relativities of human culture. For instance, Scripture points to divine revelation as its origin (2 Tim 3:16; 2 Pet 1:21). Its message transcends place and time. Jesus Christ is seen as the single source for salvation (Acts 4:12). The differences in the human situation cannotinvalidate the message of the gospel for 'the word of the Lord stands forever' (1 Pet 1:25). The Scriptures are *the* 'norm of truth by which all human thought is tested (Heb 4:12–13; John 10:35)'.[6]

Such a one-sided view of the Bible places it in a unique position from which it operates as 'the source for a metahistorical and metacultural framework within which one can understand and communicate across historical eras and cultures'.[7] It seems to me that such a position is open to the twin dangers of either ignor-

---

3. *Ibid*, 21.
4. Ellen White expresses these concepts well in *Selected Messages* (Washington, DC: Review & Herald, 1958), 1:15–23.
5. The literalistic view has been vigorously attacked by John Shelby Spong, *Rescuing the Bible from Fundamentalism: A Bishop Rethinks the Meaning of Scripture* (San Francisco, CA: HarperCollins, 1991), and by Ian Plimer, *Telling Lies for God* (Milsons Point, NSW: Random House, 1994). Plimer's work, written from a humanistic standpoint contains a particularly strong polemic against a literalistic reading of the Genesis creation and flood narratives.
6. William J Larkin, Jr, *Culture and Biblical Hermeneutics: Interpreting and Applying the Authoritative Word in a Relativistic Age* (Grand Rapids, MI: Baker, 1988), 192.
7. *Ibid*.

ing the fact that the biblical books were written and conditioned by the culture pertaining at the time of writing as well as by the personality, etc. of the various culturally conditioned writers, or that of assuming that the culture of the Bible is 'Christian' culture.

Such presuppositions tend to overlook or rationalise away the differences between the Old and New Testaments as well as the differences between the various books within each of the Testaments. The ambiguities of Scripture are well illustrated by a selection of the 'strange' laws that formed part of the divine code at least from the time of the Exodus onwards. The death penalty was prescribed for cursing one's parents (Exod 21:17); fair and equal treatment was required for the first wife when a second was taken (Exod 21:10); Israelites were admonished against boiling a baby goat in its mother's milk (Exod 34:26); and Ammonites and Moabites were not allowed to join the congregation of Israel, even to the tenth generation (Deut 23:3).[8]

Now, it is important to point out that although we may consider such commands as 'strange', Moses 'found none of them strange or even burdensome'.[9] On the contrary, he pointed out the privileges offered to Israel in divine code: 'What other nation is so great as to have such righteous decrees and laws as this body of laws I am setting before you today' (Deut 4:8 NIV). The hermeneutical and logical difficulties of applying such laws to twenty-first century society are immense.[10]

The Old Testament laws of levirate marriage illustrate quite dramatically the difficulties we have in bracketing out the strangeness of Scripture. How are we to interpret the 'grimy' story of Genesis 38? Aren't we more than a little sympathetic with Onan who refused to fulfill his obligations to his sister-in-law? Aren't we somewhat scandalised by the statement that 'What he did was wicked in the LORD'S sight, so he put him to death ... '? Was Judah's conduct less reprehensible in the sight of God than that of his sons, Er and Onan? So it seems, for Judah escapes the punishment of God for his 'one night (day?) stand' with his daughter-in-law, whom he mistakes for a 'shrine prostitute' (Gen 38:21).

There is no easy explanation for some of the most obviously culturally conditioned passages of Scripture. Perhaps the best solution is that of John Calvin who maintained that God 'accommodates' himself to the human situation by adjusting to human 'ignorance' when he 'prattles to us in Scripture in a rough

---

8. These examples are derived from Alden Thompson, *Who's Afraid of the Old Testament God* (Grand Rapids, MI: Zondervan, 1989), 71–73.
9. Ibid, 73.
10. A rather tongue-in-cheek attempt is found in AJ Jacobs, *The Year of Living Biblically: One Man's Humble Quest to Follow the Bible as Literally as Possible* (New York, NY: Simon & Schuster, 2007).

and popular style'[11] and in 'mean and lowly words'.[12] Alden Thompson similarly concludes that,

> ... divine laws are no more enduring than that human situation that makes them necessary. The beauty of the divine condescension is precisely that God recognised the human condition and moulded his revelation accordingly. Different people in different culture need to have great enduring principles of divine government applied in different ways.[13]

The only other solution is to selectively apply some of the passages of the Bible to the contemporary situation, while ignoring the force of others. The result is a rather opportunistic primitivism and a jaundiced rejection of almost anything pertaining to modernity.

To take such a stance pits Christ against culture. As Richard Niebuhr aptly points out, the results are a radical disjunction between reason and revelation that stresses the transcendence of God over his immanence in the world through his Spirit and his community, the church.[14]

The Problem of Subjectivity

Conservative Christians are very nervous about acknowledging that the Bible is, in any way, culturally conditioned. After all, where will it stop? Are there any absolutes left if God expresses himself in the context of human culture and society?[15] What can we really know about God and the world? If the biblical writers used the thought forms and world view of their own day in which to express the divine story, how are we to separate their presuppositions from the truth?

---

11. John Calvin, *Calvin's Commentaries* (Edinburgh: Oliver and Boyd, ca. 1960), on John 3:2.
12. John Calvin, *Institutes of the Christian Religion*, Library of Christian Classics, volumes 20–21, edited by JT McNeill, translated by FL Battles (Philadelphia, PA: Westminster, 1960), 1.8.1. Calvin used his idea of accommodation to explain such biblical features as anthropomorphic references to God, metaphorical references of various kinds, apparent errors in quotations and lists, etc. See also Dirk W Jellema, 'God's "baby-talk": Calvin and the "Errors" of the Bible', in *Reformed Journal* (April 1980): 26.
13. Thompson, *Who's Afraid?*, 79. This same idea is extended (with New Testament examples) in Thompson's *Inspiration: Hard Questions, Honest Answers* (Hagerstown, MD: Review and Herald, 1991), 147–50.
14. H Richard Niebuhr, *Christ and Culture* (New York, NY: Harper & Row, 1951), 76–82. Although now somewhat dated, Niebuhr's work remains the classic discussion on Christianity and culture.
15. It seems to me that conservative Christians are justified in their fear that cultural relativism will tear the heart out of the Christian message. They have seen too many illustrations among those engaged in the liberal experiment.

Let us sharpen the issue just a little. The Bible does not appear averse to using a wide range of literary genres in order to transmit what had been revealed to its writers.[16] But are we open to allowing them 'the liberty . . . to choose their forms of literary composition, even if it shocks us and contravenes our standards of writing'?[17] I do not wish to infer that we must travel the route of the liberal biblical critics in rejecting traditional interpretations just because they are traditional. Still, if Jesus could tell fictional parables, as is the case with the parable of the rich man and Lazarus, then perhaps not all of the biblical narratives are to be read as if they were sections in a modern historical or scientific textbook.[18]

Clark Pinnock maintains that 'despite history being crucial to the biblical message, we have to grant the Bible its freedom to employ styles of historical writing it wants to'.[19] It seems that to demand that God could not do otherwise then to always 'write' his revelation in a strictly historical format is to ignore the testimony of the data of Scripture as well as to lock ourselves into a doctrine of total divine control which is presupposed by biblical inerrantism.[20]

---

16. The biblical writers did not just use different literary forms in which to express their ideas. They also engaged a wide range of metaphors in order to translate the divine actions into understandable terms. For instance, salvation can be spoken of in terms of atonement, reconciliation, sacrifice, justification, etc. See Richard Rice's discussion of theories and models of the atonement in his *Reign of God: An Introduction to Christian Theology from a Seventh-day Adventist Perspective* (Berrien Springs, MI: Andrews University Press, 1997), 188–99. Millard Erickson remarks that 'in the doctrine of the atonement we see perhaps the clearest indication of the organic character of theology . . . ' See Erickson, *Christian Theology*, second edition (Grand Rapids, MI: Baker, 1998), 799.
17. Clark H Pinnock with Barry L Callen, *The Scripture Principle: Reclaiming the Full Authority of the Bible*, second edition (Grand Rapids, MI: Baker, 2006), 145
18. This perspective has always made Seventh-day Adventists extremely nervous. What would happen if they were to read the Genesis creation story as a symbolic narrative rather than a descriptive account? Certainly, they should keep in mind that they bring to the creation story their own 'story' that has been developed in opposition to evolutionary biology. However, it seems that the intention of the biblical writer is to counteract the errors contained in the creation myths of the ancient world. See for instance Gerhard F Hasel, 'The Polemic Nature of the Genesis Cosmology', in *Evangelical Quarterly* 46 (974): 81–102. For an engaging portrayal of the evangelical struggle to interpret the creation texts, see Clark H Pinnock, 'Climbing out of a Swamp: The Evangelical Struggle to Understand the Creation Texts', in *Interpretation* 43 (1989): 143–55.
19. Pinnock and Callen, *The Scripture Principle*, 145.
20. For an introduction to the lively discussion on inerrancy and divine control, see Randall and David Basinger, 'Inerrancy, Dictation and the Free Will Debate', in *Evangelical Quarterly*, 55 (1983): 177–80. Norman L Geisler critiques the Basingers in his 'Inerrancy and Free Will: A Reply to the Brothers Basinger', in *Evangelical Quarterly*, 57 (1985): 352, while the Basingers continue the debate in their 'Inerrancy and Free will: Some Further Thoughts', in *Evangelical Quarterly* 58 (1986): 351–54. For my own discussion of Clark Pinnock's paradigm shift from divine control inerrancy to a free-will model of biblical authority see Ray CW Roennfeldt, *Clark H. Pinnock on Biblical Authority: An Evolving Position* (Berrien Springs, MI: Andrews University Press, 1993), 349–61.

But, does not a more flexible view of the origin and nature of Scripture place the reasoning powers of the human interpreter over the Bible, rather than God's Word judging the reader? That is clearly the result when some engage in radical, even agnostic, biblical criticism. However, the committed Christian is not about to pronounce as unreliable a book that has introduced her or him to Jesus Christ.[21] In fact, it appears that only those readers who are submitted to Jesus will actually know what the Bible teaches (John 7:17).

Some Limits on Subjectivity

Although we do not always recognise it, the very subjectivity of the hermeneutical process is an acknowledgment of the Bible's power and genius. It actually speaks to all of us across a wide variety of situation. Thus, biblical hermeneutics is far more than merely analysing the meanings of words or unraveling the grammar of sentences, as important as that task may be.[22] But we are not left with the kind of 'chaos' which results when we bring our 'text' to the biblical text and make it mean whatever we want it to.[23] There are a number of very vital controls.

There is, of course, the control implicit in the text itself. 'Any claim to interpretation has to appear credible in the light of the text itself and must be a legitimate and possible use of it'. There, there is also the 'counsel' of the interpretational tradition. 'Tradition plays a stabilising role in hermeneutics', and protects the church against Scripture twisting and heresy. Finally, there is the community of believers who 'collectively hear the Word and assess the interpretation'.[24]

How? A Personal Note

How will we then read and apply Scripture? I cannot speak for everyone as to the best way to interpret the Bible, but I can share how it operates in my experience. I have found the idea of the Bible as 'case-book' helpful in understanding the Bible

---

21. Thus, the ultimate criterion for the authenticity of the Christian as well as for the credibility of Scripture is primarily subjective: 'The Spirit testifies with our spirit that we are God's children', (Rom 8:16 NIV).
22. It should be observed that one can approach lexical and grammatical studies from an inerrantist perspective which assumes that the biblical writer must mean 'such and such' because he has used a particular word or construction. While that may often be the case, it should be kept in mind that large portions of Scripture are 'occasional' rather than having been carefully constructed.
23. Pinnock with Callen, *The Scripture Principle*, 240.
24. *Ibid*, 240–42. Pinnock notes that 'The authority of tradition is one of counsel, not of command. It is fallible, not infallible'. He concludes that tradition 'cannot be set aside without harming the identity of the faith community'. *Ibid*, 242.

as God's Word.[25] Given the power of narrative in the formation of individuals and communities,[26] as well as the fact that far-and-away the most common form of literature in the Bible is narrative, would appear to indicate that one should learn to listen to the story/stories of the Bible.

The narratives of the Old Testament, for instance, are not just accounts of the lives of the various characters. Rather, they operate as divine stories on a least three levels: the level of the working out of the universal plan of God; that of God's specific call to Israel; and the level of the individual narratives that combine to make up the other two levels.[27]

It is clear that the Old Testament does not just tell us about the people who lived in those times. Instead, the stories function primarily as divine narratives. Thus, Old Testament narratives do not directly teach doctrines (although they may illustrate doctrines); they record what happened rather than what should have happened (and so do not always provide us with a perfect example); they invite us to judge for ourselves as to whether a particular course is right or wrong; they are always selective and incomplete; they do not answer all of our theological questions; and they consistently portray God as their hero.[28]

The Joseph narrative (Gen 37, 39–50), while having Joseph as the central character—a personality flawed by arrogance and parental favoritism—is clearly identified as a divine narrative. The biblical writer emphasises again and again that in spite of Joseph's imperfections and 'ups-and-downs' that 'the LORD was with him' (Gen 39:2-5, 21). 'The focus is on God. He can accomplish what He wills. Using such unlikely vehicles as Joseph, his family, and the Pharaoh, God preserved many people and began to create for himself a special people.'[29] Scripture invites us into the story, not to replicate the life of Joseph by doing what he did, but to actively respond to God's involvement in our own sphere.[30] As a Christian, I bring

---

25. This is the perspective of Alden Thompson in his *Inspiration: Hard Questions, Honest Answers*, although it is not exclusive to him. A similar viewpoint can be found in the evangelical version of narrative theology as espoused by Gabriel Fackre, *The Christian Story: A Narrative Interpretation of Basic Christian Doctrine*, revised edition (Grand Rapids, MI: Eerdmans, 1984). For a critique of Thompson's 'casebook/codebook' approach from an inerrantist perspective see Samuel Koranteng-Pipim, 'An Analysis and Evaluation of Alden Thompson's Casebook/Codebook Approach to the Bible', in *Issues in Revelation and Inspiration*, edited by Frank Holbrook and Leo Van Dolson (Berrien Springs, MI: Adventist Theological Society, 1992), 31–67.

26. For a discussion of the power of narrative in the secular sphere consult Khachig Tölölyan, 'Narrative Culture and the Motivation of the Terrorist', in *Texts of Identity*, edited by John Shotter and KJ Gergen (London: SAGE, 1989), 99–118. One cannot spend time working in a Two-Thirds World context (as I have) without recognising the formative function of stories.

27. This three-tiered distinction is made by Fee and Stuart, *How to Read*, 91–93.

28. This list is based on *ibid*, 92–93.

29. *Ibid*, 86.

30. This is probably the way that Hebrew 11 uses the Old Testament narratives. Since the Old Testament 'witnesses' were faithful, how much more are Christians exhorted to 'throw off everything

to my decision-making process and to my worldview not just divine imperatives, but also a bank of stories of genuine divine-human encounters which mould and inform my own walk with God.[31]

Conclusion

It is obvious that not all of Scripture can be read as narrative. Some portions are composed of prophecy, others constitute hymns, and still others provide a store of wisdom. If we are to gain optimal benefit, we must recognise that we cannot interpret everything in the same way and that the Spirit waits to guide us into all truth (John 16:13). Still, there is a 'story', for instance, behind Paul's instructions regarding food offered to idols and the participation of women in worship. To know that story (or context) provides us with a large amount of hermeneutical assistance. Finally,

> Books about interpretation are no more a substitute for interpreting than recipes are a substitute for cooking. They need correcting, but the final test is not whether they stimulate further methodological reflections: it is whether they encourage good cooking. As the aim of cooking is to promote nourishment, so the Bible is to be heard, read, marked, learned, and inwardly digested. That involves interpretation, whether this task is performed by the reader who appropriates the Bible, or by some intermediary like Philip, who offered help to the Ethiopian eunuch.[32]

> Genuine biblical interpretation is not easy, nor does it arise in a vacuum. It means grappling with the biblical text as well as interfacing it with our immediate situation. However, it also means that Scripture will only be interpreted fruitfully if adequate account of the nature of the text is accounted for. An inerrantist view of Scripture will very likely predetermine a literalistic pattern of interpretation while a

---

that hinds and the sin that so easily entangles, and let us run with perseverance the race marked out for us'? (Heb 12:1 NIV).

31. This is *my* way of reading the story of Joseph. Other readers may not come to the same conclusions. See, for instance, Gerald West, 'Difference and Dialogue: Reading the Joseph Story with Poor and Marginalised Communities in South Africa', in *Biblical Interpretation: A Journal of Contemporary Approaches* 2 (1994): 152–70.
32. Robert Morgan with John Barton, *Biblical Interpretation* (Oxford: Oxford University Press, 1988), 29.

more realistic view of the nature of the Bible may allow greater scope for continuing illumination from the Holy Spirit. Perhaps we have not yet 'scratched the surface' of the treasure that is Scripture!

PART TWO

The Relationship Between The Testaments

New Testament Use of the Old Testament

Jon Paulien

Introduction

The issue of the New Testament use of the Old Testament is a major one, involving research on every book of the Bible. My particular area of study has been the use of the Old Testament in the Book of Revelation, so I will focus on the scholarly debate as it pertains to Revelation, but the implications of that debate extend to all the other books of the New Testament. After surveying the debate regarding Revelation as a basis for outlining the primary issue, I will use a well-known passage in Matthew 2 as a test case.

In the broad sense, intertextuality has to do with the interplay between written texts. The writers of the New Testament were conscious of the Old Testament as they wrote, and often pointed readers to significant background texts to support and clarify the point they were making. Intertextuality seeks to understand an author's intention in the use of earlier literature. The understanding of intertextuality in biblical studies has recently expanded as New Testament scholars have begun to employ literary critical strategies, categories and understandings. The appropriateness of this expansion has been the subject of an ongoing debate between Steve Moyise and GK Beale. After a brief review of the broader field, specific attention needs to be given to that debate and its implications for future study of Revelation.

Revelation Is Related to the Old Testament, but How?

No one would argue that an understanding of the Old Testament is irrelevant to an understanding of the Apocalypse. The reader is fully plunged into the atmosphere of the Old Testament.[1] No other New Testament book is as saturated with the Old.[2] The symbolism of the book cannot be penetrated without careful attention to its Old Testament antecedents.

---

1. To borrow language from Henri Stierlin, *La vérité sur L'Apocalypse* (Paris: Editions Buchet/Chastel, 1972), 55.
2. Pierre Lestringant, *Essai sur l'unité de la révélation biblique* (Paris: Editions 'Je Sers', 1942), 148, suggests that one-seventh of the substance of the Apocalypse is drawn from the words of the Old Testament.

On the other hand, Revelation seems to resist efforts to understand its relationship to the Old Testament. Rather than quoting or citing the Old Testament, the book interacts with it in the most allusive manner. A word here, a phrase there, and the barest hint of an echo in another place is the essence of how Revelation evokes the Old Testament, and that is only the beginning of complications. While there is a general consensus that Revelation was written in Greek,[3] there is much dispute as to the language and text tradition of the Old Testament John uses.[4] There are also a number of striking irregularities in the Greek grammar of the Apocalypse.[5]

So granted the central place of the Old Testament in the Book of Revelation, it is still difficult to determine exactly how it is being used there. While various aspects of the above issue have been addressed in scores of books, articles and commentaries, since the middle of the 1980s a number of major specialised works have addressed the larger picture. According to GK Beale,[6] the most significant

---

3. David Tabachovitz, *Die Septuaginta und das Neue Testament*, Skrifter Utgivna av Svenska Institutet I Athen, Series 8, Volume 4 (Lund: CWK Gleerup, 1956), 125–126. See further Raymond E. Brown, *The Gospel According to John*, 2 Volumes, Anchor Bible, Volumes 29 and 29a (Garden City, NY: Doubleday, 1981), 1:cxxix; Joseph A Fitzmyer, *A Wandering Aramean: Collected Aramaic Essays*, SBLMS 25 (Missoula, MT: Scholars, 1979), 6–8, 38–43

4. Selected literature reflective of the debate: RH Charles, *The Revelation of St John*, 2 Volumes, ICC (Edinburgh: T&T Clark, 1920), 1:lxvi; Ugo Vanni, 'L'Apocalypse johannique. Etat de la question', in *L'Apocalypse johannique et L'Apocalyptique dans le Nouveau Testament*, BETL, edited by J Lambrecht (Gembloux: Leuven University Press, 1980), 53:31; Charles C Torrey, *The Apocalypse of John* (New Haven: Yale University Press, 1958), 27–48; [Leonhard] P Trudinger, 'Some Observations Concerning the Text of the Old Testament in the Book of Revelation', in *Journal of Theological Studies* 17 (1966): 82–88; G Mussies, *The Morphology of Koine Greek as Used in the Apocalypse of John*, Supplements to *Novum Testamentum* 27 (Leiden: EJ Brill, 1971): 10–11; Henry B Swete, *The Apocalypse of St. John* (London: MacMillan, 1906), cl, clv; Pierre Prigent, *Apocalypse et liturgie*, Cahiers Théologiques 52 (Neuchâtel: Editions Delachaux et Niestlé, 1964), 10; James A Montgomery, 'The Education of the Seer of the Apocalypse', in *Journal of Biblical Literature* 45 (1926): 73–74; D Moody Smith, Jr, 'The Use of the Old Testament in the New' in *The Use of the Old Testament in the New and Other Essays*, edited by JM Efird (Durham, NC: Duke University Press, 1972), 61; and A Vanhoye, 'L'utilisation du livre d'Ezékiel dans l'Apocalypse', in *Biblica* 43 (1962): 436–476.

5. Note the following discussions on this issue: RH Charles, *Studies in the Apocalypse* (Edinburgh: T&T Clark, 1913), 79–102; Heinrich Kraft, 'Zur Offenbarung des Johannes', in *Theologische Rundschau* 38 (1973): 93; G Mussies, 'The Greek of the Book of Revelation', in *L'Apocalypse johannique et L'Apocalyptique dans le Nouveau Testament*, BETL, edited by J Lambrecht (Gembloux: Leuven University Press, 1980), 53:167–170; G Mussies, *Morphology*, 6; Tabachovitz, *Die Septuaginta*, 125–126; Torrey, *The Apocalypse of John*, 13–58. Martin McNamara, *The New Testament and the Palestinian Targum to the Pentateuch*, Analecta Biblica, Volume 27a, second printing with supplement (Rome: Pontifical Biblical Institute, 1978), 10–117, 124–125, 189–190 points to the Aramaic Targums as the explanation for Revelation 1:4 and many other irregularities.

6. GK Beale, *John's Use of the Old Testament in Revelation*, JSNTSupplement 166 (Sheffield: Shef-

of these works are those of Beale,[7] Jeffrey Marshall Vogelgesang,[8] Jon Paulien,[9] Richard Bauckham,[10] Jan Fekkes,[11] and Jean-Pierre Ruiz.[12] These works all focused on John's intentions with regard to his use of the Old Testament. In spite of the allusive nature of the evidence, attempts were made to catalogue John's choices of Old Testament texts and to consider the impact of such allusions on understanding his purposes in the book.[13] Increasing attention was also given to the criteria for determining when and where the author intentionally alluded to portions of the Old Testament. These concerns seemed weighty and problematic enough to engage teams of scholars for generations to come. However, the enterprise was complicated by the arrival of new literary approaches to the topic.

Devorah Dimant and New Literary Approaches to Apocalyptic

This new direction was signaled by the research of Devorah Dimant on the use of the Old Testament in the Apocrypha and Pseudepigrapha.[14] Her research led her to the conclusion that these Jewish writers used the Old Testament according to a 'compositional use' or an 'expositional use'.[15] According to her, these two categories represent two 'fundamentally different attitudes to the biblical material', leading to correspondingly different literary genres and styles.[16]

---

field Academic Press, 1998), 13–59.

7. GK Beale, *The Use of Daniel in Jewish Apocalyptic Literature and in the Revelation of St John* (Lanham, MD: University Press of America, 1984).
8. Jeffrey Marshall Vogelgesang, 'The Interpretation of Ezekiel in the Book of Revelation', (PhD dissertation, Harvard University, 1985).
9. Jon Paulien, *Decoding Revelation's Trumpets: Allusions and the Interpretation of Rev 8:7–12*, Andrews University Seminary Doctoral Dissertation Series 11 (Berrien Springs, MI: Andrews University Press, 1988)..
10 Richard Bauckham, *The Climax of Prophecy: Studies on the Book of Revelation* (Edinburgh: T&T Clark, 1993).
11. J Fekkes, *III Isaiah and Prophetic Traditions in the Book of Revelation: Visionary Antecedents and their Development*, JSNTSupplement 93 (Sheffield: JSOT Press, 1994).
12. Jean-Pierre Ruiz, *Ezekiel in the Apocalypse: The Transformation of Prophetic Language in Revelation 16, 17–19,10*, European University Studies, Series 23, Volume 376 (Frankfurt am Main: Peter Lang, 1989).
13. All the specialised works address these issues to one degree or another.
14. Devorah Dimant, 'Use and Interpretation of Mikra in the Apocrypha and Pseudepigrapha', in *Mikra: Text, Translation, Reading and Interpretation of the Hebrew Bible in Ancient Judaism and Early Christianity*, edited Martin Jan Mulder (Philadelphia: Fortress, 1988), 381–384. My attention was drawn to Dimant's work by the article of Louis Painchaud, 'Use of Scripture in Gnostic Literature', in *Journal of Early Christian Studies*, Volume 4, No. 2 (1996):129–146, which I became aware of thanks to a conversation with Leonard Thompson.
15. *Ibid*, 382–383.
16. *Ibid*, 382.

Dimant defines 'expositional use' as a literary strategy in which the Old Testament text is presented explicitly, with a clear external marker.[17] In expositional use the biblical text is introduced as the object of interpretation.[18] The aim of the writing is to explain the biblical text. This usually involves the use of fixed terminology and special syntactical patterns, in order to separate the biblical element from the author's exposition. Genres utilising this category include rabbinic midrash, Qumranic pesher, the commentaries on the Torah by Philo and certain types of quotations in the New Testament.[19]

On the other hand, 'compositional use' occurs when the biblical elements are interwoven into the work without external formal markers.[20] The biblical element is subservient to the independent aim and structure of its new context. Genres employing compositional use do not have the same exegetical or rhetorical aims as exposition, but instead create a new and independent text. The biblical material becomes part of the texture of these works. Typical compositional genres include narratives, psalms, testaments, and wisdom discourses, which use biblical elements for their own patterns, style and terminology.[21]

While Dimant does not mention apocalyptic among the genres in which compositional use is employed, studies in Revelation clearly demonstrate that John was utilising the Old Testament compositionally, rather than expositionally. While a handful of scholars argue for anywhere from one to eleven 'quotations' of the Old Testament in the book of Revelation,[22] the overwhelming majority of scholars conclude that there are none.[23] There are certainly no explicit citations of the

---

17. This would seem to correspond to what I call a citation (Paulien, *Decoding Revelation's Trumpets*, 102), of which a number of instances can be seen in the Gospel of Matthew, for example. Some have called these citations in Matthew 'Formula Quotations', cf Merrill C Tenney, *Interpreting Revelation* (Grand Rapids, MI: Eerdmans, 1957), 102; Richard B Hays and Joel B Green, 'The Use of the Old Testament by New Testament Writers', in *Hearing the New Testament: Strategies for Interpretation*, edited by JB Green (Grand Rapids, MI: Eerdmans, 1995), 226.
18. Dimant notes that similar distinctions have been made by Heinemann and Perrot, cf Dimant, 'Use and Interpretation', *op cit*, 382, footnote 16.
19. *Ibid*, 382-383.
20. This corresponds roughly to the categories of direct allusion and echo that I worked with in my dissertation on Revelation. Paulien, *Decoding Revelation's Trumpets, op cit*, 175-178.
21. Dimant, 'Use and Interpretation', *op cit*, 382-383.
22. See, for example *Old Testament Quotations in the New Testament*, edited by Robert G Bratcher (London: United Bible Societies, 1967), 74-76; Johann Christian Carl Döpke, *Hermeneutik der neutestamentlichen Schriftsteller* (Leipzig: Friedrich Christian Wilhelm Vogel, 1829), 288; David McCalman Turpie, *The New Testament View of the Old* (London: Hodder and Stoughton, 1872), 323.
23. Selected examples: *The Greek New Testament*, third edition, edited by Kurt Aland, et al (NY: United Bible Societies, 1975), 903; Werner Foerster, 'Bemerkungen zur Bildsprache der Offerbarung Johannis', in *Verborum Veritas: Festschrift für Gustav Stählin*, edited by Otto Böcher and Klaus Haacker (Wuppertal: Theologischer Verlag Rolf Brockhaus, 1970), 225; Roger Nicole, 'A Study of the Old Testament Quotations in the New Testament with Reference to the Doctrine

expositional type.²⁴ If Dimant's observations can be verified within the context of New Testament studies, they would have large implications for understanding of John's use of the Old Testament.²⁵ Regardless of the degree to which other New Testament writers may respect the context of their Old Testament antecedents,²⁶ the author of Revelation would be signaling a generic preference for creativity in his use of Scripture.

The Moyise-Beale Debate

While Dimant's distinctions and their potential significance do not seem to have impacted studies of Revelation so far, the debate regarding John's use of the Old Testament in Revelation broke new ground with the published monograph by Steve Moyise in 1995.²⁷ Moyise provides the first serious attempt to apply the literary perspective of intertextuality to the use of the Old Testament in Revelation.²⁸

---

of the Inspiration of the Scriptures', (MST Thesis, Gordon College of Theology and Missions, 1940), *passim*; Ernest Leslie Peerman, *Living Messages from Patmos* (NY: Pyramid, 1941), 51; Pierre Prigent, *L'Apocalypse de Saint Jean*, Commentaire du Nouveau Testament, second Series, Volume 14 (Lausanne: Delachaux et Niestlé), 368; Jürgen Roloff, *Die Offenbarung des Johannes*, Zürcher Bibelkommentare NT (Zürich: Theologischer Verlag, 1984), 18:20; F Stagg, 'Interpreting the Book of Revelation', *Review and Expositor*, 72 (1975): 333; Henry B Swete, *An Introduction to the Old Testament in Greek* (Cambridge: University Press, 1902), 392; RV G. Tasker, *The Old Testament in the New Testament* (London: SCM, 1946), 168; Vanhoye, *op cit*, 436–437; Yarbro Collins, *Crisis and Catharsis*, *op cit*, 42.

24. The only 'citation' of the Old Testament occurs in Revelation 15:3, the 'Song of Moses', which seem an evident reference to Exodus 15. But the content of the 'song' in Revelation 15:3-4 is a mosaic of language from the Psalms and the prophets, not Exodus. There are, therefore, no citations of the OT of the expositional type.
25. Dimant, 'Use and Interpretation', *op cit*, 384–419.
26. Beale offers a representative anthology of the literature on this topic with some bias in favour of respect for context. *The Right Doctrine from the Wrong Texts? Essays on the Use of the Old Testament in the New*, edited by GK Beale(Grand Rapids: Baker, 1994).
27. Steve Moyise, *The Old Testament in the Book of Revelation*, JSNT Supplement 115 (Sheffield: Sheffield Academic Press, 1995). Beale chose to review Moyise in *John's Use* precisely because Moyise was the first to apply postmodern hermeneutical perspectives to the debates surrounding John's use of the Old Testament. GK Beale, 'Questions of Authorial Intent, Epistemology, and Presuppositions and Their Bearing on the Study of The Old Testament in the New: A Rejoinder to Steve Moyise', in *Irish Biblical Studies* 21 (1999): 152.
28. Literary approaches to the book of Revelation have been around for about fifteen years, beginning with the work of David Barr in the mid-80s. David L Barr, 'The Apocalypse as a Symbolic Transformation of the World: A Literary Analysis', in *Interpretation* 38 (1984): 39–50; 'The Apocalypse of John as Oral Enactment', in *Interpretation* 40 (1986): 243–256; *Tales of the End: A Narrative Commentary on the Book of Revelation* (Santa Rosa, CA: Polebridge, 1998). Note also the work of Elizabeth Schüssler Fiorenza, *Revelation: Vision of a Just World*, Proclamation Commentaries, edited by Gerhard Krodel (Minneapolis: Fortress Press, 1991), and Tina Pippin, *Death and Desire: The Rhetoric of Gender in the Apocalypse of John* (Louisville, KY: Westminster/John Knox, 1992). Barr argued for a more oral and narrative approach to the book in contrast

The literary perspective broadens the process of intertextuality by a concern for the impact of the reader on the process of intertextual interpretation.

According to Moyise, 'The task of intertextuality is to explore how the source text continues to speak through the new work and how the new work forces new meanings from the source text.'[29] 'By absorbing words used in one context into a new context or configuration, a metaphorical relationship is established.'[30] 'The reader "hears" the Old Testament text, but its meaning is affected by the new context or configuration.'[31] When a reader of Revelation who is not conscious of an allusion reads allusive words in their new context, that reader will naturally read connotations into those words that were not present in the Old Testament context. When (s)he becomes aware of the allusion, a 'cave of resonant signification'[32] is opened up that affects the reading of that part of Revelation.[33]

Moyise compares the use of the Old Testament in Revelation with Thomas Greene's four 'forms of imitation'.[34] Based on this research he argues that John deliberately leaves his use of Old Testament allusions open-ended. He invites the reader to engage in thought and analysis of his text (Rev 13:8; 17:9). Thus, there

---

to its critical analysis as a historical document. In doing so he helped open the field to literary and social approaches to the book. In 1990, under the auspices of the Society of Biblical Literature, he guided the establishment of the 'Literary Criticism and the Apocalypse Consultation', which was replaced after two years by the 'Reading the Apocalypse Seminar'. The two groups were largely made up of younger scholars eager to move the debate forward. The purpose of the seminar was to explore the 'intersection between literary and social readings of the Apocalypse'. I sense that Barr was hoping to avoid the quagmires of both pre-critical and critical readings of the Apocalypse and to develop some consensus among those advocating more contemporary approaches to the book. As the years went by, however, I sensed his increasing frustration as the fifteen to twenty members of the group seemed to fragment in a variety of directions; literary, structuralist, feminist, rhetorical, theological, liturgical, and so on. The publication of a couple of books that highlight a variety of reader responses to Revelation is still in process. With regard to the issue that has exercised Beale and Moyise, the group seemed to divide almost 50/50 between those who prefer to retain an interest in the original author's intention and those who are primarily interested in how contemporary readers respond to the book. However, the work of the group did not cover the area of intertextuality, so I have not chosen to highlight its literary critical work here.

29. Moyise, *The Old Testament, op cit*, 111.
30. *Ibid*, 110.
31. *Ibid*, 110–111.
32. Quoted from John Hollander, *The Figure of Echo: A Mode of Allusion in Milton and After* (Berkeley, CA: University of California Press, 1981), 65.
33. Moyise, *The Old Testament, op cit*, 118.
34. *Ibid*, 118–132. Based on Thomas M Greene, *The Light in Troy: Imitation and Discovery in Renaissance Poetry* (New Haven: Yale University Press, 1982), 16–53. Greene's four categories are reproductive, eclectic, heuristic, and dialectic. Moyise concludes that there is nothing in Revelation that could fairly be described as reproductive, and little that fits the eclectic category (Moyise, *The Old Testament, op cit,* 120–123). The heuristic and dialectic categories seem worthy of exploration in Revelation (*ibid*, 123–132).

may be no gap between the author's intention for Revelation and the process of reader response to the 'cave of resonant signification.'[35]

GK Beale quickly called Moyise's approach into question in the most comprehensive single work ever written on the subject of allusions to the Old Testament in Revelation.[36] The book is not a coherent whole, but reads like a series of independent units written at different times with a common general purpose. In fact many of the parts had already been published separately.[37]

The main purpose of the book seems to be an extension of the thesis that drove Beale's earlier anthology on the use of the Old Testament in the New.[38] Beale argues that John uses the Old Testament with sensitivity to its original context. The Old Testament is not just the servant of the gospel, but is also a guide. In other words, New Testament writers not only simply impose their understanding on the Old Testament; the Old Testament also becomes a source of their understanding of the events they have experienced.

Beale develops the analogy of a basket of fruit. An apple removed from a tree and placed in a basket of fruit does not lose its identity as an apple; it simply acquires a new context. So when New Testament writers quote an Old Testament text, they are not altering what the original writer means. They are simply giving it new significance in a new context.[39] While others have articulated such a viewpoint with respect to the New Testament as a whole,[40] no one else has articulated it in such detail with regard to Revelation.[41] Beale considers his position to be in serious disagreement with that of Moyise.[42]

In a short response Moyise expresses puzzlement over this disagreement.[43] He feels that Beale's distinction between meaning and significance is a hermeneutical

---

35. *Ibid*, 133–134.
36. GK Beale, *John's Use of the Old Testament in Revelation*, Journal for the Study of the New Testament Supplement Series, 166 (Sheffield: Sheffield Academic Press, 1998).
37. The sources of the book are detailed in James E West's review of GK Beale, *John's Use of the Old Testament in Revelation*, in *Review of Biblical Literature* found at www.bookreviews.org/Reviews/1850758948.
38. 'The Right Doctrine from the Wrong Texts?' The book *John's Use of the Old Testament in Revelation* is an expansion of the ideas laid out in Beale's chapter of the anthology, 'The Use of the Old Testament in Revelation', 257–276.
39. Beale, *John's Use, op cit*, 51–52.
40. In his anthology, *The Right Doctrine from the Wrong Texts?* Beale includes articles favoring respect for context by CH Dodd, I Howard Marshall, Beale himself, and David Seccombe.
41. I have benefited from the brief summary of Beale's *John's Use of the Old Testament in Revelation*, by Kenneth Newport in *Review of Biblical Literature* found at www.bookreviews.org/Reviews/1850758948.
42. Beale, *John's Use, op cit*, 50–59.
43. Steve Moyise, 'The Old Testament in the New: A Reply to Greg Beale', in *Irish Biblical Studies*, 21 (May 1999): 54–58.

cover-up,[44] and then articulates a threefold difference between their positions. In contrast to Beale, Moyise believes that the New Testament writers give Old Testaments texts new meanings;

1. the New Testament writers take Old Testament texts out of context; and
2. meaning does not derive solely from an author's intention, but also from the creative process of reading.[45]

Moyise prefers the analogy of a fruit salad to Beale's fruit basket. In a fruit salad there are no more shiny apples, but pieces of apple mixed with other fruits and covered with syrup. While the connection remains between the apple on the tree and the apple in the fruit salad, one is more struck with the differences between the two forms of apple than in the fruit-basket analogy.[46]

Moyise seems to believe that he has been unfairly characterised as a radical reader-response critic who believes a text can mean whatever a reader wants it to mean.[47] He argues instead that readers are not free to make a text mean whatever they like, but in order to arrive at a coherent interpretation, readers must make choices regarding what constitutes evidence and how it should be construed. He feels that the differences between himself and Beale demonstrate that there is no consensus on how to make such choices. More often people such as Beale interpret according to their own presuppositions and presume that they have attained the author's intention.[48]

A few months later Beale responds to Moyise with a vigorous and lengthy defense of his position on authorial intention and respect for context.[49] He argues that the debate is fundamentally about aspects of epistemology that require specific book-length treatments.[50] He seeks to summarise the parameters of such a lengthy treatment in his twenty-nine-page page article, clarifying that his approach is based on the work of ED Hirsch, KJ Vanhoozer and NT Wright.[51] No

---

44. Ibid, 55.
45. Ibid, 54.
46. Ibid, 55–56. As Moyise himself acknowledges, both analogies break down as attempts to explain what is happening in the interpretation of texts. Regardless of how it is interpreted, the original text remains intact. Once removed from a tree, however, an apple can never be replaced. The tree is fundamentally changed by the 'interpretation' whether it is a fruit basket, a fruit salad, or applesauce that results!
47. He expresses some doubt that such radical reader-response critics actually exist. Ibid, 57.
48. Ibid, 57–58.
49. GK Beale, 'Questions of Authorial Intent, Epistemology, and Presuppositions and Their Bearing on the Study of The Old Testament in the New: a Rejoinder to Steve Moyise', in Irish Biblical Studies, 21 (1999): 152–180.
50. Ibid, 153, 173.
51. ED Hirsch, Validity in Interpretation (New Haven: Yale University Press, 1967); KJ Vanhoozer,

interpretation ever reproduces an author's original meaning in full, but adequate understanding is possible.[52] Understanding can never be fully certain, but it is possible.[53] Beale insists on maintaining Hirsch's distinction between meaning and significance.[54] He considers it critical that good interpretation be judged by the degree to which it conforms to essential elements of the author's original meaning.[55]

I sense a certain amount of frustration in Beale's response. He believes that Moyise's own statements do rank him with the more radical reader-response critics that can make a text mean whatever they like.[56] For Beale this is an unnecessary abandonment of 'commonsense,' which implies that the probability of one interpretation being superior to another consists in the degrees to which there are fundamental correspondences between that interpretation and its source text.[57]

With regard to respect for context, Beale lays out a number of arguments against Moyise's position:

1. In a number of instances it can be demonstrated that New Testament writers did interpret an Old Testament text in harmony with its original intention.
2. Twenty years of detailed research have led Beale to the conclusion that John generally and consistently uses the Old Testament with significant recognition of its context.
3. When New Testament writers do shift from the exegetical meaning, they often do so using presuppositions that are rooted already in the Old Testament itself.
4. Allegory, as a method, is not found in the New Testament; therefore its writers were not haphazard in their methodology.[58]

Is There a Meaning in This Text? The Bible, The Reader, and the Morality of Literary Knowledge (Grand Rapids, MI: Zondervan Publishing House, 1998); NT Wright, *The New Testament and the People of God*, Christian Origins and the Question of God, Volume 1 (Minneapolis: Fortress Press, 1992), *passim*.

52. Beale, 'Questions of Authorial Intent', 155.
53. Beale takes up Wright's analogy of the historian (161). Historians do not record events fully as they actually happened. Neither are they unable to record anything that happened. Wright calls this 'critical realism'.
54. *Ibid*, 155–159.
55. *Ibid*, 159.
56. *Ibid*, 162–163, 173–174.
57. *Ibid*, 164–166, 175–178.
58. *Ibid*, 167–170.

He notes that Moyise has done little exegesis of Revelation in the public arena and implies that the burden of proof is on Moyise to show that the results of Beale's textual observations are incorrect.[59]

Beale also challenges Moyise to show that his rejection of authorial intention is not part and parcel of a rejection of a faith-based perspective on the claims of Scripture. Ultimately texts need to be approached from a 'hermeneutic of love' that avoids the twisting of another author's perspective to serve one's own selfish ends or the caricaturing another's position to enhance one's own.[60] A 'loving' approach to Scripture would take seriously its claim to a comprehensive worldview in which, ultimately both Old and New Testaments are the product of a single, divine, authorial purpose.[61]

In response, Moyise argues that the term 'intertextuality' has become a generic label for a lot of different practices in New Testament scholarship regarding the use of the Old Testament.[62] Instead of having its technical meaning in the world of literature, it has become an umbrella term, requiring the use of sub-categories in order to be rightly understood.[63]

Moyise proposes three such categories in the article. The first category he calls 'intertextual echo'. Grounded in the work of Richard Hays,[64] this approach maintains that a particular allusion or echo can be more important to the meaning of a text than its minor role in the wording might indicate.[65] The second category he proposes is 'dialogical intertextuality'. In this category the interaction between text and subtext operates in both directions.[66] The third category is 'postmodern intertextuality'. Postmodern intertextuality seeks to demonstrate that the process of tracing the interactions between texts is inherently unstable. While meaning can result from interpretation, it only happens when some portions of the evidence are privileged and other portions are ignored.[67] Beale appears to be comfortable with the first two categories;[68] it is the third that troubles him. Beale's great fear, according to Moyise, is the suggestion that readers 'create' meaning.[69]

---

59. *Ibid*, 166.
60. *Ibid*, 178–179.
61. *Ibid*, 165.
62. Steve Moyise, 'Intertextuality and the Study of the Old Testament in the New Testament', in *The Old Testament in the New Testament: Essays in Honour of JL North,* JSNT Supplement 189, edited by Steve Moyise (Sheffield: Sheffield Academic Press, 2000), 16.
63. *Ibid*, 17.
64 Richard Hays, *Echoes of Scripture in the Letters of Paul* (New Haven: Yale University Press, 1987).
65. Moyise, 'Intertextuality', *op cit*, 17.
66. *Ibid*.
67. *Ibid*, 17–18.
68. For him the Old Testament is both servant and guide to the writers of the New Testament. Among many occurrences of this expression in Beale note *John's Use,* 127, in context.
69. Moyise, 'Intertextuality', *op cit*, 31.

Moyise attempts to bridge the gap by elaborating 'postmodern intertextuality' in the light of John 4:16–20.[70] He is aware that many will ask the question, 'What possible benefit is it to show that all interpretations are inherently flawed?'[71] He offers three answers to the question:

1. Postmodern intertextuality is not saying that meaning, in the sense of communication, is impossible, but that it always comes at a price. Interpretation is not arbitrary, but the openness of texts like John 4:16–20 allows for interpretational choice.
2. Demonstrating that a text can point in a number of directions reveals something about the potentiality of the text. There is more than one valid reading possible. All readings based on genuine potential within the text tell us something about the text as it really is. This is different from making a text mean whatever one likes.
3. Since it is clearly impossible for any individual to grasp the meaning of a text perfectly, particularly a text like Revelation, it seems to Moyise that postmodern intertextuality must be true *'to some degree'*.

Moyise concludes with a fresh analogy from the world of music. Every performance of Beethoven's Fifth Symphony will be different. Regardless of the extent of the differences, however, there will be no doubt that one is hearing Beethoven's Fifth Symphony and not his Sixth. The differences are real and worthy of study since they enrich enjoyment of the performance, but they should not be used to suggest that nothing can be done with the symphony! Likewise, postmodern intertextuality can contribute a great deal to our understanding of text without eliminating all meaning or understanding.[72]

In personal email correspondence, Moyise suggests four points of difference between himself and Beale.[73]

1. Moyise is attempting to describe the product John has produced; Beale seeks to describe the author's intention for that product.
2. Moyise sees himself in the middle between Beale, who sees John as a serious exegete of the Old Testament, and Elizabeth Schüssler Fiorenza, who sees John 'using scripture as a language arsenal for rhetorical purposes'.

---

70. Whether one blames the Samaritan woman for exploiting the six men in her life or the men for exploiting her depends on the standpoint from which one views the text. The text itself is silent on the matter, invoking the reader's involvement.
71. Moyise, 'Intertextuality', *op cit*, 37–40.
72. *Ibid*, 40.
73. Steve Moyise, e-mail messate to author, Friday, August 4, 2000.

3. Beale believes that John's four 'presuppositional lenses' produce one true meaning for the text; Moyise sees those various lenses providing the basis for multiple readings of the text, none having preference over the others.
4. Moyise sees himself as seeking to describe texts as dynamic entities, interacting with each other; he sees Beale as describing 'a static reality, how things are'.
5. Moyise allows for the possibility that these differences might reflect differences in personality. Beale has a natural preference for an either/or approach to textual options and Moyise has a natural preference for a both/and approach.

Making Sense of the Debate

It is difficult to say how much the discussion between Beale and Moyise is semantic or real.[74] In some ways it seems to be a replay of the epistemological debate framed by Hirsch on the one hand and Martin Heidegger and Jacques Derrida on the other.[75] Beale and Moyise are each defending against the perceived extremes of the other, which he believes, if left unchecked, will undermine his own contribution to scholarship. Each, to some degree, seems to be reacting to a caricature of the other's position. Beale fears the rebirth of allegory, which he understands as the indiscriminate 'creation of meaning' when interpreting texts. Moyise also fears allegory, which he understands as the indiscriminate bias of interpreters picking and choosing textual evidence that fits their presuppositional lens, then declaring that their resulting generalisations reflect the author's intention.

Beale is afraid that in approaching texts without the goal of attaining the author's intention, interpreters will be mired in a sea of subjectivity, where any interpretation of the text will be of equal validity. On the other hand, Moyise is

---

74. At the root of the debate seems to be the 'meaning of meaning'. Beale defines meaning as the intention of the author. Moyise defines meaning as communication.
75. ED Hirsch, Jr, *Validity in Interpretation* (New Haven: Yale University Press, 1967); ED Hirsch, Jr, *The Aims of Interpretation* (Chicago: University of Chicago Press, 1976); Martin Heidegger, *Poetry, Language, Thought*, trans. Albert Hofstadter (NY: Harper and Row, 1971); Jacques Derrida, *Of Grammatology*, translated by Gayatri Chakravorty Spivak (Baltimore: Johns Hopkins University Press, 1976); Jacques Derrida, *Writing and Difference*, trans. Alan Bass (London: Routledge and Kegan Paul, 1978). For a general introduction to the complexities of Derrida's thought see Jonathan Culler, *On Deconstruction: Theory and Criticism after Structuralism* (Ithaca, NY: Cornell University Press, 1982). On the relationship between Heidegger and Derrida see Herman Rapaport, *Heidegger and Derrida: Reflections on Time and History* (Lincoln: University of Nebraska Press, 1992). On the tension between the thought of Hirsch and Derrida see Kevin J Vanhoozer, *Is There a Meaning in This Text? The Bible, The Reader, and the Morality of Literary Knowledge* (Grand Rapids, MI: Zondervan, 1998).

concerned that we pay serious attention to literary critics who caution against arbitrary and totalising interpretations that draw their authority from overconfidence in having attained the author's authoritative intention. Could it be that this is one of those times when both sides are right, at least in part? Read separately, one can easily get the impression that the issue between them is life and death. Read together, one wonders at times if it is much ado about nothing. While both seem to agree that the nature of the issue is difficult to grasp, my impression is that each is right in what he affirms, but wrong in what he denies.

Does anyone, even Beale, seriously argue that indisputable and complete access to an author's intention can be achieved, even by the author? Does anyone, including Beale, seriously argue that New Testament writers were doing academic exegesis when they 'respected the context' of Old Testament antecedents? On the other hand, does anyone, even Moyise, seriously think that all interpretations are equally valid (that the seven seals could be seriously interpreted as aquatic animals, for example)?[76] Do any literary critics seriously apply such an extreme view of reader response to their students' papers? Are life and death issues really at stake here?

When the debate is approached from a positive direction rather than from a 'hermeneutic of suspicion', Beale and Moyise don't seem so far apart. My sense is that if Moyise were to write a commentary, it would not differ hugely from Beale's. The differences between them may be more on points of emphasis than over a serious divide. It seems to me that the real division between Beale and Moyise arises from another place. Hirsch's defense of authorial intention makes a lot of sense to me, I'm not sure he would agree with the specific use that Beale has made of his work in relation to Revelation.

If by 'meaning' we are speaking of an author's intention, how can New Testament writers be said to respect the original meaning and intention of Jeremiah as a human author? They are clearly not 'exegeting' Jeremiah in the sense that we would do so today. New Testament writers had an immediate and pragmatic purpose in their use of the Old, rather than a scientific, descriptive and exegetical one. When they studied the Old Testament, they were not driven by the need to understand the human intentions of an Ezekiel or a Jeremiah, but by the desire to be more effective in communicating the gospel, as they understood it.[77] At the same time, they are not reckless in their reading, as Beale has pointed out. They are operating under consistent principles and assumptions that were not radically

---

76. My appreciation to Leonard Thompson, 'Mooring the Revelation in the Mediterranean', (paper presented at the annual meeting of the Reading the Apocalypse Seminar of the Society of Biblical Literature, Philadelphia PA, November 23, 1992) for the pointed illustration.

77. Norman R Ericson, 'The NT Use of the OT: A Kerygmatic Approach', in *Journal of the Evangelical Theological Society* 30 (1987): 338.

different than those of similar groups in the Jewish environment of the Roman world.

I believe Beale is right when he says New Testament writers respect the larger context of Old Testament writings given two realities. Firstly, they are reading Old Testament writers in terms of their understanding of the total context of 'Scripture' not primarily in terms of an individual writer's intention for a specific time and place. Secondly, they are reading the Old Testament from the perspective of where they understood themselves to be in the context of the divine plan for history. If Jesus of Nazareth is the fulfillment of a divine plan announced in the context of Scripture as a whole, then the New Testament is a reasonable and contextual reflection on that whole.[78] New Testament writers are offering an interpretation of the Old Testament they believe the Old Testament writers themselves would give if they were alive to encounter Jesus.

Here is where I think the disconnection occurs. For Beale the 'author's intention' is not limited to the perspective of the individual Old Testament author, but includes the divine superintendence and authorship of Scripture as a whole. Consequently, his approach to the New Testament use of the Old is normative, comprehensive and global. On the other hand, for Moyise, the concept of 'author's intention' is limited to what a human writer intends at a specific point in history. His approach to the Old Testament is therefore descriptive, immediate and local. Given these differing starting points, it is not surprising that Beale and Moyise disagree on whether or not New Testament writers respect the context of the Old.

Beale implies that the divide between him and Moyise is grounded in a different faith perspective.[79] He accepts the idea of divine superintendence in Scripture; Moyise (by implication) does not. Whatever Moyise's actual faith perspective, I do not believe that this assumption is accurate. Even faith-based scholars generally agree that there is a human element in the Scriptures and that this human element is an important aspect of the scriptural message. A believer in the divine superintendence of Scripture may also be interested in the human writer's intention, without denying the global insights of a Dodd or a Beale. I believe the divide here is more a matter of semantics than substance.

I am naturally attracted to Hirsch's position, and therefore to Beale's. It seems to me that all genuine human knowledge is a reflection of past experience. Our own personal experiences are expanded by the experiences of others, conveyed to us through conversation, observation and reading. The collective wisdom of the human race comes to us in books and other media. For us to truly learn from

---

78. I wonder whether Moyise discounts this 'christocentric' principle in the New Testament too much. See, for example, his thoughts on presuppositional lenses in an as yet unpublished article entitled, 'The Use of Analogy in Biblical Studies'.
79. Beale, 'Questions of Authorial Intent', *op cit*, 165, 171–172.

reading, we must go beyond our own impressions of the text and ascertain something of the understanding and intention of the author. The experiences of others will be worthless to me unless I at least partially understand and appreciate them. The human race progresses from generation to generation as the learning, experience, and values of earlier generations are accurately passed on. For me, an understanding and appreciation of authorial intention seems to be a critical part of this process.

The strong element of common sense in the previous paragraph is underscored for me by the very debate we are here discussing. Moyise is just as eager as Beale to understand the intention of the others' communication. He also is concerned about the misuse of the term 'intertextuality' within New Testament scholarship.[80] 'Reader response' as a literary approach is very compelling in the abstract, but in practice when your own work is at stake, you reflexively resist open-ended interpretation.

Nevertheless, we cannot live as though Derrida (or Moyise) have never existed.[81] Far too often authoritative appropriations of significant texts are not based on careful exegesis, but on presupposition-laden 'reader responses' treated as accurate reflections of the text's intent. The ground of such readings has been the drive for power and control more than for faithfulness to the authoritative text. Calling attention to such abuse of texts is a valuable contribution to human experience. By increasing our awareness of human limitations to understanding, and of the effect that readers have on texts, literary critics may instill greater humility into the process of interpretation.

While I find Beale's fears understandable, Moyise's brief scholarly contributions to the exegesis of Revelation have been insightful and not very different to the work Beale has done. Profiting from the experience of others entails not only seeking authorial intention, but also discovering the limits of our ability to learn. The ultimate goal of authentic existence is enhanced by attention both to authorial purpose and attention to reader limitations.[82]

I would conclude that Beale and Moyise have brought to the topic two sides of a necessary dichotomy. Both a hermeneutic of suspicion and a hermeneutic of

---

80. Moyise, 'Intertextuality', *op cit*, 15–17.
81. Kirsten Nielsen, 'A Shepherd, Lamb, and Blood: Imagery in the Old Testament Use and Reuse,' *Studia Theologica: Scandinavian Journal of Theology*, Volume 46, No. 2 (1992): 126.
82. Kirsten Nielsen offers a fascinating observation that mediates the divide in a unique way for the study of Revelation. She argues that in a book like Revelation, where allusion is central to the imagery, the concepts of authorial intention and reader response come together. In other words, whenever we are dealing with allusion, we are dealing with an author that is also a reader (*ibid*, 126-127). The author of an allusive text begins as reader of an earlier text. For Nielsen, then, 'we cannot proclaim the death of the author without proclaiming the death of the reader, because every author is a reader as well. And conversely, if we claim the existence of the reader, we must accept the author as well.' (*ibid*, 127)

retrieval are needed and provide a necessary balance for interpretation.[83] While a given interpreter may prefer to spend more time on one side or the other of the dichotomy, awareness of both sides is valuable to developing understanding. We all want to be understood and to make a contribution to the human endeavor. We all want our ideas and intentions to be heard and taken seriously. At the same time we must acknowledge that authorial intention will always remain a goal of interpretation. We will not fully arrive, and seeking authorial intention will always be a process. As long as human existence goes on, we will continue to raise questions and strive to understand.

A Case Study of the Debate on Matthew 2:14–15

My colleague at Andrews University, Richard Davidson, has in the past expressed concern that I give too much credence to the human element in Scripture. I have often said that New Testament writers rarely use the Old Testament in an exegetical way. On the other hand, Davidson prefers to say that the New Testament writers use the Old Testament in harmony with its context. It is not surprising that students have sometimes felt our views were diametrically opposed. As with Beale and Moyise, I do not believe that this is the case.

Under other circumstances, it might have been preferable for me to illustrate the Beale/Moyise debate with an example from the book of Revelation. But since Davidson has included a essay here on Matthew's use of Hosea,[84] I thought it would be helpful for me to use the same pair of texts independently as an example of the method I prefer, then to see whether our results differ a great deal. You are invited to be the judge.

The point at issue is Matthew's use of Hosea 11:1 in Matthew 2:14, 15. Joseph gets up during the night and takes Jesus and his mother to Egypt to escape Herod. Matthew concludes, 'And so was fulfilled what the Lord had said through the prophet: "Out of Egypt I called my son."' The statement, "Out of Egypt I called my son," is clearly a quotation from Hosea 11:1. But a look at that verse in its immediate context suggests that it is not a direct prophecy about Jesus.

Is Matthew 2:14–15 an exegesis of the immediate intention of Hosea?[85] Hosea 11:1–4 is not a prophecy of the Messiah; it is a summary description of the Exodus in the form of an analogy based on the parenting of a small child.

---

83. I was intrigued by this pair of phrases in a Listserve reply to David Barr by Ian Paul at rev-list@sunsite.auc.dk on August 24, 2000. Paul stated there that the language was based on the work of Paul Ricoeur.
84. See below,.
85. For my definition of exegesis, see above, .

> When Israel was a child, I loved him, and out of Egypt I called my son. But the more I called Israel, the further they went from me. They sacrificed to the Baals and they burned incense to images. It was I who taught Ephraim to walk, taking them by the arms; but they did not realise it was I who healed them. I led them with cords of human kindness, with ties of love; I lifted the yoke from their neck and bent down to feed them (Hos 11:1–4).

The image is similar to the narrative of Matthew 2, but it seems to be a stretch of the imagination to say Hosea is here discussing a future Messianic figure.

Is Matthew's use of Hosea completely out of context? No. While Matthew is not doing exegesis of Hosea in a technical sense, he is using Hosea 11:1–4 in the light of the entire theological context of the Old Testament.

> Will they not return to Egypt and will not Assyria rule over them because they refuse to repent? Swords will flash in their cities, will destroy the bars of their gates and put an end to their plans. My people are determined to turn from me. Even if they call to the Most High, he will by no means exalt them (Hos 11:5–7).

Hosea here switches from the past to the future tense. If the people continue to turn away from Yahweh, enemies will invade their cities and rule over the people. So Hosea 11 is not merely a summary of the Exodus experience; it includes the captivity in Egypt as a model for the return to captivity that will occur if the prophet's message is not heeded. But like the first captivity in Egypt, this second captivity will not last forever.

> How can I give you up, Ephraim? How can I hand you over, Israel? How can I treat you like Admah? How can I make you like Zeboiim? My heart is changed within me; all my compassion is aroused. I will not carry out my fierce anger, nor will I turn and devastate Ephraim. For I am God, and not man—the Holy One among you. I will not come in wrath. They will follow the LORD; he will roar like a lion. When he roars, his children will come trembling from the west. They will come trembling like birds from Egypt, like doves from Assyria. I will settle them in their homes, declares the LORD.

Hosea 11:1–4 is one of the many places in the prophets where the Exodus experience is recalled.[86] The Exodus, God's mighty act at the founding of the nation of Israel, becomes the model for His next mighty act, the return from Babylon. While

---

86. I cover the Exodus theme in the prophets in some detail in my book *Meet God Again for the First Time* (Hagerstown, MD: Review & Herald, 2003), 45–54. See a broader, less specific treatment in *What the Bible Says About the End-Time* (Hagerstown, MD: Review & Herald, 1994), 55–64.

Israel has failed God, He retains his passion for them, like a loving husband for a wayward wife (Hos 2:8-15) or a loving parent for a wayward child (Hos 11:1-11). He *will* bring them back from far away places, just as He once brought them back from Egypt.

But the spectacular New Exodus of the prophets never happens. The actual return bears few direct resemblances to the Exodus. A handful of exiles return to a broken-down city and for those who saw the old temple, the new temple evokes only disappointment (Hag 2:1-4). God nevertheless assures them that the fulfillment has occurred, and that an even greater fulfillment lies ahead (Hag 2:5-9). This greater fulfillment is what Matthew is inviting the reader to embrace when he quotes the text, 'Out of Egypt I have called my Son my Son' (Matt 2:15). For Matthew, Jesus is the new Moses who leads a new Israel out of spiritual Egypt to the promised Kingdom of Heaven.

Like Moses, Jesus experiences an attempt on His life as an infant (*cf* Exod 1:15 - 2:10; Matt 2:16-18b). These two stories are remarkably parallel. There is nothing quite like them in the entire Bible. In both cases it is a hostile king and not just a random mugger. In both cases the child is seen as a threat to the throne. In both cases, many babies are destroyed in order to attack the one, and the one targeted escapes.

Moses fasts for forty days in the wilderness and then gives the law on a mountain (Exod 24:18; 34:28). Jesus fasts for forty days in the wilderness, then goes up on a mountain and gives the law of his new kingdom, the Sermon on the Mount (Matt 4:5). Both Moses and Jesus are glorified on a mountain (Exod 34:29-35; Matt 17:1-8). Moses gives Israel manna in the desert (Exod 16) and Jesus feeds 5,000 in the desert (Matt 14:13-21). In the Old Testament, the writings of Moses are collected into five books. Jesus' sayings are scattered throughout the Gospel of Luke. But as any red-letter edition of the Bible shows, his sayings in Matthew are grouped into five distinct sermons (Matt 5-7, 10, 13, 18; 24; 25). In Matthew, Jesus is clearly a new Moses who reveals the ways of God as Moses did.

But for Matthew Jesus is not only a New Moses; he is also a New Israel. Jesus is Mary's firstborn son (Matt 1:18-25). Israel is collectively God's firstborn (Exod 4:22-23). Jesus passes through the waters of baptism just as Israel passed through the waters of the Red Sea (Exod 14:10-31; Matt 3:13-17). He spends forty days in the wilderness just as Israel spends forty years in the wilderness (Num 14:33-34; Matt 4:1-2). Matthew is using the language of the past mighty act of God in the Exodus to set the background for God's mighty act in Jesus Christ.

Jesus relives the experience of Old Testament Israel. He is faithful to God where Israel was unfaithful. But not only does He relive the life of Israel and redeems it. He also takes upon Himself the consequences for Israel's disobedience, as per the curses of Deuteronomy 28:15-68. Disobedient Israel was stripped of its wealth and forced to live in poverty (Deut 28:15-20). Jesus has nowhere to lay His head

(Matt 8:20). The cursed ones of Deut 28 were to be 'smitten' before their 'enemies' (verse 25). Jesus was certainly smitten on the cross. On the cross, Jesus experienced darkness (Matt 27:45), being mocked (Mark 14:19, 31), thirst (John 19:28), and nakedness (Matt 27:35). In the wilderness He experienced hunger (Matt 4:2). The climax of the curses is to suffer with an anxious mind and a despairing heart (Deut 28:65-67). In the middle of the night the Israelites would groan and say, 'Oh, I wish it were morning', and in the middle of the day they would say, 'Oh, I wish I could go to bed, life is just not worth living anymore.' Jesus experiences an anxious mind and a despairing heart at Gethsemane.

When Matthew calls on Hosea 11:1 as a prophecy of an event in Jesus' life as an infant, he is not treating Hosea 11:1 as a direct prophecy. Instead he is using Hosea 11:1 as a pointer to the whole Old Testament pattern of the Exodus as a model for God's future saving activity. Time after time in the Old Testament prophets the Exodus becomes the model for what God will do in Babylon and beyond. So when Hosea recalls the Exodus in the context of a future exile and return, it is appropriate that Matthew finds an echo of Jesus' experience.

Hosea himself may not have understood the full significance of what he wrote. But subsequent history and the guiding hand of God open up the deeper meaning of Hosea's language. The statement, 'Out of Egypt I called my Son', is an excellent New Testament pointer to a theological reading of the Old Testament Exodus.[87] Matthew's use of Hosea is not exegetical in a technical sense, but is it valid as an exercise in biblical theology.

There is one final dimension in this Matthew text I would like to note. Hosea reference to Israel as God's son (Hos 11:1) is an individualisation of the concept of Israel as a nation. This individualisation is not original with Hosea (Exod 4:22, 23). Embedded deep within the Pentateuch is the Hebraic concept of 'corporate personality'. The whole nation can be represented by a single individual and the individual can stand for the whole.[88] The way is thus paved for the New Testament,

---

87. The New Testament scholar who first noticed how New Testament writers use Old Testament wording as pointers to the larger context was CH Dodd, *According to the Scriptures* (London: Nisbet & Co, 1952). See also CH Dodd, *The Old Testament in the New* (London: Athlone Press, 1952).

88. I am indebted to Jiri Moskala for the following list of helpful resources on the subject of corporate personality or representation. The concept hit the scholarly scene with a lecture by H Wheeler Robinson published in *Werden und Wesen des Alten Testaments*, beiheft 66 zur *Zeitschrift für die alttestamentliche Wissenschaft*, edited by P Volz, F Stummer and J Hempel (Berlin: Alfred Töpelmann, 1936); reprinted with an introduction by Gene M Tucker as *Corporate Personality in Ancient Israel* (Philadelphia: Fortress Press, 1980). While Robinson's thesis was based on some questionable socio/psychological assumptions, most scholars continue to see the concept of 'corporate representation' as having validity with reference to the biblical materials. The following represent various sides of the ongoing debate. JW Rogerson, 'Corporate Personality', in *Anchor Bible Dictionary*, edited by DN Freedman (Garden City, NY: Doubleday and Co, 1992),

which sees in the person of Jesus the one who represents the entire people of God, including Old Testament Israel.[89] His life relives the experiences of the nation (Matt 2:14–15). His death reaps the consequences of the whole nation's failure (Luke 9:31). When Hosea has God say, 'Out of Egypt I called my son', he is individualising the nation in a way natural to the theology of the entire Old Testament, from the Pentateuch onwards. While Matthew 2:14–15 is not an exegetical reading of Hosea 11, it is a natural extension of the theological purpose of the Exodus motif throughout the Old Testament. The wording of Hosea becomes a pointer to that entire context. Matthew has properly understood the inspired trend of the Law and the Prophets.[90]

Conclusion

I reaffirm that both Beale and Moyise are right with regard to the New Testament use of the Old Testament. The crucial issue is how theology and exegesis are defined, as discussed in the first essay of this volume. Beale is correct in the broad theological sense, that Matthew and Revelation are sensitive to the overall inspired context of the Old Testament. Moyise is correct that New Testament writers do not use the Old Testament in the sense of the human author's original setting and explicit intention.

Beale and Moyise have highlighted the two great dangers of intertextual study. One is the tendency to raise doubts about the integrity of the New Testament writers by assuming that all New Testament use of the Old Testament is fast and loose. The other is the tendency to claim an exegetical precision in such use that doesn't hold up to careful scrutiny. While the latter position may seem to be faithful to a high view of Scripture, it raises doubts in the minds of those who cannot buy into the overstatement.

A balanced view of intertextuality allows both the human and the divine authors of Scripture to assume their proper roles. It invites careful and prayerful study. It respects the integrity of Scripture, including its human elements, while inviting obedience to the divine intention of the Word. A balanced view of inter-

---

1:1156–1157; Philip Kaufman, 'The One and the Many: Corporate Personality', in *Worship* 42 (1968): 546–558; Cuthbert Lattey, 'Vicarious Solidarity in the Old Testament', in *Vetus Testamentum* 1 (1951): 267–274; JR Porter, 'Legal Aspects of "Corporate Personality" in the Old Testament', in *Vetus Testamentum* 15 (1965): 361–380; Stanley E Porter, 'Two Myths: Corporate Personality and Language/Mentality Determinism', in *Scottish Journal of Theology* 43 (1990): 289–299.

89. For a detailed outline of the New Testament application of OT history to Jesus see my book *Meet God Again for the First Time* (Hagerstown, MD: Review & Herald, 2003), 55–75.

90. Although I came to this understanding of Matthew 2:14–15 on my own and don't agree with everything Walter C Kaiser says on this subject, I am indebted in a couple of places to Kaiser's book, *The Uses of the Old Testament in the New* (Chicago: Moody, 1985), 47–53.

textuality allows that many passages of Scripture will not be fully understood until we reach the heavenly kingdom. It is content to rejoice in what we know, while acknowledging with Paul, 'We know in part . . . we see through a glass darkly' (1 Cor 13:9, 12; 2 Cor 5:7; Gal 3:6–14).[91]

---

91. For an excellent but challenging outline of this corporate understanding of Jesus and Israel, see NT Wright, *The Climax of the Covenant* (Minneapolis: Fortress Press, 1992).

Did Matthew 'Twist' the Scriptures?
A Case Study in the New Testament Use of the Old Testament

Richard M Davidson

Introduction

One of the most crucial issues in biblical theology is the question of the relationship between the Old and New Testaments, and in particular, the use of Old Testament quotations by New Testament writers.[1] Those who maintain a high view of Scripture recognise the Bible's self-testimony affirming the fundamental unity and harmony among its various parts.[2] Accepting this affirmation has in the past led to the assumption that the New Testament writers remain faithful to the original Old Testament contexts in their citation of Old

---

1. That the relationship between the Old Testament and the New Testament is one of the major, if not the major, issue in biblical theology, is widely recognised. See Henning Graf Reventlow, *Problems of Biblical Theology in the Twentieth Century*, translated by John Bowden (Philadelphia, PA: Fortress, 1986), 11, citing and translating NH Ridderbos, 'De verhouding van het Oude en het Nieuwe Testament', in *Gereformeerd theologisch Tijdschrift* 68 (1968): 97: 'The relationship between Old and New Testaments: that is just about the whole story; the whole of theology is involved in that.' Likewise, Walter Kaiser, Jr, *The Uses of the Old Testament in the New* (Chicago: Moody, 1985), 2, writes: 'the relationship between the OT and the NT stands as one of the foremost, if not the leading, problems in biblical research of this century.' Of course, there are many areas of concern in the study of the relationship of the Testaments. We have limited ourselves in this article to the explicit citations of Old Testament passages in the New Testament. Here, again, our study could go in many directions, such as examining the text types underlying the various citations. We have restricted discussion to the central question we are addressing: do the New Testament citations of Old Testament Scripture remain faithful to the original Old Testament contexts, or do they reinterpret these passages by reading back into the Old Testament a meaning that is imported from the New Testament? More specifically, we focus on Matthew's use of the Old Testament. Much of the material in this study is an update of my previous article, 'New Testament Use of the Old Testament', in *Journal of the Adventist Theological Society*, Volume 5, No. 1 (1994): 14–39.
2. See my discussion of the unity of Scripture according to the Bible writers' self-testimony in 'Interpreting Scripture: An Hermeneutical Decalogue', in *Journal of the Adventist Theological Society*, Volume 4, No 2 (Autumn 1993): 99–100.

Testament passages. This has been the consistent position of Christian scholarship until the rise of the historical-critical method in the wake of the Enlightenment.

The rationalistic presuppositions and procedures of historical criticism have led to an entirely different view of the relationship between the Testaments. A corollary of the historical-critical method posits a fundamental disunity among and between the Testaments, since they are seen as the product of a long development of oral tradition and various written sources redacted by fallible human writers with differing theological agendas.[3] According to the still widely prevailing view of current critical scholarship,[4] Jesus and the New Testament writers often take Old Testament passages out of context, reinterpret and reapply them in light of the Christ event, and thus impose an alien New Testament meaning upon the Old Testament. Raymond Brown summarises the historical-critical perspective with regard to the New Testament use of Old Testament statements as predictions of the Messiah: '[T]his conception of prophecy as prediction of the distant future has disappeared from most serious scholarship today, and it is widely recognised that the NT "fulfillment" of the OT involved much that the OT writers did not foresee at all'. He continues, '[T]here is no evidence that they [the Old Testament prophets] foresaw with precision even a single detail in the life of Jesus of Nazareth.'[5]

Even among evangelical scholars, it is frequently asserted that the New Testament methods of interpreting the Old Testament passages often do not incorporate sound exegesis, but rather offer Christological reapplication based upon first-century interpretational techniques such as rabbinic midrash, Hellenistic allegory, and/or Qumran-style *raz pesher* ('mystery interpretation').[6] It is suggested that

---

3. See my discussion of this development in 'The Authority of Scripture: A Personal Pilgrimage', in *Journal of the Adventist Theological Society,* Volume 1, No. 1 (Spring 1990): 43, 51–52.
4. In the last couple of decades there has arisen a new emphasis upon studying the 'final form' of the biblical text, but most of this new canonical exegesis and theology still presupposes the historical-critical reconstruction of the history of the text, even though these historical issues may be bracketed out of the discussion. Many of the most potent quotations of those disparaging the New Testament use of the Old Testament come from the period of the 1960s and 1970s before the rise of postmodernism, which has made it less fashionable to use heavily judgmental language and encouraged the acceptance of a pluralism of readings. By means of reader-oriented criticism and deconstructionism, the postmodern reader is encouraged to engage in his/her own reinterpretation of biblical passages.
5. Raymond Brown, *The Birth of the Messiah: A Commentary on the Infancy Narratives in Matthew and Luke* (Garden City, NY: Doubleday, 1977), 147.
6. See for example, Richard Longenecker, *Biblical Exegesis in the Apostolic Period* (Grand Rapids, MI: Eerdmans, 1975), 218: 'I suggest that we cannot reproduce their [the NT writers'] pesher exegesis . . . Likewise, I suggest that we should not attempt to reproduce their midrashic handling of the text, their allegorical explications, or much of their Jewish manner of argumentation. All of this is strictly part of the cultural context through which the transcultural and eternal gospel was expressed.' *Cf* E Earle Ellis, 'How the New Testament Uses the Old', in *New Testament Interpretation*, edited by I Howard Marshall (Grand Rapids, MI: Eerdmans, 1977), 201–208.

since the New Testament writers (and Jesus) are inspired, they have the right and authority under the Holy Spirit's guidance to reinterpret and reapply to Jesus what originally in the Old Testament does not refer to him.[7] There is an implied need to modify the traditional view of inspiration to accommodate the New Testament distortions of Old Testament passages.[8]

But is it necessary to dilute the historic high view of the inspiration of Scripture? Is it true that the New Testament writers follow a common first-century Jewish practice of reapplying and thus distorting the contextual meaning of the Old Testament passages they cite?

A Cambridge dissertation by David Instone-Brewer may be destined to rock the presuppositions and even topple the 'assured results' of current critical scholarship regarding first-century Jewish exegetical methods. Brewer's monograph demonstrates that 'the predecessors of the rabbis before 70 CE did not interpret Scripture out of context; did not look for any meaning in Scripture other than the plain sense; and did not change the text to fit their interpretation, though the later rabbis did all these things'.[9] Brewer then throws down a challenge: 'If the conclusions of this work are correct it demands a fresh examination of the New Testament, which may yet provide a model for the modern exegete.'[10]

This 'fresh examination' of New Testament exegetical methods has already begun. A growing number of studies re-examining New Testament citations of Old Testament passages conclude that New Testament writers (and Jesus Himself) were careful exegetes, faithfully representing the original plain contextual meaning of the Old Testament texts for New Testament readers.[11]

From my own research I have become increasingly convinced—contrary to my previous understanding—that the New Testament writers do not take Old Testament Scriptures out of context in their citations and do not read back into the Old Testament what is not there, but instead consistently remain faithful to

---

7. See for example, Norman Hillyer, 'Matthew's Use of the Old Testament', in *Evangelical Quarterly*, 36 (1964): 25; E Earle Ellis, *Paul's Use of the Old Testament* (Grand Rapids, MI: Eerdmans, 1957), 83; and Longenecker, *Biblical Exegesis, op cit*, 207. This view has been taken further by some Seventh-day Adventist scholars, who claim that such doctrines as the pre-advent/investigative judgment are not taught in the Book of Daniel, but that Ellen White, as an inspired prophet, had the right, like the New Testament writers, to reinterpret the Old Testament prophecies.
8. See for example, the view of Alden Thompson, *Inspiration: Hard Questions, Honest Answers* (Hagerstown, MD: Review and Herald, 1991), especially 205–213.
9. David Instone Brewer, *Techniques and Assumptions in Jewish Exegesis before 70 CE* (Tübingen: Mohr, 1992), 1.
10 *Ibid.*
11. See for example, the collection of such studies in *The Right Doctrine from the Wrong Texts? Essays on the Use of the Old Testament in the New*, edited by GK Beale (Grand Rapids, MI: Baker, 1994).

the Old Testament intention, and consistently engage in solid exegesis of the Old Testament passages using sound hermeneutical principles.

I have gradually come to this conclusion by re-examining the major New Testament passages commonly alleged to have taken Old Testament texts out of context.[12] We will concentrate on passages in the Book of Matthew that scholars frequently insist represent a twisting of the Old Testament Scriptures.[13] We will look at the following passages from Matthew:

Matthew 1:23, citing Isaiah 7:14.
Matthew 2:15, citing Hosea 11:1.
Matthew 2:18, citing Jeremiah 31:15.
Matthew 2:23, citing 'the prophets'.
Matthew 12:40, citing Jonah 2.
Matthew 27:35, 36 (and parallels), citing Psalm 22.

The Virgin Birth: Matthew 1:23, Citing Isaiah 7:14

Isaiah 7:14 has been called 'the most difficult of all Messianic prophecies'[14] and is perhaps the most studied text in biblical scholarship.[15] McCasland sees Isaiah 7:14 as a prime example of Matthew twisting the Scriptures. 'It is well known that this saying of Isaiah refers to an event of his own time, and that the Hebrew word *almāh*, for the mother of the child, does not mean a virgin but only a young woman.'[16] A recent article comes to the same conclusion.[17] It is not possible in this study to delve into all the exegetical issues in this passage.[18] Rather, our focus is on the question: Does Matthew

---

12. The number of such examples is actually not large. Of the more than 300 formal Old Testament quotations by New Testament writers (The UBS Greek New Testament lists 318), the majority are uncontested as representing a literal usage that is faithful to the original context. In this study we are not dealing with the multitude of New Testament allusions to the Old Testament. New Testament writers, steeped in OT language and imagery, often employ Scriptural language in passing without formal quotation.
13. See for examle, note the title of S Vernon McCasland's article, 'Matthew Twists the Scriptures;, in *Journal of Biblical Literature*, 80 (1961): 143–148. McCasland insists that 'Matthew felt free in changing and distorting the Scriptures', in *ibid*, 146.
14. J Barton Payne, *Encyclopedia of Biblical Prophecy* (Grand Rapids, MI: Baker, 1973), 291, citing Milton S Terry, *Biblical Hermeneutics* (New York, NY: Phillips and Hunt, 1883), 331
15. For a representation of the immense bibliography, see John DW Watts, *Isaiah 1 – 33*, Word Biblical Commentary (Waco, TX: Word, 1985), 24:95–103.
16. McCasland, 'Matthew Twists the Scriptures,' 144.
17. Warren C Trenchard and Larry G Herr, 'The Interpretation of the Old Testament in the New: Isaiah, Matthew and the Virgin', in *Spectrum* , Volume 28, No. 1 (Winter 2000): 16–23.
18. For further discussion of this passage, see especially Gleason Archer, *Encyclopedia of Bible Difficulties* (Grand Rapids, MI: Zondervan, 1982), 266–268; and John N Oswalt, *The Book of Isaiah; Chapters 1 – 39*, NICOT (Grand Rapids, MI: Eerdmans, 1986), 192–248.

remain faithful to the Old Testament context of this passage when in Matthew 1:23 he cites it as a prediction of the virgin birth of the Messiah? The interpretations of Isaiah 7:14 fall into three major categories: (1) those that maintain only a local fulfillment in the time of Isaiah; (2) those that posit a reference in the text only to the virgin birth of the Messiah; and (3) those that argue for both.

A careful look at the immediate context of Isaiah 7:14 clearly reveals a local dimension to the fulfillment of the prophecy. The historical setting is the Syro-Ephraimite War (ca. 734 BCE) when the northern kingdoms of Syria and Israel band together to attack their southern neighbor, Judah (Isa 7:1,4-6). Ahaz, King of Judah, is terrified of the impending invasion, but God sends Isaiah with the comforting word that the northern coalition will not succeed in their plans to overthrow Ahaz (Isa 7:2, 3, 7-9). In this situation God gives Ahaz a sign through Isaiah: 'Behold, the virgin [is, shall be] pregnant,[19] and she shall bear a son, and she shall call his name Immanuel' (verse 14).

The succeeding verses give the time frame of the local fulfillment of this sign: 'For before the child shall know to refuse the evil and choose the good, the land that you dread will be forsaken by both her kings' (verse 16). The child clearly would be born in the time of Ahaz, and before it reached the age of accountability, the Syro-Ephraimite coalition would be dissolved. This local interpretation is confirmed in the succeeding chapter. Isaiah goes in to 'the prophetess' (his wife, who at the time of the prophecy may have been a virgin), she conceives, and bears a son (Isa 8:3). The link between this son and the prophecy is made in Isaiah 8:4 by a statement clearly parallel with Isaiah 7:16: 'for before the child shall have knowledge to cry "my father" and "my mother", the riches of Damascus and the spoil of Samaria will be taken away before the king of Assyria'. The time elements implied in Isaiah 7:16 and 8:4 were fulfilled precisely: in 732 BC (within two years of the prophecy of 7:14, before the child could say 'father' or 'mother') Damascus fell, and in 722 BC (before the child was twelve and had reached the age of accountability) Samaria fell.

Thus Isaiah 7:14 does have a dimension of local fulfillment. But is this all that is implied in the text, and in its larger context? Let us look more closely. First, that the prophecy of Isaiah 7:14 is not addressed only to Ahaz, but to the 'house of David' (verse 13). When Isaiah records that 'The Lord Himself will give *you* a sign', the word 'you' is in the plural, not the singular, implying a wider application

---

19. Literal translation. Note that this is a nominal clause in Hebrew, that is, it does not supply the verb 'to be'. At first sight there is thus an ambiguity about whether the woman already 'is' pregnant or later 'will be' pregnant. It is not possible, however, to translate the clause as 'Behold, the pregnant woman', as though she is already standing there, obviously preg-nant for the king to behold. If such were the case, the adjective *hārāh* 'pregnant' would need to be attributive rather than predicative, that is, it would need the definite article to match the definite article attached to *'almāh* (See *Gesenius' Hebrew Grammar* Par. 126 u).

than just to Ahaz. Second, in Isaiah 7:14 the Hebrew word *'almāh* ('virgin, young woman'), translated in the LXX and Matthew 1:23 by *parthenos* or 'virgin', means more than just a 'virgin'. There is another Hebrew word that means 'virgin', namely *bᵉthûlāh*. But *bethûlāh* does not specify the age or marital status of the virgin. The word ᵈ*almāh*, however, means 'a young woman of marriageable age, sexually ripe', who is unmarried, and therefore (unless she is an unchaste woman) a virgin.[20] Thus ᵈ*almāh*, like the English equivalent *maiden*, has 'overtones of virginity about it',[21] even though virginity is not the primary focus of the term. If it did not have such overtones, the Septuagint translation as *parthenos* 'virgin' would be inexplicable. In this prophecy, Isaiah uses a term that does not stress virginity, and thus could have significance for Ahaz's situation with a local, partial fulfillment; but that at the same time m has connotations of virginity, thereby pointing beyond the local setting to the ultimate sign in the virgin birth of the Messiah.

What is hinted at in the text is made explicit in the larger context. Scholars generally agree that Isaiah 7:14 is part of a larger literary unit of Isaiah encompassing Isaiah 7–12, often called the 'Volume of Immanuel'. However, they often fail to view Isaiah 7:14 within the whole of this larger setting. When Isaiah's son is born, he is not named 'Immanuel', as Isaiah 7:14 predicts. God tells Isaiah to name him Maher-shalal-hash-baz, 'Speed the spoil, hasten the booty' (Isa 8:1). The name Immanuel is next used in a context that seems to move from the local to the cosmic level (Isa 8:8).

Isaiah and his sons are said to be 'signs' in Israel (Isa 8:18) of future events to be brought about by God. These events move from the local level at the end of Isaiah 8 to the eschatological Messianic level in Isaiah 9. The land which was in *gloom* and *darkness* (8:22) will become a land where the *gloom* is removed (9:1) and 'the people who walked in *darkness* have seen a great light' (9:2). Most significantly, Isaiah's son is a sign to Israel, but in the Messianic age a greater Son, the ultimate fulfillment of Isaiah 7:14, will appear: 'For unto us a Child is born, unto us a Son is given, and the government will be upon His shoulder. And His name will be called Wonderful Counsellor, Mighty God, Everlasting Father, Prince of Peace' (Isa 9:6). This coming and work of the Messiah is expanded in Isaiah 11:1–9.

---

20. The eight other occurrences of *'almāh* in the Old Testament are in the following passages: Genesis 24:43; Exodus 2:8; 1 Chronicles 15:20; Psalm 46:2 (English verse 1); 68:26 (English verse 25); Proverbs 30:19; Cant 1:3; 6:8. Numerous scholars cogently argue that in none of these passages does *'almāh* refer to a married woman or one who is no longer a virgin. See John Oswalt, *The Book of Isaiah, Chapters 1 – 39*, NICOT (Grand Rapids, MI: Eerdmans, 1986), 210–212.
21. *Ibid*, 210. Though the word 'maiden' does not directly mean virgin, it does imply someone who is unmarried, in contradistinction to the word 'matron' (thus 'maid of honour' and 'matron of honour' to denote unmarried and married woman respectively). Thus if a maid is chaste, she is a virgin.

The prediction will have local fulfillment in the birth of a son in the time of Ahaz. However, Isaiah himself, under divine inspiration, indicates that this local fulfillment is a type of the ultimate Messianic fulfillment in the divine Son, Immanuel. We may diagram the typological relationships in Isaiah's volume of Immanuel as following:

1. Type		Isaiah 7:14 (Immanuel prophecy)
		Isaiah 8:1–4 (local fulfillment of Isaiah 7:14)
2. Antitype		Isaiah 9:1–7 (ultimate fulfillment in the Messiah)
		Isaiah 11:1–9 (further description of the Messiah)

Matthew, therefore, far from taking Isaiah 7:14 out of context, has recognised the larger Messianic context of Isaiah 7 – 12, which critical scholarship has usually ignored. Did Matthew twist the Scriptures with regard to this passage? No! He saw the dual focus of the prophecy, with the ultimate fulfillment climaxing in the virgin birth of the Messiah.

'Out of Egypt I Called My Son': Matthew 2:15, Citing Hos 11:1

Matthew 2:15 is another instance where critical scholars charge Matthew with unfaithfulness to the Old Testament context. For example, S Marion Smith states that in citing Hosea 11:1 Matthew employs 'a method that can be rejected outright as an untenable use of Scripture . . . '[22] However, I suggest that these critical scholars fail to discern the larger context of Hosea 11:1.

It is true that in its immediate historical context, Hosea 11:1 refers to the past historical exodus of ancient Israel from Egypt: 'When Israel was a child, I loved him, and out of Egypt I called my son'. The next verse describes the historical circumstances of national Israel's turning away from Yahweh to serve the Baals.

However, it is also crucial to see the wider context of this verse.

CH Dodd, in his classic work, *According to the Scriptures*, has demonstrated how the New Testament writers often cite a single Old Testament passage as a pointer for the reader to consider the whole larger context of that passage. Dodd has shown that the larger context of Hosea 11:1, both in the book of Hosea itself and in other eighth-century prophets, describes a future new exodus connected with Israel's return from exile and the coming of the Messiah.[23]

---

22. Marion Smith, 'New Testament Writers Use the Old Testament', in *Encounter*, 26 (1965): 239.
23. CH Dodd, *According to the Scriptures* (London: Collins, 1952), 74–133. Especially note Hosea 2:14–15; 12:9, 13; 13:4–5; Isaiah 11:15–16; 35; 40:3–5; 41:17–20; 42:14–16; 43:1–3, 14–21; 48:20–21; 49:3–5, 8–12; 51:9–11; 52:3–6, 11–12; 55:12–13; Amos 9:7–15; Micah 7:8–20. *Cf* Jeremiah 23:4–8; 16:14–15; 31:32.

In fact, the typological interconnection between ancient Israel's exodus and the Messiah's exodus from Egypt is already indicated in the Pentateuch. In the oracles of Balaam, there is an explicit shift from the historical exodus to the Messianic exodus. In Numbers 23:22 Balaam proclaims, 'God brings *them* out of Egypt; He [God] has strength like a wild ox'. In the next oracle, Balaam shifts to the singular, 'God brings *him* out of Egypt' (Num 24:8), and in the next and final oracle, referring to the 'latter days' (24:14), Balaam indicates the Messianic identification of the 'him': 'I see Him, but not now; I behold him, but not near; a Star shall come out of Jacob; a scepter shall arise out of Israel, and batter the brow of Moab, and destroy all the sons of tumult' (24:17).[24]

In a recent article John Sailhamer demonstrates that 'Hosea's entire message throughout the book is grounded in a careful and conscious exegesis of the pentateuchal text' and that when Hosea recalled the event of the exodus he likely had in mind 'its central messianic meaning within the Pentateuch'.[25]

Thus the Pentateuch and the classical prophets (especially Hosea and Isaiah) clearly recognise that Israel's exodus from Egypt is a type of the new exodus, centered in the new Israel, the Messiah. Matthew remains faithful to this larger Old Testament context in his citation of Hoseah 11:1. In harmony with the Old Testament predictions, Matthew depicts Jesus as the new Israel, recapitulating in his life the experience of ancient Israel, but succeeding where the first Israel failed.

The first five chapters of Matthew describe Jesus as the new Israel experiencing a new exodus: coming out of Egypt after a death decree (Matt 2:15) and going through His antitypical Red Sea experience in His baptism (Matt 3; *cf* 1 Cor 10:1, 2). This description is followed by the depiction of his wilderness experience of forty days; parallel to the forty years ancient Israel was in the wilderness. During this time Jesus indicates His own awareness of His role as the new Israel in the new exodus by consistently meeting the devil's temptations with quotations from Deuteronomy 6 – 8 (where ancient Israel's temptations in the wilderness are summarised). Finally, Jesus appears on the mount as a new Moses, with His twelve disciples representing the tribes of Israel, and repeats the law as Moses did at the end of the wilderness sojourn. Matthew, Mark, and Luke also depict the death and resurrection of Jesus as a new exodus.[26]

---

24. See John H Sailhamer, *The Pentateuch as Narrative: A Biblical-Theological Commentary* (Grand Rapids, MI: Zondervan, 1992), 407–409, and the recent published Andrews University dissertation by Friedbert Ninow, *Indicators of Typology within the Old Testament: the Exodus Motif* (Frankfort am Main; New York: P Lang, 2001). Ninow deals not only with this Pentateuchal 'New Exodus' indicator, but also with the entire scope of Old Testament exodus typology passages

25. John H Sailhamer, 'Hosea 11:1 and Matthew 2:15', in *Westminster Theological Journal*, 63 (2001): 87-96 (quotation from 91).

26. Now how at the transfiguration, the first Moses speaks to the New Moses about the latter's *exo-*

Thus, rather than distorting the Old Testament context of Hos 11:1, Matthew,

> quoted a single verse not as a proof text, but a pointer to his source's larger context. Instead of interrupting the flow of his argument with a lengthy digression, he let the words of Hosea 11:1 introduce that whole context in Hosea.[27]

Matthew faithfully captures the wider eschatological, Messianic context of this exodus passage as portrayed by Hosea and his prophetic contemporaries, and as already set forth in the Pentateuch.

'Rachel Weeping for Her Children': Matthew 2:18, Citing Jeremiah 31:15

LS Edgar considers Matthew 2:18 to be 'the most striking case of disregard of context in the NT'.[28] What does Rachel's weeping for her children killed by the Babylonians or taken into captivity, have to do with the slaughter of the Bethlehem babies at the time of Jesus' birth?

It is true that the local historical context of Jeremiah 31:15 has to do with the inhabitants of Judah at the time of their going into exile in Babylon: 'A voice was heard in Ramah, lamentation and bitter weeping, Rachel weeping for children, refusing to be comforted for her children, because they are no more'. It is in Ramah that Nebuzarhadan, the captain of the Babylonian guard, assembles the Judean captives, before taking them in chains to Babylon (Jer 40:1). Rachel, the 'mother' of Israel (Ruth 4:11), is portrayed as weeping for her descendants, especially the children who are 'no more' (Jer 31:15), apparently put to death by the Babylonians near her tomb at Ramah (see Ps 137:8, 9; cf Isa 13:16), or ready to be taken into exile.

But while the immediate context of Jeremiah 31:15 is the Babylonian exile, the larger context in this chapter involves the eschatological gathering of Israel from exile (verses 7–8) as part of the Messianic new covenant (verses 31–34). Walter Kaiser details the larger context:

> Even though Jeremiah clearly says that the Babylonian Exile will last for seventy years (Jer. 25:11, 12; 29:10), it is just as clear that he

---

dus, which he is to accomplish at Jerusalem (Luke 9:31). Jesus' death is his Red Sea experience. After his resurrection, he remains in the wilderness of this earth forty days (like Israel's forty years in the wilderness) and then as the New Joshua enters heavenly Canaan as the pioneer and perfector of our faith. See George Balentine, 'Death of Christ as a New Exodus', in *Review and Expositor*, 59 (1962): 27–41; and *idem*, 'The Concept of the New Exodus in the Gospels', (ThD dissertation Southern Baptist Theological Seminary, 1961).

27. Kaiser, *The Uses, op cit*, 52.
28. SL Edgar, 'Respect for Context in Quotations from the Old Testament', in *New Testament Studies*, 9 (1962): 58.

knows that the Exile will not end until the coming of the new David. The whole book of comfort (Jer. 30–33) offers not only the renewal of the ancient covenant with the inhabitants of Judah and Israel, but a new David who will sit on the throne of Israel once again (30:8-9; 33:14-15, 17) . . . Clearly, the context of Rachel's weeping lies within the bounds of the ultimate hope of God's final eschatological act . . . The whole context of the book of comfort must be brought to bear on the total understanding of this passage. Thus, Rachel must weep yet once more in Herod's time before that grand day of God's new David and new Israel.[29]

Kaiser's conclusion with regard to the use of Jeremiah and Hosea in Matthew 2 is on the mark: 'Matthew displayed a sensitivity for the whole context of Hosea and Jeremiah, one that involved an awareness of their canonical, theological, and eschatological contexts in addition to their historical context.'[30]

'He Shall Be Called a Nazarene': Matthew 2:23, Citing 'the Prophets'

Matthew 2:23 reads: 'And he came and dwelt in a city called Nazareth, that it might be fulfilled which was spoken by the prophets, "He shall be called a Nazarene."' In this case, no specific Old Testament passage is cited. Many scholars have seen here a reference to the law of the Nazirite in Numbers 6 (*cf* Judges 13:4-5), and have pointed out how the context simply does not fit the situation of Jesus.

It is true that Jesus is not a Nazirite. He does not refrain from drinking the juice of the grapes or from shaving His head. But the problem of this passage is not with Matthew in mistakenly connecting Nazareth with the Nazirites; it is with those scholars mistakenly attributing such a connection to Matthew.

What needs to be recognised is that the Greek letter *zeta* or 'z' is used to transliterate two Hebrew letters, *zayin* (or 'z') and *tsade* (or 'ts'). The Hebrew for the town Nazareth comes the Hebrew root *nsr*, not *nzr*. The OT noun built on this stem is *n'tser*, which means 'sprout, shoot, branch'. This Hebrew word is the technical term for the Messiah utilised in the prediction of Isaiah 11:1: 'There shall come forth a Rod from the stem of Jesse, and a Branch [*n'tser*] out of his roots'.

Matthew, far from positing a false connection between Jesus and the Nazirite, is instead recognising the connection between the name of the town 'Nazareth' and the title of the Messiah. Messiah, the Branch [*n'tser*], grows up [*ntsr*] in the City of the Branch [*nāt□sāret*]! Again, Matthew is remaining faithful to the original Messianic context of the Volume of Immanuel (Isa 7 – 12), in his allusion to Isaiah 11:1.

---

29. Kaiser, *The Uses, op cit,* 55–56.
30. *Ibid,* 57.

Two additional passages in the book of Matthew have been frequently cited as examples of taking the Old Testament out of context. Matthew, however, reports these as words of Jesus Himself.

The Sign of Jonah: Matthew 12:40, Citing Jonah 2

In a previous study on biblical typology,[31] I point out how various persons, events, and institutions are called 'types' in the New Testament, and are already indicated as such in the Old Testament. I briefly note how this is true in the case of Jonah. Here, let us look more closely at the typology of Jonah referred to by Jesus.

Already in Jonah's prayer during the three days and nights in the belly of the great fish, the language the prophet employs goes well beyond his own literal experience. What he describes is a virtual 'death-resurrection' experience: 'out of the belly of Sheol [the grave] I cried'; 'the earth with its bars closed behind me forever; yet you have brought up my life from the pit [the grave]' (Jonah 2:2, 6). This language is clearly metaphoric, representing his traumatic experience in the watery depths, and thus has a local primary application to his own near-drowning.

But only a few short years after Jonah's experience, Hosea 6:1–3 clearly refers to Israel's captivity and restoration as a 'death' and 'resurrection' on the 'third day',[32] parallel to the experience of Jonah. Israel is 'like a dove', a *yônāh* or 'Jonah', who goes to Assyria (Hos 7:11). It is 'swallowed up' (Hos 8:8) just as Jonah is by the great fish (Jonah 1:17). In its 'death-resurrection' experience, Hosea sees Israel as recapitulating Jonah's experience.

In the same eighth-century BC context, as we have already seen, Isaiah clearly describes the Messiah as a new Israel. Isaiah reveals that the Messianic Servant will represent and recapitulate the experience of the first Israel, especially through his death and resurrection.[33]

To summarise, Hosea indicates that Israel is another Jonah, experiencing 'death' followed by 'resurrection' on the third day. Isaiah shows that the Messiah

---

31. See Richard M Davidson, 'Sanctuary Typology', in *Symposium on Revelation—Book I*, Daniel and Revelation Committee Series 6, edited by Frank Holbrook (Silver Spring, MD: Biblical Research Institute, 1992), 106, 128.
32. See Bertrand C Pryce, 'The Resurrection Motif in Hosea 5:8 – 6:6: An Exegetical Study', (PhD dissertation Andrews University, 1989), for an examination of the exegetical evidence for the death-resurrection motif in this passage.
33. In the Servant Songs of Isaiah 42 – 53, the frequent alternation between the corporate and the singular aspects of the servant is striking. In this way the prophet indicates that the Messianic Servant would be the New Israel. See HH Rowley, *The Servant of the Lord and Other Essays* (London: Lutterworth, 1952). On the death-resurrection motif with reference to the Messianic servant in Isaiah, see Duane F Lindsey, *The Servant Songs: A Study in Isaiah* (Chicago, IL: Moody Press, 1985).

is a new Israel, undergoing a death and resurrection like the first Israel. It remains for Jesus, the master exegete, to call attention to these connections between God's 'servant' Jonah (2 Kgs 14:25), the servant Israel, and the Messianic Servant. Based upon the typological relationships already set forth in the Old Testament, Jesus can confidently proclaim the sign of Jonah: as Jonah was in the belly of the great fish for 'three days and three nights' so the new Jonah/Israel will be in the heart of the earth and rise after three days.[34] Jesus remains faithful to the wider Old Testament context of Jonah's experience, and accurately announces the fulfillment of the Jonah/Israel typology indicated by the Old Testament prophets.

The 'Psalm of the Cross': New Testament References to Psalm 22

Numerous New Testament passages cite Psal, 22 as being fulfilled in events surrounding the death and resurrection of Christ.[35] The problem arises because the Psalm itself does not explicitly indicate that it is referring to the Messiah. It is written by David in the first person, and apparently describes David's own personal experience.[36] How can the New Testament writers see this psalm as pointing to the Messiah? Many scholars assume that the New Testament is engaging in reinterpretation, reading back into the Old Testament something that is not there. However, the Old Testament itself provides verbal indicators that identify the typological nature of the messianic psalms.

Despite Davidic authorship and use of the first person, various commentators have recognised that 'the features of this psalm far transcend the actual experi-

---

34. Also apparently based upon these OT typological connections among Jonah, Israel, and Jesus, it is possible for Paul to say that Christ 'rose again the third day *according to the Scriptures*' (1 Cor 15:4). The third-day timing of the Messiah's resurrection is also probably indicated in the typology of the wave sheaf in Leviticus 23. A sheaf of barley was to be waved 'on the day after the Sabbath' of Passover week (Lev 23:11). If the Sabbath referred to here is the first day of the Feast of Unleavened Bread (Nisan 15), as interpreted by the Pharisees, and indicated by Josephus (*Antiquities* 3.10.5), then the wave sheaf would always be waved on Nisan 16, the third day from Nisan 14 when the Passover was celebrated. Paul recognises that Jesus in his resurrection is the antitypical wave-sheaf, the first-fruits of the coming harvest (1 Cor 15:20, 23).
35. Matthew 27:35 and parallels (Mark 15:24, Luke 23:34, John 19:24), cite Psalm 22:18; Matthew 27:39 and Mark 15:29 cite verse 7; Matthew 27:43 cites verse 8; Matthew 27:45 and Mark 15:34 cite verse 1; and Hebrew 2:12 cites verse. 22.
36. The superscription (Ps 22:1) reads, *mizmôr l⊠david*, 'A Psalm of David'. For evidence supporting the authenticity of the superscriptions in the Psalms and David's authorship of Psalms with this superscription, see, for example, Derek Kidner, *Psalms 1 – 72: An Introduction and Commentary on Books I and II of the Psalms*, Tyndale Old Testament Commentaries (London: Tyndale Press, 1973), 32–35; HC Leupold, *Exposition of the Psalms* (Grand Rapids: Baker, 1959), 5–8.

ences of David'.[37] 'David's language overflows all its natural banks.'[38] It is 'not a description of illness, but of an *execution.*'[39] The executed one is actually brought 'to the dust of death' (verse 15); and yet in verses 22ff. he is again alive and well, declaring Yahweh's name to His brethren! 'In Psalm 22 David descends, with his complaint into a depth that lies beyond the depth of his affliction, and rises, with his hopes to a height that lies far beyond the height of the reward of his affliction.'[40]

The way that Psalm 22 moves beyond David's own personal experience is clarified in connection by the first Messianic psalm of the Psalter. In Psalm 2, also written by David (Acts 4:25), there is striking evidence that the anointed Davidic king is seen as a type of the future Messiah. The psalm moves from the local level of the earthly installation of the Davidic king as Yahweh's 'son', to the cosmic level of the divine Son, the Messiah. The final verse indicates this typological movement: 'Kiss the Son, lest he [the Son][41] be angry, and you perish in the way, when His [the Son's] wrath is kindled but a little. Blessed are all those who put their trust in Him [the Son].' The phrase 'take refuge in' is always reserved for the deity in Scripture, and therefore the Son of verse 12 is none other than the divine Son of God.[42] This internal typological indicator in Psalm 2 sets the tone for the remainder of the Davidic Psalter: the Davidic $m^e\check{s}iach$ or 'anointed one' is a type of the eschatological divine Messiah.

What is implicit in the Psalms becomes explicit in the prophets. Numerous Old Testament prophets, under inspiration, predict that the Messiah will come as the new antitypical David, recapitulating in his life the experience of the first David.[43] Thus the Davidic psalms relating to David's experience of suffering and royal reign as the anointed one are already announced in the Old Testament as types of the coming Davidic Messiah. The New Testament writers in citing these psalms are simply announcing the fulfillment of what is already anticipated in the Old Testament.[44]

---

37. Leupold, *Psalms*, 21.
38. Kidner, *Psalms 1–72*, 109.
39. A Bentzen, *King and Messiah* (Lutterworth, 1955), 94, note 40.
40. Franz Delitzsch, 'Psalms', in *Commentary on the Old Testament in Ten Volumes*, by CF Keil and F. Delitzsch (Grand Rapids, MI: Eerdmans, 1976 [original 1867]), 5:306.
41. The most natural antecedent to the pronoun is the nearest noun, the Son, rather than Yahweh in the previous verse.
42. For a discussion of the New Testament Messianic fulfilment of Psalm 22, see Hans LaRondelle, *Deliverance in the Psalms* (Berrien Springs, MI: First Impressions, 1983), 53–60.
43. See for example, Jeremiah 23:5; Ezekiel 34:23; 37:24; Isaiah 9:5, 6; 11:1–5; Hoseah 3:5; Amos 9:11; Zechariah 8:3.
44. Other Davidic psalms thus cited typologically include: Psalm 35:19 (John 15:25); Psalm 40:6–8 (Heb 10:5–9); Pslam 41:9 (John 13:18); Psalm 69:4 (John 15:25), 9 (John 2:17; Rom 15:3), 21 (Matt 27:34 and parallels); Psalm 109:8 (Acts 1:20). There is also David's reference to the 'son

In Daniel 9:26, the angel Gabriel refers to the death of the Messiah and specifically alludes to Psalm 22. Jacques Doukhan notes that the expression $^e\hat{e}n\ l\hat{o}$ 'he has no ...' is a contracted form of $^e\hat{e}n\ ^d\hat{o}zer\ l\hat{o}$ 'he has no help' in Daniel 11:45, parallel to the phrase $^e\hat{e}n\ ^d\hat{o}zer$ 'no help' in Psalm 22:11.[45] Doukhan thus shows that Daniel 9:26 indicates that the Messiah will fulfill the words of Psalm 22. This typological indicator points to Psalm 22 as the special psalm of the Messiah at his death.

Jesus, as a careful exegete of the messianic prophecy of Daniel 9, apparently understands his death to be linked in fulfillment to Psalm 22. In fact, it is possible that Jesus faces the experience of Calvary fortified by the words of Psalm 22, perhaps even mentally moving through the psalm as the events of His crucifixion unfold.

It seems no coincidence that as His unity with the Father is breaking up, separated by the sins of the world which He bears, Jesus cries out using the opening words of Psalm 22: 'My God, my God, why have you forsaken me?' As He hangs on the cross, He cannot see through the portals of the tomb, but by naked faith holds on to the assurances of this Psalm and sees the events it describes transpiring before Him All around Him mockers use the very words of Psalm 22:8: 'He trusted in the Lord, let Him rescue Him; let Him deliver Him, since He delights in Him!' (Matt 27:43; Luke 23:35). All his disciples have forsaken him: 'there is none to help' (Ps 22:11).In His thirst, He experiences Psalm 22:15: 'My strength is dried up like a potsherd, and my tongue clings to my jaws'. In the pain coming from the nail-pierced hands and feet, there is reminiscence of Psalm 22:17: 'they have pierced my hands and feet'. As the soldiers cast lots for his garment, Psalm 22:18 comes true before His eyes: 'They divide my garments among them, and for my clothing they cast lots'.

Jesus' faith may well have pierced the gloom as He recalled the words that come in the second half of the psalm, starting with the abrupt affirmation in verses 21-22: 'You have answered me! I will tell your name to my brethren.' Here is the assurance of the resurrection from the 'dust of death' of Psalm 22:15. Is it not only a coincidence that Jesus' first instructions to the women at the tomb after

---

of man' (Ps 8:3-8), an allusion to Adam (Gen 1:26, 28), that in light of Psalm 80:17 and Daniel 7:13, 14, establishes the basis for Adam-Christ typology and the citation in Hebrews 2:6-9. Psalm 68 describes the activity of Yahweh. In the Old Testament the Angel of Yahweh is already recognised as Yahweh (Gen 16:7-13; 18:1, 2, 33; 19:1; Gen 31:11-13; 32:24, 30; 48:15-16; Exod 3:2-7; Judg 13:17-22) and the New Testament identifies Yahweh with Christ (for example, John 8:58). Ephesians 4:8 therefore readily applies Psalm 68:18 to Christ. The Davidic Psalm 110 is directly messianic, when the Lord [the Father] speaks to David's Lord [the Messiah]. This latter passage is faithfully exegeted in Matthew 22:41-46 and Hebrews 5:5-11; 7:11-27. Compare the non-Davidic psalms, Psalm 97:7, cited in Hebrews 1:60, and Psalm 102:25-27, cited in Hebrew 1:10-12].

45. Jacques Doukhan, 'The Seventy Weeks of Daniel 9: An Exegetical Study', in *Andrews University Seminary Studies*, 17 (1979): 18-19.

his resurrection echo the words of Psalm 22: 'Go and tell my brethren . . . (Matt 28:10)?

Perhaps Jesus' faith is fortified in those last minutes on the cross by the encouragement of the final verses of Psalm 22, describing the future spread and acceptance of His testimony in 'all the ends of the world' and succeeding generations (verses 27–31). The final words of Psalm 22 may be translated either as 'He has done [it]' or 'It is done!' If we accept the latter translation, then Jesus dies in triumph with the closing message of the psalm on his lips!

Whether or not Jesus consciously works his way through Psalm 22 in His crucifixion, it is clear that the fulfillment of this psalm in His death and resurrection is no reapplication in the light of the Christ-event. The Old Testament has already indicated that the ultimate meaning of the psalm moves beyond David to the antitypical David, the Messiah, and to his suffering and death.

Conclusion

In light of the evidence examined for this article, my understanding has grown into a settled conviction that the Matthean citations of Old Testament passages do not involve 'christological reinterpretation', Hellenistic allegory, rabbinic midrash, Qumran-type *pesher*, or other methods of interpretation that distort the original meaning of the Old Testament citations. Rather, the New Testament writers consistently remain faithful to the original passages in their immediate and wider Old Testament contexts.

We have concentrated on the book of Matthew, which scholars insist represent a twisting of the OT Scriptures. Far from substantiating charges by scholars like McCasland that 'Matthew felt free in changing and distorting the Scriptures,'[46] we find Matthew (and Jesus) remaining faithful to the Old Testament context, and upholding unity and harmony between the Testaments.

There is further work to be done in examining New Testament citations of the Old Testament. We have not looked at every alleged instance of Matthew's distortion of the Old Testament, let alone the alleged distortions on the part of other biblical writers, and the ones we have treated call for more detailed analysis. But there is enough evidence for a tentative conclusion to emerge. Matthew's use of the Old Testament faithfully and accurately reflects the deeper meaning inherent in these passages when they are viewed in the light of their broader Old Testament contexts. Matthew does not 'twist' the Scriptures!

---

46. McCasland, 'Matthew Twists the Scriptures', *op cit*, 146.

Paul and Moses in 2 Corinthians 3: Hermeneutics from the Top Down
David H Thiele

Introduction

Paul's argument in his discussion of the new covenant in 2 Corinthians 3 is difficult for any reader. A steady stream of articles and monographs on various features of the chapter bear eloquent testimony to its difficulty.[1] The flow of Paul's argument is not immediately transparent. 'It seems as though the obscurity of this passage is impenetrable and that the commentaries lead us to the conclusion: "so many men, so many minds".'[2] Letters written with ink on parchment—letters of recommendation (2 Cor 3:1)—morph into the letters of the law engraved on stone tablets (verse 3). The veil on Moses' face (verse 13) becomes the veil over the minds of Jews in Paul's day (verses 14, 15). The old covenant ministry (verse 14) is glorious (verses 7, 9-10) and yet it is a ministry of death and condemnation (verses 7, 9). The veil is placed over Moses face because the people are not able to gaze on its glory (verse 9) but also because he does not want them to see that the glory is fading (verse 13)[3].

---

1. Charles FD Moule describes the unit of thought in 2 Corinthians 3:1-4:6 as 'one of the most elaborately studied of all New Testament *cruces*, II Cor iii.18b, kathaper apo; kuriou pneumatos', *Essays in New Testament Interpretation* (Cambridge: Cambridge University Press, 1982), 227.
2. WC van Unnik, "With Unveiled Face', An Exegesis of II Corinthians iii 12-18', in *Novum testamentum*, 6 (1963): 153-169. 'Unfortunately, 2 Corinthians 3, though squeezed and prodded by generations of interpreters, has remained one of the more inscrutable reflections of a man who had already gained the reputation among his near-contemporaries for writing letters that were "hard to understand" (2 Peter 3:16).' Richard B Hays, *Echoes of Scripture in the Letters of Paul* (New Haven, CN: Yale University Press, 1989), 123.
3. The exact meaning of pros to mē atenisai tous huious Israēl eis to telos tou katargoumenou ('to keep the people of Israel from gazing at the end of the glory that was being set aside') is disputed. The dispute revolves around whether telos here means 'end' or 'goal/purpose' and *tou katargoumenou* means 'what was/is fading' or 'what was/is being abolished'. The majority of scholars would translate telos here as 'end' and *tou katargoumenou* as 'fade' here. These renderings certainly fit with the thesis being argued in this essay but are not essential to it.

2 Corinthian 3 as Midrash

The twenty-first century reader's difficulty with the passage is intensfied by Paul's exegetical approach, which has much in common with ancient Jewish midrash,[4] and little in common with contemporary methods of exegesis.[5] Describing 2 Corinthians 3 as midrashic emphasises the following characteristics of the passage:

---

4   Morna D Hooker, 'Beyond the Things which are Written? St Paul's Use of Scripture', in *New Testament Studies*, 27 (1981): 297; Joseph A Fitzmyer, 'Glory Reflected on the Face of Christ (II Cor 3:7 – 4:6) and a Palestinian Jewish Motif', in *Theological Studies*, 42 (1981): 632; Anthony T Hanson, 'The Midrash in II Corinthians 3: A Reconsideration', in *Journal for the Study of the New Testament*, 9 (1980), 22; R Bloch, 'Midrash', in *Approaches to Ancient Judaism: Theory and Practice*, Brown Judaic Studies 1, edited by WS Green (Missoula, MA: Scholars, 1978), 48.

The term 'midrash' is notoriously difficult to define, because some scholars understand it in literary terms, and others in terms of content, process, function, or attitude. They have not been 'discussing the same phenomenon in a similar manner', Gary G Porton, 'Defining Midrash', in *The Study of Ancient Judaism, 1: Mishnah, Midrash, Sidduy*, edited by J Neusner (New York: KTAV, 1981), 61. Porton's own definition is 'a type of literature, oral or written, which stands in direct relationship to a fixed canonical text, considered to be the authoritative and the revealed word of God by the midrashist and his audience, and in which this canonical text is explicitly cited or clearly alluded to', *ibid*, 62.

This definition would include virtually any bible commentary (ancient or modern) and most sermons. This may be one reason that Richard Hays suggests the term is not helpful when discussing the New Testament's use of the Old. Hays, *Echoes, op cit*, 11–14. He argues that it closes analysis where it should be starting, by precluding detailed study of *how* scripture is actually read by New Testament writers. However, if Hays' criticism were valid, it would surely apply equally to the study of rabbinic and other ancient Jewish literature.

Similarly, Wright declares Paul's argument is not midrashic '[b]ut follows the line of thought in Galatians 3:15–22, or even Mark 10:2–9. Difference in style of ministry is occasioned by difference in the spiritual condition of the hearers.' NT Wright, *The Climax of the Covenant* (Edinburgh: T&T Clark, 1991), 180. A more relevant test of whether or not the argument is midrashic may be whether or not it follows the argument of Exodus 34.

Clearly, scholars who apply the term 'midrash' to Paul's use of scripture in 2 Corinthians 3 intend something different to Porton's definition. Porton, 'Defining Midrash', *op cit*, 70–84, himself divides ancient Jewish midrash into four clearly distinguishable groupings: targumim, pious rewritings of biblical narratives, pesher, and rabbinic midrash. All these forms are characterised by an approach to the biblical text that adds detail to the biblical account. Many scholars have noted how easily ancient midrashic exegesis is able to interpret the text in ways that are neither simple nor self-evident, *ibid*, 59.

Some scholars claim that Paul has taken over an existing midrash, developed and/or used originally by his opponents, and used it against them. for examle, Ernst Käsemann, 'The Spirit and the Letter', in *Perspectives on Paul* (Philadelphia, PA: Fortress, 1971), 149; Dieter Georgi, *The Opponents of Paul in Second Corinthians* (Edinburgh: T&T Clark, 1986), 264–271. The fact that 2 Corinthians 3 coheres so well with the surroundings chapters is a strong argument against this claim.

5. Two basic approaches to the general question of the use of Old Testament in the New have been identified: historical and intertextual. Richard Hays and Joel Green, 'The Use of the Old Testament by New Testament Writers', in *Hearing the Old Testament: Strategies for Interpretation*, edited by JB Green (Grand Rapids, MI: Eerdmans, 1995), 229–230. Although I agree with Hays

1. It is a piece of 'applied exegesis',[6] in which the primary purpose is not to explicate the meaning of the text but to apply the text to the contemporary situation.
2. It comments on an Old Testament passage in a somewhat atomistic way.
3. Other Old Testament passages are imported into the discussion of the primary text on the basis of such phenomena as 'hook words' and principles such as the *gezirah shawah* ('from lesser to greater').
4. The exegetical conclusions do not necessarily harmonise with those of modern historical exegesis.

A related problem is that Paul's interpretation of Exodus 34 in 2 Corinthians 3 appears to be at odds with the original story. Paul makes the following points regarding Moses:

1. Moses' face is glorified in connection with the giving of the law (2 Cor 3:7).
2. His face is too glorious for the people of Israel to look at (2 Cor 3:7).
3. This glory is temporary and fading (2 Cor 3:7, 10, 12).
4. Moses veils his face so the people will not see the fading of the glory on his face (2 Cor 3:12).

A comparison with the original story in Exodus 34 is revealing:

1. Moses face is glorified in connection with the giving of the law (Exod 34:29).[7]
2. The people, led by Aaron, are initially afraid of the glorious appearance of Moses' face (Exod 34:30), but Moses calls the people to himself and spoke to them (verse 31).
3. Moses veiled his face *after* speaking to the congregation (Exod 34:32), presumably to indicate the finish of his 'official' communication of God's revelation.[8]

---

and Green that these two approaches are not necessarily mutually exclusive, my own sympathies lie primarily with the historical approach.

6.
7. In Exodus the 'glory' on Moses face is clearly intended to echo the Sinai theophany and to indicate that he is God's messenger. See, John I Durham, *Exodus*, Word Bible Commentary, Volume 3 (Dallas, TX: Word, 1987), 466–467.
8. *Ibid*, 467. This point is explicitly noted by Hays, *Echoes*, 140, even though he regards Exodus 34 as 'generative' of Paul's comments in 2 Corinthians 3, *ibid*, 132. For Hays, 'generative' does not imply a literal, historically accurate exegesis. Rather, Paul only finds Exodus 34 'generative' because he reads it in a radically new way in the light of the Christ event, *ibid*, 124. He points out that Paul uses Exodus 34 as a complex 'parable', *ibid*, 144. 'The only thing that interests Paul about the story is its compelling image of a masked Moses whose veil is removed

4. There is no indication that the glory on Moses' face is temporary. On the contrary, Moses thereafter keeps his face veiled, except when he speaks to Yahweh in the tabernacle. When he then communicates Yahweh's message to the people, they again see his glorified face (Exod 34:34–35).

Paul's argument seems to centre on the glory and the veil, and it is precisely here that he is furthest away from the meaning of Exodus. It is difficult not to sympathise with Morna D Hooker's observation: 'Often one is left exclaiming: whatever the passage from the Old Testament originally meant, it certainly was not this.'[9]

Two other Seemingly Intractable Problems

Resolution of the difficulties inherent in 2 Corinthians 3 is compounded by two other seemingly intractable problems in the book. First is the question of the literary integrity of the epistle. 'There are almost as many partition theories as there are commentaries on 2 Corinthians.'[10] Scholars have seen this letter as a collection of up to six fragments from originally independent letters.[11] However, several recent works have affirmed the essential unity of at least chapters 1–7,[12] if not of the entire letter.[13] This study accepts the unity of 2 Corinthians as a working hypoth-

---

when he enters the presence of the Lord. That image becomes for Paul the center and substance of an *imaginative interpretation* that is—despite [Phillip] Hughes' conscientious efforts to cover it up—*mystical and eschatological*, ibid, 140 (emphasis added)..

9. Hooker, 'Beyond the Things', *op cit*, 295.
10. Ben Witherington III, *Conflict and Community in Corinth: A Socio-Rhetorical Commentary on 1 and 2 Corinthians* (Grand Rapids, MI: Eerdmans, 1995), 328.
11. Hans D Betz understands the letter to be a compilation of the following fragments from originally independent letters: (a) 2:14–6:13, 7:2–4; (b) 10:1–13:10; (c) 1:2–13, 7:5–16, 13:11–13; (d) 8; (e) 9; (f) 6:14 – 7:1. See his 'Corinthians, Second Epistle to the', in *Anchor Bible Dictionary*, edited by DN Freedman (New York: Doubleday, 1992), 1:1149–1150. The same schema is followed by many others, for example, Günther Bornkamm, 'The History of the Origin of the So-called Second Letter to the Corinthians', in *New Testament Studies* 8 (1961 – 62):258–264; S Maclean Gilmour, 'Corinthians, Second', in *Interpreter's Dictionary of the Bible*, edited by GA Buttrick (Nashville, TN.: Abingdon, 1962), 693–695.
12. Linda L Belleville, 'Reflections of Glory: Paul's Polemical Use of the Moses-Doxa Tradition in 2 Corinthians 3:1–18', in *Journal for the Study of the New Testament* Supplement Series 52 (Sheffield: Sheffield Academic, 1991), 84–104; David A deSilva, *The Credentials of an Apostle: Paul's Gospel in II Corinthians 1 – 7*, Biblical Monograph Series 4 (North Richland Hills, TX: Bibal, 1998), 1–29; Victor P Furnish, *II Corinthians*, Anchor Bible 32A (Doubleday, New York, 1984), 30–41.
13. Witherington, *Conflict and Community*, *op cit*, 327–339; Paul Barnett, *The Second Epistle to the Corinthians*, New International Commentary on the New Testament (Grand Rapids, MI: Eerdmans, 1997), 15–25; Werner G Kümmel, *Introduction to the New Testament* (London: SCM, 1975), 287–293; DA Carson, *From Triumphalism to Maturity: An Exposition of 2 Corinthians 10 – 13* (Grand Rapids, MI: Baker, 1984), 1–16.

esis, although the difficulties inherent in this position, particularly with regard to the relationship of chapters 1 – 9 to chapters 10 – 13, are recognised.[14]

The second problem concerns the identity of Paul's opponents Paul in 2 Corinthians. Scholarly identifications fall into four basic groups: Judaisers, Gnostics, 'divine men' akin to those supposedly found in Hellenistic Judaism, or pneumatics.[15] Each of these suggestions is problematic. There is a paucity of data from the Greco-Roman environment.[16] The data concerning the opponents must therefore largely be drawn from a 'mirror-reading' of Paul's comments. However, this procedure is fraught with difficulties and can easily be overdone.[17] The evidence is so ambiguous that a definitive answer is impossible.

The second problem is clearly intertwined with the first. Are the opponents 2 Corinthians 3 the same as the opponents in chapters 10 – 13? Numerous parallels can be drawn between the pictures of the opposition in ach of these sections.[18] Nothing in the description of the opponents unsettles the hypothesis of the original unity of the letter.

The precise identity of Paul's opponents is not an issue that has to be definitively answered before 2 Corinthians 3 can be discussed. However, it will remain near the surface in any discussion of that chapter. Paul's defense of his apostleship against the claims and charges of his opponents provides a key for understanding it.[19] Linda Belleville sees the nature of apostleship as the theme of the letter represented in the fragment 2 Corinthians 1–7.[20] In fact, it seems to provide the theme for the entire epistle, as we now have it.[21]

---

14. Carson, *Triumphalism*, 16, correctly observes that no solution to this problem is without difficulties.
15. Jerry L Sumney, *'Servants of Satan','False Brothers' and Other Opponents of Paul*, JSNT Supplement 188 (Sheffield: Sheffield Academic, 1999), 79.
16. For example, Georgi, *passim*, suggests that the opposition should be understood as being in the category of 'divine man' (*theios anēr*). However, other scholars dispute whether *theios anēr* represents a clearly defined category in the ancient world, seeing the phrase instead as 'a fluid expression . . . [which] could vary dramatically in meaning.' Jack D Kingsbury, 'The 'Divine Man' as the Key to Mark's Christology – The End of an Era?', in *Interpretation*, 35 (1981): 249. *Cf* Carl H Holladay, *Theios Aner in Hellenistic-Judaism*, SBLDS 40 (Missoula, MT: Scholars, 1977).
17. John MG Barclay, 'Mirror-Reading A Polemical Letter: Galatians as a Test Case', in *Journal for the Study of the New Testament* 31 (1987): 73–93.
18. Sumney, *Opponents of Paul*, 130–133; Hays, *Echoes*, 126.
19. Hays, *Echoes*, 125, notes that 2 Corinthians 3 forms part of Paul's defence of his apostolic ministry, but finds the key to understanding the chapter elsewhere.
20. Belleville, *Reflections, op cit*, 165–166.
21. Sumney, *Opponents of Paul, op cit*, 130–133.

Paul's Defense of His Apostolic Ministry

The importance of Paul's defense of his apostleship for understanding of 2 Corinthians 3 is clear even at a casual reading. Paul opens his epistle with stereotypical greetings and then launches immediately into an explanation of his hardships and sufferings (2 Cor 1:3–11). His opponents understand apostleship in terms of glory, power, and majesty.[22] For them, Paul's sufferings discredit him as an apostle. However, Paul boasts of his share in the suffering of Christ (2 Cor 4:7–12; 11:21b–30; 12:8–10).

Paul defends his integrity in the light of his changing travel plans (2 Cor 1:12–2:4). His opponents accuse him of being a different person at a distance than he is when actually in Corinth (2 Cor 10:10). He makes it clear that his change in plans is neither the result of a lack of consistency nor of a failure of integrity. Rather, he is motivated by his concern for the Corinthians (2 Cor 1:23), especially in the light of their strained relationship during his last visit (2 Cor 2:1). The root of the problem concerns a church member in Corinth who has now been disciplined by the church (2 Cor 2:5–11).

Paul stresses the concern he feels for the Corinthians (2 Cor 3:12–13). He declares the authenticity of his ministry:

> Who is sufficient for these things? For we are not peddlers of God's word like so many; but in Christ we speak as persons of sincerity, as persons sent from God and standing in his presence. Are we beginning to commend ourselves again? Surely we do not need as some do, letter of recommendation to you or from you, do we? (2 Cor 2:16b–3:1)[23]

Paul's opponents are again clearly in view. It is they who are 'peddlers of God's word'. In contrast to Paul, who cares for the church community, they abuse it (2 Cor 11:20). And in contrast to him, they have letters of recommendation.

It is instructive to notice how the issues introduced in the opening two chapters of the epistle run throughout chapters 3–5. Paul rhetorically asks, 'Who is sufficient for these things?' (2 Cor 2:16). His answer is that his competence and confidence come from Christ (2 Cor 3:4–6), and that the 'extraordinary power' in-

---

22. A word frequency study in 2 Corinthians is revealing: doxa (glory) occurs sixteen times; dunamis (power) occurs nine times; kauchaomai (to boast) is used sixteen times—more often then in the rest of the Pauline corpus combined—and kauchēma (boast) occurs three times. That there is an issue between Paul and his opponents over these matters is clear.
23. Carol K Stockhausen argues that 2 Corinthians 3:1–6 is a distinct unit separated from what precedes it by the introduction of the new topic of 'letters'. *Moses' Veil and the Glory of the New Covenant*, Anchor Bible 116 (Rome: Editrice Pontificio Instituto Biblico, 1989), 34. Her point is well taken. However, the new topic arises directly from the concerns expressed in the introductory chapters.

volved belongs to God not himself (2 Cor 4:7). He therefore ministers with boldness (2 Cor 3:12).

Is Paul recommending himself again (2 Cor 3:1)? No, he is giving the Corinthians an opportunity to boast about him (2 Cor 5:12a), so that they can answer 'those who boast in outward appearance and not in the heart' (2 Cor 5:12b), that is, his opponents.

Does Paul suffer hardships? Yes, his experience is that of 'clay jars' containing hidden treasure (2 Cor 4:7). He is afflicted, perplexed, persecuted, struck down, 'always carrying in the body the death of Jesus . . . always being given up to death for Christ's sake' (2 Cor 4:8-12). His 'outer nature' is being destroyed (2 Cor 4:16), as is his earthly tent (2 Cor 5:1). There is no shining glory on his face as there is on Moses' (2 Cor 3:7). People can look at Paul and see nothing extraordinary.

Is Paul lacking in integrity and consistency? No, his conscience is clear. Nothing is hidden behind a veil (2 Cor 4:2-3 *cf* 3:12-13). He is confident that he will not be found naked (and ashamed) on the day of judgment (2 Cor 5:2).[24]

Paul's basic approach is to use a set of parallel polarities: the visible and the hidden; the present and the future; the earthly and the heavenly. He is certainly responding to positions taken by his opponents, as he makes clear in 2 Corinthians 2:5-12b. His visible experience is that of the abused clay jar, but there is treasure hidden within (2 Cor 4:7). The visible outer nature is wasting away, but the hidden inner experience grows stronger and stronger (2 Cor 4:16). The visible earthly tent is in the throes of destruction, but the heavenly house, now visible only by faith, remains eternal in heaven (2 Cor 5:1), ready to be occupied at the *parousia* (2 Cor 5:4).[25] Paul's suffering, evident to any observer, is dismissed as 'this slight momentary affliction', when it is compared to 'the eternal weight of glory beyond all measure' (2 Cor 4:17). How can this be? 'Because we look not at what can be seen but at what cannot be seen; for what can be seen is temporary but what cannot be seen is eternal.' (2 Cor 4:18). It is faith that counts, not sight (2 Cor 5:7). To take any other perspective is to judge from a human point of view that fails to recognise the decisively new thing God has accomplished in Christ (2 Cor 5:16-21).

The same polarities are clearly seen in chapter 3. The following contrasts are either explicitly or implicitly made:

---

24. On the connection between 'naked' and 'ashamed' in this verse, see E Earle Ellis, 'The Structure of Pauline Eschatology (II Corinthians 5:1-10)', in *Paul and his Recent Interpreters* (Grand Rapids, MI: Eerdmans, 1961), 35-48 [= *New Testament Studies*, 6 (1959-60) 211-24].
25. 2 Corinthians 5:1-11 is often read as if it focused on the moment of death. However, its correct orientation is to the *parousia*. So Ellis, *op cit, passim*.

Letters of commendation – visible (2 Cor 3:1)	Letters on the heart – hidden (2 Cor 3:2)
Letter written with ink – visible (verse 3)	Letters written by the Spirit – hidden (verse 3)
Law written on stone – visible (verse 3)	Gospel engraved on the heart – hidden (verse 3)
Letter – visible (verse 6)	Spirit – hidden (verse 6)
Ministry of condemnation/death – visible (verses 7, 9)	Ministry of Spirit/justification/life – hidden (verse 9)[1]
Glory of the ministry of death/ Moses – visible (verse 7)	Glory of the ministry of the Gospel/ Paul – hidden (verse 8)
Temporary visible glory (verse 7)	Permanent (although currently hidden) glory (verse 11)
Outward appearance – visible (verse 12)[2]	Heart – hidden (verse 12)[3]

The conclusion is clear. Paul's primary purpose in 2 Corinthians 3 is not to develop a theology of covenants, to expound on the role of the law in the Christian life, or to exegete Exodus 34. It is to defend his apostolic ministry against opponents who denigrate it.[26]

Paul's Starting Point

Paul's starting point is not the Old Testament story of Moses. He is not asking, 'How can I get these people to understand Exod 34?' Rather, his starting point is his certainty regarding the gospel he preaches and his apostolic calling. His question is, 'How can I explain the validity of my apostleship to these people?' With this starting point,

---

26. Wright comments, 'If the main thrust of the argument is thus a defence of Paul's ministry, both in that he does not need "Letters of recommendation" and in his paradoxical apostolic boldness and confidence, the main weapon with which he begins this thrust is the concept of the new covenant.' Wright, *Covenant, op cit*, 176. This may be an overstatement. Wright himself acknowledges that 'covenant' is only explicitly mentioned in vs. 6. Paul nowhere describes the old covenant as abolished. His focus is on models of ministry, not on the old and new covenants *per se*. In his discussion of 2 Corinthians 3, Wright allows Paul's urgent concerns about the nature of Christian ministry to fall too much into the background.

Paul's argument becomes clearer. He may appear to be dealing with Moses and the Old Testament story, but his focus is actually on his opponents and their false theology of ministry.[27]

Moses is the obvious example of a biblical character with outward glory.[28] Since Paul's opponents stress outward glory, it is only a small step to make Moses a symbol of the opponents and their theology.[29] Paul describes the ministry of Moses as a ministry of condemnation and death (2 Cor 3:7, 9), but it is the ministry of his opponents that is his true target. It is universally recognised that Paul only defends his apostleship because his gospel is also at stake.[30] He may seem to portray Moses as dishonest and deceptive in covering his face to hide the fading glory, but it is the ethics of his opponents that Paul really has in mind. He makes this point with particular clarity. He stresses his 'sincerity' in contrast to those who are 'peddlers of God's word' (2 Cor 2:17). This is neatly parallel to his stress on his own 'boldness' in contrast to Moses self-veiling.[31] He declares that his gospel is utterly unveiled, except to those who have been blinded by the devil, because 'we have renounced the shameful things that one hides; we refuse to practice cunning or to falsify God's word' (2 Cor 4:2).[32] Clearly Paul is here either defending himself against the attacks of his opponents or launching an attack on them.[33]

---

27. Ralph P Martin's comments on 2 Corinthians 3:7 are revealing in this regard: 'The entrée to Paul's thought may well be as simple as Jervell (*Imago Dei*, 178f) surmises: the gramma refers primarily to the "letters of recommendation" (3:1–3), and points to the controversy with the "false brethren" who carried them. By contrast, Paul's ministry is authenticated by the "power" (*Vollmacht*) of the Spirit who has produced a different kind of letter—one that is "spiritual" (*geistig*).' *2 Corinthians*, Word Bible Commentary 40 (Waco, TX: Word, 1986), 60.
    It is interesting to note that in his apologetic treatment of 2 Corinthians 3, Nichol does not refer to Paul's opponents at all. Nichol, *Answers, op cit*, 72–76.
28. Adam is really the only other contender. However, the story of Adam stresses his rebellion and consequent loss of glory. In some Jewish traditions, Moses is seen as receiving the glory Adam lost. In this sense he become a 'new Adam'. See Belleville, *Reflections, op cit*, 63–75.
29. The opponents themselves probably hold Moses in high regard. Their exact position is open to dispute, hinging, as it does, on their identity. Regardless of the *precise* position which they take, they certainly argue that God's messengers ought to be glorious, powerful and majestic, as, in fact, Moses is. It is therefore unnecessary to insist that Paul's opponent are already using Moses as a model of ministry and contrasting him with Paul. So Hays, *Echoes, op cit*, 126; Wright, *Covenant, op cit*, 177. This position need not imply acceptance of Wright's overall approach to the text.
30. Carson, *Triumphalism*, 20; K Kertelge, 'Letter and Spirit in II Corinthians 3', in *Paul and the Mosaic Law*, edited by James DG Dunn (Grand Rapids, MI: Eerdmans, 1996), 119; FF Bruce, *I and II Corinthians*, New Century Bible (Grand Rapids, MI: Eerdmans, 1971), 173.
31. Van Unnik, 'With Unveiled Face', *op cit*, 153–169.
32. Hays, *Echoes, op cit*, 126, also notes the close connection between 2 Corinthians 2:17 and 4:2 as part of Paul's counter-attack on his opponents.
33. In other words, Paul speaks in terms of the contrast between Moses and himself, but is actually focused on the contrast between his ministry and his opponents'. Wright, *Covenant, op cit*, 180, seems to reduce the tension between the speech and the focus, by suggesting that Paul's primary

A number of puzzling features of the chapter can now be seen in a clearer light. What are the implications of Paul's comments on the 'covenant' and the 'letter' (gramma) of the law? He is certainly developing neither a theology of covenant or law, nor a philosophy of hermeneutics.[34] Rather, his point is correct his opponents' misapprehension of the role of the law in Christian life. Paul's target does not seem to be the law as such, but its misuse: 'legalism', to use a contemporary word.[35]

The 'glory' and the 'veil' can now also be understood more clearly. Paul does not deny that his opponents' ministry is marked by a certain impressiveness, but suggests that it is only so 'from a human point of view' (2 Cor 5:16). The various uses of 'veil' in 2 Corinthians 3 – 4 cohere at exactly this point. The face of Moses was truly glorified through his encounter with the same God who now transforms Christians 'from one degree of glory to another' (2 Cor 3:18). The ancient Israelites responded 'from a human point a view,' and a veil separates them from this glory.[36]

---

contrast is not between Paul and Moses or between Christians and Moses, but rather between Christians and the Israelites, both in Moses' day and his own day. Paul does contrast the Jews of his own day and Christians (2 Cor 3:14–16). However, he *never* explicitly contrasts the Israelites of Moses with day with Christians. On the other hand, he does draw an explicit contrast between himself and Moses (verses 12, 13). This fact, combined with the repeated contrasts between the ministries of the old and new covenants (verses 7–11), suggest that the primary contrast is indeed between Paul and Moses. See Georgi, *Opponents of Paul,* 254–264; *cf* Martin, *2 Corinthians, op cit,* 61. Wright's argues that the Old Covenant ministry requires the veil because the people are unable to look upon the glory. This argument, of course, fails to take into account the fact that according to the Old Testament, Moses removed the veil when he conveyed messages from God to the people.

The significance of Wright's overstatement is perhaps reduced by his acknowledgment that 'The contrast, then, is between the necessary style of Moses's ministry to Israel and the proper and appropriate style of Paul's ministry to Christian who, as in verses 1–3, are themselves the "letter" written by the Spirit.' Wright, *Covenant, op cit,* 80.

34. Peter Richardson, 'Spirit and Letter: A Foundation for Hermeneutics', in *Evangelical Quarterly,* 45 (1973): 208–21; Hays, *Echoes, op cit,* 149: '2 Corinthians 3 is neither a practical discussion of how to do exegesis nor a theoretical treatise on the problems of continuity and discontinuity between the testaments.'

35. Thomas E Provence "Who is Sufficient for these Things?': An Exegesis of II Corinthians 2:15–3:18', in *Novum Testamentum,* 24 (1982): 65–68; *cf* Martin, *op cit,* 61. The term 'legalism' is fraught with difficulties, not least of which is the fact that it is often used to describe the heresy being combated in Galatians. However, Paul's opponents in Galatia and Corinth appear to be significantly different. At least, Paul polemicises against them in significantly different terms. See E Earle Ellis, 'Paul and his Opponents', in *Prophecy and Hermeneutic in Early Christianity* (Grand Rapids, MI: Baker, 1978; reprint 1995), 80–115.

36. Paul does not use the words *kata sarka* in 2 Corinthians 3 – 4, but he does say 'their hearts were hardened' (2 Cor 3:14), a statement with similar connotations to *kata sarka* in 2 Corinthians 5:1. For Paul, sarx does not specifically denote the physical aspects of reality, but rather expresses human existence in its concrete reality. The fact that this concrete reality is typified by sin and rebellion against God means that sarx is readily used for humanity in a state of rebellion and alienation. See E Schweizer, 'sarx, sarkina, sarkinos', *TDNT,* 7:98–151, and particularly 125–135.

The Israel of Paul's day also judges his gospel from a human perspective. The veil remains.[37] However, Paul's message is unveiled, except to those Satan has blinded (2 Cor 4:2-3), that is, to those whose hearts are hardened, who judge from a human point of view. Paul proclaims that in contrast to them, he and his fellow Christians enjoy the privilege of Moses: viewing the glory of God and being changed into his likeness (2 Cor 3:18).[38]

Conclusion

What conclusions may be drawn from all of this? The insight that 2 Corinthians 3 focuses on the conflict between two competing ministries is scarcely new.[39] However, it has not always been taken seriously enough. There has been an evident anxiety to get to the hot issues for the interpreter: covenant, or hermeneutics. However, to understand Paul on his own terms, we must take his own emphasis as seriously as he himself does.

A further implication may be drawn from Paul's use of the Old Testament. He operates from a base of certainty: the gospel of Christ. The glory of God that he sees on the Damascus road is now far more important to him than the glory of God on the face of Moses.[40] For Christians the Old Testament remains Scripture, but its use in the formation of doctrine and standards of practice is mediated through the great certainties revealed with clarity in the New Testament (*cf*, Heb

---

    In the Bible hardening of the heart similarly signifies an action of rebellion and the rejection of God's grace. See J Behm, 'kardia(i), kardiognvsth~, sklhrokardiva', *TDNT*, 3:605–614.

37. Paul says the veil remains when the Israel of his day reads the Old Testament. The Old Testament is at this time the only Scripture the Church possesses. It preaches the gospel from the Old Testament. However, the majority of Jews reject it, ostensibly because they find a glorious rather than a humiliated Messiah in the Old Testament. They proclaim a different Christ even as Paul's opponents proclaim 'a different Jesus' (2 Cor 11:4), although the exact import of that phrase is hotly disputed. See, Furnish, *II Corinthians, op cit*, 500–502.
38. Both Charles FD Moule, 227–234, and James DG Dunn argue that the Lord who is Spirit here is not Christ, but God the Father. See Dunn's 'I Corinthians 3:17-"The Lord is the Spirit"', in *The Christ and the Spirit*, Volume 1, *Christology* (Grand Rapids, MI: Eerdmans, 1998), 115–125. They admittedly hold a minority position, but it certainly harmonises well with the understanding of 2 Corinthians 3 presented here.
39. For example, Bornkamm, 'The History', *op cit*, 259, refers to 2 Corinthians 2:14 – 7:4 as 'the great apology for the apostolic office'.
40. Barnett, *Second Epistle*, 38. Paul's own experience certainly lies behind many of his comments in 2 Corinthians 3. He himself has in many ways played the role now filled by his opponents. He elsewhere delineates the 'glory' of his pre-Christian experience (2 Cor 11:22–23a; Phil 3:4b–6) which has involved him in a ministry of condemnation and death (Acts 9:1–2; 22:4–5; 26:10–11). He has seen the glory of God but been unable to gaze upon it (Acts 9:3, 8–9; 22:6,11; 26:13). See Martin, *2 Corinthians, op cit*, 61.

1:1–2).⁴¹ To seek 'light in the shadows,'⁴² however noteworthy the shadows may be, reflects a non-pauline approach. More pauline is the endeavor to shed the light of the New Testament on the teachings of the Old.⁴³

---

41. Hays, *Echoes, op cit,* 148, quotes Klaus Koch approvingly when he states 'Paul moves in a hermeneutical circles with the citation of Exodus 34:34a: it is possible for Paul to adduce this citation in favor of the thesis that he proposes here–that Scripture can be understood appropriately only in Christ–only because he, for his part *has already interpreted the citation "in Christ"'* (emphasis added). This statement suggests Paul would not find this meaning in the text (even if it is there!) if he starts with the text. Rather, the meaning becomes plan when the text is read in the light of the clarifying light of the revelation of God given in Christ.
42. This phrase comes from the title of an article from Frank B. Holbrook, 'Light in the Shadows: An Overview of the Doctrine of the Sanctuary', in *Journal of Adventist Education,* Volume 46, No. 1 (October-November, 1983): 17–35.
43. Norman H Young has recently made a similar point with regard to the use of the Old Testament in Hebrews. See 'The Day of Dedication or the Day of Atonement? The Old Testament Background to Hebrews 6:19–20', in *Andrews University Seminary Studies,* 40 (2002): 68.

PART THREE

Bringing Our Text To The Text

Our Story as Text

Ray CW Roennfeldt

Introduction

Biblical interpretation is a crucial subject for all Christian believers. If the Bible is the Magna Carta for the Christian community (2 Tim 3:16–17), it is important that the community and individuals within it understand and apply the Scriptures correctly. The Seventh-day Adventist Church is an example of a denomination that has long recognised the necessity of following proper hermeneutical rules. For instance, the Millerites, clearly spelled out their 'rules' as follows:

1. The Bible contains a revelation from God to humankind, and of course must be the best, plainest and simplest that can be given. It is a revelation in human language, to human beings, and must be understood by the known laws of language.
2. The Bible is always to be understood literally, when the literal sense does not involve contradictions, or is not unnatural.
3. When the literal sense involves the passage in contradiction, or expresses ideas, which are unnatural, it is figurative, or parabolic, and is designed to illustrate rather than reveal the truth.
4. When a passage is clearly figurative, the figure is to be carefully studied, and the passage compared with, other parts of the Word where the same or similar figure may be employed.[1]

This close interest in hermeneutical principles has been an increasing preoccupation among Seventh-day Adventists through to the present day.[2] It is commend-

---

1. 'Second Coming of Christ No. 1', in *Signs of the Times*, April 15, 1840, cited in Kai Arasola, *The End of Historicism: Millerite Hermeneutics of Time Prophecies in the Old Testament* (Uppsala, Sweden: Datem, 1990), 218.
2. Especially notice the section on 'Biblical Interpretation: General Principles', by Gerhard F Hasel, in the *Australasian Division Bible Conference 1978* notebook ([Wahroonga, NSW:] Australasian Division of the Seventh-day Adventist Church, 1978. An even greater portion of the *North American Bible Conference 1974* notebook (Washington, DC: Biblical Research Committee of the General Conference of Seventh-day Adventists, 1974) was devoted to biblical interpretation.

able that a community of Christians considers the correct interpretation of Scripture to be vital. However, could it be that in their desire to present a unified front on matters of biblical interpretation or doctrine, they have produced apathetic Christians on the one hand, and theological fundamentalists on the other?

Putting Biblical Interpretation into Perspective

Let me illustrate the former and the latter dangers. Recently, a second-generation Adventist who is a pastor's wife told me that she found the study of the Bible 'totally boring'. When I asked her, 'Why?', she replied, 'Because we know it all. Everything is laid out for us in such detail that there is no room for individual interpretation or belief. The possibility of discovering something new in Scripture is almost nonexistent.'

While apathy and boredom is personally destructive, the fundamentalist ideal of absolute doctrinal uniformity is devastating for the unity of the Christian community.[3] There will always be some diversity of belief in the local or corporate church. Yet, that variation should not interfere with Christian unity. On the contrary, unity, compassion, understanding, and love are most evident where there are differences of perspective (1 Cor 12–14).

If our biblical interpretation is designed to build a system of coherent and consistent doctrines we have done a good thing. The Bible writers commend true doctrine and condemn false doctrine (for example, Tit 2:7–8; 2 John 9). The Bible is 'useful for teaching' (2 Tim 3: 16), but what is truly profitable is doctrine that functions 'so that the man of God may be thoroughly equipped for every good work' (2 Tim 3:17). Biblical interpretation that does not take into account real life is inadequate and irrelevant at best, and divisive and damaging at worst.[4]

See also *A Symposium of Biblical Hermeneutics*, edited by Gordon M HydeWashington, DC: Biblical Research Committee of the General Conference of Seventh-day Adventists, 1974).
3. I am using the term 'fundamentalist' in its wider sense as applying to those who profess 'strict adherence to (especially Protestant) orthodoxy in the matter of Biblical interpretation. See, eds., "Fundamentalism," *The Oxford Dictionary of the Christian Church*, edited by FL Cross and EA Livingstone (Oxford: Oxford University Press, 2005, third edition, revised), 650. For a wider perspective and an historical overview of the fundamentalist phenomenon see Karen Armstrong, *The Battle for God: Fundamentalism in Judaism, Christianity and Islam* (London: HarperCollins, 2000). Samuel Koranteng-Pipim's *Receiving the Word: How New Approaches to the Bible Impact Our Biblical Faith and Lifestyle* (Berrien Springs, MI: Berean Books, 1996) appears to be cast in the mould of fundamentalism from an Adventist perspective.
4. The early Adventist idea of 'present truth' is relevant here. Richard Rice remarks that 'good theology is creative and constructive. It brings to the task of interpreting the biblical message the conviction that our present experience may enable us to see things that have never been as fully appreciated before.' Therefore 'the work of theology is never once and for all'. Richard Rice, *The Reign of God: An Introduction to Christian Theology from a Seventh-day Adventist Perspective* (Berrien Springs, MI: Andrews University Press, 1997), 8–9.

Therefore our emphasis in biblical interpretation must be on how to apply the biblical teachings in our lives and in the life of the church community, rather than on creating an information bank of Christian doctrines. Do not misunderstand. I am not setting up a dualism between Christian life and church doctrines, but I am emphasising that good interpretation involves application to real-life situations.[5]

If interpretation is so important, how will we go about it? I do not intend to address the general principles of scriptural interpretation at this point. I am assuming ministers and teachers have long been familiar with such matters as the relationship between interpretation and the original text of the Bible; biblical translation, understanding specific scriptural words, sentences, units, books, and authors; and the importance of taking into account the entire canon.[6] Nor do I wish to detail the individual steps involved in interpreting and applying particular scriptural texts.[7] Rather, I want to discuss the two basic matters that we need to keep in mind if we are to interpret rather than interrupt: the listener/reader and the Word of God.

The Beginning Point: My Situation

I am taking as my starting point the human situation. Some conservative Christians may object that I have chosen the wrong place to begin. Surely, one should begin with the Bible, since it provides us with a platform that is fixed and objective. I agree, that would be the ideal place to start, but I am convinced that none of us actually begins there. Instead, our own situation provides the launching pad for our study of Scripture, and it is vital that we realise that such is the case.

Allow me to illustrate this from personal experience. I have to confess that one particular facet of my background has influenced the way I interpret the Bible more than any other. The eight years I spent pastoring and teaching in Papua New Guinea mean that I can no longer read the Word of God in the way that I did before I left Australia. I was thrown into the 'deep end' of another culture where people reason in radically foreign ways and read the Old Testament in a seemingly more consistent and less opportunistic fashion. They cannot always see the connections I draw between the gospel message and personal and social eth-

---

5. For instance, the details provided to the Thessalonian believers in regard to the coming of Christ are not given merely for the sake of information, but in order that they might not 'grieve like the rest of men, who have no hope' (1 Thess 4:13), and for their encouragement (1 Thess 4:18).
6. For information on these matters see Gerhard F Hasel, 'Biblical Interpretation: General Principles', *Australasian Division Bible Conference 1978* (separate pagination for each section).
7. For a convenient summary of the processes involved in biblical interpretation and application see John Goldingay, *Models for Interpretation of Scripture* (Grand Rapids, MI: Eerdmans, 1995), 2–7.

ics, and are constantly aware of the closeness of supernatural forces (both divine and demonic). I have been forced to make some wide-ranging alterations to the familiar theological paradigms I have learned in church from my infancy through to my theology degree at Avondale College.[8]

Some of us have lost a child to sudden infant death syndrome, or have watched as a partner is gradually stripped of his/her strength and dignity by multiple sclerosis, or have had a daughter forsake family, friends, and God for the shadow land of drugs and prostitution. They will also know that they can no longer read the Bible in the same way as before.[9]

If your 'text' and mine is the place where we start our reading of the biblical text, what does our 'text' look like? Its appearance obviously varies from person to person, yet we can probably generalise. The following factors will certainly not be equally important for each of us, but most of them are common among us.

Gender

Undoubtedly, one very dominant factor in biblical interpretation throughout Christian history has been the fact that most biblical study is carried out from a male perspective. Of course, a strong biblical case can be made for insisting that women should not have a teaching/interpreting role in the church (1 Tim 2:11–15), but is it not a masculine bias which insists on a literalistic reading of the pauline instructions regarding women, while ignoring his desire that 'men everywhere . . . lift up holy hands in prayer' (1 Tim 2: 8)?[10]

Whatever one's viewpoint on the role of women in the church, the pastoral heart cannot ignore the fact that some women find the Bible, especially Paul, 'hurtful, unhelpful, not revealing of God, and not worth the effort to come to grips with.'[11]

---

8. For further details see my 'How Melanesia Shaped My Hermeneutics and Theology: Some Personal Reflections', in *Avondale and the Pacific: 100 Years of Mission*, edited by Barry Oliver *et al* (Cooranbong, NSW: Avondale Academic Press, 1997), 93–97.
9. This idea is well expressed by Ingrid Rosa Kitzberger: 'When I approach biblical texts I do so with a text already *written on my soul*, that is, with my life-experience and my own story. Key is my socialisation and history, as well as everyday experience, as a woman in a patriarchal and sexist society and church. Key also is my theological training within male-dominated and patriarchally structured and shaped discipline with its—at least until recent years—dominating sexist interpretations of the bible' (emphasis, Kitzberger). Kitzberger also observes that the idea of 'reader as text' applies 'as much to the first readers as to any subsequent reader'. Kitzberger, 'Love and Footwashing: John 13:1–20 and Luke 7:36–50 Read Intertextually', in *Biblical Interpretation: A Journal of Contemporary Approaches* 2 (1994): 192.
10. An excellent place to begin an excursion into feminist theology is with Katharine Doob Sakenfield's excellent summary article, 'Feminist Uses of Biblical Materials', in *Feminist Interpretation of the Bible*, edited Letty M Russell (Philadelphia, PA: Westminster, 1985), 55–64.
11. *Ibid*, 64. This reaction to Scripture is not unique to feminists. I have experienced the same reac-

Privilege

It is difficult for those who are part of the privileged segments of society to place themselves in the 'Bible-reading shoes' of the 'have-nots', the 'have-beens', the 'might-have-beens', the powerless, and the disenfranchised. For example, it comes as a shock to western Christians to realise that some Latin American theologians emphasise a completely different set of texts on the subject of salvation.[12]

Age

Sensitive though this issue is, one should keep in mind that we bring our particular age to the study of the Scriptures. Studies reveal that with increasing age there is usually increasing intolerance for ambiguity, although education and personality are important factors as well. This increasing rigidity may be expressed religiously in fundamentalism and in the heightened probability of an authoritarian approach to religion.[13]

Race and Culture

The culture, nationality, and place of birth of the biblical reader provide a large part of the 'text' which (s)he brings to Scripture. For example, in Australia and New Zealand, non-Anglo-Saxon Adventists at times cannot understand why Anglo-Saxon church members do not 'see' in the Bible what is absolutely plain to them. East Coast and Mid-West American Adventists look askance at Southern Californian Adventists. Tragically we tend to label people who do not interpret the Bible in the same way we do as conservative or liberal, concrete-thinkers or abstract thinkers, educated or non-intellectual, and biblically literate or scriptural neophytes.

Imagine what a wealth of biblical insight we might find if we were to listen to the insights of those who approach the Book from quite different cultural, racial

---

tions from Christians who are in the process of grieving, dealing with marital breakdown, or coping with teenagers. Also see Norman H Young's thought-provoking article, 'Women: The Silenced Majority', *South Pacific Record*, 14 January 1995, 911.

12. For instance, Gustavo Gutierrez (one of the fathers of liberation theology) explains that 'to believe ... is to be united with the poor and exploited of this world from within the very heart of the social confrontations and 'popular' struggles for liberation'. Gutierrez, 'Freedom and Salvation: A Political Problem', in G Gutierrez and R Shaull, *Liberation and Change*, edited by RH Stone (Atlanta, GA: John Knox Press, 1977), 92.
13. For example, see the cross-sectional data from the 'Adventist Family Study, 1994', by Bradley J Strahan with Bryan Craig, *Marriage, Family and Religion* (Sydney: Adventist Institute of Family Relations, 1995), 51–65. This study focuses on a randomly selected sample of 996 Seventh-day Adventist adults from nineteen to ninety-two years of age. For a more general discussion of age-related cognitive changes, see Kathleen Stassen Berger, *The Developing Person Through the Life Span* (New York, NY: Worth Publishers, 1988, second edition).

and family perspectives, especially we Westerners, for whom 'calculation is more obviously characteristic of modern life than reflection'.[14]

Adventist

It is important to recognise that members of any given particular religious affiliation will tend to bring to Scripture a system by which they attempt to organise the material that they discover there. Accordingly, Seventh-day Adventists tend to read the Bible through 'Adventist spectacles'. For example, we view matters such as sin, salvation, God's sovereignty, and human freedom, through the lens of the 'great controversy' motif. Such an approach can be positive, if the organising principle applied to biblical data arises from the Bible itself. However, we fail to really listen to Scripture if we press the biblical story into our own mould so forcefully that we lose sight of its ambiguities.[15]

Ministerial

Whether or not they know it, pastors tend to treat the Bible as 'their' book, which they have been trained to dispense to the laity as needed. Even the way they conduct a Bible study is seen by the uninitiated as something they cannot possibly imitate. It is all too easy for one to hold a position of power over how the Bible is interpreted and applied. While we should not underestimate the advantages of theological training, we should also recognise that it has prepared people for exit from the culture of 'Jane Citizen' and for entrance into the 'peculiar' culture of ministers.

Sin

As sinners we have a tendency to circumvent the plain meaning of Scripture. Our natural tendency to disobedience can cause us to rationalise the radicality of the Bible. 'The heart is deceitful above all things and beyond cure. Who can understand it?' (Jer 17:16). It is essential that we ponder the fact that there are two primary ways of evading the text of Scripture. One is by twisting the text in such a way that the gospel is transformed into a form suiting our own liking.[16] The other type of rebellion is 'orthodox legalism' which tithes the mint and cumin while 'the

---

14. Robert Morgan with John Barton, *Biblical Interpretation* (Oxford: Oxford University Press, 1988), 290.
15. It is vital to notice that at times our biblical interpretations arise out of the perspectives of Ellen G White. I do not wish to call into question her inspiration, but I think she would be disappointed to find that we have not individually or collectively put ourselves into the biblical story as she herself attempted to do.
16. This attitude is condemned in 2 Timothy 4:3–4 and 2 Peter 3:16.

real meaning of the text is passed over'.[17] Is it not the sin of pride that causes us to think that we know more about God and his heaven than he has revealed to us in the written or incarnate Word?

Personality

Last, but not least, the personality type of the reader or interpreter will have a large bearing on the meaning found in Scripture.[18] For instance, the overly serious will not notice humor or irony in Scripture. More than likely (s)he will read such material in a flat, black/white, and literalistic fashion. Think of the exegetical contortions that some biblical interpreters and preachers have engaged in as they have tried to explain Jesus' 'ridiculous' statement that 'it is easier for a camel to go through the eye of a needle than for a rich man to enter the kingdom of God' (Matt 19:25).[19]

Conclusion

All of us come to the Bible as biased readers. Conservative Christians have long warned how 'contemporary beliefs and presuppositions seem to block the way and distort all our interpretations.' How then, can the text assume 'a determining role over us, given our own place in history' when it is impossible to remove distorting assumptions?[20]

Naively thinking that we can bracket out our own story is not the answer. Rather, we 'have to take account of the bias factor when we go about hermeneutics'. One must be cognisant of the fact that it is harder to get at the original meaning than we may have previously thought and 'it calls for greater effort'.[21] If that is the case, it is not surprising that Paul should command Timothy: 'Do your best to present yourself to God as one approved, a workman who does not need to be ashamed and who correctly handles the word of truth' (2 Tim 2:15).

---

17. Clark H Pinnock makes this distinction in his *The Scripture Principle* (San Francisco: Harper and Row, 1984), 199. In commenting on the twin dangers of rebellious liberalism and orthodox legalism, Pinnock observes that the wise course must be for us to attend to the error we ourselves may be guilty of and correct that, hoping others will do the same. 'For it is not right to point out the beam in our brother's eye when there is a speck in our own.' *Ibid.*
18. A handy but somewhat outdated introduction to this aspect of biblical interpretation is found in Cedric B Johnson, *The Psychology of Biblical Interpretation* (Grand Rapids, MI: Zondervan, 1983).
19. The overly scrupulous can miss the larger picture as 'gnats' are strained and 'camels' are swallowed (Matt 23:24).
20. Pinnock, *The Scripture Principle, op cit,* 207.
21. *Ibid,* 208.

'To be an interpreter means to be an incessant seeker.' We do not possess absolute knowledge; hence the necessity of interpretation. Neither do we have absolute goodness; so we must continually apply Scripture to our lives.[22] Nor do we come as unbiased seekers. Therefore, we must be always open to the corrections of God's Spirit as He applies God's Word to us.

---

22. Kevin J Vanhoozer, 'The World Well Staged? Theology, Culture, and Hermeneutics', in *God and Culture: Essays in Honor of Carl F.H. Henry*, edited by DA Carson and JD Woodbridge (Grand Rapids, MI: Eerdmans, 1993), 30.

The Use of Scripture in Cross Cultural Context

Matupit Darius

Introduction

> In the past God spoke to our forefathers through prophets at many times and in various ways, but in these last days he has spoken to us by his Son, whom he appointed heir of all things, and through whom he made the universe.[1]

When 'God spoke to our forefathers', he used their language, customs, symbols, modes of dress, value systems, and ways of dealing with each other. For example, when God and two angels appeared to Abraham 'near the great trees of Mamre' (Gen 18:1), they participated in the local customs. After accepting Abraham's hospitality, the men washed their feet with water that was brought by Abraham. Then, they ate what his catering service provided: curd, milk, bread, and a roasted calf. Abraham did not eat with them, but participated in their conversation as he stood nearby and watched (Gen 18:8). He took on the role of a servant.

On another occasion, God had promised Abraham (then Abram) that he would possess the land where he was now wandering as a nomad (Gen 15:7). Abram accepted the promise, but wanted something to back the promise: '. . . [T]he patriarch begged for some visible token as a confirmation of his faith and as evidence to after-generations that God's purpose toward them would be accomplished.'[2] God's reply to Abram is noteworthy. God asked him to bring a heifer, a goat, a ram, a dove and a young pigeon. 'Abram brought all these to him, cut them in two and arranged the halves opposite each other; the birds, however, he did not cut in half' (verse 10).

What is the significance of the animals being cut in two and arranged opposite each other? God was simply resorting to a cultural practice that Abram was

---

1. Hebrews 1:1, 2. All Bible quotations are from the New International Version, unless otherwise indicated.
2. *Ibid*, 132.

familiar with, a standard ritual of the day to authenticate, validate, and legalise transactions.[3]

'In these last days he [God] has spoken to us by his Son' (Heb 1:2). At the end of His ministry, Jesus declares that anyone who has seen Him has seen the Father (John 14:9). This is a fascinating statement, because to date Jesus has talked, walked, dressed, slept, wept, and looked very much like any ordinary man of his day; that is how God has chosen to reveal Himself to humanity. That revelation of the Father is clothed in culture humans can identify with. 'The evidence of His divinity was seen in its adaptation to the needs of suffering humanity. His glory was shown in His condescension to our low state.'[4]

Parables of the Kingdom

Matthew makes two very important observations about Jesus' method of teaching. 'Then he told them *many things in parables* . . . Jesus spoke all these things to them in parables; *he did not say anything to them without using parables*' (Matt 13:3, 34, emphasis added). He frequently introduces these parables with the expression, 'The kingdom of heaven is like . . .' However, to illustrate the kingdom of heaven, He uses stories, objects, customs, incidents, nature and other things from Palestine. He uses the seen to illustrate the unseen, the known to explain the unknown, and the familiar to reveal the unfamiliar. Jesus realises that illustrations from within a culture are the best tool for bringing the realities and values of heaven to His audience.

Using Culturally Specific Material to Illustrate the Kingdom

Using culturally specific material to illustrate the kingdom of heaven is very productive. We do this all the time in our preaching. When an American is preaching to an American audience (s)he uses American stories, practices, and news items to illustrate his sermon. Likewise, when an Australian is preaching to an Australian audience (s)he uses Australian stories and slang. The preacher uses many Australian stories, events, humor, characters and customs that make the presentation appealing to Australians. This can be a very successful approach because it meets them where they are. They do not have to sit with Bible dictionaries, commentaries or an encyclopedia to find the meaning of the slang, figures of speech and idioms that are used.

However, there is another side to the coin. I participated in two Christian meetings in Papua New Guinea, in which the presentations by Australia preach-

---

3. *Anchor Bible* (Garden City, NY: Doubleday & Company Inc, 1964), 1:113.
4. Ellen G White, *The Desire of Ages* (Mountain View, CA: Pacific, 1940), 217.

ers were beamed in via satellite. One was at Pacific Adventist University (PAU), where I am the church pastor, while the other was at Wewak, where most of the young people come from rural villages. The students at PAU enjoyed the program, but missed much of what the Australian audience was laughing at. In Wewak, the young people could not understand all that happened before the sermon. It went over their heads. However, they were able to follow the sermons, though with some difficulty. Even those who thought they had a good grasp of English had difficulty following the use of idiom.

The Negative Impact of Cultural Perceptions on Reading the Bible

The Bible has universal appeal because it is written in narrative form. Each culture interprets the Bible narratives according to its cultural beliefs, value system and worldview. This has very serious implications.

Let's take three examples. First, the Old Testament gives vivid accounts of certain prominent characters, like Jacob and David, acquiring more than one wife, plus concubines. In Western cultures, polygamy is non-issue and this facet of the stories has little impact. In polygamous cultures, these Bible stories are perceived as supporting the practice.

Second, Abraham sends his servant Eliezer to Mesopotamia in search of a wife for Isaac (Gen 24). When Eliezer finally strikes a 'successful deal' with Rebecca's parents and brother, he gives them very expensive gifts. People who come from a tribal society like mine instantly draw two conclusions:

1. Parents and relatives must arrange marriages, with very little input from the young people involved.
2. The Bible supports the payment of 'bride price', because the 'friend of God' pays bride price for his daughter-in-law.

Western missionaries tell our people that polygamy and bride price are heathen practices and that the church should discipline those involved in them. Our people usually react negatively, saying, 'The Bible we read talks about God's people having more than one wife and paying and accepting bride price? Which Bible are you reading? Is this a Bible conspiracy?' Of course we are reading the same Bible. The difference is in the 'cultural reading glasses' or cultural background and perceptions we bring to interpretation.

Third, let's suppose that a Bible teacher has students in his class from both third world and western backgrounds. When they discuss the story of Joseph in Egypt, the teacher asks what is the most important lesson to be drawn. Students from Western backgrounds suggest that Joseph's refusal to commit adultery with

Potiphar's wife is extremely important. This response comes from a Western preoccupation with sexual sins and marital infidelity. However, the third world students come from a background where family loyalty and solidarity are highly valued emphasised. For them, Joseph's active concern for his father and brothers during the famine is the key to the story.[5]

The Positive Impact of Cultural Perceptions on Reading the Bible

Sometimes cultural perspectives help us understand Bible stories better. For example, in contrast to the western world, sorcery is a very big issue in many third world animistic cultures. In Papua New Guinea, sorcery permeates the whole society. I am sorry to admit that it affects our Christian communities as well. Because I come from that background, Bible stories concerning sorcery jump out at me. Some of these stories are obvious to any reader (for example, Acts 19:19, 1Sam 28:7–25), but there are others that a westerner would not easily connect to sorcery.

For example, when Aaron throws his walking stick onto the floor in front of Pharaoh it turns into a snake. Pharaoh summons his magicians; they throw their walking sticks on to the floor and their sticks also turn into snakes (Exod 7:10–12). Many Christians from animistic cultures relate well to this story. Our cultural beliefs tell us that spirits can transform themselves into whatever form they want to take, just as Satan is able to transform those sticks into snakes. In Papua New Guinea, people who are able to transform themselves into other forms, through the power of the devil, have a specific name: '*sanguma*'.

When my father was young, an old sorcerer wanted to pass his witchcraft onto him. One day the sorcerer taught him how to disguise himself as an old woman. He recited a formula, which the sorcerer had given him, and they were instantly transformed. When some people saw my father and the sorcerer walking up from where they had been practicing, these people actually saw two old women carrying baskets on their heads. The people greeted the two men in the way they normally greet women.

In the middle of last year (2002), I preached a sermon against sorcery, and in the second half of the sermon I used Job 1–2. A faculty member later commented to me later that in his whole life he had never seen any hint of, or allusion to sorcery in those chapters. He honestly could not, because he comes from a culture that does not take sorcery very seriously. I have no difficulty seeing the connection. My animistic background colours my reading of Job in such a way that it is hard for me to miss it.

In animistic societies, people believe that there are good spirits as well as evil ones. The evil spirits can inflict terrible harm on anyone who happens to be in

---

5. Borge Schantz, *Ministry*, (June 1992): 8.

their way. To protect themselves from evil spirits and sorcery, people usually carry magic charms with them. To protect their homes, they grow certain plants around the house. Sometimes they even bury magic potions under the house or hang them above the doorway.

In the first chapter of Job, Satan the arch-sorcerer admits to God that he cannot penetrate the hedge that God had put around Job, his family and his property. Satan can touch Job and his property only when God withdraws that protective hedge. Animists perceive the protective hedge around Job as something similar to the protection provided by the magic charms they carry around.

> For our struggle is not against flesh and blood, but against the rulers, against the authorities, against the powers of this dark world and against the spiritual forces of evil, in the heavenly realms. Therefore put on the full armor of God, so that when the day of evil comes, you may be able to stand your ground, and after you have done everything, to stand (Eph 4:12).

In western Christianity, Satan and evil spirits are involved in tempting, seducing, and leading people to break the law of God. However, this is a foreign concept in animistic cultures, especially in Papua New Guinea, in which evil spirits are rather believed to be involved in making people sick and bringing death; causing accidents, deformity, storms, rain, and drought; breaking marriages; and bringing bad luck.

In Papua New Guinea, we have often preached sermons on Ephesians 6:12–16 using the historical-grammatical method of interpretation, dramatising the passage with cardboard armor and weapons. But what has been the result? It has been just another western sermon that does not have any relevance to the people in their every-day life and their fear of evil spirits, sorcery and *sanguma*.

The above passage has a very meaningful and powerful message for people in animistic societies of today. The passage would be readily understood and appreciated if it is illustrated with things the people are familiar with. The question is: How do we do that? I suggest three steps:

1. Use the historical/grammatical method to study the passage in order to get the real message the author is trying to convey.
2. Isolate that message from the cultural vehicle the author is using.
3. Select and use illustrations from within the culture that will best convey the original message without distorting it.

Summary

The Bible presents an effective model for communicating the gospel to the various cultures of the world. That model was designed and used by God in the Old Testament. Jesus used the same model during His incarnation. This model uses the culture, customs, language, stories and objects from within a culture to convey the Gospel to people of that culture.

Cultural backgrounds, value systems, and worldviews often colour people's interpretation of Bible stories. Sometimes cultural backgrounds enhance the reader's appreciation and reception of Bible truths. Recipients readily appreciate and accept Bible truths when they are presented through illustrations that are culturally relevant to them. Communication technology has reduced our world to a global village. But we still need to learn as much as we can about the cultures of our congregations so that we can explain the Bible effectively to them.

My Reading? Your Reading? Author(ity) and Postmodern Hermeneutics
Grenville JR Kent

We believe that each man must find the truth that is right for him.
Reality will adapt accordingly.
The universe will readjust.
History will alter.
We believe that there is no absolute truth
Excepting the truth that there is no absolute truth.
We believe in the rejection of creeds.
- Steve Turner, 'Creed'[1]

Abstract: This essay examines postmodern theories relevant to biblical hermeneutics, then examines two 'special interest' readings of the book of Ruth—Queer and Postcolonial—and evaluates them. It examines James Barr's critique of postmodern 'readings', then attempts an original reading—Racist—as a *reductio ad absurdum* to demonstrate that postmodern relativity can sustain no arguments against fascism. It examines fundamentalist flirtation with postmodernism and critiques Walter Brueggemann's early optimism. It then evaluates the usefulness and otherwise of postmodern hermeneutics.

Introduction

Postmodernism, a loosely related group of memes in philosophy, cultural theory, gender relations, design, the arts and popular culture, also has its own literary hermeneutics. Its philosophical stance is skepticism, as expressed by Jean-Francois Lyotard's 1979 call to rebel against 'grand narratives', those inherited 'universal theories of Western culture'.[2]

One key concept is Jacques Derrida's late-60s term 'deconstruction', which means to read a text not for one 'true' meaning but for many possibilities of mean-

---
1. Steven Turner, *Up To Date* (London: Lion, 1982), 138–139.
2. Jean-Francois Lyotard, 'The Postmodern Condition: A Report on Knowledge', in *The Routledge Companion to Postmodernism*, edited by Stuart Sim (London & New York: Routledge, 2001), 3.

ing, including those contrary to the author's apparent intentions. Derrida advocated close reading to notice 'hierarchies', 'repressed contradictions and inherent vulnerabilities' rather than a consistent viewpoint, and saw the text as an unfinished network of other texts rather than a representation of reality. He wanted to 'expose, reverse and dismantle binary oppositions', the (structuralist) use of chaos and order, darkness and light, etc, where one term is always privileged and the other denigrated.[3] Derrida attacked 'logocentricity', 'the assumption that words can unproblematically communicate meanings'; he claimed that the meanings of words lacked 'internal stability'.[4] Postmodern literary theory emphasises the reader's role in constructing meanings, rather than text containing truth from the Author-Authority. (Ironically these authors used words themselves, and expected readers to understand.)

In 1968, Roland Barthes wrote of 'The Death of the Author'.[5] He argues that the Author is merely 'a modern figure', an Enlightenment construct of 'positivism' and 'capitalist ideology', and that one can never know who is speaking in literature—the author? the hero? wisdom?—because 'writing is the destruction of every voice', and the text's history is irretrievable or irrelevant: 'every text is eternally written *here and now*'.[6]

> We know now that a text is not a line of words releasing a single 'theological' meaning (the message of the Author-God) but a multi-dimensional space in which a variety of writing, none of them original, blend and clash.

Barthes' brief essay does not demonstrate this point, but merely asserts that 'we' (a term not defined) 'now know'.

> Once the Author is removed, the claim to decipher a text becomes quite futile. To give a text an Author is to impose a limit on that text, to furnish it with a final signified, to close the writing.
> [But] 'refusing to assign . . . an ultimate meaning . . . to the text (and to the world as text) liberates what may be called an anti-theological activity, an activity that is truly revolutionary since to refuse to fix meaning is, in the end, to refuse God and his hypostases—reason, science, law.

This is a creedal statement of postmodern hermeneutics, leaving meanings open and doubting whether ultimate meaning exists. Postmodern thinkers would in-

---

3. After Lyotard, 'Postmodern Condition, *op cit*, 222.
4. See Sim, *Companion to Postmodernism*, 306–307.
5. Roland Barthes, *Image, Music, Text* (New York: Noonday Press, 1978), 142–148.
6. *Ibid*, 143, italics his.

deed refuse God, reason, science and law as self-serving meta-narratives constructed by society's power elites.

The social and historical location of the first postmodernists suggests revolutionary political motives—manning the intellectual barricades to end the reign of Ultimate Truth, crying *Liberte!* and bringing in the mob rule of self-made meaning. Barthes was a Communist organiser in the 1968 Paris riots and his authorship is unmistakably alive here:

> We are now beginning to let ourselves be fooled no longer by the arrogant antiphrastical recriminations of the good society ... the birth of the reader must be at the cost of the death of the Author[7]

Barthes distinguished between 'readerly' and 'writerly' texts. Readerly texts make one a reader, passively consuming and responding in a predetermined way: eg a 19th century realist novel with a careful plot, omniscient narrator and moral purpose. In 'writerly' texts, by contrast, the reader 'is actively involved in the production of textual meaning', filling in gaps and even writing endings. Barthes claimed writerly texts rebel against hegemony[8] and free the reader. Yet later critics have argued that writerly texts are equally manipulative in a covert way.[9]

Michel Foucault also problematised the notion of Author, suggesting the 'author-function' was an Enlightenment construct,[10] as was the very notion of 'man' or a stable, unified 'self' (hence the phrase 'death of man'[11]). Foucault analysed the relationship between power and knowledge, and described 'discourses', the 'specialised languages and the networks of power relations operating in and defining a given field.'[12]

These theories were initially wildly controversial, but by about the 1990s they were widely accepted. After an intellectual 'trickle-down effect' they were eventually picked up by biblical studies, encouraging varied readings including political/economic,[13] postcolonial, feminist, gay/lesbian, environmental/'Vegetarian',[14]

---

7. *Ibid,* 143. Antiphrasis is '[u]se of words in a sense opposite to their customary meaning', OED.
8. Hegemony is the way the ruling class imposes its ideology on the mass of the population so that it seems to be the natural order of things. After Lyotard, 'Postmodern Condition', *op cit,* 275.
9. Roland Barthes, *S/Z* (Paris: Editions du Seuil, 1970). See Lyotard, 'Postmodern Condition', *op cit,* 347–348, 382.
10. Michel Foucault, 'What is an Author?', in *Language, Counter-Memory, Practice,* ed. D. F. Bourchard, translated by DF Bourchard and Sherry Simon (Ithaca, NY: Cornell University Press, 1977), 124–127.
11. Lyotard, 'Postmodern Condition', *op cit,* 246.
12. *Ibid,* 245.
13. For example, Ched Myers, *Binding the Strong Man: A Political Reading of Mark's Story of Jesus* (Maryknoll, NY: Orbis Books, 1991).
14. See David JA Clines, *Job 1 – 20,* Word Biblical Commentary (Dallas: Word Books, 1990), l–lii.

Christian,[15] and even atheistic.[16] For postmodern theology, authority is not sited in an ancient text but in the reader's reception, or in the political power of 'reading communities' (for example, church tradition, magisterium,[17] lobby groups).

Let us now consider two contemporary applications of postmodern hermeneutics:

Queer Readings

In *Queer Commentary and the Hebrew Bible*,[18] Ken Stone welcomes 'the development of "queer theory" out of the intersection of lesbian and gay studies and so-called 'postmodern" thought'.[19] He welcomes the 'rapid transformation' of Biblical studies 'with the appearance of a range of new interpretive questions and types of reading, many of which are now . . . grouped together . . . under the rubric of "postmodern" biblical interpretation'. For Stone, 'the proliferation of queer readings of the Bible seems today like a real future possibility—if not, unfortunately, very much of a present reality'.[20]

Timothy Koch, in 'Cruising as Methodology: Homoeroticism and the Scriptures',[21] deploys an interesting reading strategy. Koch owns his social location: 'I am a gay man and therefore my own guiding sensibility is homoerotic . . . I cannot and do not presume to speak for anyone else.' He declares his motive as 'hunger for an effective strategy to deal with the attacks . . . putatively based on . . . anti-homosexual Scriptures.' He rejects three 'hermeneutics currently employed by gay men': one, piling up arguments (philological etc) to win control, which for Koch seems like power-grabbing modernism; two, using the trump-card argument of love and acceptance (his example is Bishop Spong), which Koch sees as another attempt to control behaviour; three, trying to fit gay people into other scriptural categories (for example, eunuchs). Koch's hermeneutic clearly locates authority in the reader, not the text:

> I name the locus of my authority as intrinsic, and do not look to these or any texts to be normative for my life or my ethics . . . I seek to allow my own deep knowing, my own homoerotic power, to be the light by which I do my reading, thinking, believing.[22]

---

15. *Ibid*, liv-lvi.
16. Mark Taylor, *Erring: A Postmodern A/theology* (Chicago: University of Chicago Press, 1984).
17. Anthony C Thiselton, *et al*, *The Promise of Hermeneutics* (Cambridge: Eerdmans, 1999), 158.
18. *Queer Commentary and the Hebrew Bible,* edited by Ken Stone (Cleveland, OH: The Pilgrim Press, 2001).
19. *Ibid*, 20.
20. *Ibid*, 11.
21. Koch, 'Cruising as Methodology: Homoeroticism and the Scriptures', in Stone, *Queer Commentary, op cit*, 169–180.
22. *Ibid*, 174.

His hermeneutic involves 'using our [gay men's] own ways of knowing', and is called 'cruising' (a term which usually means looking for gay partners) 'in a bar, in an internet chatroom, or in the pages of Holy Scripture'.[23] His goal is not 'institutional validation', but reading 'because we want to, because we can'.[24]

Koch cruises 'Elijah, the Hairy Leather-Man'[25] and is attracted to him. He cruises Elisha,[26] who he says is wearing baldness as a sign of mourning for his lost 'companion' and who refuses taunting by young men. 'This scenario felt to me, in my bones, just like a queer-baiting'. Koch footnotes Ruth and Naomi as a queer couple.[27] He acknowledges that you may doubt his conclusions, but counters that you may also doubt whether a man is gay or not.

Rebecca Alpert, in 'Finding Our Past: A Lesbian Interpretation of the Book of Ruth,'[28] sketches contemporary Jewish lesbian liturgy and experience. She seeks 'lesbian role models' through 'imaginative reconstruction of the texts', which must be 'read through the lens of lesbian feminist experience'. Alpert writes:

> A Jewish lesbian midrash on Ruth requires that we read between the lines of the text and imagine Ruth and Naomi to be lovers. To lesbians, this is not implausible ... We insist on our right to find hints of the existence of women like ourselves in the past where we can.[29]

Postcolonial Readings

In 1978, Edward Said's *Orientalism* used Foucaultian theory to expose Eurocentric hegemony in representation of non-Europeans as 'the Other'. Since then postcolonial theorists and have applied postmodern theory of language, gender, subjectivity and race,[30] doing to cultural studies what the anti-western *Dances With Wolves* did to the Western film genre: reversing the point of view and political polarity, seeing 'them' as 'us'. One early application to biblical studies was Robert Allen Warrior's 1989 reading of the exodus narrative, 'A Native American Perspective: Canaanites, Cowboys and Indians'.[31]

---

23. *Ibid*, 180.
24. *Ibid*, 175.
25. 2 Kings 1:2–8.
26. 1 Kings 2:23–25.
27. Koch, 'Cruising as Methodology', *op cit*, 180.
28. Rebecca Alpert, 'Finding our Past: A Lesbian Interpretation of the Book of Ruth', in *Reading Ruth: Contemporary Women Reclaim a Sacred Story*, edited by JA Kates and GT Reimer (New York: Ballantine Books, 1994).
29. *Ibid*, 92–93.
30. See Lyotard, 'Postmodern Condition', *op cit*, 336.
31. Reproduced in RS Sugirthirajah, *Voices from the Margin: Interpreting the Bible In the Third World* (London: SPCK, 1991), 235–241.

Laura Donaldson's essay 'The Sign of Orpah: Reading Ruth Through Native Eyes'[32] favors Orpah and the Moabite point of view. It begins:

> The act of reading the Bible has been fraught with difficulty and contradiction for indigenous peoples . . . and [has] facilitated what we now call culturecide . . . [Yet] Native peoples have actively resisted deracinating processes by reading the Bible on their own terms, for example, choosing with which characters to identify rather than accepting colonisers' values.[33]

She outlines the Israelite perspective of Moabites as sexually corrupting, based on a name suggestive of incest,[34] on history[35] and on their legal exclusion from worship for ten generations.[36] Citing Randall Bailey's article, 'They're Nothing but Incestuous Bastards',[37] she argues 'dehumanisation through graphic sexual innuendo' is used to justify David's mass slaughter of Moabites.[38] Donaldson also finds Native American women being equated with Moabites in early US Christian readings of *Ruth*, including statements by Thomas Jefferson, second US president and co-framer of the Constitution. For Jefferson, she claims, Ruth-like assimilation was the 'final solution to the seemingly irresolvable "Indian problem"'.[39] Donaldson quotes Cherokee scholar Rayna Green on this 'Pocahontas Perplex', where Ruth links up with a man whose nation is bent on destroying her national culture and blotting out its memory,[40] as a rewriting of 'one of Euramerica's most important master narratives about Native women'.[41] Donaldson derives the name Orpah from '*orep (BDB*7686) meaning the back of the neck because Orpah turns her back and leaves Naomi; she is the 'abandoner'.[42] 'To Cherokee women . . . Orpah connotes hope rather than perversity, because she is the one who does not reject

---

32. Laura Donaldson, 'The Sign of Orpah: Reading Ruth Through Native Eyes', in *Ruth and Esther: A Feminist Companion to the Bible*, second series, edited by Athalya Brenner (Sheffield: Sheffield Academic Press, 1990), 130–144.
33. *Ibid*, 130–131.
34. The traditional derivation, reflected in Genesis 19:36–37, is from *min* (from) and *'ab* (father), producing a pun on *me'abihen* ('from their father') in verse 36.
35. Numbers 25:1–3.
36. Deuteronomy 23:3.
37. Randall Bailey, 'They're Nothing but Incestuous Bastards: The Polemical Use of Sex and Sexuality in the Hebrew Canon Narratives', in *Reading from This Place. Social Location and Biblical Interpretation in the United States*, edited by GF Segovia and MA Tolbert (Philadelphia: Fortress Press, 1995), 121–138.
38. 2 Samuel 8:2; and the Ammonites who were (very!) closely related (2 Sam 12:26–31).
39. Donaldson, 'The Sign of Orpah', 137.
40. Deuteronomy 12:3.
41. Donaldson, 'The Sign of Orpah', *op cit*, 139.
42. *Ibid*, 141–142.

her traditions or her sacred ancestors.'[43] For Donaldson, Orpah is 'the story's central character'.[44]

Sugirtharajah would call this postcolonial 'reading as resistance', which sees liberation 'not as something hidden or latent in the text, but rather as born of public consensus in democratic dialogue between text and context', and which is 'not confined to a particular religious source'.[45] This contrasts with liberation hermeneutics, which sees 'liberation as something . . . located in the biblical texts', and which stays 'within the bounds of Christianity'. The key difference is whether the text or one's own ethical platform has higher authority.

Musa Dube, in 'Divining Ruth for International Relations',[46] borrows her hermeneutic from a custom of the 'Batswana and other southern Africans': 'reading a divining set [of carved bone characters] with a professional diviner healer' to diagnose social and relational problems. They request divine guidance, have the reader select a character (eg a young woman-shaped piece), then study the relations among the pieces. Thus each reader 'writes and reads her/ his own story with the diviner healer in the reading session'. The Batswana, hearing the Bible from early missionaries, took it as a divination set, and many healers still use it as such.

> These readers attest that Ruth, like any other text, is a mine or mosaic of social relations, where readers can take their pick . . . [and] see and relate these social relations to their own social relationships.[47]

Dube selects the 'experiences of Ruth in Judah and the experiences of Naomi in Moab.'[48] Her conclusion: African 'nations need to acknowledge and develop a relationship of liberating interdependence.'

Evaluation

These readings provide intriguing reception-history. They demonstrate the tendency of a group or individual to read according their presuppositions, a valuable caution for any reader.

Koch's reading is creative, but could be critiqued for its lack of attention to textual details. It adduces no evidence that Elisha was Elijah's lover, or that the taunting was anti-homosexual. Koch feels that in his bones, an 'osteo-herme-

---

43. *Ibid*, 143.
44. *Ibid*, 142.
45. RS Sugirtharajah, *The Bible and the Third World: Precolonial, Colonial and Postcolonial Encounters* (Cambridge: Cambridge University Press, 2001), 261–262.
46 Musa W Dube, 'Divining Ruth for International Relations' in *Other Ways of Reading: African Women and the Bible*, edited by Musa W Dube, (Atlanta, GA: Society of Biblical Literature, 2001), 179–195.
47 Dube, 'Divining Ruth,' 180.
48 Dube, 'Divining Ruth,' 187.

neutic' that is subjective and offers little or nothing to convince readers outside Koch's reading group. Such reading 'through a glass queerly'[49] compares unfavorably to the work of William Countryman[50] who argues for similar conclusions on the basis of serious scholarly exegesis. Koch's reading ignores standard interpretive practices and could be seen as using a hermeneutic of convenience for 'spin-doctoring' purposes.

Alpert's article commendably opposes discrimination. It is quite 'imaginative', and frank about reading 'between the lines', 'through the lens of lesbian experience'. It briefly cites Ruth 1:16-17 as a lesbian couple's vow without giving reasons for this view, and otherwise ignores textual details. Other views are not engaged. Its appeals are emotive and personal: 'Making room for lesbian interpretations of the Book of Ruth is a way of welcoming lesbians into the contemporary Jewish community.' To question that, then, could seem personally prejudiced and exclusive. Alpert frankly acknowledges that 'less plausible midrashim have been accepted throughout the ages', and hopes 'our midrash will find an honored place in Jewish tradition'[51], a political process which creates accepted truths or, in postmodernist terms, a reading group which creates meaning for a text. Queering *Ruth* may make synagogue or church feel more inclusive and appealing for some, yet it cannot genuinely be sustained as *Ruth*'s theme, or aligned with other texts in the canon[52], including laws that are anything but open, writerly texts.[53] It is wish fulfillment without a textual word in its favor.

Donaldson's conclusions would be welcomed by anyone concerned for human rights, yet the reasoning behind them is debatable. Can Orpah really be the hero and central character of a narrative that mentions her twice and ignores her for its last three-quarters? Orpah is introduced in parallel with Ruth[54] and functions as a foil, providing negative contrast to Ruth's positive choice (as the unnamed relative does for Boaz in Ruth 4:1-6). Donaldson's derivation of Orpah's name is inventive but debatable. The name may be Moabite rather than Hebrew, and many derivations are suggested: the Hebrew *'arp* (BDB7446) 'to drop like dew'; the Ugaritic *'rpt* and Hebrew *'arip* meaning 'clouds', with a possible link to Baal the rider of clouds; or as cognate with the Arabic *'urf* 'mane' and referring to luxurious hair, or

---

49. Lori Rowlett, 'Violent Femms and S/M: Queering Samson and Delilah', in *Queer Commentary and the Hebrew Bible*, edited Ken Stone (Cleveland, OH: The Pilgrim Press), 106–115.
50. William Countryman, *Dirt, Sex and Greed* (Philadelphia, PA: Fortress, 1988). For a response, see Thomas E Schmidt, *Straight & Narrow: Compassion and Clarity in the Homosexual Debate* (Downers Grove, IL: InterVarsity Press, 1995).
51. Alpert, 'Finding our Past,' 95–96.
52. Genesis 19, Judges 19, Ezekiel 16:49–50. For Christians, Rom 1:26, 1 Corinthians 6:9–11; 1 Timothy 1:9–11; 2 Peter 2:6–7; Jude 7.
53. Discussions often include Leviticus 18:22; 20:13. Deuteronomy 22:5; 23:17,18.
54. Robert L Hubbard, Jr, *The Book of Ruth* (Grand Rapids, MI: Eerdmans, 1988), 94.

'arf 'scent'. Further, Donaldson's reading simplistically equates Israel with the invading, colonising culture and Moab with the indigenous colonised. This ignores Israel's regular victimisation by superpowers in biblical history, and particularly the immediate context when Moab oppressed Israel.[55] More nuanced sociological analysis is required. Donaldson's reading also ignores the canonical statement that Yahweh's order to destroy Moabite culture was based on moral judgment,[56] not on a racist model of genetic inferiority as in nineteenth century Darwinism. Ruth's acceptance into Israel's royal genealogy suggests the exclusion was not based on genes[57]. The Moabites anyway shared ancestry with Israel.

Donaldson commendably aims to advance human rights, and subordinates the text to this political agenda. Yet, ironically, lamentable abuses of human rights occurred when colonisers subordinated Scripture to their society's political consensus, rather than recognising the Bible's ethical authority. Texts were made to serve a colonialist worldview and the power relations of empire were seen as natural—as postmodernism ably exposes. (This cautionary tale that should make Westerners check our cultural sureties today.) Yet Scripture portrays Yahweh as freeing slaves. Would that not suggest that a Bible featuring Yahweh (and claiming Yahweh's inspiration) would be a liberationist text and one deserving to be properly understood rather than resisted? The Bible claims to be a text with moral power, not simply a blank screen for each generation or social group to project whatever ethics are convenient.

Dube's method is fascinating cross-culturally, yet the conclusions come more from the diviner rather than the text: why then use the Bible rather than a newspaper, or Rorshach ink blots? And the Bible is hardly compatible with divination.[58]

---

55. See Judges 3:14.
56. See Deuteronomy 23:3–6; Leviticus 18, especially 1–4. Contra Randall C Bailey, 'The Danger of Ignoring One's Own Cultural Bias', in *The Postcolonial Bible*, edited by RS Sugirtharajah (Sheffield: Sheffield Academic Press, 1995), who argues that Canaanites and Egyptians are racially maligned as practitioners of sexual taboos in Leviticus 18:2–30, just as Gentiles are sexually labelled in Ephesians 4:19 and Galatians 5:19. Yet the Galatians reference does not mention race; it concerns fallen humanity, so is irrelevant to this question. Bailey also takes Rom 1:26–27 as applying to Jews, which is inaccurate since it concerns 'mankind' (*cf* 1:18) and would in any case be race-neutral from a Jewish writer. Bailey reads in sexual innuendoes about Blacks ('more sexually endowed and active', 'voracious' and 'animal like'). He says these were a 'lynchpin in our oppression' (p 78) which regrettably may well be true, and yet he does not make the case that these views come from the Scriptures. Israel's disapproval of Gentile practices is too easily equated with racism.
57. Further see Mark G Brett, *Ethnicity and the Bible* (Leiden: EJ Brill, 1996), 161–165.
58. For example, Deuteronomy 18:10–12; Jeremiah 14:14; Ezekiel 12:24.

Questioning Postmodernism

Text critic James Barr turns the hermeneutics of suspicion onto postmodernism itself:

First, postmodern readings can 'sound incredibly individualistic: anyone can read anything in any way he likes', but reader-responses need sensible limits and controls. 'For . . . people just to read their own ideas and ideologies into the Bible is an invitation to folly and chaos.'[59] Are texts mere ventriloquists' dummies that will let any hand move their mouths? Few writers set out to produce blank screens for anyone's psychological projections. Is the reader morally equipped to ignore past insights and seize the authority of the author? If so, why write at all?

Second, whose values should be read in? Postmodernism prefers de-centering, anti-oppression values. But why these? Will there be 'organised discussion of these and other possible values . . . or will it be decided by power and influence?'[60] Barr claims these values have become 'the essential dogmas of the modern liberal churches and institutions. They have replaced the older ecclesiastical dogmas but assumed a similar function of control.'[61] Today, some ideas are 'canonical or authoritative, at least in the sense that it will be dangerous to dispute them.'[62]

Third, 'why should the Bible, once detached from its church connections and academic captivities, be so important for us to read at all?' If it is only one text among many, the Bible can be labeled the sexist, racist empire building of dead white males and ignored—unless one lobby group wants to co-opt the Bible's remaining influence over some other groups.

Fourth, many 'readings' are shallow and unscholarly: we see 'the dominance of theory over serious knowledge, the absence of connection with religious traditions . . . '[63] Barr's nightmare is that 'Derrida and Foucault will become more familiar than . . . Brown, Driver and Briggs.'[64]

Fifth, readings should not be done in isolation, despite post-modern suspicion of totalising metanarratives. Readings are not theology unless 'related to a network of conceptions of God and his relations with the world.'[65]

Sixth, many theological readings display uncritical acceptance of postmodernism, and many scholars have not critically read the post-modern philosophers but are merely following fashion.[66]

---

59. James Barr, *History and Ideology in the Old Testament: Biblical Studies at the End of a Millennium* (Oxford: Oxford University Press, 2000), 156.
60. Barr, *History and Ideology,* 154–155.
61. *Ibid,* 152.
62. *Ibid,* 152–153.
63. *Ibid,* 156.
64. *Ibid,* 28.
65. *Ibid,* 155.
66. *Ibid,* 158.

Seventh, I would add that the term 'reading' is antiphrastical, fuddling or even deceptive in phrases like 'oppositional reading', 'subversive reading' or 'reading against the grain'. Barthes frankly differentiated writerly and readerly texts, and some of what are today called readings should be called re-writings.

Racist Reading: A Reductio Ad Absurdum

Postmodernism can self-deconstruct when taken to its logical conclusion. To demonstrate the extreme malleability of postmodern hermeneutics by a *reductio ad absurdum*, let us now attempt a racist reading of *Ruth*.

I am writing as a fool[67] to make a point, yet it would not be hard to find a racist reading group among white supremacist Bible-readers today, or a centuries-old interpretive tradition such as the covenant theology behind South Africa's *apartheid* era, which read Africans as 'unbelieving black "Canaanites"' ('certainly not among the "elect"'), the British Army as Pharaoh, and the Voortrekkers as the new covenant race, 'God's people' who 'acted according to His will', so that 'He delivered them out of the hands of their enemies and gave them their freedom in the promised land'.[68] There may be an even more ancient rabbinic tradition of Philistine-hating:

> Gender and race fantasy about the Philistines reaches an extreme in the rabbinic story that Goliath was descended from Orpah ... As Orpah returned home ... she was raped by a hundred Philistines and a dog (the dog comes from 1 Sam. 17:43, the hundred Philistines from the foreskins of chap 18). David and Goliath descend in parallel lines from Ruth and Orpah.[69]

So to attempt a racist reading, *Ruth* is a warning against miscegenation and corruption by foreigners: God put them in their own countries,[70] and *Ruth* shows the dire results of interfering with that. Foreigners promise loyalty to anyone for citizenship, preying on the old and the vulnerable, moving on to the ruling class using their unnatural sexual appetites as a weapon. They trade on sympathy.

---

67. In good company, *cf* 2 Corinthians 11:23.
68. T Dunbar Moodie, *The Rise of Afrikanerdom: Power, Apartheid and the Afrikaner Civil Religion* (Berkeley, LA & London: University of California Press, 1975), 5, 26, 28. He cites President Paul Kruger as an example of this belief.
69. David Jobling and Catherine Rose, 'Reading As A Philistine', in Brett, *Ethnicity, op cit*. They cite *Midrash Rabbah* Ruth 1:14.
70. Deuteronomy 32:8; Acts 17:26. In his chapter in Dr G Cronje's 1947 book *Regverdige Rasseapartheid* (English translation: A Just Racial Separation), the eminent Dutch Reformed theologian Professor EP Groenewald quoted these texts, along with Genesis 11, to argue God had ordained racial separation. See WA De Klerk, *The Puritans in Africa: A Story of Afrikanerdom* (London: Rex Collings, 1975), 221.

Their desperation work ethic brings cutthroat competition that destroys the labor market, displacing national workers. This relentless greed and social climbing of ethnic minorities will destabilise society and threaten the integrity of the nation's highest institutions—family, economy, nobility, leadership. Witness how the conspiracy of world Jewry has seized such power in the USA and globally! Boaz was vulnerable to weak-minded sympathy for foreigners because he was the son of the Canaanite whore Rahab[71]. Later King David, a product of inferior genetic stock, struggled with the Moabite sexual appetite, which was a major factor in his temptations and even the incest amongst his children[72]. Its example corrupted Solomon, whose wives (foreigners again[73]) turned his heart away from God, and his example was repeated throughout *Kings*, which ends tragically. In more enlightened times, like Hitler's Reich, racial purity laws would have excluded David. God's law was even more discerning in excluding Moabites from the temple even when diluted by ten generations of assimilation . . .

Enough of this ridiculous racist reading! Yet postmodernism provides no objective criteria to combat it, nothing beyond personal preference, group disapproval and Nietzschean power reductionism. This reading would be welcome to some reading groups, and quite powerful if backed with violence. Personally I find this racist reading offensive and as justified intellectually as 'reading' *Mein Kampf* as a document of Jewish liberation or *Schindler's List* as a romantic comedy. Yet for postmodernism, any reading is equally valid. Richard Rorty famously admitted he was unable to find within postmodernism a rationale against fascism:

> [W]hen the secret police come, when the torturers violate the innocent, there is nothing to be said to them of the form 'There is something within you which you are betraying . . . there is something beyond these principles which condemns you.'[74]

Rorty cannot mount moral critiques because of his relativism:

> There is nothing deep down inside us except what we have put there ourselves, no criterion that we have not created in the course of creating a practice, no standard of rationality that is not an appeal to such a criterion, no rigorous argumentation that is not obedience to our own conventions.

---

71. See Matthew 1:5. Donaldson makes this point, 'The Sign of Orpah', *op cit*, 138.
72. Amnon's rape of his half-sister Tamar, 2 Samuel 13:1–22.
73. 1 Kings 11:1–11.
74. Richard Rorty, *Consequences of Pragmatism* (Minneapolis, MN: University of Minnesota Press, 1987), 189–190.

How ironic that postmodern philosophers, who suffered Nazi invasion as teens, tried to decenter power and ended up failing to offer a logical defense against fascism.

The best defense against this racist reading is the text itself. Given more space, it could be argued that the text commends Ruth the Moabite, both in other characters' words and the narrator's depictions of kind actions. It accepts her into the faith community, narratively rewards her with affirmation (3:11), food security and even wealth (3:16; 2:1), love (4:13), progeny (4:13), public acceptance (4:11–12, 15), and the honour of royal descendants (4:17–22) and even, in canonical context, Messiah as descendant (Matthew 1:5). This Moabite woman is taken under the wings of 'Yahweh, the God of Israel' (Ruth 2:12).

Can a hermeneutical method that allows such extreme relativism really be useful and valid? (Of course this is a different question from asking whether it is true, but asking whether a relativistic philosophy is true is a self-deconstructing question.)

Idealism About Postmodernism

Walter Brueggemann, widely respected for his intuitive, synchronic, literary approach, heralded a brave new hermeneutical era of post-modernism some twenty-five years after its French theorists wrote. His 1993 work *Texts Under Negotiation: The Bible and Postmodern Imagination*[75] is upbeat that the 'wholly new interpretive situation' of postmodernism is a 'positive opportunity' for the 'the liberation of the Biblical text'[76] since

> church interpretation (especially where historical criticism has been taken with excessive seriousness) has tended to trim and domesticate the text not only to accommodate regnant modes of knowledge, but also to enhance regnant modes of power.

This is classic postmodern vocabulary;[77] Brueggemann even fears the 'tyranny' of 'positivism'. Yet otherwise his sketch of postmodernist bears little resemblance to that of its founding writers, whose works he does not cite. He acknowledges having 'no expertise about the historical and philosophical issues involved in the

---

75. Walter Brueggemann, *Texts Under Negotiation: The Bible and Postmodern Imagination* (Minneapolis, MN: Fortress, 1993).
76. *Ibid*, vii.
77. See Michel Foucault, 'On Power', in *Politics, Philosophy, Culture: Interviews and Other Writings, 1977–1984*, edited by LD Kritzman, translated by Alan Sheridan *et al* (New York & London: Routledge, 1988), 96–109; or Michel Foucault, *Power/Knowledge: Selected Interviews and Other Writings, 1972–1977*, edited by Colin Gordon (London: Harvester, 1981).

critique of modernity'.[78] Brueggemann's construct of postmodernism can airily dismiss the problem of relativism:

> [T]he threat of unbridled relativism is not, in my judgment, much of a threat. In reality, the dispute boils down to a few competing claims on any issue, and this is not the same as 'anything goes'. I regard relativism as less of a threat than objectivism.[79]

Since then, postmodern interpretations have moved well beyond just a few. One outlying example of this is the atheist reading of Mark Taylor, *Erring: A Postmodern A/theology*.[80] Assuming God is dead, 'Taylor argues for the elimination of such concepts as self, truth, and meaning. Language does not refer to anything, and truth does not correspond to anything'.[81] One could then ask: Why write in words? Why not paint dada or throw bombs?

Brueggemann opines that a 'postmodern climate recognises that there is no given definition and that rival claims must simply be argued out'.[82] This misunderstands postmodernism, which suspects logic itself as another metanarrative 'claiming to provide universal explanations and to be universally valid'.[83] It critiques 'logocentricity', the 'assumption that words can unproblematically communicating meanings'.[84] So rational argument and free speech (both Enlightenment ideas) have no place in Foucault's world of Nietzschean power reductionism. There is no basis for reasoning together, and no external standard agreed for rational argument or moral debate, so the ideology with the most voters, lobbyists and spin doctors likely wins. Postmodernist culture-forming is not an international dialogue moving towards truth, but new tribes locked in a Darwinist struggle where might is right—which sounds, with painful irony, like fascism. Since you cannot reason with your enemies, crush them with political or media power.

Brueggemann believes that 'general scientific positivism is breaking down'.[85] Yet few scientists are postmodern about their work. In *Fashionable Nonsense: Postmodern Intellectuals' Abuse of Science*, physicists Alan Sokal and Jean Bricmont devastatingly show how later postmodern intellectuals have 'repeatedly abused scientific concepts and terminology'; they target the 'epistemic relativism,

---

78. Brueggemann, *Texts Under Negotiation*, viii.
79. *Ibid*, 10.
80. Taylor, *Erring, op cit*.
81. McGrath, *Bridge-Building, op cit*, 105.
82. Brueggemann, *Texts Under Negotiation, op cit*, 15.
83. Lyotard, 'Postmodern Condition', *op cit*, 316.
84. *Ibid*, 306–307.
85. Brueggemann, *Texts Under Negotiation, op ci*, 2.

namely the idea ... that modern science is nothing more than a "myth", a "narration" or a "social construction" among many others.'[86]

Brueggemann sees postmodernism as breaking up hegemonies and opening up discussion. Yet has not debate in biblical studies been ever with us?

Despite questioning this idealism about postmodern hermeneutics, it should be said that Brueggemann's commentary is usually commendably fresh, perceptive, challenging to the power elites of his culture, and concerned for the weak and poor.

Fundamentalist Postmodernism?

Support for postmodern hermeneutics has recently come from an unlikely quarter: resurgent neo-fundamentalism. The common ground is a loathing of critical study of the Bible. Barr believes fundamentalists are attracted to a-historical postmodern readings because 'the Bible can be read without all that historical stuff!'[87] Robert Chisholm observes this in evangelicalism:

> Some well-meaning evangelicals deemphasise historical setting and cultural background, arguing that the 'meaning resides in the text'. This affirmation is true as far as it goes, but one must remember that the text is rooted in a historical-cultural context that is inextricably linked to its meaning. To understand what the text meant, we must try to reconstruct this context to the best of our ability, utilising the linguistic and archaeological evidence at our disposal. When a so-called text-centered interpreter fails to do this, one's approach easily degenerates into a reader-oriented analysis ... [88]

Barr seems surprised that fundamentalists are not more wary of postmodern hermeneutics. First, their bedfellow is a 'totally non-Christian and non-religious philosophy and practice'.[89] Michel Foucault, for example, was a Marxist involved in the 1968 Paris riots,[90] homosexual,[91] reported practitioner of sexual torture

---

86. Alan Sokal and Jean Bricmont, *Fashionable Nonsense: Postmodern Intellectuals' Abuse of Science* (New York, NY: Picador, 1998). (French *Impostures Intellectuelles*, 1997). They stick to 'epistemic/cognitive relativism, not 'the more delicate issues of moral or aesthetic relativism'. Foucault comments on the institutional coercive power of science in Foucault, 'On Power', 96–109.
87. Barr, *History and Ideology, op cit,* 150.
88. Robert B. Chisholm Jr, *From Exegesis to Exposition: A Practical Guide to Using Biblical Hebrew* (Grand Rapids, MI: Baker Books, 1998), 149–150.
89. Barr, *History and Ideology, op cit,* 150–151.
90. His disappointment at the defeat of these riots and advocacy of smaller, more local causes may be behind his postmodernist suspicion of *grand recits* or meta-narratives like Marxism.
91. Although he rejected the term and others suggesting fixed identity or stable selfhood. See also Michel Foucault, *The Will to Knowledge: The History of Sexuality: 1* (London: Penguin, 1978),

(claimed to have knowingly passed on AIDS in San Francisco sadomasochistic bath-houses[92]), and understood as advocating child sex.[93] This is not an attempted *ad hominem* attack on his theory, but for Christians to expect hermeneutical help from the rebel against textual authority and morality would be ironic. Second, do conservatives really want to abandon claims that the Bible is historically true? 'They may not want critical history, but they do need historical fact'. Third, 'to have truth and rationality disappear out of the window is uncomfortable'. Fourth, reader-response theories may seem to legitimise evangelical readings, but it legitimises anyone's readings and 'this is slippery ground. A more secure foothold is offered if one goes the other way and thinks that the Bible has its own, clear, meaning, which anyone can perceive'.[94]

Responding To Postmodernism

So what can evangelicals do with postmodernism? James Barr dismisses it out of hand: '[T]o utter the word "postmodern" is equivalent to saying "I am now going to start talking nonsense"'.[95] John Barton also rejects it:

> As 'a theory' (sometimes, with staggering imperialism, just 'theory' with no article!) claiming to explain or expose culture, art, meaning and truth, I find postmodernism absurd, rather despicable in its delight in debunking all serious beliefs, decadent and corrupt in its indifference to questions of truth ... But as a game ... a way of having fun with words, I find it diverting and entertaining. I enjoy the absurd and the surreal, and postmodernism supplies this in ample measure.[96]

Robert Carroll presents a nuanced view. He critiques the 'theory-driven scholars' who, after the cold precision of structuralism,

> emerged after the 1960s determined to read themselves into the text and to construct reading strategies ... which would reflect the points of view of their own reader-response approaches to the biblical text.[97]

---

and *The Use of Pleasure: The History of Sexuality 2* (London: Penguin, 1984).
92. Roger Kimball, 'The Perversions of Michel Foucault', www.newcriterion.com/archive/11/mar93/foucault.htm, citing and reviewing Foucault's biography ('hagiography'), James Miller, *The Passion of Michel Foucault* (New York: Simon and Schuster, 1993). (Accessed January 2003).
93. See his co-interview on French radio, 1978, transcribed as 'Sexual Morality and the Law', in *Politics, Philosophy, Culture: Interviews and Other Writings, 1977–1984*, edited by LD Kritzman, translated Alan Sheridan *et al* (New York & London: Routledge, 1988), 271–285.
94. Barr, *History and Ideology, op cit*, 150–151.
95. *Ibid*, 30.
96. John Barton, *Reading the Old Testament*, second edition (London: Darton, Longman & Todd, 1996), 235.
97. Robert P Carroll, 'Poststructuralist approaches New Historicism and postmodernism', in *Ibid*, 50.

Yet Carroll acknowledges 'real strengths' in postmodern method when applied to 'specific biblical narratives', especially the 'sophisticated blending of modernist and postmodernist approaches' which 'gives birth to the reader as an active subject in the construction of meaning', and shows 'concerns other than the old-fashioned ones of finding objective meanings in texts which may then be imposed on all readers in authoritarian modes'. These, Carroll finds, can 'rescue . . . the Bible from its ecclesiastical and academic captivities in hermeneutic forms which have become sclerotic over the centuries', and so postmodern-informed readings are 'some of the best work now being done in biblical studies'.[98]

From his different perspective, Anthony Thiselton argues for balance: 'A hermeneutic of promise . . . will steer between the Scylla of Cartesian individualism, which has orphaned itself . . . and the Charybdis of an intralinguistic indeterminacy.'[99] That is, good hermeneutics avoids two extremes: one, taking Descartes ('I think, therefore I am') to the extreme where only my thoughts matter; the other, getting lost in the belief that language has no meaning. Thiselton argues:

> The biblical writings cannot be reduced to a Cartesian textbook of information that permits the response of only wooden replication of ideas or idiosyncratic novelty outside the clear boundaries of the text . . . On the other hand, while many passages of the biblical writings operate with literary productivity that seduces, challenges, surprises, provokes and transforms the expectations of readers, the biblical writings also contain creeds, doctrines, traditions, beliefs, and assertions that cannot be reduced without doing violence to the status of 'literary' or 'open' texts . . . [In the Bible] every degree of coding between fully 'closed' and fully 'open' texts can be found.[100]

How might one tell the difference between open texts and closed texts? One major way is sensitivity to genre and literary techniques. Legal texts aim to preclude other understandings,[101] and one closed part of Ruth is the public legal declaration (4:9–10).[102] An open part of *Ruth* is the scene where Boaz gives Ruth grain (3:15). At a literal level, he is showing *chesed* by giving 30–45 kg of food to a poor im-

---

98. *Ibid*, 60-6`
99. Thiselton *et al, Hermeneutics, op cit*, 151. In Greek mythology, Scylla was a dog-headed monster and Charybdis variously a whirlpool or monster that spewed water three times a day, endangering sailors. Hence they represent opposite extremes to steer between.
100. Thiselton *et al, Hermeneutics, op cit*,153.
101. It would be difficult to misread the legalese, purposely redundant command to 'destroy, kill and annihilate' (Esther 3:13).
102. Though even this can be read allegorically as Christ securing the legality of the believer's salvation.

migrant woman after a famine. Yet so soon after the near-seduction scene and her marriage proposal, he asks her to remove part of her clothing and then gives her seed, and one need not be a Jungian analyst to see that he is offering her not just grain but seed—physical love, descendants, parental immortality. Perhaps high modernist scholarship needed postmodernism to centre the pendulum, but faith communities have long known Biblical stories were amazingly adaptable and universally relevant; Robert Alter writes of narratives multi-layered enough to 'generate three thousand years of exegesis, with no end in sight'.[103]

Postmodern hermeneutics, while no natural ally of Bible-believing Christianity, can be catalytic in some ways:

> 1. They challenge one's presuppositions, easy assumptions and traditions, and make one *look again at the text,* which can humble interpretive arrogance. Yet, 'while "right" understandings remain dynamic, polymorphic and irreducible to a single simplified concept, some "understandings" are clearly *wrong.*'[104]
>
> 2. Postmodern writers encourage readers to confront 'the Other' rather than just one's own ego.[105] The assumptions of one's own gender, class, socio-economics, race, etc. seem only natural, yet postmodernism shows how the same story reads differently in Beverly Hills and Baghdad. However, postmodernism too easily allows readers to shop for a like-minded reading group, to de-emphasise confronting truths and find teachers for itching ears, and to remain self-serving. Less textually respectful postmodern 'readings' cross the line between genuine re-interpretation and mere spin. Readers need to ask ourselves the question: do we want to understand the text or project our own views onto it? Perhaps the ancient proverb is relevant: 'Fools have no interest in understanding; they only want to air their own opinions.'[106] Reason-based discussion, however modernist, is a valuable preventative against 'solipsism and relativism'.[107]
>
> 3. In raising awareness of radically different ways audiences read Scripture, postmodern hermeneutics can offer insights for cross-cultural ministry. Yet this should not be a license for the reader to

---

103. Robert Alter, *Canon and Creativity: Modern Writing and the Authority of Scripture* (New Haven & London: Yale University Press, 2000), 16.
104. Thiselton *et al, Hermeneutics, op cit,* 142.
105. *Ibid,* 133–134.
106. Proverbs 18:2, NLT.
107. David Jasper, 'Literary readings of the Bible', in Barton, *Old Testament, op cit,* 27. Solipsism is 'in philosophy, the view or theory that only the self really exists or can be known. Now also, isolation, self-centredness, selfishness.' (OED).

assume God-like powers over the text. Readers should approach the text expecting to learn something, and should be changed by the text rather than vice-versa. Writers should be assumed to have some skill in making their thoughts understood. Language may not be perfectly accurate, but it works: a kiss is still a kiss, whether literal[108] or metaphoric.[109] Beyond this, Divine inspiration should be considered (*cf* Prov 30:5, 6).

4. Postmodern scholars often encourage readers to question power, even though postmodernism itself lacks the necessary motivation to do so. Robert Morgan points out this irony:

> The recent explosion of biblical study into a bewildering variety of literary possibilities is likely to weaken its revolutionary potential and indirectly support the *status quo*. It requires a strong belief in rationality for biblical scholarship and interpretation to speak with a sufficiently strong common voice to achieve institutional change.[110]

Morgan claims traditional Christian ways of reading already challenge power, stimulating positive revolutionary thinking and action in Christian communities beyond what postmodernist readings will do.

5. Postmodern hermeneutics tend to bring contemporary concerns to the text. These are crucial in keeping an ancient text relevant across time; yet equally crucial are objective controls, notably those of historical-grammatical exegesis. Some contemporary questions can be answered only in principle or by analogy, and some perhaps not at all. For example, what does *Ruth* say about the ethics of new reproductive technologies or genetic engineering? One may seek precedents in the Mosaic principles of levirate marriage narrated in Ruth, or the answer may be, 'Nothing'.

These contributions can be valuable but ultimately the text itself, in 'canonical-historical context' and with help from 'historical, literary, and canonical controls', must define its own interpretation, otherwise readings can multiply infinitely and become 'embarrassingly narcissistic', yielding 'shallow politicisation instead of convincing interpretation'.[111]

---

108. Song of Songs 1:1 (Heb 1:2).
109. Psalm 85:10.
110. Morgan, in Barton, *Old Testament, op cit,* 126.
111. Michael S Moore, *The Book of Ruth*, NIBC (Peabody, Massachusetts: Hendrickson, 2000), 298.

Scripture records a model of how to respond. Apostolic preaching was, in postmodern terms, a new Christian 'reading' of the Hebrew Bible and quite threatening to the reading group(s) of Judaism. Synagogue members in Berea[112] were commended for not blindly holding a traditional reading. They searched (not just superficially browsed) the Scriptures (the text, not traditions or theory) daily (not just once as if there was nothing left to learn) to see (which suggests one can know and see, at least with reasonable certainty) whether these things were true (suggesting truth exists and is knowable, however imperfectly).

Understanding ancient texts requires linguistic and historical competence humbly provided by experts trained in using rational controls and dialogue with others, and applied by faith communities forging a theology through the struggles of life experience. Thus there can be proper confidence as well as constant searching for new understanding. Without becoming lost in literary games or falling down the epistemological mineshafts of postmodernism, people can use various methods to search the text for principles that speak to contemporary questions.

If space permitted, we could outline the major themes and many sub-themes of *Ruth*—God's character and interventions; *chesed,* both human and divine; the gospel of grace and redemption; Gentile inclusion and world mission; self-righteousness and ethnocentrism; marriage; ethical workplace relations, and many more. Clear themes can be seen, yet no explanation can claim to be the last word. 'People yet unborn'[113] should see fresh relevance and gospel liberation in the story.

---

112. Acts 17:10–11.
113. Psalm 22:30–31

PART FOUR

Issues In The Interpretation Of Ellen G White

Learning from Ellen White's Perception and Use Of Scripture: Toward An Adventist Hermeneutic For The Twenty-First Century

Arthur Patrick

Introduction

Abstract: Ellen White, the most voluminous of all Seventh-day Adventist authors, held a high view of Scripture and used the Bible copiously. Studies of the past three decades have the potential to illumine the way in which White's writings support and inform the current need of the church in Western cultures to enhance its hermeneutic for the biblical canon.

Ellen Gould Harmon White (1827–1915) is the most prolific, most published and most influential author amongst some thirteen million Seventh-day Adventists (SDA) distributed within 204 nations.[1] White's literary career began in New England during the 1840s and endured into the second decade of the twentieth century, involving extended travels in the United States of America as well as in parts of Europe and Australasia.[2]

Early attempts at analysis of White's concepts and use of Scripture were hampered by the difficulty of achieving access to her entire literary corpus and the absence of adequate search aids for her voluminous writings. Beyond individual attempts, the church has fostered effective indexing and to that end it has produced useful publications, especially in 1926, 1962–3, 1977 and 1992. It has also

---

1. See Marilyn C Crane, *Bibliography of Ellen G White Titles* (Loma Linda, CA: Loma Linda University Library, revised 1990) for an alphabetical list of nearly 600 titles used up to that time for pamphlets and books by Ellen White. For a list of publications available in the 1990s, see *Ellen G White Books and Pamphlets* (Silver Spring, MD: Ellen G White Estate, 1996). Note that hereafter in the text of this essay only Ellen White's married surname is used.
2. A brief account relevant for Seventh-day Adventists in the territory of the South Pacific Division is available in Arthur Patrick, 'Ellen White's Antipodean Exile, 1891–1900: Reflections on Her Australian Years', October 2002. This and other sources cited in this essay are available for study in the Ellen G White/SDA Research Centre, Avondale College.

published illuminating compilations from White's writings and increasingly facilitated better access to her unpublished manuscripts and letters, especially since the 1940s.[3] Although the effects of these related initiatives have flowered with the advent of computer technology, analyses of White's perception and use of Scripture are still indicative rather than definitive.[4] This essay builds on existing studies of these related matters, offering examples of the type of development that characterised her thought during seven decades of prophetic ministry, and citing illustrations of the variety of ways the Scriptures are treated within her writings.[5] However, its ultimate purpose is to inform one facet of Seventh-day Adventist hermeneutics in ways that have significance within Western cultures early in the twenty-first century.

Some Illustrative Dilemmas

A theology student spends countless hours with the four gospels establishing the order of the events in Christ's earthly life. In part, his method is to correct the gospel harmonies available to him on the basis of the only source the student believes to be definitive: White's writings. The conclusions reached are recorded systematically with a mapping pen in the student's wide-margin Bible. While the effort is prodigious, one of its outcomes is a sense of chronological and sequential certainty for a couple of decades during the delivery of sermons and Bible studies. However, a simple comparison of *The Spirit of Prophecy*, II (1877), with *The Desire of Ages* (1898) shows that White adjusted her understanding of the order of events. This revision has the potential to influence applications made of biblical statements. For instance, when describing the experience of the disciples during a storm on Galilee, the 1877 account states, 'In their agony of fear they turn to him, remembering how he had once saved them in a like peril' (307–8). But if the 'like peril' is in the future, it cannot be remembered. In other words, an altered sequence may invalidate an interpretation or necessitate the reinterpretation of comment made in an earlier piece of writing.[6] Therefore, the core of the student's

---

3. The *Manuscript Release* process, initiated in the 1940s, accelerated slowly until it led to the publication of twenty-one volumes between 1981 and 1993.
4. A short review is offered in Arthur Patrick, 'Reflections on Unfinished Business: Ellen White Studies in Historical Perspective', January 2003.
5. Selected aspects of this development are expressed in Arthur Patrick, 'Ellen White, Yesterday and Today: Understanding and Affirming the Ministry of the Most Creative Sabbatarian Adventist', September 2003. Accessed 14 September 2010 at http://www.sdanet.org/atissue/white/patrick/egw-scripture.htm.
6. Compare Chapter 21, 'Walking on the Water', of Ellen G White, *The Spirit of Prophecy* (Washington DC: Review and Herald, 1969), 2:267–274; Chapter 25, 'Christ Stills the Tempest', *ibid*, 305–310; Chapter 35, 'Peace, Be Still', from Ellen G White, *The Desire of Ages* (Nampa, ID: Pacific, 2006), 333–341; Chapter 40, 'A Night on the Lake', *ibid*, 377–382. It should be noted that

research project and the way it informed years of ministry are brought into serious question.

A biblical scholar concludes that the Old Testament offers a 'good' revelation of God that meets the needs of its time and place but the New Testament makes an even 'better' disclosure, culminating as it does in the life and teachings of Jesus Christ and the founding of Christianity. He discovers that a similar type of development is apparent in White's experience and writings. He illustrates this reality by noting the change in White's emphasis from the awesome 'power' of Sinai to the winsome 'goodness' of Calvary. The *Adventist Review* publishes an abbreviation of his research in a five-part series, an action that remains a point of concern for some earnest believers.[7]

A respected district pastor with an earned MA degree and a reputation for a constructive understanding of Scripture and history decides to offer a series of seminars on the twenty-seven Fundamental Beliefs of Seventh-day Adventists. His most vigorous congregation, in a city approaching thirty thousand people, includes several congregants noted for their determination to monitor ministerial orthodoxy. They bring a number of White's books to church week by week and leaf through these volumes diligently during the pastor's presentations, preparing questions to pose as the pastor greets members in the foyer. With a sense of triumph, on the day the seminar focuses on 'The Church,' a member avers that the SDA church is 'teaching heresy' because Fundamental 11 states that the church is the bride of Christ, whereas White declares in *The Great* Controversy (426–7) that 'the people of God are said to be guests at the marriage supper' and therefore 'cannot be represented as the bride' of Christ.[8]

These dilemmas are cited from the experience of three ordained SDA ministers who are actively teaching and preaching in 2003.[9] A survey of

---

nowhere does White imply that she is an authority on such matters as chronology. The theology student was merely following a belief that seemed to be so pervasive in the church that it was beyond question.

7. See Alden Thompson, 'From Sinai to Golgotha,' a five part series in *Adventist Review,* December 1981; Alden Thompson, *Who's Afraid of the Old Testament God?* (Exeter: Paternoster Press, 1988), 15–17; Alden Thompson, *Inspiration: Hard Questions, Honest Answers* (Hagerstown, MD: Review and Herald, 1991), especially Appendix E, pages 285–298; Alden Thompson, 'From Burdensome Asceticism to Joyous Simplicity: The Interplay of Theology and Experience in the Life of Ellen White' (paper presented at the Pacific Northwest Region meeting of the American Academy of Religion/Society of Biblical Literature, Eugene, Oregon, 5 May 2002).

8. S Ross Goldstone reports this event in a two-page statement dated November 2002. Goldstone's document is located in the same Research Center file as the original copy of this paper.

9. Compare such of my papers as 'Visioning and Re-Visioning Seventh-day Adventist Tertiary Education in Australia: A Centennial Assessment of Avondale College', The Inaugural Murdoch Lecture, August 1997, in *Avondale Reader,* Volume 1 (July 1999); 'Re-Visioning the Role of Ellen White for Seventh-day Adventists Beyond 2000', in *Adventist Society for Religious Studies Annual Meeting Papers* (November 1997), 107–132; 'Historians of Adventism: Their Agony, Ecstasy, and

ministers might quickly multiply such illustrations, for they are frequent within the regional and the world church. More than that, the church's archival collections include abundant evidence that dilemmas of this type have surfaced within Sabbatarian Adventism repeatedly since its early decades, often creating career uncertainties even for well-known and respected leaders.[10] This reality has helped to provide a rationale for heterodoxy and it has supplied grist for the mills of heresy. Also, it has helped fuel internal controversies and construct effective weapons for persons who criticise the church.[11]

Clearly, it is a matter of importance for the church to foster an adequate understanding of White's writings in general and their inspiration in particular. For pastors who face situations like those cited above, a doctrine of inspiration grounded in reality may be expected to facilitate more effective Bible study and preaching; it may support a sustainable application of White's counsels; and it may help to transmute divisive controversy into more effective relationships within the church and fuller cooperation in the church's mission to the world. However, while this essay acknowledges the importance of the doctrine of inspiration, it will only address that issue in an oblique fashion. Its purpose is to offer comment toward the development of a sustainable hermeneutic for Scripture in terms of White's writings.

Ellen White and the Bible

Most Seventh-day Adventists are well aware that White affirms Scripture as the church's only rule of faith and practice, the foundation of faith and the test of Christian experience.[12] As she reflected on her role during the church's formative

---

Potential' (April 1998); 'Ellen White, the Adventist Church and Its Religion Teachers: A Call for Transformed Relationships' (April 1998), Adventist Society for Religious Studies Annual Meeting, Orlando FL. A summary of central ideas embodied in these papers is attempted in a brief presentation, 'Ellen White and Adventists in the 1990s' (May 1998). I have benefited greatly since 1998 from critiques sent to me by scholars and pastors serving in many parts of the world, after they read one or more of these papers on sdanet.org in the AT ISSUE section.

10. For one of many potential illustrations, consult Gilbert M Valentine, *The Shaping of Adventism: The Case of W. W. Prescott* (Berrien Springs: Andrews University Press, 1992).
11. For instance, note the frequently stated expectations of *The Remnant Herald* regarding the church's understanding and presentation of White's ministry, up to and including the issue dated December 2002. These expectations form an important strand in many of the forty volumes written and published by Drs Russell and Colin Standish.
12. 'God will have a people upon the earth to maintain the Bible, and the Bible only, as the *standard* of all *doctrines* and the *basis* of all *reforms*', Ellen G White, *The Great Controversy* (Mountain View, CA: Pacific, 1950), 595 (emphasis added). Several hundred similar passages refer to the Bible as *standard, foundation, basis* and *rule*. To extend the search, juxtapose such words as *faith, doctrine* and *practice* with *Bible, Scripture* and *Word of God*. This essay does not include extended lists of quotations in that computerised technology is readily available to most readers

years, she indicated that often it was to confirm steps already taken on the basis of prayerful yet diligent Bible study. She also describes her ministry as a 'lesser light' leading to the 'greater light' of Scripture.[13] It is instructive to observe the way in which she refused to settle theological debates, even when her legitimacy was thereby brought into serious question. Her lifelong attitude is well illustrated by the occasion in 1901 when she quite bluntly counseled assembled leaders to lay her writings aside until they understood the Scriptures.[14]

White is often described as a co-founder of the Seventh-day Adventist Church. From the vantage point of nineteenth-century historians, this makes her one of a group of innovative people who account in part for clusters of thought identified as Mormon, Seventh-day Adventist, Christadelphian, Christian Scientist, and Jehovah's Witness.[15] Of the founders of these religious bodies, White used Christian authors most extensively as background material for her writings. This fact, in addition to her Methodist upbringing, helps to make her more orthodox than the others, from the perspectives of historic Christianity. In a number of ways, she cogently pointed her spiritual descendants toward an effective relationship with the Bible. This fact has tended over time to narrow the gap between Seventh-day Adventists and mainstream Christianity.[16] How, then, may White's perception and use of Scripture be described?

At the outset it is important to observe that White made a concerted attempt to understand, employ and apply the whole of Scripture. This reality alerts those who value her writings to the fact that she will lead their Bible study in directions quite different from those fostered by the founders of the other religious movements that arose in nineteenth-century America. Her persistence in encompassing the

---

who may wish to check the statements.
13. The 'lesser light' expression is used by White to refer to the moon, the Jewish age and the ministry of John the Baptist, in addition to illustrating the relationship between her writings and the Bible.
14. For a contextual appraisal of this statement in terms of the three extant stenographic reports, see Arthur Patrick, 'An Adventist and an Evangelical in Australia? The Case of Ellen White in the 1890s', in *Lucas: An Evangelical History Review* 12 (December 1991): 42–53, especially footnote 20 in relation to *Manuscript Release* 115:12. For an edited version of this article, see *Ministry* (February 1995): 14–17.
15. The most instructive comparison of White and other female religious founders of her time is Ronald D. Graybill, 'The Power of Prophecy: Ellen G White and the Women Religious Founders of the Nineteenth Century' (PhD dissertation, Johns Hopkins University, 1983).
16. This process invites exploration from a number of perspectives, especially those of historians and sociologists. The most cogent contemporary analyses are available in the numerous journal articles by an expatriate Australian, Ronald Lawson. Lawson's initial PhD studies at the University of Queensland embraced both history and sociology. His long career at the City University of New York and his extensive research undertaken in various parts of the globe locate his interests progressively within the discipline of sociology, but his writings demonstrate the benefits of an ongoing engagement with historical studies.

thought of the entire Bible is intimated visually by indices to her writings. For instance, seldom in a relative sense is a chapter in the *SDA Bible Commentary* devoid of citations to White's writings.

Secondly, White maintained for seven decades a focus on the apocalyptic literature of Scripture, demonstrating thereby both the promise and the problems of millenarian thought. Her experiences as a Millerite, as a 'Shut Door' Sabbatarian Adventist, as an 'Open Door' Adventist, as a pioneer of Health Reform and Righteousness by Faith, were impacted by the apocalypticism of Daniel and Revelation in particular. Even as there is a creative tension between the classic prophets of the Old Testament and those suffused with the characteristics of the apocalyptic mind, there is a tension in White's writings between the *now* and the *not yet*, between occupation and imminence. This is a tension which must never be resolved if the Christian is to balance the teachings of Scripture. White's experience and diary-like comment on the relevant issues during the founding years and early maturity of Adventism illumine the past and offer instructive comment for the ongoing present.[17]

Thirdly, White revealed during her ministry a growing interest in basic principles of exegetical Bible study. Exegesis requires attention to linguistic, syntactical and contextual considerations, openness to the illumination provided by historical and archaeological studies, and recognition of the immediate life setting of the text under consideration and the relationships that exist between the various parts of the Bible. While White was not an academician in these respects, her writings demonstrate a genuine interest in Bible study that either takes account of or leaves room for exegetical endeavours.[18] Unlike some of her most ardent supporters at the present time, she welcomed translation initiatives that improved upon the delivery of God's Word through the King James Version.

A fourth consideration is the way in which major themes in White's literary endeavours led her to persistent Bible study. One of the best examples is the 'Great Controversy' theme. Fortunately, the development of her writing on this concept is now well documented and widely understood.[19] Ten years after her introduc-

---

17. The recent study by Douglas Morgan indicates how the church has attempted to understand and apply Revelation 13:11–18 over a period of sixteen decades. A shelf of similar books could well be written about other important passages in Daniel and Revelation. See Morgan, *Adventism and the American Republic: The Public Involvement of a Major Apocalyptic Sect* (Nashville: University of Tennessee Press, 2001).
18. A trusted colleague warns that this sentence may overstate the case. After careful consideration of his caution, I have retained the concept but admit it needs thorough exploration in a single-issue paper.
19. Note the attention given to the Great Controversy theme in Herbert E Douglass, *Messenger of the Lord: The Prophetic Ministry of Ellen G White* (Nampa, ID: Pacific Press, 1998). See also Frank B Holbrook, 'The Great Controversy', in *Handbook of Seventh-day Adventist Theology* Commentary Reference Series twelfth, edition, Raoul Dederen (Hagerstown, MD: Review and

tion to the idea, she began to express it in *Spiritual Gifts* (1858–1864), followed by four *Spirit of Prophecy* volumes (1870–1884), and five *Conflict of the Ages* tomes (1888–1917). These books illustrate her engagement with the theme, but they do not encompass it. Indeed, the controversy between Christ and his angels and Satan and his angels provides the most comprehensive framework for her entire corpus. *Early Writings* is probably the most accessible early expression of this strand within White's writings; it both illustrates the concept and resonates with the way New England's religious culture understood and applied the related insights of John Milton. She continued to explicate the theme throughout her life in the books mentioned above and in many others, especially *Testimonies for the Church* (1855–1909), *Thoughts from the Mount of Blessing* (1896) and *Christ's Object Lessons* (1900). This engagement continues in many of her five thousand periodical articles and in uncounted numbers of letters, manuscripts, and oral discourses.

Twenty-five years ago, Adventists in the South Pacific Division started to hear about Walter Rea's research into the sources that White used so copiously in her extensive writings. Four years later, near the highest point of the intense controversy surrounding Rea's claims, an article was published suggesting that the literary relationship between White's writings and the work of other authors is in the order of 0.002 per cent.[20] It was no doubt motivated by a commendable desire to stabilise the understanding of the church in the South Pacific. However, the painstaking, four volume study by Fred Veltman and suggests a figure 15,000 times higher may apply to fifteen randomly selected chapters of *The Desire of Ages*. In a public lecture during September 2002, Rea offered evidence that the discovery of literary parallels is ongoing, significant and includes the content of such books as *The Great Controversy*. The debate over percentages will remain contentious until we examine candidly a range of models that take account of all the known evidence and foster sustainable configurations.

White states that 'scenes', 'views', and 'representations' were disclosed to her mind in prophetic visions and dreams. Her son, William White, who more than any other person associated with her during her long literary career, described these experiences as 'flashlight' or 'panoramic' scenes. If her 1858 Great Controversy vision was like a two-hour video of the war between righteousness and sin, subsequently reinforced by flashbacks and similar experiences, there was every reason for her to explore and select from the multiple sources she used in writing on the Old Testament, the New Testament, and on Christian and Adventist history. There was rationality in her reliance on literary assistants, advisers and

---

Herald, 2000).
20. Robert J Wieland, 'Ellen White's Inspiration: Authentic and Profound', in *Australasian Record* (31 May 1982): 9.

editors in the initial process of preparing her writings for publication and in the subsequent revision of such works as the 1888 edition of *The Great Controversy*. When Bible and history teachers met with administrators during 1919, the recorded discussion makes it clear that such processes were remembered within the group quite adequately. However, obscurantist impulses were so apparent at the time that the records of the 1919 discussions were packaged, stored and lost to the memory of even the church's thought-leaders. So, during the next six decades, the entire Adventist community largely forgot the vibrant lessons offered by this aspect of its past. It moved White's writings away from their historic role toward making them the definitive and authoritative encyclopedia of Adventist thought and practice. Therefore, the church needed the factual disclosures of the 1970s and 1980s, even though these revelations seemed traumatic to some at the time. Because of the church's failure to remember the way the Lord had led and taught it during its past history, there was much for it to fear and it experienced great loss.[21]

There remains a tendency amongst some Adventist apologists to continue to claim too much for White's writings, a fact that undermines her credibility. For instance, the McAdams' study of sources for the John Huss chapter in *The Great Controversy* indicates that she followed known historians 'page after page, leaving out much material, but using their sequence, some of their ideas, and often their words', even their 'historical errors and moral exhortations'.[22] Such practice

---

21. In papers referenced above I refer to analyses of the three reactions likely to occur when a religious group is inundated with new information: reversion, rejection, or transformation. The interpretation of Adventist history since 1970 in particular is illumined usefully in terms of such sociological insights. Perspectives relating to White from the pioneering study of sociologist Robert Wolfgramm (1983) are now extended by other doctoral studies. For example, see Michael Chamberlain, 'The Changing Role of Ellen White in Seventh-day Adventism with Reference to Sociocultural Standards at Avondale College' (PhD thesis, University of Newcastle, 2001). Currently Rick Ferret is researching and writing an illuminating doctoral thesis on the impact of the routinisation of charisma, identity and sectarian change within Adventism.'
22. Donald R McAdams, 'Shifting Views of Inspiration: Ellen G White Studies in the 1970s', in *Spectrum* 10 (March 1980): 27–41. See page 34 for McAdams' abbreviated account of his research on the Huss chapter. The McAdams' article remains the best overview of the 1970s, the decade in Adventism during which the most significant data about White's life and thought became available. Over 900 pages of material were generated for the 1982 International Prophetic Guidance Workshop, thereby making crucial information a matter of public record. Data discovered since that time has added further illumination and offered additional confirmation of some positions that were still tentative at that time. For the past two decades the task of the church has been located more within the area of interpretation than in the realm of discovery. The indefatigable research of Fred Hoyt is one of the best examples of the importance of this process. For instance, Hoyt's ongoing research has illumined the charismatic milieu of White's early ministry, confirming the picture that in 1982 was available only in outline form. In similar fashion, Hoyt's research demonstrates that while the fact of the literary relationship between White's writings and those of other authors was well known by 1982, the implications of this reality are still being

is consistent with the 'divine video' understanding of White's experience, which presented Huss as a man of God who stood for truth and righteousness. This visionary input may well have left White to determine a host of related matters: When and where did Huss live? What were the main events of his life? Who were his contemporaries? How was his witness received within his time and place? The common Adventist mistake when reading volumes like *The Great Controversy* is to think White was *writing* history. In actual fact she was *interpreting* history. The first is a human endeavor; the latter needs divine disclosure, if it is to rise above the level of human analysis and offer a sustainable theology of human experience.

Such remarks are predicated on the belief that White's work has an inner consistency, whether she is interpreting Scripture, history, or other matters. The overarching themes she treats disclose the essence of her unique advantage over other authors. However, we do her a great disservice when we hold her to ransom over mundane details. God gave us what we needed: a trail blazed by an intrepid explorer, for a journey during which we are sustained by his grace as we follow the Guidebook illumined by the Holy Spirit. God chose not to give us the equivalent of a paved and lighted freeway with controlled access to facilitate an unthinking glide into the kingdom of glory. To change the metaphor, we should be grateful for a direction-setting, panoramic vision of a vast landscape with evident landmarks, rather than lamenting the lack of a contour map and a street directory.[23] Ours is a journey to be undertaken by faith, not by sight. Our decisions are to be made after considering the weight of evidence, not on the basis of 20/20 vision. We are to seek the level of Christian maturity intimated in Ephesians 4 and illustrated aptly by such authors as Kohlberg and Fowler.[24]

The picture that emerges from these considerations is reinforced by reference to other areas of White's writings, including the theme of healthful living. The research of a Melbourne surgeon, Don McMahon, provides the church with another useful window into White's world with particular reference to her health counsels. A number of competent observers imply that McMahon's findings merit careful consideration.[25] McMahon's studies indicate that White's 'what'

---

defined by new discoveries. See, for one telling example, Hoyt's reconstruction of the context of White's comments on the Civil War; in particular, her reference (Ellen G White, *Testimonies to the Church* (Mountain View, CA: Pacific, 1948) 1:266–7) to the First Battle of Manasses.

23. Note the expression of this concept in Arthur Patrick, 'Landmarks and Landscape', in *Adventist Review* (27 October 1983): 4. The church would be greatly helped if a range of appropriate metaphors was developed and popularised.
24. For a useful application of the insights of Lawrence Kohlberg and James Fowler in relation to the doctrine of the Holy Spirit and the need for inclusive worship styles, see Barry Oliver, 'Worshipping in the Joy of the Holy Spirit', in *The Ministry of the Holy Spirit,* edited by Gerhard Pfandl (Wahroonga: South Pacific Division of Seventh-day Adventists, nd [circa 1995]). Especially note page 44, footnote 5.
25. Dr Russell Standish, a medical doctor, strongly contests these suggestions; note his comment

and 'why' health statements achieve about twice the credibility rating of the 'what' and 'why' health statements of her contemporaries. This is evidence that she received input from a Source far more reliable than Graham, Alcott, Jackson, and Kellogg combined.[26] Those who take her health counsels seriously are apt to live seven or more years longer than the general population.[27] However, even as White's writings leave room for continued biblical enquiry, they also leave room for the development of medical science on the bases of diligent observation and intentional research. Thus the health emphasis that she initiated now embraces scientific medicine and its advocates are able to hold their heads high in a world that is very different from that of her lifetime.[28] It is remarkable indeed that, according to McMahon's findings, her 'health and medical statements' in books like *Spiritual Gifts* (1864) and *The Ministry of Healing* (1905) may merit about a seventy per cent credibility score amongst health professionals, and that this score may improve as medical research continues to develop.

The evidence that White's biblical and theological writings are related to the North American and Adventist cultures of her time is well documented. A similar clarity derives from the evidence that her historical writings are related to those of Protestant historians and that her health writings are related to those of American health reformers. William White notes that her literary dependence was especially significant in the general areas of prophetic and doctrinal exposition.[29] The reversionist response within Adventism has continuing problems with the recognition and application of such data. From a polar opposite position, the rejectionist response seeks resolution from acute cognitive dissonance by creating distance from the prophet and in some instances from the Adventist community. By contrast, the transformationist response accepts all the known data

---

filed with the original of this paper in the Research Centre.
26. I am indebted to Dr McMahon for the way he has shared both his methodology and his conclusions with me orally over several years. For a short introduction to his research, see Don S McMahon, 'Adventist Health: Inspired or Acquired?' However, a far more comprehensive report is available on the CD that McMahon has produced. McMahon's research corrects the impulse to claim 100 per cent accuracy for White's health counsels, even as it undermines the claim that she borrowed all her health concepts from her contemporaries.
27. Dr Gary Fraser's forthcoming volume will offer a context for interpreting this remark. Fraser, a researcher based at Loma Linda, intimates that his book may be entitled *Diet and Chronic Disease: Studies of Seventh-day Adventists and Other Vegetarians*. He expects it to be published by Oxford University Press.
28. More than a thousand hours of research and writing about Sydney Adventist Hospital convinces me that this theme merits careful investigation. See Arthur Patrick, *The San: 100 Years of Christian Caring, 1903–2003* (Warburton: Signs Publishing Company, 2003).
29. Observe the way this concept is placed within a helpful context in Graeme Bradford's forthcoming volume on White's writings. Bradford's content, honed with the help of some twenty readers, has been intimated in his preaching, teaching and writing of the past decade (*cf Ministry*, August 1999, 25–27).

and searches for ways to be faithful to the entire body of evidence as conclusions are formed and applications are made. Only the latter pattern is sustainable and unifying.[30]

It may well be claimed that these remarks are theoretical. The next section will, therefore, seek to concretise them by noting examples of the way in which White related to biblical themes and employed specific Bible passages during her long literary career.

Ellen White, Biblical Themes and Selected Passages

Theology is literally word or discourse about God.[31] For about seven of Sabbatarian Adventism's founding years, White along with most other leaders and members denied saving truth about God, Christ, and the Holy Spirit. To declare that God had rejected the sinful world and that the time for the salvation of sinners was past meant that serious heresy was proclaimed.[32] The process whereby the church has dealt with this matter is instructive. In the early years, White's writings were edited to remove problematic expressions and ephemeral items were lost sight of as the movement developed. Thus, over time, relevant evidence became hard to access until effective archives were established throughout the Adventist world during the 1970s. Therefore, even a prominent author like Francis D Nichol could expend great energy in denying the reality of the problem.[33] Since 1982 the church has placed this matter increasingly within a coherent framework. It is clear that God leads his people step by step; indeed, the orthodoxy of one period may become the heresy of the next and, contrariwise, the heresy of one era may develop into the orthodoxy of the next. White is emphatic that the Adventist movement has many, many lessons to *unlearn* as well as many things to *learn*.[34] Examples of the essential unlearning process are numerous from the 1840s to the present. For instance, Miller used fifteen evidences to identify 1844 as a prophetic

---

30. Probably the finest manual for implementing a transformationist response within Adventism is Fritz Guy's volume, *Thinking Theologically: Adventist Christianity and the Interpretation of Faith* (Berrien Springs, MI: Andrews University Press, 1999). Rejectionist responses are available currently from a plethora of websites as well as via videos and publications. Reversionist responses are also plentiful; in magazines, books and websites. For a brief comment on one outspoken author, Samuel Kooranteng-Pipim and his volume *Receiving the Word*, see Alden Thompson, *Spectrum*, Volume 26, No. 4 (January 1998): 50–52. Pipim's 2001 volume may be as tangential as his 1996 one. His sincerity is not under question, but the concept of inspiration he proposes leads either to the denial of data that is beyond dispute, or to the destruction of White's prophetic ministry in the way Roger Coon warned (1982).
31. For a much more adequate definition, see Guy, *Thinking Theologically, op cit*, 3–19.
32. For some of the data basic to this statement and an attempt to interpret it constructively, see Patrick, 'Ellen White Yesterday and Today'.
33. Francis D Nichol, *Ellen G White and Her Critics* (Washington DC: Review & Herald, 1951).
34. Ellen G White, *Review and Herald*, 26 July 1892.

date, whereas in 2003 probably no informed Australian Adventist could conscientiously support fourteen of them. More than that, Miller was wrong about the event that he predicted would occur in 1844. Yet we firmly believe that God led Miller and his colleagues to proclaim an essential 'present truth'. Similarly, we are now able to demonstrate cogently that the evidence used by early Adventists to adduce the idea that the door of mercy closed in 1844 is invalid. However, the 'Shut Door' teaching served an important purpose, holding the fledgling movement together while it established a membership base with more viable biblical and organisational foundations.[35]

White's perception of 'present truth' is a crucial consideration for those who would place such theological development within a sustainable and constructive context. God is infinite truth but human perceptions of truth are always partial. Therefore, within the Adventist community of faith, truth is well defined as 'progressive'. Our constant expectation is that 'the Lord will send us increased truth'. Conversely, it is a satanic deception to conclude that 'we have all the truth essential for us as a people'. The faithfulness and zeal of our forebears are exemplary for us; however we may well be judged and condemned if we do not 'improve our light as they improved theirs'.[36]

Critics of White and the Seventh-day Adventist church are apt to hurl a host of colorful missiles in their attempt to demolish her credibility and that of the movement with which she sustained a symbiotic relationship. It has proved impossible to parry some of these missiles in the way Nichol and other apologists tried to do. Conversely, White's prophetic ministry is not imperiled by the actuality of such minor mistakes.[37] Her understanding of the descent of the human race into iniquity is a case in point. Genesis 6 expresses this concept in unmistakable terms. White reaches into her culture and employs a nineteenth-century idea to illustrate antediluvian degeneracy. Her understanding of amalgamation, interpreted as the interbreeding of humans and animals, is clarified by Uriah Smith's *Review and Herald* defense of her statement. James White's action clinches the interpretation decisively: he republished Smith's apologetic in book form for wide distribution at Adventist camp meetings.[38] From our vantage point it is evident that a minor

---

35. A doctoral student commented on this point by saying that the Shut Door provided time, necessary time, much like when a basketball team takes 'time out' to consider its options. Compare Arthur Patrick, 'Mount Exmouth and the Adventist Journey', in *Record*, 27 October 2001: 2; Bruce Manners, 'The Challenge of "Present truth"', in *Record*, 26 October 2002: 2.
36. See *Signs of the Times*, 26 May 1881, 26 May 1890, White, *Testimonies*, 1:261.
37. As in the way in which Ellen White acknowledges the possibility that there are mistakes in the Bible yet avers the reliability and sufficiency of Scripture in terms of its Divine purpose.
38. Gordon Shigley, 'Amalgamation of Man and Beast', *Spectrum*, 12 (June 1982): 10–19.

flaw like White's adoption of such an idea does not militate against her credibility for those who have developed an adequate understanding of her inspiration.[39]

Often the reader of White's writings is helped to understand their appropriate application by learning more about how she did her work. For instance, the theology student described earlier who sought to develop a definitive chronology of Christ's life needed to reshape his approach after reading a pamphlet from White Estate, 'How *The Desire of Ages* Was Written'.[40] This document and its exhibits make it apparent that White laid no claim to ultimate knowledge about matters such as the order of the events in Christ's earthly life. Rather, with the help of her staff, she used the best harmony that happened to be available to her at the time. She was open to consider insights from the people around her, such as those gleaned by her longest-serving literary assistant, Marian Davis, from attendance at classes in the Melbourne Bible School. White's *Life of Christ* project was located within responsible nineteenth-century Evangelical Christian thought in terms of the thirty known sources that she valued. The nature of the revision that White implemented for her writings is illustrated aptly by her response to 105 suggestions made by W.W. Prescott for the 1911 edition of *The Great Controversy*. In short, many of the conclusions reached by the theology student distorted the author's intent for her classic volume. The student's studies might have proceeded usefully had he read page 22 of *The Desire of Ages* as an indication of the book's theme: 'to know God is to love Him.' The book is a peerless production within Adventism because it is such a winsome invitation to develop a loving relationship with God through Jesus Christ.

As for the 1888 statement discussed earlier that the church *is not* the bride of Christ, it is only a problem if White's subsequent statements are unheeded, declaring without reservation that the church *is* the bride of Christ. The concept of development within her understanding of Scripture illumines a host of apparent contradictions. As already noted, Alden Thompson's *From Sinai to Golgotha* series has identified and described a helpful example of the constructive development that characterises her thought. Rolf Poehler provides a comprehen-

---

39. For a representative list of such flaws, see Robert W Olson, 'The Question of Inerrancy in Inspired Writings' (Washington, DC: Ellen G White Estate, 12 April 1982). Olson's statement should be read in the context of several thousand pages included in or referred to in Document Files 65 and 739. Clearly the church will benefit when a competent author (such as George Knight) presents it with a comprehensive analysis of relations between Adventism and Fundamentalism. Whereas in the 1920s and 1930s many Adventists adopted the fundamentalist notion of inerrancy, by the 1970s it was evident that this concept would either require unfaithfulness to evidence or abandonment of White's prophetic ministry. The Adventist debate over inspiration in the 1990s was impaired by failure to recognise this reality; note, for instance, the way in which chapters by Frank Hasel and Samuel Koranteng-Pipim were promoted by the Adventist Theological Society.

40. Robert W Olsen, 23 May 1979.

sive framework for understanding continuity and change in Christian doctrine, Adventist heritage, and White's thought.[41] Fritz Guy offers 'how to' ideas that will help the church rise above controversy and develop a constructive future.[42] Therefore, instead of being threatened by the reality of doctrinal development that is evident in White's personal experience and writings, Adventist pastors should enable their members to understand and rejoice that God leads errant human beings (including prophets) toward the increasing light of His perfect day.

Due to limitations of space, we shall notice only three further illustrations of the way in which White related to important biblical concepts over time: 'the daily', 'the schoolmaster' and 'the holiest'. Each of these expressions might be interpreted fruitfully in the light of decades of discussion within the church, but we must focus upon them chiefly in terms of White's perspectives.

Daniel 8:13 and its reference to 'the daily' was an important theme within Millerism before it became a staple in Sabbatarian Adventism. Linked with 'the transgression of desolation' and the treading under foot of 'the sanctuary and the host', the daily has demonstrated a potential to both engage constructive dialogue and create divisive controversy. Was it to be interpreted in terms of 'sacrifice', the supplied word in the King James Version? Was the attack upon the sanctuary by paganism in its Babylonian, Greek, or Roman manifestations? Or was the attack by apostate Christianity, as in the papacy, or by a non-Christian religion, as in Islam? Was the sanctuary under discussion was a Jewish temple on earth or the 'true tabernacle' in heaven. Once the relations between the daily, 'the little horn' and 'the king of the north' were included in the discussion, the potential for controversy was intensified. Adventist heritage collections preserve accounts of debates point by point in books, periodicals, document files, and microform materials. Some of these controversies persisted for decades, often subsumed under titles (like 'The Eastern Question') that have long since lost their earlier intensity.[43]

In the post-1844 years, White supported Owen Crosier and his colleagues as they began to move away from identifying 'the daily' as paganism. During the controversy of 1850, White saw a need to divert the Sabbatarians from an interest in a physical return to a literal Jerusalem that was associated with continued date

---

41 Rolf J Poehler, 'Change in Seventh-day Adventist Theology: A Study of the Problem of Doctrinal Development' (PhD diss, Seventh-day Adventist Theological Seminary, Andrews University, 1995). The Adventist focus of this 591-page study has since become more accessible in such publications as Rolf J. Poehler, *Continuity and Change in Adventist Teaching: A Case Study in Doctrinal Development* (Frankfurt: Peter Lang, 2000).
42 See his *Thinking Theologically*.
43 For an historical introduction to such matters, see Richard Schwarz, *Light Bearers to the Remnant: Denominational History Textbook for Seventh-day Adventist College Classes* (Mountain View, CA: Pacific, 1979), especially Chapter 24, 'Debates Over Nonessentials.'

setting. Therefore she returned to the Millerite concept as 'the correct view' of the daily. This support seemed to put White at variance with the 'new' view propounded fifty years later by though-leaders like LR Conradi and WW Prescott, that 'the daily' was Christ's ministry in the heavenly sanctuary. Some observers believed that White was reversing her earlier position by being open to the new view. This perception raised deep concern about her prophetic reliability and even about the integrity of Adventism. However, a century later the entire issue is much clearer and can be discussed without fear or rancor.[44]

In the 1840s White fostered an embryonic view that proved fruitful in the long term prove the most fruitful, because it best apprehended the ministry of Jesus Christ. In the 1850s she seemed to revert to the Millerite position, to steer the young Sabbatarian movement away from a destructive heresy. In the early 1900s she was open to a more inclusive attempt to exegete the Bible, understand history and emphasise the Christ-centered nature of the biblical revelation. At no stage did she present her writings as the final authority in the matters of biblical interpretation that were in focus. Always her counsel sought to limit destructive controversy by helping to envision and implement a present that would develop a productive future for the Advent movement.[45]

In Galatians 3:24, the Apostle Paul presents the law as 'our schoolmaster to bring us unto Christ, that we might be justified by faith'. The Adventist discussion over whether this law is ceremonial or moral has simmered for much of the history of the movement. Like Mount Vesuvius it has proved able to erupt with destructive force, as it did in the context of the Minneapolis General Conference of 1888. Once again White's relation to the issue is instructive. For a time she had seemed to support the concept that Paul's opposition to law should be understood as directed against the ceremonial law. That position enabled a fitting apologetic for the perpetuity of the moral law and hence for the continuing significance of the Seventh-day Sabbath. At a later time, when the identity and continuance of the Sabbath were well established, the burning issue was the problem of the misuse of law by legalistic thought and behaviour. The perception that White had altered her understanding of the schoolmaster distressed Adventist literalists, who feared identifying the schoolmaster as the moral law may would

---

44. This interpretation is based on about twenty statements White made with reference to the daily between the 1840s and 1911, read within the context of the discussions taking place in the church. Obviously these two paragraphs on the daily need at least an entire article to treat the subject adequately. For a succinct and illuminating introduction to 'the Daily', see *Seventh-day Adventist Encyclopedia*, Commentary Reference Series, second edition, edited by Don F Neufeld (Hagerstown, MD: Review & Herald, 1996), 10:429–433.

45. Perhaps the most perceptive published account of the daily in relation to White's ministry is Valentine's Chapter 13, 'Theological Controversy and a Change of Job', in *The Shaping of Adventism*, op cit, 185–203.

imperil the Sabbath and destroy White's prophetic authority. Reversionist concern and rejectionist criticism of White's stances on the schoolmaster are not well founded when they are viewed in the light of varying historical contexts or in the glare of present research.[46]

In the Epistle to the Hebrews, the apostle is intent on showing that Jesus Christ is a better high priest offering a better sacrifice and ministering in a better sanctuary. The reading of such passages as Hebrews 6:19, 20, and 10:19–22 has raised concerns for Adventists ever since Crosier sought to distinguish between a daily atonement for the *forgiveness* of sins and a yearly atonement for the *blotting out* of sins. After the Great Disappointment, Hebrews created a landmark for Sabbatarian Adventists as they began to focus on Christ as minister of 'the true tabernacle, which the Lord pitched' (Heb 8:2). But for some believers, Hebrews seemed to erode the very landmark that it helped to create, by implying that Jesus at his ascension entered 'within the veil' (Heb 6:19), indeed 'into heaven itself' to appear there 'in the presence of God for us' (Heb 9:24). How could it be that even New Testament Christians may have 'boldness to enter into the holiest by the blood of Jesus'?

Once again White's writings offer enormous help to the Advent Movement. She affirms the stances of Crosier and Edson in the 1840s, but she moves far beyond both of them in later decades. We can now discern more clearly that Crosier and Edson led the young movement in the *right direction*, but did not arrive at the *ultimate destination* of consummate understanding. Even the 'Shut Door' concept embodied a 'present truth,' despite its biblical inadequacy. James White and Uriah Smith continued the Adventist journey, as did major doctrinal statements of the 1870s, 1890s and 1930s. Fundamental 23 adopted in May of 1980 formed a new and important climax in a long process, but even its refined understanding was not the church's last word. In August of the same year, at the largest-ever assemblage of Adventist thought-leaders convened for study of the sanctuary doctrine, the conferees probably came closer to agreement with the biblical data than any other Adventist assembly had previously been able to do. Thousands of pages of documents indicate that since that time the process of constructive development has continued as Adventists have diligently studied their Bibles. In hindsight, White's potential as a coalescing agent within Adventism can be discerned with increasing clarity. The sincerity of those who have used her writings as a centrifugal force may merit deep respect, but both the hermeneutical

---

46 Again, at the press of a few computer keys, White's writings can be searched on this issue. Most useful are her comments preserved in White, *Selected Messages,* volume 1; *Seventh-day Adventist Bible Commentary,* volume 6, edited by Francis D Nichol (Washington DC: Review & Herald, 1953); *Review and Herald* articles; *1888 Materials, Manuscript Releases,* volume 1; and the biography, Arthur L White, *Ellen G White Biography,* volume 3 (Washington DC: Review & Herald, 1985).

evidence and documented historical results call loudly for continuing change in attitude and practice.

How can such matters be understood coherently? A cluster of considerations must be noted. The maturation of biblical understanding within Adventism had been enhanced by the production of the *SDA Bible Commentary* and other factors. The experiences and the studies of the 1950s moved some believers toward a more sustainable view of the biblical doctrine of judgment. The concept of theodicy, so deeply imbedded in the Book of Daniel, was emerging into a matter of importance, enhanced by linguistic and other aspects of biblical studies. The implications of the doctrine of Righteousness by Faith were being integrated more effectively into the church's thinking. There was a perceived need to redefine the church's understanding of White's writings in relation to Scripture, following the effervescent discussions of the 1970s.

This latter need was achieved in principle by a short statement voted during August 1980 but the component ideas were not spelled out clearly until 1982 and 1983. At last the church was readied to read Hebrews without threat to its faith and to appreciate more fully White's *historical* reviews of the sanctuary doctrine, her *experiential* reflections on its process, and her intimations of what Calvary meant in terms of the Letter to the Hebrews.[47] A landmark statement of 'affirmations and denials' was formed, discussed, amended and published during 1982 and 1983. Welcomed by some church members, its import was little understood by the majority. Therefore, its essence merits restatement at this point.

Before its final publication, the single-page statement was read and commented upon by more thought-leaders worldwide than most other documents have been in the history of the denomination. This reality means it has less authority than a statement voted at a General Conference Session, but it has greater credence than most other articles in such centrist publications as *Adventist Review*, *Ministry* and *Record*.[48] The document lists ten affirmations. The first four statements relate to Scripture as divinely revealed and inspired in a canon of sixty-six books, a canon that provides 'the foundation of faith and the final authority in all matters of doctrine and practice' and constitutes 'the Word of God in human

---

47. One again, computer-assisted research can identify readily some forty Ellen White comments that provide the backdrop for these brief remarks.
48. The statement is one of the few carried in all three of these publications as well as many others worldwide. See 'The Inspiration and Authority of the Ellen G White Writings: A Statement of Present Understanding', in *Adventist Review*, 23 December 1982; *Record*, 22 January 1983; *Ministry*, February 1983. For a straightforward application of such principles that a pastor might share profitably with a local congregation, see the article by Woodrow W Whidden, 'Ellen White, Inerrancy, and Interpretation', in *Ministry* (December 2002): 24–28. Of great value in this regard is George Knight's *Ellen White Series* of four books, especially *Reading Ellen White* (Hagerstown, MD: Review and Herald, 1997).

language'. The next three statements affirm that 'the gift of prophecy will be manifest in the Christian church after New Testament times', that 'the ministry and writings of Ellen White were a manifestation of the gift of prophecy', and that, as the product of inspiration, they 'are applicable and authoritative especially to Seventh-day Adventists'. Affirmation eight focuses on the purpose of White's writings as including 'guidance in understanding the teaching of Scripture and application of these teachings, with prophetic urgency, to the spiritual and moral life'. The final two affirmations emphasise the importance White has for the nurture and unity of the church, and they emphasise that her 'use of literary sources and assistants finds parallels in some of the writings of the Bible'.

These affirmations are followed by ten important denials, as follows:

1. *We do not believe that the quality or degree of inspiration in the writings of Ellen White is different from that of Scripture.*
2. *We do not believe that the writings of Ellen White are an addition to the canon of Sacred Scripture.*
3. *We do not believe that the writings of Ellen White function as the foundation and final authority of Christian faith as does Scripture.*
4. *We do not believe that the writings of Ellen White may be used as the basis of doctrine.*
5. *We do not believe that the study of the writings of Ellen White may be used to replace the study of Scripture.*
6. *We do not believe that Scripture can be understood only through the writings of Ellen White.*
7. *We do not believe that the writings of Ellen White exhaust the meaning of Scripture.*
8. *We do not believe that the writings of Ellen White are essential for the proclamation of the truths of Scripture to society at large.*
9. *We do not believe that the writings of Ellen White are the product of mere Christian piety.*
10. *We do not believe that Ellen White's use of literary sources and assistants negates the inspiration of her writings.*

These affirmations and denials were intended to foster 'a correct understanding of the inspiration and authority of the writings of Ellen White' and, therefore, to avoid two extremes: first, regarding these writings as functioning on a canonical level identical with Scripture', or, secondly, 'considering them as ordinary Christian literature'. These 1982 statements form the parameters within which this essay seeks to examine and interpret the studies of White's writings undertaken within the church during the past three decades.

Two statements White made before important church assemblies seem to epitomise her life-long intent. Amidst the turmoil of Minneapolis she stood tall and enjoined warring Adventists to solve their destructive debate by a deeper study of the Word of God.[49] In the charged climate of the 1901 General Conference she pointedly called for her writings to be laid aside in favor of the Scriptures, the precious source of truth she so often challenges her readers to duly search, rightly understand, and faithfully apply.[50] Such counsels focus attention upon the crucial question: How should responsible Seventh-day Adventists envision from her writings a viable hermeneutic for Scripture in the twenty-first century?

Preliminary Hermeneutical Considerations

Although this section of the essay needs a book-length treatment, it must be profiled in a few words, much like an artist may try to depict an event or narrate a story with a few strokes. The questions are several yet closely related. What perceptions did White have of the Bible and its study? What example does she model and what counsel does she offer Adventists toward the development of a viable hermeneutic? How does she enjoin the application and outcomes of Bible study? Such an exploration might well begin with the 1962–3 indices of her published writings by looking up three expressions: *Bible*, *Scripture* and *Word of God*.[51] That exercise will lead to fifty pages listing several thousand references; the scanning of these will yield key words that can be tested and extended with the help of subsequent printed indices and used in a more comprehensive computer-assisted exploration. For convenience, a number of words and phrases that will especially reward a computer search are presented below in italics. Effective packaging for this vast body of material may include headings such as the following.

Orientation: reverence in the presence of Scripture

The attitudes and presuppositions of the *Bible student* are crucial. The *sacred* or *holy Word* of the living God is to be approached with *awe*, *reverence* and the attitudes of '*a learner in the school of Christ*'. The student may be confident in seeking

---

49. Read in context White's sermon, 'A Call to a Deeper Study of the Word', delivered 1 November 1888, printed in AV Olson, *Thirteen Crisis Years, 1888–1901* (Washington, DC: Review & Herald, 1966, 1981): 303–311.
50. Note the references given in footnote 14, above.
51. Here, too, it is appropriate to explore the rich heritage of the Seventh-day Adventist community and its engagement with Bible study. For a recent conspectus see Richard Davidson, 'Biblical Interpretation', in *Handbook of Seventh-day Adventist Theology*. Hagerstown MD: Review and Herald, 2000, 58–104. Davidson offers in five pages an illuminating selection of 'Ellen G White Comments'.

the guidance of the *Holy Spirit*. However, *diligent effort* is indicated, along with awareness that the *mine of truth* can never be exhausted.[52]

The human interpreter: responsible but limited

Every *rational being* is responsible for learning the *truth* from the Scriptures, for exemplifying it and sharing it with others. Yet, because of the scope of the task, the conclusions of any one person are unlikely to convey the fullness of truth. Therefore, the task is best pursued within a community of faith. Disagreements are likely but should be checked by grace and humility as well as by continuing efforts to understand *'the truth as it is in Jesus'*. Strong convictions may be a result of the guidance of the Holy Spirit and as such are to be respected as essential in the experience of Christians.[53]

Process and method: respecting text, canon and historical context

The recovery of the authentic text of the Bible and its accurate translation lays a foundation for understanding the Word of God effectively. Linguistic information is useful in this regard. The Bible is its own *expositor*, so it is fruitful to *compare Scripture with Scripture*. The recovery of the life setting of any given text may be instructive and may be assisted by reference to the biblical writer, his experience and circumstances as the well as local customs and practices. White's practice demonstrates that it is legitimate to read widely in books about the Bible and to seek to understand the way any given text has been interpreted and applied elsewhere in Scripture as well as in Christian experience and Adventist history. It is likewise fruitful to use White's writings as a lesser light leading to the greater light of Scripture.[54]

Theme and purpose: God, Christ, the Holy Spirit, and salavation

The *Old Testament* (624) whether it treats *history* (3,606), *precept* (1,516) or *prophecy* (1,992), is *irradiated* (33) with the glory of *Christ* (69,227) *Jesus* (37,038) The *New Testament* (450) has the same *grand* (1,403) *theme* (629). *Scripture* (1,942) discloses *God's* (133,323) *original* (642) *purpose* (6,514) for this *earth* (16,508), it

---

52. See 'The Imperative Necessity of Searching for Truth', in *The Advent Review and Sabbath Herald*, 8 and 15 November 1892, and many other references. More than 500 times in White's published writings, the context within which she refers to the Word of God includes a reference to the Holy Spirit. (Note that all such statistics usually include repetitions due to thematic compilations.)
53. Of a great many references, note especially White, *The Great Controversy*, 598. More than six hundred times Ellen White speaks of 'the truth as it is in Jesus'.
54. White's support for these sentiments is evident more from personal example than explicit injunction. Many *Signs of the Times* articles are of value in this regard, not least the following: 'The Weapon Against Satan's Delusions' 18 September 1892; 'Our Great Treasure House', 21 March 1906 to 17 October 1906. See also 'Able to Make Us Wise unto Salvation', 1 May 1907.

describes the origin and development of the *great controversy* (960) and it profiles the work of *redemption* (2,742). Every theme in the *Bible* (8,492) clusters around the plan of *salvation* (10,090).[55]

Outcomes and effeccts: the application of Bible study for the individual, the church, and the world

Bible study is to find application in the individual life, in the community of faith and in the church's mission for the world. God's Word received into the soul shapes thought and develops character. Truths learned are to be applied in daily experience. Every dimension of church life is to be guided by Scripture. The truth of the Bible is a trust from God.[56] A typical example of White's perception of Scripture exemplifies the mood of many expressions:

> The Bible is full of the richest treasures of truth, of glowing descriptions of that heavenly land. We should search the Scriptures, that we may better understand the plan of salvation, and learn of the righteousness of Christ, until we shall exclaim in viewing the matchless charms of our Redeemer, 'Thy gentleness hath made me great.' In the word of God we shall see the infinite compassion of Jesus. The imagination may reach out in contemplation of the wonders of redeeming love, and yet in its highest exercises we shall not be able to grasp the height and depth and length and breadth of the love of God; for it passeth knowledge.[57]

The extensive body of material so fleetingly reviewed in this section portrays White as one who stimulates biblical enquiry rather than circumventing it on the basis of superior understanding or prophetic authority. An assumption that guided in the production of the *SDA Bible Commentary*, that no comment should be seen to challenge any statement by White, is inappropriate as a rubric under which to conduct biblical enquiry in the twenty-first century, not least because of the new circumstances into which the church has been thrust.[58] More than that,

---

55. Note White, *The Desire of Ages*, 211; Nichol, *The SDA Bible Commentary*, 7:907; White, *Christ's Object Lessons*, 129; 'Build on a Sure Foundation', in *Review and Herald*, 24 September 1908. The bracketed numbers in this paragraph indicate the number of times the italicised word is used in White's published writings. By combining qualifying words with key words a mass of comment can be made more accessible.
56. From a host of potential references, note in particular 'The Scriptures a Sufficient Guide', Week of Prayer Reading for Sabbath 15 December 1888, B-209-1888, printed in 'The Ellen White Materials, Volume 1, 196–202. Compare 'The Value of Bible Study', *Advent Review and Sabbath Herald*, 17 July 1888; 'The Truth as it is in Jesus', *The Signs of the Times*, 16 June 1898.
57. 'The Beatitudes', *The Signs of the Times*, 30 May 1892.
58. As early as the 1974 Bible Conference, within the Biblical Research Institute there was recognition of 'the great variety of ways' in which White uses the Bible. See Raymond F Cottrell, 'Ellen

it is useful to understand the *Gestalt* within which White wrote, for the symbiotic relationship she sustained with the Seventh-day Adventist community of faith deeply influenced her counsel and hence the specific applications that she made of Scripture. It is as perilous to claim adequacy for the pious but uninformed studies of the theology student as it is to follow the approach of the earnest congregants. One of the most cogent expressions of the doctrine of inspiration applicable to White's corpus as well as the biblical canon has been on the church's corporate desk for over a decade.[59] Therefore, the church needs to take seriously its opportunity to offer effective pastoral care, shepherding wisely the substantial portion of its members who are unlikely to perceive adequately the dynamic nature of the development evident in White's writings, or to understand unaided the historical context that may illumine any given statement.[60] The responsibility to offer balanced pastoral leadership is enlarged by the fact that most Adventist members do not have access to the full range of thought represented in White's voluminous literary output, so their anxieties and their criticisms will often be nourished by inadequate information. One of the hopeful indicators that the church may experience enhanced unity, a clearer focus on its identity and a greater commitment to its mission in the near future is the present opportunity to implement comprehensively the South Pacific Division strategy document (1999) with reference to White's writings.

Conclusion

Carl Schurz suggests that 'ideals are like stars' in that we cannot touch them with our hands but they are useful as guides.[61] Four decades ago as an evangelist and pastor my ideals included the purpose to translate from the Hebrew and Greek originals all the texts used as bases for sermonic communication, and then to read everything White had written about these Bible passages prior to the delivery of any particular discourse. My frail hands have seldom grasped either of these ideals adequately over extended periods of time. The life of a minister and a teacher tends to be a daily response to a tumult of immediate demands. In an age when serious Bible study is too readily supplanted by lower order matters, the will to listen as prophets, apostles and Jesus Christ speak to us in their own tongues remains a worthy ideal for preachers of the Word. For Seventh-day Adventists who are moving rapidly into a world that is radically different from that of their

---

G White's Evaluation and Use of the Bible', in *A Symposium on Biblical Hermeneutics*, edited by Gordon M Hyde (Washington, DC: Review and Herald, 1974), 142–161.
59. Thompson, *Inspiration, op cit*.
60. See Barry D Oliver, 'The Development of an Adventist Lifestyle: Some Contemporary Implications', in this volume for a thoughtful essay that discusses related issues with pastoral sensitivity.
61. John P Neff, *Gleanings* (Washington, DC: Review and Herald, nd), 62.

founders, it remains a helpful ideal to seek a comprehensive understanding of the writings that witness to their rich heritage, and in particular those of the author whose prophetic ministry spanned the first seventy years of Sabbatarian Adventism. It is my hope that the cursory remarks offered in this essay may foster the development of a hermeneutic that will enhance the ministry of those who would proclaim 'present truth' with a constructive awareness of the way the Lord led and taught the Advent Movement in its earlier years.

Hermeneutics of Parable Interpretation in Ellen White Compared to Those of Archbishop Trench
Robert K McIver

Introduction

It is probably an exaggeration to date the interpretation of parables BJ and AJ—before Jülicher' and 'after Jülicher'—but only a slight one. From the second to the nineteenth centuries there was one dominant way to expound parables, that of allegory.[1] Jülicher's work and publications changed that. His decisive contribution was to gather all previous comment on each of the parables, almost all of them allegorical in nature. An allegorical approach to a particular parable may well have had persuasive force when it was given, whether during the time of the church Fathers or during the Reformation. However, changing circumstances and perspectives, and the opportunity to read a number of mutually incompatible

---

1. This is generally true, despite well known statements by some individuals to the contrary. For example, with typical dramatic flare, Luther disparages the allegorisation of Origen: 'When I was a monk I was a monster in the use of allegories. I allegorised everything' [54:47 this and following citations are from *Luther's Works*, edited by Helmut T Lehmann (Philadelphia: Fortress, 1959)]. 'When I was young I dealt with allegories, tropologies, and analogies and did nothing but clever tricks with them. If somebody had them today they'd be looked upon as rare relics. I know they're nothing but rubbish.' [54:406]. Instead of allegory, Luther urged the interpretation of Scripture in its 'plain sense': 'The literal sense does it—in it there's life, comfort, power, instruction, and skill. The other is tomfoolery, however brilliant the impression it makes' [54:406]. While Luther wrote commentaries on the Psalms, Galatians, Romans, he did not write one on the Gospels, so it is not possible to know how he would have treated the parables. He does refer to them from time to time in his sermons, but always in the service of illustration of another point he is making. This references to three parables which illustrate the Christian's need to given generously to the poor is typical: '... there is the parable of the rich reveller in Luke 16[:19-31]. He was not damned because he robbed or did evil with respect to these goods, for he feasted and clothed himself sumptuously every day with his own goods. He was damned rather because he did not do good to his neighbour, namely, Lazarus. This parable adequately teaches us that it is not sufficient merely not to do evil and not to do harm, but rather that one must be helpful and do good.' [51:8] From this, and other uses he makes of parables, it is apparent that his disparagement of allegory does not prevent Luther using the parables rather allegorically. On the other hand, John Calvin has provided commentary on all the parables, which is generally well considered, and still useful to modern commentators. He feels no compunction against using allegory where he considers that this is the best way to approach a particular parable, but compared to most ancient writers, Calvin uses it very cautiously.

allegorical interpretations at the same time, meant that after the publication of volume 1 of Adolf Jülicher's book *Die Gleichnisreden Jesu,* serious scholarship decisively rejected allegory. Any trace of it was ruthlessly eliminated from almost all scholarly interpretation of the parables for the first seven or eight decades of the twentieth century.[2] To this day, many serious commentators reject the authenticity of the interpretations of Jesus of the parables of the sower and the tares in Matthew 13:18–23, 36–43, mainly on the basis that they are allegorical.[3] Conservative scholarship, though, generally accepts their authenticity, and they are not alone is doing so.[4] Conservative scholarship, while learning from the excesses of the past, is not averse to using a mildly allegorical approach to those parables which appear to warrant it, although it eschews the method in parables for which the method it clearly inappropriate.[5]

Ellen White's major work on the parables, *Christ Object Lessons,* was first published in 1900, fourteen years after Jülicher had published *Die Gleichnisreden Jesu.*[6] Yet it is highly unlikely that she ever heard of Jülicher's work, which in any event has yet to be translated into English.[7] Indeed, the new thinking about parables subsequent to Jülicher did not reach English-speaking circles for some time. CH Dodd's important short work, *The Parables of the Kingdom,* decisively

---

2. Despite some protests, such as that of Matthew Black, 'The Parables as Allegory', in *Bulletin of the John Rylands Library,* 42 (1959–60): 273–87.
3. As does Rudolf Schnackenburg, in his recently translated commentary, *The Gospel of Matthew* (Grand Rapids, MI: Eerdmans, 2002), 127. Schnackenburg and others, have found the extensive arguments of Joachim Jeremias persuasive, in his *The Parables of Jesus,* revised edition (London: SCM, 1972), *passim,* especially 66–89.
4. For example, Craig S Keener, *A Commentary on the Gospel of Matthew* (Grand Rapids, MI: Eerdmans, 1999), 383 states that 'although parables generally exhibit a central thrust and the details are sometimes merely part of the story, one cannot exclude some allegory from even their earliest form (pace Jülicher, Dodd . . .).' WD Davies and Dale C Allison, *A Critical and Exegetical Commentary on the Gospel of Matthew* (Edinburgh: T&T Clark, 1991), 2:397–99, discusses the arguments for and against the authenticity of Matthew 13:18–23. This volume concludes that 'the case against authenticity is not conclusive', but 'At the same time, the case for a dominical origin, in our estimation, falls short of proof.'
5. As this is not a essay on modern parable interpretation, little more can be said. These readers interested in reading further about parable interpretation might wish to consult my book, *The Four Faces of Jesus* (Boise, ID: Pacific Press, 2000), 47–72. Also useful is Robert H Stein, *An Introduction to the Parables of Jesus* (Philadelphia, PA: Westminster, 1981), 15–26, 42–81. On the place of allegory in Rabbinic parables with a consideration for the implications for the use of allegory by Jesus in His parables, see Harvey K McArthur and Robert M Johnston, *They Also Taught in Parables* (Grand Rapids, MI: Academie, 1990).
6. Adolf Jülicher, *Die Gleichnisreden Jesu* (Tübingen: Mohr, 1886 followed by further editions in 1888 and 1889; second edition 1910).
7. An English-language survey of the history of parable interpretation is available in Warren S Kissinger, *The Parables of Jesus: A History of Interpretation and Bibliography* (London: Scarecrow, 1979).

rejected of allegory, but was not published until 1935.[8] Joachim Jeremias' influential book, *The Parables of Jesus* was not made available in English until 1954.[9] So it is safe to conclude that anything that Ellen White wrote about parables is written BJ (before Jülicher).

These days there is scarcely an undergraduate student let alone a commentator who has not been exposed to the work of Jülicher.[10] We are all working AJ (after Jülicher), and it is just not possible to unlearn what has been brought to our attention by the nearly one hundred years of serious scholarship on parables that has taken place since the publication of *Christ's Object Lessons*. Consequently, it is perhaps unfair to consider the hermeneutics visible in Ellen White's interpretation of parables alongside contemporary approaches. Instead, it would be better to compare her with another writer on parables who also wrote before Jülicher, and who better to represent that period than Richard Chenivix Trench?

Richard Chenivix Trench—Principles of Interpretation

Trench published *Notes on the Parables of our Lord*[11] in 1841. The popularity of Trench's book is shown by the number of copies that are available in most second hand bookstores. It has provided materials for countless sermons in the past and continues to do so.[12]

Trench began by outlining where a parable differs from a Aesopic Fable, from mythus, and from proverbs.[13] They differ from allegory 'in form rather than es-

---

8. CH Dodd, *The Parables of the Kingdom*, revised edition (London: Fontana, 1961; first published by James Nisbet in 1935). Of Jülicher, Dodd comments: 'It was the great merit of Adolph Jülicher . . . that he applied a thoroughgoing criticism to this method [allegorical interpretation], and showed, not that the allegorical interpretation is in this or that case overdone or fanciful, but that the parables in general do not admit of this method at all.' (*Ibid*, 14).
9. My copy is the third revised edition of Jeremias, *The Parables of Jesus* (London: SCM, 1972).
10. For example, the conservative writer Robert Stein devotes a significant amount of space to Jülicher. See Stein, *op cit*, 53–58.
11. New York, Revell, nd.
12. One of my 2002 students left me momentarily at a loss for words. I had asked him why, if he had read Jeremias, he had included in his paper one particular incorrect item of historical background. He said that he had indeed read Jeremias on the topic, but reminded me that I had stressed to the class that what Jeremias says must always be evaluated carefully, as conservatives such as Seventh-day Adventists would find much in Jeremias that they would not accept. He had also read Trench, who had said that he had done some research on the topic in question. So, of the two, Trench seemed the more reliable scholar to the student!
13. Re fables: 'The parable is constructed to set forth a truth spiritual and heavenly: this the fable, with all its value, is not. It is essentially of the earth, and never lifts itself above the earth. It never has a higher aim than to inculcate maxims of prudential morality, industry, caution, foresight and the like . . .' (Tench, *Notes, op cit*, 8); re mythus: 'inasmuch as in the mythus the truth, and that which is only the vehicle of the truth, are wholly blended together' (*Ibid*, 10).

sence' (13). He then devoted a chapter to the reason Jesus taught in parables. He used them to illustrate and prove truths

> Their power lies . . . in the harmony unconsciously felt by all men, and by which all deeper minds have delighted to trace, between the natural and spiritual worlds (16). . . . the earthly relation is indeed but a lower form of the heavenly, on which it rests, and of which it is the utterance (17). For such is the condition of man . . . Around him is a sensuous world, yet one which need not bring him into bondage to his senses, being so framed as, if he will use it aright, continually to lift him above himself—a visible world to make known the invisible things of God, a ladder leading him up to the contemplation of heavenly truth (19).
> Had our Lord spoken naked spiritual truth, how many of His words, partly from His hearers' lack of interest in them, partly from their lack of insight, would have passed away from their hearts and memories, and left no trace behind them (26).

Trench devotes his third Chapter to discussing the interpretation of parables:

First, most of the details of the parable can convey meaning:
'There is one question of more importance than any other . . . How much of them is to be taken as significant?' There are those who say that much of the parable has no meaning other than to round out the story. 'On the other hand, Augustine, though himself sometimes laying down the same canon, frequently extends the interpretation through all the branches and minutest fibres of the narrative; and Origen no less, despite the passage which I have just quoted' (32). He criticises Calvin and Storr, for leaving the 'parables bare trunks, stripped of all their foliage and branches (33). After he cites the example of Jesus' interpretation of Sower and Tares (33), he says, '. . . it must be confessed that no absolute rule can be laid down beforehand to guide the expositor how far he shall proceed. Much must be left to good sense, to spiritual tact, to that reverence for the word of God, which will show itself sometimes in refusing curiosities of interpretation, no less than at other times in demanding a distinct spiritual meaning for the words which are before it' (34). He quotes with approval:

> . . . similitude is perfect in proportion as it is on all sides rich in application; and hence, in treating the parables of Christ, the expositor must proceed on the presumption that there is import in every single point, and only desist from seeking it when either it does not result without forcing, or when we can clearly show that this or that

circumstance was merely added for the sake of giving intuitiveness to the narrative (34–35).

Second, it is often helpful to keep in mind the main point being made in the parable: 'It will much help us in this matter of determining what is essential and what not, if, before we attempt to explain the particular parts, we obtain a firm grasp of the central truth which the parable would set forth, and distinguish it in the mind as sharply and accurately as we can from all cognate truths which border upon it' (35).

Third, one should pay heed to the context, particularly how a parable is introduced and summed up (36).

Fourth '. . . *it is good evidence that we have discovered the right interpretation of a parable, if it leaves none of the main circumstances unexplained*' (37).

Fifth, '. . . *the parables may not be made first sources and seats of doctrine.* Doctrines otherwise and already established may be illustrated, or, indeed, further confirmed by them; but it is not allowable to constitute doctrine first by their aid' (37).

Richard Chenivix Trench—On the Parable of the Ten Virgins

Trench's exposition of the parable of the ten maidens in Matthew 25:1–13 serves as an illustration of his methodology and as a useful point of comparison with Ellen White, who has commented at length on this parable. Trench first outlines the marriage scene, which he describes as typical of Palestine. He then expounds the meaning of the parable, and true to his principles he seeks meaning in every possible detail. His interests show through in his exposition. He highlights points of personal application and of good doctrine, and does not neglect to draw out ethical implications. The meanings he attaches to each of the elements of the parable are as follows

> Virgins: 'the fact that they are virgins implies the "profession of a pure faith (195).
> Foolish Virgins: '. . . we may . . . contemplate the foolish virgins, unprovided with oil, as those going through a round of external duties, without life, without love, without any striving after inward conformity to the law of God, whose religious is all husk and no kernel . . . It is clear that whatever is merely outward in the Christian profession is the lamp—whatever is inward and spiritual is the oil reserved in the vessels' (196–97).

Oil: [see also comments above on foolish virgins]: '... before we have exhausted all the meaning of the oil, we must get beyond both the works and the faith to something higher than either, the informing Spirit of God, which prompts the works and quickens the faith, of which Spirit oil is ever in Scripture the standing symbol' (197).

Bridegroom delayed: 'We may number this among the many hints given by our Lord, that the time of his return might possibly be delayed very far beyond the expectation of his first disciples' (199).

Sleep: The fact that all slept does not mean that not all are unready, but rather is a reference to the sleep of death.

Trimming the lamps: 'In a higher sense, every one at the last prepares to give an account of his works, inquires into the foundations of his faith ... When the day of Christ comes, it will be impossible for any to remain longer ignorant of their true state...' (202).

Refusal of oil: 'The request, with the refusal which it meets, –like the discourse between Abraham and Dives, –can only be the outer garb of the truth; but of truth how momentous! –no other than this, that we shall look in vain from men for that grace which God only can supply...' (208). 'In the reason which the wise virgins give for declining to comply the with other's request, *'lest there be not enough for us and you'*, there lies a witness against the works of supererogation, however Roman Catholic expositors may resist the drawing of any such conclusion from the words (203–4).

The above is perhaps enough to illustrate Trench's general interpretative strategy with regard to this parable. Attention will now be given to Ellen White's parable interpretation.

Ellen Gould White—Principles of Interpretation

At the time of her death, Ellen G White owned several copies of Trench's book on the parables.[14] It is not unreasonable to suppose that she had read the book prior to writing her principal work on the parables, *Christ's Object Lessons*. However, the materials consulted for this essay, while clearly written in the same era, were equally clearly formed in-dependently.[15] Thus it makes sense that Ellen White's work be first

---

14. 'A Bibliography of Ellen G White's Privet and Office Libraries', compiled by Warren H Johns, Tim Poirier and Ron Graybill (available as a 'shelf document' from the Ellen G White Research Centre, Cooranbong, NSW 2265).

15. Fred Veltman's extensive list of works contemporaneous to Ellen White in his 'Full Report of the Life of Christ Research Project', (unpublished manuscript, available at the Ellen G White Research Centre, Cooranbong, NSW 2265), IV:W1–Z11, lists several works of Richard C Trench, but not his *Notes on the Parables of Our Lord*. None of the works of Trench are listed as major or

considered independently of Trench, before a final comparison is made between the two.

The book, *Christ's Object Lessons,* begins with a chapter entitled 'Teaching in Parables', in which Ellen White sets out the principles by which parables should be approached and understood.

First, parables link earthly things with spiritual truths. The first words of Ellen White's book are as follows: 'In Christ's parable teaching the same principle is seen as in His own mission in the world... Men could learn of the unknown through the known; heavenly things were revealed through the earthly' (17). This theme is developed over five pages, concluding with the words: 'The scenes upon which the eye daily rests were all connected with some spiritual truth, so that nature is clothed with the parables of the Master' (20).[16]

Second, through his parables, '*Jesus desired to awaken inquiry*' (20).

Third, '*Christ had truths to present which the people were unprepared to accept or even to understand*' (21).

Fourth, 'Jesus sought an avenue to every heart ... He ... *appealed to the different hearers*' (21).

Fifth, Jesus was surrounded by enemies, and by using parables *he avoided giving them occasion to act against him,* while at the same time rebuking them (22).

Comments later in the book reveal another principle. *Sixth,* one should be careful about the danger of over-enthusiastic allegory. For example, she says of the parable of the unforgiving servant: 'This parable presents details which are needed for the filling out of the picture but which have no counterpart in its spiritual significance' (244).

Seventh, parables may have more than one application. This will be demonstrated in the next section of the essay.

Ellen Gould White—On the Parable of the Ten Maidens

The writings of Ellen White have two extended treatments of the parable of the Ten Maidens (Matt 25:1–13), one in *Christ Object Lessons* and one in *The Great Controversy.*[17]

---

minor sources of the chapters from *Desire of Ages* that Veltman analyses (883–888). The chapters which Veltman chose to investigate involved no exposition of parables, and Trench's *Notes on the Parables* would have been a highly unlikely source. In her library Ellen White also had a copy of Trench's *Christ the Desire of All Nations, or the Unconscious Prophecies of Heathendom.*

16. 'So through the creation we are to become acquainted with the Creator', (Ellen G White, *Christ's Object Lessons* (Washington DC: Review and Herald, 1941), 24).

17. The other place one might fairly expect to find a lengthy treatment of the parable is in Ellen G White, *Desire of Ages* (Mountain View, CA: Pacific, 1970). The scriptural index at the back of my copy contains seven closely typed pages of scriptural citations (*Ibid*, 735–41). However, there are no references to any verse in Matthew 25:1–13.

The chapter in *Christ's Object Lessons*, 'To Meet the Bridegroom', begins by painting the picture of Jesus and his disciples overlooking a marriage party from the Mount of Olives. The basic outline of the parable of the five wise and five foolish maidens is told, then the basic approach that Ellen White takes to this parable is outlined in a few words:

> He told His disciples the story of the ten virgins, by their experience illustrating the experience of the church that will live just before His second coming.
> The two classes of watchers represent the two classes who profess to be waiting for their Lord. They are called virgins because they profess a pure faith. By the lamp is represented the word of God . . . The oil is a symbol of the Holy Spirit [pp 406–407]

The points made in the rest of the chapter are more fully developed than those made above. Some attention is given to the 'class represented by the foolish virgins' (411). They have a 'regard for truth, . . . they are attracted to those who believe the truth, but they have not yielded themselves to the Holy Spirit's working. They have not fallen upon the Rock, Christ Jesus, and permitted their old nature to be broken up' (411). When the cry goes forth, 'Behold the Bridegroom,' it is revealed that the foolish 'have not entered into fellowship with Christ' (413). The last eight pages are devoted to developing the implication of what is means to be a wise virgin who has enough oil to be a light giver: '. . . in the night of spiritual darkness God's glory is to shine forth through His church in lifting up the bowed down and comforting those that mourn' (417). In other words, the light which the Christian sheds in this time dominated by the darkness of evil is expressed in very practical terms. Indeed, 'Practical work will have far more effective than mere sermonising. We are to give food to the hungry, clothing to the naked, and shelter to the homeless' (417).

In sum, in *Christ Object Lessons*, Ellen White uses a mildly allegorical approach to the parable which she sets in the context of the church just before the second coming of Jesus. Each of the various items are explained, and great care is taken to highlight the spiritually edifying message of the parable.

The treatment in *Great Controversy* has some elements in common with that in *Christ's Object Lessons*, but also some significant differences. Chapter 22, 'Prophecies Fulfilled,' deals with the seventh-month movement, or developments within the Millerite movement between the time of Spring 1844 and Oct 22, 1844. Spring 1844 passed without the second coming of Jesus, and the Millerites were disappointed. Ellen White cites the theme of delay found in Hab 2:1–4; and Ezek 12:21–25, 27–28, then states, 'The parable of the ten virgins of Matthew 25 also illustrates the experience of the Adventist people' (392-393[18]). Matthew 24 points to the signs of the second coming. '*Then* [original italics] shall the kingdom of heaven be likened unto ten virgins.' Here is brought to view the church living in the last days' (393-94). The wise 'had reviewed the grace of God, the regenerating, enlightening power of the Holy Spirit, which renders His words a lamp to the feet and a light to the path... These had a personal experience, a faith in God and in His word, which could not be overthrown by disappointment and delay' (393-94). 'By the tarrying of the bridegroom is represented the passing of the time when the Lord was expected, the disappointment, and the seeming delay' (394-95). During this time, an element of fanaticism appeared among the Millerites, which Ellen White attributes to the work of Satan. Then, 'In the summer of 1844, midway between the time when it had been first thought that the 2300 days would end, and the autumn of the same year, to which it was afterward found that they extended, the message was proclaimed in the very words of Scripture: 'Behold, the bridegroom cometh!' (398-99). A page is devoted to pointing out that feasts which are associated with the first-coming of Jesus (such as Passover) were spring feasts, while those associated with the second coming (primarily the Day of Atonement) were autumn feasts. The tenth day of the seventh- month, the day of atonement, fell on Oct 22 in 1844. 'In the parable of Matthew 25 the time of waiting and slumber is followed by the coming of the bridegroom. This was in accordance with the arguments just presented, both from prophecy and from the types. They carried strong conviction of their truthfulness, and the 'midnight cry' was heralded by thousands of believers. Like a tidal wave the movement swept over the land... Fanaticism disappeared before this proclamation' (400-1). From this point, the chapter describes the spiritual wholesomeness of the movement and the terrible nature of the disappointment which followed when Jesus did not come on Oct 22, 1844.

It is clear that what is said about the parable of the ten maidens in *Great Controversy* is of quite a different character to the exposition found in *Christ's Object Lessons*. It is nearly a typological approach to the parable. The experience of the wise and foolish maidens 'illustrates' (392-93) the experience of the Adventist people. Here Ellen White, of course, is doing nothing more than using the language and interpretation of the 1844 Millerites. Yet she does so with apparent approval and without any comments that such use was inappropriate. Her two expositions are complimentary, rather than contradictory. What is said in *Great Controversy* about the experience of the wise maidens corresponds significantly with what is said in *Christ's Object Lessons*, and they both place the interpretation of the parable in the context

---

18 Page numbers to *Great Controversy* are given in terms of the standard pagination from the 1911 edition, and found printed at the bottom of my 1974 paperback edition. Pp. 392-393 corresponds to p. 347 in this paperback edition.

of the Church in the last days. At the very least, on the basis of these two expositions of the parable of the ten maidens, one must say that Ellen White is comfortable that a parable has several applications. In fact, she explicitly gives more than one application in her *Christ's Object Lessons* exposition of the Parable of the Rich Man and Lazarus: on pages 267–69 we have the 'Application to the Jewish Nation', while on pages 269–71, we have the application of the parable, 'In the Last Days'.

Conclusions

Archbishop Trench's work on the parables is indeed closer to that of Ellen G White than to a contemporary scholarly treatment of parables. In Trench's work there is little of the divide that exists in contemporary writing between the type of objectivity that is found in scholarly works and the warm personal application that is found in sermons. Trench considers himself at liberty to move freely from a discussion of a Greek term, interaction with Augustine, Tertullian, and the academic writers of his time, to the application of a parable to the personal spiritual life of his reader. Ellen White likewise moves freely from commenting on relevant historical backgrounds and detailed exposition of the text to personal and spiritual application. Both Trench and White are comfortable with what might be described as 'natural theology'. God, as creator, has revealed himself in nature, as well as in his Son and in Scripture.[19] The parables of Jesus are but an extension of this idea. In his parables Jesus reveals the spiritual truths already inherent in nature.

Both Trench and White are very comfortable with using allegory as a method of interpreting the parables, although there is a difference between them in this regard. Compared to Trench, White is relatively conservative in the amount of allegorisation. Not every element of the parable is pressed for a meaning—only those that are most important to the meaning.

The biggest contrast between the two authors lies in the relative importance given to the imminence of the eschaton. Trench does consider the near return of Christ an important teaching of the Church. As he discusses the hint of the delay of our Lord contained in the phrase 'while the bridegroom delayed', he says:

> It is not that He desires each succeeding generation to believe that in their day He will certainly return; for He cannot desire our faith and our practice to be founded on a misapprehension, but then the faith and practice of all but the last would be. But it is a necessary ele-

---

19. 'The universe is a source of theology. The Scriptures assert that God has revealed himself in nature ... The systematic exhibition of these facts, wether derived from observation, history or science, constitutes natural theology', in Augustus Strong, *Systematic Theology* (Old Tappan, NJ: Revell, 1907), 26.

ment of the doctrine concerning the second coming of Christ, that it should be possible at any time, that none should consider it improbable in theirs.[20]

For Ellen White, alongside of her consistent personal and spiritual applications, is clear in her consciousness that the message is urgent because of the soon expectation of the second coming of Jesus. Jesus is not just coming in some generation. Jesus is coming soon, *very* soon. This gives an urgency to her exposition: an urgency that, let it be said, represents the New Testament well.

---

20. Trench, *Notes, op cit*, 199.

Lifestyle And Hermeneutics:
A Hermeneutic for the Writings of Ellen White and Contemporary Adventist Lifestyle Issues

Barry D Oliver

Introduction

How do Adventists who live in the twenty-first century understand the observations of Ellen White with respect to lifestyle? Most of her instructions were written over one hundred years ago in a very specific cultural and historical context. What does Adventists' practical application of her instructions tell us about the way in which they are interpreting her writings? And why do some say that her writings are no longer relevant? These are fascinating questions that should be addressed candidly and openly by Seventh-day Adventists who are committed to fulfilling the gospel commission of Jesus and take seriously the mandate that they believe has been given to this Church.

The purpose of the essay is to derive from a discussion of some of Ellen White's counsel on lifestyle issues some guidelines with respect to the manner in which we interpret and apply the Bible and the writings of Ellen White. Because of the volatile nature of the topic, any conclusions reached or suggestions made in this essay are to be regarded as tentative. The intention is that this discussion should encourage ongoing dialogue and research by responsible, committed, Seventh-day Adventists.[1]

The conclusions will be sought using an inductive methodology. That is, the conclusions will be derived from the data presented rather than presented to support a preconceived hypothesis. Further, the research does not follow a strictly conventional historical method. Rather, the history of the Seventh-day Adventist Church is engaged only in terms of a dialogue with the present. This method of approach has been followed because:

1. No effort is made to discuss any particular lifestyle issue in depth. The purpose of this essay is to emphasise the necessity of an adequate meth-

---

1. The perspective is unashamedly Seventh-day Adventist. This unique perspective on theology and history is presuppositional to the discussion and is not to be compromised.

od of interpretation or hermeneutic. It is not intended to be a detailed apology for specific viewpoints on specific lifestyle issues;
2. The challenges exist in the present, the twenty-first century. These challenges need solutions that are applicable now. Historical reflection is intended to be a useful tool which may assist in the formulation of present solutions

Why is this essay important? First, it provides foundational principles that will assist Adventists to articulate a hermeneutic for the Bible and the writings of Ellen White. Second, it provides the foundation whereby proper hermeneutical principles can assist in understanding and applying the principles of authentic Adventist lifestyle.

The Context of this Discussion

The results of the Valuegenesis studies conducted in the early nineties in the North American and South Pacific Divisions of the Seventh-day Adventist Church have demonstrated it is becoming increasingly challenging to describe contemporary authentic Adventist lifestyle. While earlier last century it may have been possible to articulate Adventist lifestyle in a specific way, the perceptions of the young adults surveyed in the Valuegenesis studies did not reflect that traditional position of the church in a number of key aspects. The results demonstrated that if the church is to remain a viable relevant presence in their lives it needs to recognise it must take very seriously the task of describing the principles that undergird Adventist lifestyle.

In the studies conducted in each of these Divisions, the respondents made it clear that there was a sharp distinction in their minds between lifestyle issues which reflected core Adventist values and lifestyle issues that did not reflect essential values. Abstinence from alcohol, tobacco, illegal drugs, and premarital sex; and proper observance of the Sabbath were widely regarded as reflecting core values. On the other hand, items that were not considered so essential included not watching movies in movie theatres, not dancing, not watching adult-only movies, and not using caffeinated drinks.[2]

This practice of assigning a different place on a scale of values for different behaviours has posed a new challenge for Adventist theology and practice. Historically, the church has not followed the practice of arranging lifestyle behaviours on a priority scale, as these youth suggested. The church has tended to list lifestyle behaviours as a set of standards, all of which appeared, at least in the eyes of the

---

2. *Valuegenesis Study 1—Core Report: A Study of Faith Development and Value Formation in Seventh-day Adventist Adolescents and Youth Aged 12–18 Years* (Wahroonga, NSW: South Pacific Division of Seventh-day Adventists, 1993), 79.

youth, to have equal value. However, those studies pointed out the inadequacy of that position. They pointed to the need for a rethinking of the manner in which we determine which are and which are not essential and appropriate lifestyle behaviours.[3]

Additionally the studies pointed to a number of perceptions which impinge on lifestyle behaviours and which need addressing:

1. Adventist youth perceive a lack of warmth in the church;
2. Adventist youth perceive a lack of acceptance in the church;
3. Adventist youth perceive that church standards are overemphasised;
4. Adventist youth perceive that the church wants unquestioning loyalty;
5. Adventist youth perceive that the church is irrelevant to the needs of its youth; and
6. Adventist youth perceive that the church lacks a grace orientation.

These perceptions do not stand in isolation from each other. If the church is to maintain its commitment to its authentic lifestyle, it must do so in the context of addressing each of these concerns of the youth of the church.

Ellen White and Adventist Lifestyle

The counsel of Ellen G White has contributed strongly to the formation of the Adventist lifestyle. While it is impossible to consider the whole body of her discussion of Adventist lifestyle in one essay, several examples of her counsel will be given and the reader invited to consider how that counsel has been applied in his/her life. It is imperative that the church adopt a hermeneutic for the writings of Ellen White that enables it to practice a lifestyle that communicates viable and authentic Christian values both within the community of faith, and in the context of the missionary endeavor of the church.

Such a task involves considerable risk. Some readers may well protest that Seventh-day Adventists do not base their lifestyle or doctrines on the writings of Ellen White. On that basis alone they may wish to dismiss everything that is said in this essay as if any reference to her writings were an appeal to an antiquated irrelevancy. For those so inclined, may I suggest that you persevere and see the line of reasoning through to its conclusion, and then make your value judgment.

---

3. In the North American study, the perceptions of young Adventists were directly compared with those of young people from six other Protestant denominations. The denominations were: Southern Baptist, United Church of Christ, United Methodist, Presbyterian Church of the USA, Evangelical Lutheran, and Disciples of Christ. This material, based on the North American study unless stated otherwise, is summarised from Steven G. Daily, *Seventh-day Adventism for a New Generation* (Portland, OR: Better Living Publishers, 1992), 7–16.

Other readers will begin to work through the argument. However, they have an absolute and unwavering commitment to the veracity of the writings of Ellen White, so they will be tempted to dispute the way in which this essay deals with the material from her work. I also urge you to persevere and form your conclusions from the perspective of all that is being said, and not from any preconceived opinions.

The problem that we face as Adventists is to remain true to our heritage, including a correct understanding of the role of the gift of prophecy, and yet live and articulate an Adventist Christianity which is authentic and relevant in the modern world. We cannot retreat into the supposed safety of a nineteenth-century, mid-western cocoon and expect to fulfill the global mission that we believe has been specifically given to this church. Nor can we betray that authentic Adventist heritage and our Christian principles. We are talking here about the viability and vitality of the Seventh-day Adventist Church in the twenty-first century.

Notice some brief statements from the pen of Ellen White in which she gives specific counsel with respect to the suitability of some behaviors.

1. Tennis and cricket
'A view of things was presented before me in which the students were playing games of tennis and cricket. Then I was given instruction regarding the character of these amusements. They were presented to me as a species of idolatry, like the idols of the nations.'[4]

2. Wedding rings
'Some have a burden in regard to the wearing of a marriage ring, feeling that the wives of our minister should conform to this custom. All this is unnecessary . . . We need not wear the sign, for we are not untrue to our marriage vow . . . Not one penny should be spent for a circlet of gold to testify we are married. In countries where the custom is imperative, we have no burden to condemn . . . let them wear it if they can do so conscientiously.'[5]

---

4. Ellen G White, *Counsels to Parents, Teachers and Students* (Mountain View, CA: Pacific, 1913), 350. Of particular interest to readers in the South Pacific Division is the fact that these words were addressed to students and staff at the Avondale School for Christian Workers.
5. White, *Testimonies to Ministers and Gospel Workers* (Mountain View, CA: Pacific, 1923), 180–181. Note well the reference to the wearing of wedding rings by people of other cultures. Ellen White wrote this article in 1895 while she was in Australia. Clearly, her exposure to cultures other than her own helped her to become aware that **despite some very strong language**, her advice on specific aspects of Christian lifestyle and appropriate behaviours were not necessarily to be regarded as absolute.

3. Chess and checkers
'Such mental exercise as . . . chess, and checkers excites and wearies the brain and hinders recovery.'[6]

'There are amusements, such as . . . chess, checkers etc., which we cannot approve, because Heaven condemns them. These amusements open the door for great evil. They are not beneficial in their tendency, but have an exciting influence, producing in some minds a passion for those plays which lead to gambling and dissipation. All such plays should be condemned by Christians, and something perfectly harmless should be substituted in their place.'[7]

4. The circus
'There is no influence in our land more powerful to poison the imagination, to destroy religious impressions, and to blunt the relish for the tranquil pleasures and sober realities of life than theatrical amusements . . . The only safe course is to shun . . . the circus, and every other questionable place of amusement.'[8]

5. Croquet
'In the place of getting exercise by jumping and playing ball or croquet, let their exercise be to some purpose.'[9]

6. Women Voting
'I do not recommend that women should seek to become a voter or an office holder.'[10]

7. Bicycles
'The exhibitions in the bicycle craze are an offence to God. His wrath is kindled against those who do such things.'[11]

'I was shown things among our people that were not in accordance with their faith. There seemed to be a bicycle craze . . . "Look ye, and behold the idolatry of My people, to whom I have been speaking, rising up early, and presenting to them their dangers. I looked that they should bring forth fruit." There were some who were striving for the

---

6. White, *Testimonies For the Church* (Mountain View, CA: Pacific, 1948), 1:555.
7. Ibid, 514.
8. White, *Testimonies, op cit*, 4:653.
9. White, *Child Guidance* (Nashville, TN: Southern, 1954), 352.
10. White, *Christian Service* (Washington DC: Home Missionary Department of the General Conference of Seventh-day Adventists, 1947), 28.
11. White, *Testimonies, op cit*, 8:66.

mastery, each trying to excel the other in the swift running of their bicycles... These things are an offence to God.[12]

In each of these examples Ellen White has worded her condemnation of the specific behaviour very strongly indeed. Yet all the Seventh-day Adventists I know choose to disregard much of her specific counsel with regard to these issues.

Please look carefully at this list of lifestyle issues. Ellen White discussed each one of these issues on a number of occasions.

Dancing	*Reading Novels*
Drinking Alcohol	*Drinking Coffee*
Drinking Tea	*Taking Morphine*
Attending Opera	*Pornography*
Wearing Fancy Ribbons	*Wearing Collars*
Gambling	*Horse Racing*
Boxing	*Playing Cards*
Entering Lotteries	*Theatre Attendance*
Using Tobacco	*Wearing a Wedding Ring*
Playing Tennis	*Playing Cricket*
Homosexuality	*Riding Bicycles*
Using Cosmetics	*Playing Checkers*
Attending the Circus	*Playing Croquet*
Bowling	*Living in Big Cities*
Wearing Jewelry	*Joining Labor Unions*
Feminism	*Attending Fairs*
Unchaperoned Dating	*Watching/Playing Football*
Playing Chess	*Listening to Worldly Music*

Most of us would agree that there are some items on the list of which Seventh-day Adventists could not approve. On the other hand, there are some items that would generally receive their approval. Finally, there are some items that many would not be too sure about. They may not be able to determine whether we approve or disapprove of these particular behaviours.

But our difficulties do not end there. Anecdotal evidence suggests that no two Seventh-day Adventists would place all of these items in identical categories! For example, while some may disapprove of theatre attendance, others may approve. Others may approve of it in some circumstances but not in other circumstances. Still others may be making up their minds. The same could be said of a number of items on the list. We may all see them somewhat differently.

---

12. *Ibid*, 51, 52.

Why is that so? How can we say 'no', 'yes', or 'maybe?' And why is it that we each respond by saying 'no', 'yes', and 'maybe' at different points on the list? Why, for example, is there a tennis court at the back of the South Pacific Division offices? And why have I personally observed people employed by the church organisation actually playing tennis on the tennis court? Believe it or not, I have played cricket on the same cricket team as a past Division President. I have played checkers and chess (and Scrabble, Monopoly and Pictionary) in the homes of many good, loyal Seventh-day Adventists. Most Adventist ladies that I know regard it as their rightful prerogative to vote along with their male counterparts and many of them have accompanied their husbands and children to the circus, or seen the circus on TV. The vast majority of Seventh-day Adventists have ridden a bicycle at some time or other. While I was a lecturer at Avondale College I used to ride a bike to work just about every day and I observed a number of my colleagues doing likewise. In fact, I dare say that we felt most virtuous for doing so because we knew it was good for our health!

But Ellen White spoke strongly against **ALL** of these lifestyle behaviours.[13]

A Hermeneutic For Authentic Adventist Lifestyle

The nature of our dilemma must surely tell us that first, great care and mutual trust is needed when we discuss this topic. Second, it tells us that we need some healthy flexibility and respect for the mature viewpoint of each other. Third, the fact that we each regard some of these behaviours as acceptable today, means we must be using a method of interpretation that is modifying some very direct counsel that was given to the Church by Ellen White at the end of the nineteenth century.

It is apparent that each of us is consciously or unconsciously using some principles of interpretation when it comes to our acceptance of appropriate lifestyle guidelines in the writings of Ellen White. Our hermeneutic tells us that certain things she wrote approximately one hundred years ago no longer apply in the twenty-first century. On the other hand, it tells us that many things she wrote regarding lifestyle are still entirely applicable. Some may wish that it were possible to maintain a hermeneutic that insists her repeated, decisive counsel against any particular lifestyle behaviour closes all discussion of the issue for Seventh-day Adventists. However, it is apparent such is just not the case, particularly for younger members of the Church.

On the basis of this discussion we can suggest some fundamental principles of interpretation for the writings of Ellen White:

---

13 Reference to the *Index to the Writings of Ellen G. White* will quickly yield a number of statements under each of these headings. Some are quoted above in this essay.

The importance of literary context

To adequately understand the counsel given by Ellen White it is essential to consider the literary context of her particular statements. The original context of each statement must be considered, rather than each statement being accepted as if it had been written in a vacuum, or as it has been condensed in a compilation. When Ellen White wrote on a lifestyle issue, she was often addressing a specific need or question. Proper research will always consider the incoming correspondence to which she was replying, as well as her written response.

The importance of priorities

When the Seventh-day Adventist Church was emerging in the late nineteenth century, it was interested in some of the big issues that were being discussed in the society of which it was a part. The issues included the abolition of slavery, temperance and prohibition, a focus on preventative medicine and public health, the role of labor unions, the separation of church and state, and a commitment to a global perspective on mission. There is no doubt that these issues were much more a driving force in Adventism in late nineteenth century than were issues of individual lifestyle. Individual lifestyle was important, but careful investigation of the climate of Adventism in the 1890s and early twentieth century indicates that larger issues set the tone and framework of Adventism and gave it its priorities.

The counsels of Ellen White must be read in the light of this larger context and applied in the larger context of the twenty-first century. Today, a whole generation is saying that it is imperative that the church follows the lead of its own history and look carefully at those contemporary issues that are priorities. In order to be true to itself, its commission, and its Lord, the church of today cannot consume its time and energy focusing on relatively unimportant matters. Our global mission is at stake.

Please do not misunderstand what is being said here. We are not saying that 'anything goes.' We would certainly betray our God-given responsibility if we went down that road. But we will just as surely betray that responsibility if we do not carefully consider the manner in which we communicate our response to the saving grace of Jesus Christ in an authentic Christian lifestyle. In a disintegrating world God calls the church to be a prophetic voice. The prophets always made the big issues their priority.

The Importance of Understanding Cultural Shift

For the emerging Adventist Church, the meaning of lifestyle behaviours articulated by Ellen White was connected to a specific time and place.[14] Lifestyle behav-

---

14. Gary Land has shown that Adventist practice in the late nineteenth century was largely derived

iours send a certain message in their context. But as the context changes, so may the message. Two specific examples will serve to illustrate the point:

A. The wedding ring

This is a good example for the South Pacific Division because it has not been a matter of polarised discussion here. For North American Adventists, taking off the wedding ring came to symbolise the establishment of a meaningful separation between believers and non-believers who were perceived as rejecting the Lordship of Christ. It symbolised the rejection of a worldly lifestyle and the acceptance of a deep loyalty to Christ and his church.

However, in this day and age when loyalties such as a marriage are treated so casually by many, **a wedding ring is probably a most appropriate symbol of loyalty to Christ and his church.** For example, have you ever noticed how many married Protestant ministers wear a wedding ring? It would seem that a person who is continuously giving counsel for troubled marriages would be very wise indeed to send an unequivocal message that he/she is happily married. Changing contexts demand changing lifestyle priorities.

B. Health issues and Victorian attitudes toward sex

Another example relates to the way in which society regards human sexuality. Bull and Lockhart have well demonstrated that the Victorian predisposition for having a negative attitude towards human sexuality had considerable impact on Adventist thinking and lifestyle in that era. Notice, for example, a summary statement in their book:

> Sex was deemed particularly injurious to the human constitution. Excess, resulting either from masturbation, fornication, or marital lust, was likely to result in general debilitation and premature death. The sexual impulse, unless firmly repressed, was liable to undermine the entire Adventist program for human betterment. It was redundant in the divine realm. The angels did not marry and bear children, nor would the saints in heaven. Sexual activity was, from the perspective of eternity, dysfunctional; it devoted valuable time to a practice that would soon be disregarded; it precipitated emotional outbursts of the kind that angels shunned; it reduced the possibility of remaining alive until the Second Advent; and it caused physiolog-

---

from what was considered appropriate in the conservative Christian cultures of which the Adventists themselves had been part. See Gary Land, 'Adventists in Plain Dress', in *Spectrum* 20 (December 1989): 42–48.

> ical malfunction, which, as there was no disjunction between body and soul, could also result in spiritual debilitation.
>
> To avoid any excitement that might release the sexual impulse, Adventists were instructed to abjure the use of alcohol, tobacco, meat, tea, and coffee. Dancing and novel reading were also prone to stimulate unholy passions and fell under similar disapproval . . . The range of Adventist taboos prompted the creation of carefully monitored social environments. The benefits of the Adventist lifestyle could be maximised within a closed situation. In a sanitarium or college, individuals could be freed from the distractions of the world, denied access to harmful substances and practices, and encouraged to develop a perfectly balanced way of life.[15]

As an example of the way Ellen White herself was influenced by the prevailing societal attitudes note the following address to Christian mothers in the *Health Reformer* of October 1871:

> The artificial hair and pads covering the base of the brain, heat and excite the spinal nerves centering in the brain. The head should ever be kept cool. The heat caused by these induces the blood to the brain. The action of the blood upon the lower or animal organs of the brain, causes unnatural activity, tends to recklessness in morals, and the mind and the heart is in danger of being corrupted. As the animal organs are excited and strengthened, the morals are enfeebled. The moral and intellectual powers of the mind become servants to the animal . . . Many have lost their reason and become hopelessly insane, by following this deforming fashion.[16]

Christian principles cannot necessarily endorse contemporary societal attitudes to human sexuality, then or now. Nevertheless, it should be obvious to the reader that even if a relationship between insanity and sexual perversion exists, it would not be stated in the same way today.

---

15. Malcolm Bull and Keith Lockhart, *Seeking a Sanctuary: Seventh-day Adventism and the American Dream* (New York: Harper and Row, 1989), 169.
16. Ellen G White, 'Words to Christian Mothers on the Subject of Life, Health, and Happiness', in *Health Reformer*, October 1871, 121. For additional relevant discussion on the subject of changing priorities over time see Delmer I Davis's treatment of the theatre in Ellen White's day in his 'Hotbed of Immorality: Seventh-day Adventists and the Battle Creek Theatre in the 1880's', in *Adventist Heritage* 7 (Spring 1982): 20–23.

The Importance of Cultural Symbolism

Despite assertions to the contrary, it is not possible to interpret any counsel without reference to the characteristics of the culture in which it was given. The most obvious characteristic of any culture is its language. It is the most persuasive and powerful symbol system in every culture. If I cannot understand this symbol system, I cannot understand any counsel, Ellen White's or anyone else's. Apart from language there are hundreds of other symbol systems in each culture. These symbol systems are continually being modified. The meaning which is derived from those systems is also being modified. The meaning derived from a particular symbol at one specific time and place will not be the same as the meaning derived from the same symbolic form in a different cultural context.

Most of our Seventh-day Adventist lifestyle behaviours are symbolic. We attach certain specific meanings to them, meanings that indicate the values or principles at the core of our being. Some of them are such important indicators we regard them as non-negotiable. The Ten Commandments are an example of such a set of behaviours, so important that God himself prescribed them verbally. They are non-negotiable. There are other lifestyle behaviors that are clearly less essential. Some of those we have referred to above.

In our zeal and commitment to the Lord and his message, Seventh-day Adventists must be very careful not to 'absolutist' a set of lifestyle imperatives which gave specific identity to believers at a particular developmental stage of their movement. However, they now place us in a situation where we are incapable of moving on and interfacing with the world we are commissioned to reach with the gospel. Jesus had the highest set of ethical values ever lived on this earth, but His values did not prevent Him from reaching the people who needed him. A symbolic form or behaviour can never assume more importance than the principle on which it is based. Meaning is derived as several principles are arranged on a scale of priority, and the specific behaviours that arise from them are accepted or rejected according to this set of values. The Christian recognises that conversion occurs when there is a radical change in worldview. This change in worldview turn brings about change in the priority of specific values.

Foundational Principles Applied to Specific Contexts

In order to avoid narrow, ethnocentric behaviour prescriptions, a church that stands for stability and continuity and has a worldwide, diverse constituency must describe its lifestyle priorities as principles. Because Ellen White's counsel was contextual, it is vital that a hermeneutic for her writings emphasise the need to understand the enduring principles that she applied to her own specific context. An example of a statement that speaks in broad principles is the following:

> There are many who try to correct the life of others by attacking whatthey consider are wrong habits. They go to those whom they think are in error, and point out their defects. They say, 'You don't dress as you should'. They try to pick off the ornaments, or whatever seems offensive, but they do not try to fasten the mind to the truth. Those who seek to correct others should present the attractions of Jesus. They should talk of his love and compassion, present his example and sacrifice, reveal his Spirit and they need not touch the subject of dress at all. There is no need to make the dress question the main point of your religion. There is something richer to speak of. Talk of Christ, and when the heart is converted, everything that is out of harmony with the Word of God will drop off.[17]

Lifestyle priorities should not be derived from the manner in which Ellen White has applied the principles to her own context, but from the principles themselves. Adventists often seem to have uncritically adopted a specific application without first distilling the principle. If they had first distilled the principle they would be in a better position to critically contextualise those lifestyle principles that are Christian and uniquely Adventist.

Of course, specific applications articulated by Ellen White may still be appropriate in the twenty-first century. Many are directly applicable. What has changed is the manner in which many lifestyle imperatives should now be articulated and, in some cases, the meaning that is attached to them. Methodological and lifestyle issues must be set in context. The work of the prophet has always been to call for radical discipleship within a specific context.

Appropriate Dynamic Equivalence

It is not the intention of this essay to enter into a detailed exegesis of relevant biblical passages. That task remains for other writers.[18] However, in order to help us understand how to approach the writings of Ellen White it is helpful for us to consider how we approach Scripture. Just as we have unconsciously applied a particular hermeneutic to the writings of the biblical authors, we have unconsciously applied a particular hermeneutic to the writings of Ellen White.[19] As the context changes, so does the way in which we apply a given principle to the new

---

17. Ellen G White in *Signs of the Times*, July 1, 1889, quoted in Ellen G White, *Evangelism* (Washington, DC: Review and Herald, 1946), 272.
18. See, for example, Madelyn Jones-Haldeman, 'Adorning the Temple of God', in *Spectrum* 20 (December 1989): 49–55; Charles Scriven, 'I Didn't Recognise You With Your Ring On', in *Spectrum* 20 (December 1989): 56–59.
19. For a most enlightening discussion, see Alden Thompson, *Who's Afraid of the Old Testament God?* (Grand Rapids, MI: Zondervan, 1988).

context. In Bible translation this is known as dynamic equivalence. Bible translators use this principle in order to successfully make the word of God accessible in a new language or culture. However, great wisdom and care must be exercised. It is entirely possible to lose the meaning altogether. What remains may well be syncretistic at best and satanic at worst.

A biblical example of the way in which we apply an interpretative approach to Scripture is found in the epistles of Paul and Peter.[20] Notice the following:[21]

1 Corinthians 16:20:	All the brothers here send you greetings. *Greet one another with a holy kiss.*[22]
2 Corinthians 13:12:	*Greet one another with a holy kiss.* All the saints send their greetings.
Romans 16:16:	*Greet one another with a holy kiss.* All the churches of Christ send greetings.
1 Thessalonians 5:26:	*Greet all the brothers with a holy kiss.* I charge you before the Lord to have this letter read to all the brothers.
1 Peter 5:14:	*Greet one another with a kiss of love.* Peace to all of you who are in Christ.[23]

It will be immediately apparent that despite the imperative mood in which the writers speak, the same imperative to 'greet all the brothers with a holy kiss' is not generally regarded as binding on Seventh-day Adventists today. How can that be, especially when there are Seventh-day Adventists in many parts of the world who see the command to greet the brothers with a kiss in exactly the way it was written, as an imperative?

It should be apparent that we are using the same hermeneutical approach to these passages of Scripture as we used when we earlier considered some examples from the writings of Ellen White. This method of interpretation takes into account the context in which we apply the undergirding biblical principles. God's

---

20. The point being made will be easily understood by persons living in some Anglo-American cultures, where the handshake is the standard greeting form. It will not be so easily understood in some other cultures, which may use variations on the kiss as the standard form.
21. I am indebted to Dr Gottfried Oosterwal for making me aware of these passages and for clarifying the meaning we derive from them.
22. All biblical references are quoted from the New International Version unless stated otherwise.
23. Other examples of the same kind are found in: Exodus 3:5 (taking off shoes on holy ground); Genesis 38; Deuteronomy 25:5–10 (levirate marriage); 1 Corinthians 11:1–16 (women covering their heads at prayer); Genesis 29:15ff (compensating the bride's family when she marries); Acts 15:29 (prohibition against eating food offered to idols); Psalm 149:3 and 150:3–5, 1 Sam 18:6 and 2 Samuel 6:12–14 (praising God with loud clashing music and dance). One example which is still the subject of much discussion is found in 1 Corinthians 14:33–35 (women keeping silence in church).

people have always found it necessary to do that. Look at the considerably different way in which New Testament authors applied some eternal principles and compare that with the manner in which Old Testament authors did. God calls us to maturity and responsibility in the way we live in the context where He has placed us.

This call is not a call to 'lower the standards.' Rather, it is a call to a more principled, self-disciplined life, filled with the presence and power of the Holy Spirit. God has given us the power of choice so that we may choose the best good as a matter of principle, not as a matter of arbitrary compliance. We make such a choice when we show we are able to apply the principles of the Bible writers and Ellen White to a context considerably different to theirs. To fail to do so is to consign our Christianity to the realm of antiquated irrelevancy, and ultimately, to fail in the mission that God has given to this church. Remember that Christ accused the religious leaders of his day of doing exactly that.

The Overriding Emphasis on Mission

No one can read the writings of Ellen White without being confronted with her overriding emphasis on the mission of the church and on the mission of each person who comprises it. It follows that any hermeneutic for her writings can only do justice to her if it reflects this priority. It also follows that unless we are prepared to grapple with the issues raised in this essay, we will be confronted by an insurmountable dilemma: How can the Seventh-day Adventist Church maintain a high commitment to win the world for Christ, when theologically and methodologically its lifestyle priorities isolate it unnecessarily from the very world it is commissioned to win?

Despite Christ's instructions to the contrary, the church will be incapable of acting as salt and light in the world if it follows an unnecessarily isolationist lifestyle. The church will become a fortress, buttressed against the world.

But the fortress cannot be the predominant image of the church and its mission in the Seventh-day Adventist Church. As necessary as it may be as a place of safety from the world, the church has historically conceived of itself in terms of its global mission and ability to reach out to the world!

So much in the example and teaching of Christ and Paul has to do with the church incarnating itself in the world, in order to win the world for the kingdom. Notice the words of Christ:

John 17:15–18:
My prayer is not that you take them out of the world but that you protect them from the evil one . . . As you sent me into the world, I have sent them into the world.

Consider likewise the words of Paul:
1 Corinthians 9:22–23: To the weak I became weak, to win the weak. I have become all things to all men so that by any possible means I might save some. I do this for the sake of the gospel, that I may share in its blessings.

I wonder how Ellen White would address the evangelistic challenges of today. How would she react to the issue of lifestyle flexibility in the evangelistic situation? We want to live and communicate the ideal, but do we realise people living in a secular, urbanised, pluralistic world may never hear the ideal, let alone accept it, unless we can communicate it in a real, hearable way?[24] To what extent are we ourselves still being discipled as we live in a world that is far from God's ideal? Can we convince our Adventist subculture to be more aware of basic principles and more willing to live those principles? Should we even try to do that? Or are we satisfied to descend into certain redundancy and irrelevancy?

> I have a hunch that there are a lot of thoughtful young people who in their souls would like to be challenged to stick with or even join a church that really was different from the rest of the culture as long as they thought the differences or 'standards' dealt with were important. For starters, what about Jesus' list: justice, mercy, and faithfulness (Matt 23:23)? Maybe he knew that these are the 'standards' that stand out in our world because they are in such short supply. Maybe the Adventist church has asked too little of its members. Maybe the price tag for membership has been high enough to pinch but too low to make a real difference.[25]

Conclusion

We have addressed some difficult questions in this essay. We have not found all the answers. Because we have not found all the answers some Adventist readers will feel dissatisfied. They will say that the essay did not specifically say that it was okay to wear jewelry, to go to the picture theatre, to drink caffeinated drinks occasionally, to play cricket or tennis or chess or croquet, or even to ride a bicycle!

Other readers will feel dissatisfied for an altogether different reason. They will feel that they do not like what is happening to Adventist standards; that the stan-

---

24. It is very easy to blame the hearer if he/she does not hear, but the fault may equally be that of the speaker. It is just as much the responsibility of the speaker (sender of the communication) to frame the message in a hearable medium, as it is for the hearer (receptor of the message) to attempt to hear and understand it. In fact, contemporary communication theory insists successful communication is more the responsibility of the sender than the receiver. If the sender does not adequately facilitate the communication process, there is no possibility that the receiver will receive the right message. Yet too often, Adventists have been content to bemoan the fact that 'they are not listening'. Maybe it is not all 'their' fault.
25. Ernest Bursey, 'Why be an Adventist?', in *Spectrum* 20 (September 1988): 12–13.

dards of the church are being eroded; that there is no longer any clear statement of lifestyle behaviours; and that Adventism is in danger of losing its essence and its identity.

If any reader is in either of these groups please reconsider very carefully what this essay has been saying. It has been saying that:

1. With respect to lifestyle behaviours, we need to become aware of the way in which we are reading the Bible so that we can follow a consistent hermeneutic. Such a hermeneutic meets the authors where they were, enables us to retain absolute integrity to the message of Scripture, and facilitates contextualisation of that message today.
2. Within the framework of a proper understanding of the role of Ellen White in the Seventh-day Adventist Church, we need to approach her writings with a similar hermeneutical method as that with which we approach the Bible. A systematic hermeneutic will be a vital ingredient enabling us to be consistent in our interpretation and practice.
3. Our hermeneutic extends beyond what is written to what is lived. Not only is exegesis required to understand scripture and the writings of Ellen White. It is also required to understand the world in which we live and the people to whom we are called to deliver the gospel of Jesus Christ in the framework of the three angel's messages. This task is cultural exegesis. It has to do with presenting the gospel so that it is hearable.

Fidelity to these basic methods will yield two further outcomes:

1. Lifestyle behaviours will be expressed in terms of principles Examples of how a principle is to be applied may be given, but the church must be careful it does not reduce the freedom to choose discipleship to mere compliance to a series of prescribed behaviours. On the other hand, each person must recognise the validity of overt behaviours as symbols of allegiance, and recognise that adherence to a set of principles will involve symbolic demonstration of that allegiance.
2. If the church and its members adopt the three broad guidelines outlined above, continuous prayer, study, and adaptation will be necessary as the church grows through time and space. As time passes, the symbolic meaning of some behaviors will change. Some behaviors once shunned may become acceptable, and some once acceptable will need to be shunned. As the church expands around the world, the demands of diversity will mean that behaviours in one place will not necessarily be acceptable in another place, and vice versa. The great principles and valuesof Christianity must be transportable across more than one symbol

system or culture, and they must be able to travel through time. If those principles and values cannot do that, Christianity itself will not endure. While the great principles of the word of God stand above all cultures and challenge all cultures, we must remember that God has chosen to communicate those principles through the medium of culture.

All things considered, it may seem to some readers that it would be best to interpret Ellen White as if she were dogmatically presenting Adventist lifestyle as a set of prescriptive behaviours, expecting unquestioned compliance. This is an option some honest souls will take. But to journey back down this road would surely bring about the demise of the church in the coming generations. The gospel must be hearable. Our lifestyle must be livable. Its context must be recognised as a viable vehicle for the communication of the gospel in this world.

Ellen White's Use of Scripture

Jon Paulien

Introduction

Seventh-day Adventist interpreters share a deep appreciation of the writings of Ellen G White. Her comments on the Bible stimulate much productive insight into the treatment of various Bible passages in light of the ultimate 'big picture;' the cosmic perspective often known as the 'Great Controversy'. She also offers many creative insights into the details of various texts and helpful summaries of the backgrounds to biblical books and their narratives. Her devotional insights, generated in passing, are inspiring and often exhilarating.

Unfortunately, there is a darker side to all of this. Well-meaning interpreters have treated her off-handed comments about biblical texts as if they were careful and scholarly exegesis. Such misuse distorts both her intention for the comments and the meaning of the Bible passage. In my experience, there is particular reason for concern when it comes to her use of the book of Revelation—a scholarly focus of mine.

Ellen White was well aware that Revelation brings together language, ideas, and types from throughout Scripture, forming a consummate conclusion to the Bible as a whole.[1] She often quotes Revelation as a major source of her Great Controversy theme. Adventist scholarship, therefore, would be remiss to ignore her perspective on the symbols and theology of the Book of Revelation.

Having said this, it is important to recognise that the difficulty interpreters have in understanding an apocalyptic book like Revelation, make its interpretation particularly vulnerable to the abuse of Ellen White's scriptural comments. She herself recognised that her work had been used by some in ways that obscured the true meaning of the biblical text and made it serve the agenda of the

---

1. Ellen G White, *The Acts of the Apostles* (Mountain View, CA: Pacific, 1911), 585.

interpreter.² Off-hand comments in various contexts can be universalised or applied in ways that run counter to the implications of the biblical text itself.³

In raising these concerns I am in no sense questioning her inspiration or her value to the Seventh-day Adventist church. What I am arguing for is respect: respect for her conscious intention in the comments she makes. When Ellen White's comments about the Bible are used in ways she did not intend, her prophetic gift is not respected and much harm can result.

Inspiration is truly handled with respect when the intention of an inspired writer is permitted to emerge from the text in its original context (exegesis). We must avoid reading into the text our own interests and presuppositions (eisegesis). Messages from living prophets can easily be clarified upon request. But once the prophet has passed from the scene, we are on safest ground when the intent of each inspired text is allowed to emerge by means of careful exegesis. The interpreter's need to establish a particular position offers no license to do with the text whatever one wants.⁴

---

2. 'Those who are not walking in the light of the message, may gather up statements from my writings that happen to please them, and that agree with their human judgment, and, by separating these statements from their connection, and placing them beside human reasoning, make it appear that my writings uphold that which they condemn.' White, Letter 208, 1906
3. When she applied the phrase 'touch not, taste not, handle not' to the use of tea, coffee, alcohol, and tobacco she was certainly echoing the language of Colossians 2:21, but not in the manner in which Paul used it! For her, the phrase had a positive use in relation to a proper abstention from harmful substances; for Paul, the phrase in context, represented an unhealthy asceticism that diverted attention from Christ (Col 2:18–23). White, *Ministry of Healing* (Mountain View, CA: Pacific, 1942), 335. When she applied the phrase 'God made man upright' to the need for good posture she never intended to imply that the author of Ecclesiastes was discussing posture in Ecclesiastes 7:27–29. White, *Fundamentals of Christian Education* (Nashville, TN: Southern, 1923), 198. In *Patriarchs and Prophets* she used the phrase in harmony with the moral intention of the biblical author. White, *Patriarchs and Prophets* (Mountain View, CA: Pacific, 1958), 49. The fact that Ellen White called for Daniel and Revelation to be published together *without comment* indicates the importance she attached to careful textual study and comparison. Cf. White, *Testimonies to Ministers and Gospel Workers* (Boise, ID: Pacific, 1962), 117.
4. 'Many from among our own people are writing to me, asking with earnest determination the privilege of using my writings to give force to certain subjects which they wish to present to the people in such a way as to leave a deep impression upon them. It is true that there is a reason why some of these matters should be presented; but I would not venture to give my approval in using the testimonies in this way, or to sanction the placing of matter which is good in itself in the way which they propose.
The persons who make these propositions, for aught I know, may be able to conduct the enterprise of which they write in a wise manner; but nevertheless I dare not give the least license for using my writings in the manner which they propose. In taking account of such an enterprise, there are many things that must come into consideration; for in using the testimonies to bolster up some subject which may impress the mind of the author, the extracts may give a different impression than that which they would were they read in their original connection.'
Ellen G White, 'The Writing and Sending Out of the Testimonies for the Church', 26. Quoted in

The role of inspiration is particularly problematic with regard to Ellen White's use of Scripture. An interpreter with a strong preconceived idea can easily use Ellen White's scriptural comments in such a way as to overthrow the plain meaning of the text in its biblical context. Inferences drawn from the text of Revelation are at times creatively combined with inferences drawn from the Spirit of Prophecy to produce a result that cannot be plainly demonstrated by either a natural reading of the text of Revelation, or of the writings of Ellen White.[5]

Though usually well intentioned, such sidetracks divert the people of God from careful attention to the plain meaning of the text, and thus encourage careless methods of interpretation that can damage the cause of God. With the goal of safeguarding her inspired intention, some tentative guidelines for the use of Ellen White in the study of Revelation and other biblical texts follow.

Basic Principles

Allusion or echo?

First, it is important to determine whether Ellen White was intending to cite a particular biblical text or was merely 'echoing' it. If the text is quoted and a reference given, the matter is fairly clear. But often she uses biblical words or phrases in isolation and without apparent reference to their original context. In such cases it is not immediately clear if she was aware that she was using biblical language, or if that language was flowing naturally from her experience with the Bible.

The same procedure applied elsewhere in this book to the Revelator's use of the Old Testament would be helpful here as well. When she echoes a text, she is certainly not expressing a judgment on the biblical writer's intention for the use of that text. She may draw a valid spiritual lesson when she echoes Scripture, but it is not necessarily the same lesson the biblical writer sought to impress upon his readers.

Arthur L White, *Ellen G White, Messenger to the Remnant* (Washington DC: Review & Herald, 1969), 86.

5. An excellent example of such 'hybrid theology' can be found in the book *Give Glory to Him* by Robert Hauser (515 Pine Hill Rd, Angwin CA, by the author, 1983), 30–32. By comparing statements from the Bible and Ellen White, Hauser seeks to demonstrate that Revelation 4:1 – 5:6 takes place in the Holy Place of the Heavenly Sanctuary and that in Revelation 5:7 Jesus moves from the Holy Place into the Most Holy Place, with 5:8–14 taking place there. As brilliant as this suggestion is, it is rendered extremely unlikely by the simple fact that no such movement between apartments is detectible in the text of Revelation 4 – 5 itself, and Ellen White nowhere describes such a movement in terms of Revelation 5. Hauser's suggestion transcends the intention of both John and Ellen White. Thus, Ellen White's use of Scripture is misused in order to demonstrate something neither she nor John the Revelator intended.

Exegetical, theological or homiletical?

Second, where Ellen White clearly refers the reader to a Scriptural passage, one should ask how she is using the passage. Is she using it exegetically—making a statement about the original meaning of the passage in the author's context? Is she using it theologically—discussing the implication that passage has for a larger theology based on Scripture as a whole and focusing particularly on God's will for the recipients of her writings? Or, is she using it homiletically—enjoying the effectiveness of the biblical language that moves people to action in a worship setting?[6]

To interpret a homiletical usage as though it were an exegetical statement will distort, not only her intention in its use, but also the meaning of the biblical statement. While more study needs to be done on this question, it is my opinion that Ellen White rarely uses Scripture exegetically (that is, being primarily concerned with the biblical writer's intent).[7] As was the case with the classical prophets of the Old Testament, her main concern was to speak to her contemporary situation. This would generally cause her to use Scripture theologically and homiletically, rather than exegetically.

To say this is not to limit Ellen White's authority. Her intention in a given statement should be taken with the utmost seriousness. At the same time we must be careful not to limit the authority of the biblical writer. We should not deny a biblical writer's intention on the basis of a homiletical usage of his passage. What I am pleading for here is that we respect Ellen White's own intention in her use of biblical material. Since she often uses Scripture in other than exegetical ways, statements quoting Revelation must be examined with great care before being dogmatically applied in the exegesis of the book.[8]

Published or unpublished?

Third, Ellen White herself made a distinction between her published writings and other material.[9] We can best understand her theological intention in the writings

---

6. See the above illustration from her use of Colossians 2:21.
7. A high percentage of her exegetical statements are probably found in the book *Acts of the Apostles* which contains specific discussions of NT books in their original setting. Many exegetical statements are also found in Ellen G White, *Christ's Object Lessons* (Washington DC: Review and Herald, 1941) and White, *Thoughts from the Mount of Blessing* (Washington DC: Review and Herald, 1956). *Cf* the comments by Robert Olson in *Ministry*, December, 1990, 17.
8. When she appears to use a text exegetically, a tension remains between her use of the text and the apparent intent of the author's language. Two possibilities should be kept in mind: (1) It is possible that the interpreter has misunderstood the intent of either the biblical writer or Ellen White, or both; and (2) An inspired person can apply a biblical passage to his/her contemporary situation in a local sense without exhausting the ultimate intention of the original writer. (Note Peter's use of Joel 2:28–32 in Acts 2:16–21 and Jesus' use of Dan 7:13, 14 in Matt 9:6.
9. Ellen G White, *Testimonies for the Church* (Mountain View, CA: Pacific, 1948), 5:696. *Cf* White,

that were written and edited by her. Off-hand comments in letters or stenographically reproduced from sermons may not reflect her settled opinion on timeless issues. Compilations of her writings by others need to be used even more cautiously, since the ordering of material can, in itself, make a theological statement. If something is found only in letters and manuscripts, particularly if it occurs only once, the interpreter needs to demonstrate that it is a true reflection of her considered and consistent intent.

Central or peripheral?

Fourth, the question should be asked, is Ellen White's use of a given scriptural text critical to the conclusion she comes to in a given portion of her writings? If her use of a given Scripture is peripheral to her central theme, it may not partake of a thought-out exegesis. As is the case with Scripture, we are on safest ground when we refer to passages where the specific topic we are concerned with is being discussed.

When it comes to the book of Revelation, her statements will be most helpful when the reason for her writing was to give an interpretation for a whole passage of Scripture.[10] If you want to know her view on Revelation 13, go to the statements where she systematically works through Revelation 13. On the other hand, much of the book of Revelation is never made central to any of her discussions. We must exercise great caution in applying off-hand and peripheral statements to our own interpretation of Revelation.

Earlier or later?

Fifth, Ellen White's later writings should be allowed to clarify positions taken in earlier writings. As her skills as a writer developed, her ability to express, accurately and clearly, the thoughts she received from God correspondingly increased. And as earlier statements were opposed or became subject to controversy, she would offer clarifying statements to make her intention clear. A well-known example of this is found in EW 85–96 where she offers a series of clarifications of earlier statements and visionary descriptions.[11]

Selected Messages (Washington DC: Review and Herald), 1:66; White, *Testimonies to Ministers*, 33.

10. Revelation is central to her discussion in chapter 57 (pages 579–592) of *Acts of the Apostles* and in much of the latter part of the book Ellen G White, *The Great Controversy* (Mountain View, CA: Pacific, 1950).

11. A theological example of her maturing clarity of expression is her understanding of the deity of Christ. No one can mistake her clear belief in the full deity of Christ as expressed in later statements such as White, *Selected Messages* book 1, 296; White, *The Desire of Ages* (Nampa, ID: Pacific, 2006), 530; White, *Review and Herald*, 5 April 1906; and White, *Signs of the Times*, 3 May

How frequent?

Finally, how often did she utilise a scriptural passage in a particular way? Generally speaking, the number of times a specific concept is repeated is in direct proportion to the writer's burden that the concept be clearly understood by readers. It is not normally wise to base an interpretation on a single passage. An idea repeated in a variety of circumstances, and by a variety of expressions, is not easily misunderstood or misused.

Summary

The main reason for suggesting these basic guidelines for determining her intent is the problem of ambiguity in Ellen White's writings. Her statements are often susceptible to more than one interpretation.[12] This is not due to confusion or lack of clarity on her part necessarily, it is due to the fact that she rarely addresses the questions that concern us most today in a direct way. An unbiased reader finds many statements that answer our concerns with less clarity than we would prefer. The biased reader, on the other hand, when confronted with an ambiguous statement, picks the option out of several which best fits his/her preconceived ideas and hammers it home to those who might not see it that way.

The reality is that many exegetical questions cannot be clarified from Ellen White's writings. The wisest course is to avoid using ambiguous statements as definitive evidence to prove a point. It is always appropriate, of course, to point out the multiple possibilities inherent in such statements.

The Principles Illustrated

To illustrate the use of these six principles it may be helpful to examine the statement in EW 279–280:

1899. But pre-1888 statements such as White, *Spirit of Prophecy, op cit,* 1:17–18 are ambiguous enough to be read as Arian if the later statements are ignored (She updates and clarifies this in White, *Patriarchs and Prophets, op cit,* 37–38). To draw her view from this statement while ignoring the later clarifying statements is to hopelessly distort her intention.

12. An excellent example of an ambiguous statement can be found in White, *Ministry of Healing,* 445. She states there that, 'The sealing of the servants of God is the same that was shown to Ezekiel in vision. John also had been a witness of this most startling revelation.' She follows with a number of items that are common to both books. Since the visions of John and Ezekiel are analogous, but certainly not identical, two possibilities of interpretation emerge: (1) The events of around 600 BC partook of the same principles that will manifest themselves in the final crisis portrayed in Revelation 7; or (2) Ezekiel describes not the events of 600 BC but the end-time. While one or the other interpretation will be considered more likely based on the prior assumptions a reader brings to the text, either is possible based on the language she chose to use in context.

> An angel with a writer's inkhorn by his side returned from the earth and reported to Jesus that his work was done, and the saints were numbered and sealed. Then I saw Jesus, who had been ministering before the ark containing the ten commandments (sic), **throw down the censer**. He raised His hands, and with a loud voice said, 'It is done'. And all the angelic host laid off their crowns as Jesus made the solemn declaration, 'He that is unjust, let him be unjust still: and he which is filthy, let him be filthy still: and he that is righteous, let him be righteous still: and he that is holy, let him be holy still.'

The context of this passage is the close of probation. Ellen White utilises language reminiscent of Ezekiel 9,[13] Revelation 8:5,[14] Revelation 16:17,[15] and then quotes Revelation 22:11. Revelation 16:17 and 22:11, clearly belong in a 'close of probation' context. Taken at face value, one could easily get the impression that her choice of language found in Revelation 8:5 indicates that all seven of the trumpets in Revelation occur after the close of probation.

Does Ellen White in fact understand the act of throwing down the censer depicted in Revelation 8:5 to be a reference to the end-time close of probation? Does this mean that she considered the seven trumpets of Revelation to portray future events from her standpoint in time? (The six guidelines already mentioned can help answer these questions).

First, it is not clear that Ellen White intended the reader to perceive an allusion to Revelation 8:5 in this passage. The phrase 'throw down the censer' is certainly unmistakable. If there is an allusion to Scripture at all when she sees Jesus 'throw down the censer,' it is clearly an allusion to Revelation 8:5. But a number of indications suggest that she is *not* alluding to Revelation 8:5 in this statement. It is Jesus that ministers the incense, not an angel, as in Revelation 8:5. He ministers before the ark, not the altar of incense. He throws down the censer in front of the ark, not to the earth. So the statement in *Early Writings* merely echoes the language of Revelation 8:5 without referring the reader explicitly to that text. It is precarious to draw specific exegetical information from an echo of language

Second, there is clearly no attempt to exegete Revelation 8:5 in her statement. It is part of a visionary description of a future event, the close of probation. As such it is a theological or homiletical usage of Revelation 8:5. The meaning of Revelation 8:5 in its original context is not addressed.

Third, the statement occurs in a published work that was edited with considerable care. This means that whatever the statement is saying should be taken seriously as a reflection of her conscious intention. Exactly what that intention

---

13. 'An angel with a writer's inkhorn by his side ... reported' Ezekiel 9:2,3,11.
14. 'Threw down the censer.'
15. 'Loud voice ... It is done.'

was with regard to Revelation 8 is not clear on account of the first and second observations.

Fourth, as mentioned earlier, the exegesis of Revelation 8:5 is not central to the issue in EW 279–280. The issue at hand is a description of the close of probation, not the context of Revelation 8. The description of Jesus throwing down the censer could be left out without materially affecting the theological content of the statement.

Fifth, the statement is an early one, thus an interpreter wishing to understand her usage here should be prepared for the possibility that a later statement may decisively clarify this one. The possible implications of this statement should not be pressed in the face of a later one, particularly if the later statement significantly alters what is said in the earlier statement.

Finally, the language of throwing down the censer occurs just one time in all of her available writings. So even if its meaning in this single context appeared clear to all interpreters, it could be questioned whether Ellen White's intention in the allusion had been rightly understood. She has certainly not gone out of her way to clarify her understanding, if any, of the relation of Revelation 8:5 to the close of probation.

To summarise: as much as we would like to have exegetical help in determining the meaning of Revelation 8:5 and its context, EW 279–280 should not be used for that purpose. It is not exegetical or central to the topic in its context, neither is it reasonably certain that Ellen White intended the reader to perceive an allusion to Revelation 8:5 in the statement.

Of great interest to this issue, however, is the fact that this statement is repeated (nearly in its entirety) in GC 613. That statement is quoted below with the italics representing all words that are identical to EW 279–280.

> *An angel returning from the earth* announces *that his work is done*; the final test has been brought upon the world, and all who have proved themselves loyal to the divine precepts have received 'the *seal of the living God.'* *Then Jesus* ceases His intercession in the sanctuary above. *He lifts His hands and with a loud voice says, 'It is done;' and all the angelic host lay off their crowns as He makes the solemn announcement: 'He that is unjust, let him be unjust still: and he which is filthy, let him be filthy still: and he that is righteous, let him be righteous still: and he that is holy, let him be holy still.' Rev 22:11.*[16]

The basic point of this passage and two-thirds of the wording are identical to EW 279–280. Even where the wording is changed the basic meaning is the same. But two significant changes in Ellen White's use of Scripture have taken place. The

---

16. White, *Great Controversy, op cit*, 613.

language of Ezekiel 9 and Revelation 8:5 has been dropped. In place of Revelation 8:5 is the statement that Jesus 'ceases His intercession in the sanctuary above.'

The *Great Controversy* passage clarifies the meaning of the earlier passage. In *Early Writings* she used the language of Revelation 8:5 as a graphic description of the end of intercession. But she apparently did not want to leave the impression that Revelation 8:5 (or Ezekiel 9 for that matter) was a description of 'the' Close of Probation. Therefore, in GC 613, explicit terminology is used instead of an echo to Revelation 8:5.

This illustration indicates that to carry out these guidelines takes patience and time. Where she makes an abundance of statements on a text or a topic, that level of patience and time may be impossible for most interpreters. In most cases the flavor of her viewpoint can be obtained by a careful surface survey of her statements. It becomes essential to follow these guidelines carefully, however, whenever a particular statement or series of statements becomes controversial, usually due to ambiguity. In such a case the burden of proof is on the interpreter to demonstrate if, were Ellen White alive, she would support his/her use of that statement as proof of a point.

In the last two major sections of this essay we will turn our attention, by way of further illustration, to a number of statements related to Revelation 4–9, perhaps the most difficult chapters in the book of Revelation. The following offers examples of how to use the method introduced above to assess Ellen White's contribution to our study of the Bible in general and the book of Revelation in particular.

Ellen White and Revelation 4–6

The purpose of this part of the essay is to clarify, as far as possible, the views Ellen White held with respect to the visions recorded in Revelation 4–6. All the statements related to these chapters in the available Scripture indexes to the writings of Ellen White have been examined. Space will permit discussion of only a few considered to be particularly pertinent to the Adventist interpretation of this passage. I do not consider the observations below to be the final word; they are offered to stimulate discussion and encourage careful application of the method to controverted points.

The Broader Context

The closest thing to a major interpretive statement for the entire first half of the book of Revelation is found in the book *Great Controversy*, pages 414–415.[17]

---

17. This statement is also found in White, *Patriarchs and Prophets*, 356. Both statements are an expansion and clarification of the earlier and more ambiguous Idem, *The Story of Redemption* (Washington DC: Review and Herald, 1947), 377.

There, Ellen White offers a clear statement regarding the significance of the sanctuary material in Revelation 4, 8, and 11:

> The holy places of the sanctuary in heaven are represented by the two apartments in the sanctuary on earth. As in vision the apostle John was granted a view of the temple of God in heaven, he beheld there seven lamps of fire burning before the throne. Revelation 4:5. He saw an angel having a golden censer; and there was given unto him much incense, that he should offer it with the prayers of all saints upon the golden altar which was before the throne. Revelation 8:3. Here the prophet was permitted to behold the first apartment of the sanctuary in heaven; and he saw there the seven lamps of fire and the golden altar, represented by the golden candlestick and the golden altar of incense in the sanctuary on earth. Again, the temple of God was opened (Revelation 11:19), and he looked within the inner veil, upon the holy of holies. Here he beheld the ark of His testament, represented by the sacred chest constructed by Moses to contain the law of God.

There is no question Ellen White had three specific Bible passages in mind as she wrote. The statement also appears to be an attempt to explain the significance of the author's original vision regarding these matters. It is drawn from one of her major works and is central to the discussion of the sanctuary in its context.[18] The purpose of the chapter is not, however, to exegete the intention of the Revelator, so the passage may qualify more as a theological statement than an exegetical one.

In any case, it is her most comprehensive statement on the meaning of Rev 4–11 and it is of first importance for understanding her view of the meaning of this portion of the book. It seems evident from this statement that Ellen White understood the events of the seals and the trumpets to be taking place under the rubric of the first apartment of the heavenly sanctuary, while the second apartment ministry comes into view only in Revelation 11:19.

While this may seem a major conclusion to draw from just a few words, Ellen White clarified this statement in a *Review and Herald* article published on Nov 9, 1905. There she repeats the above statement with the following addition:

> The announcement, 'The temple of God was opened in heaven, and there was seen in his temple the ark of his testament', points to the opening of the most holy place of the heavenly sanctuary, at the end of the twenty-three hundred days,—in 1844,—as Christ entered there to perform the closing work of the atonement. Those who by

---

18. Chapter twenty-three of White, *Great Controversy*, 409–422, is entitled 'What is the Sanctuary?'

faith followed their great High Priest, as he entered upon his ministry in the most holy place, beheld the ark of the testament.

The title of her article was 'The Ark of the Covenant'. If Ellen White had considered it appropriate to indicate that the ark could be equated with the throne in Revelation 4–5, or with the activity in Revelation 8:3, 4, this would have been the ideal place to do so. Instead, she makes it clear that Revelation 11:19 (the sanctuary introduction to chapters twelve through fourteen—the section that features the three angel's messages) is the point at which the book of Revelation begins to concentrate on the end-time judgment. These Ellen White citations call into question the assertions some make that the writings of Ellen White can be used to support a Day of Atonement or end-time setting for the seals and trumpets as a whole. Such a position cannot be maintained in light of the fact that there are no clear and explicit statements from her pen to that effect, and the citations we have quoted do not support this hypothesis.

The End-Time Significance of Revelation 5

There is only one statement I am aware of that imputes unusual importance to any part of Revelation 4–6 and 8–9. That statement is found in *Testimonies to the Church*:

> Those who humble their hearts and confess their sins will be pardoned. Their transgressions will be forgiven. But the man who thinks that should he confess his sins he would show weakness, will not find pardon, will not see Christ as his Redeemer, but will go on and on in transgression, making blunder after blunder and adding sin to sin. What will such a one do in the day that the books are opened and every man is judged according to the things written in the books?
> The fifth chapter of Revelation needs to be closely studied. It is of great importance to those who shall act a part in the work of God for these last days. There are some who are deceived. They do not realise what is coming on the earth. Those who have permitted their minds to become beclouded in regard to what constitutes sin are fearfully deceived. Unless they make a decided change they will be found wanting when God pronounces judgment upon the children of men. They have transgressed the law and broken the everlasting covenant and they will receive according to their works.[19]

---

19. White, *Testimonies*, 9:266–267.

This statement is part of an address read to the General Conference session of 1909 entitled 'Distribution of Responsibility'[20]. The first half concerns the need to make wise choices where the leadership of the church is concerned.[21] The latter half is a series of warnings made up largely of quotations from Matthew 11:20–30, Revelation 6:12–17, Revelation 7:9–17, Luke 21:33–36, and Matthew 24:42–51.[22] The above statement precedes the quotation of Revelation 6:12–17.

The statement is more ambiguous than we would like. It is clear that Revelation 5 is intended to play a significant role for those who are to act a part in the closing up of earth's history, but it is not clear what that role is. Does Ellen White understand the chapter itself to be end-time? Is there an event portrayed there that is of particular importance to those who live at the end? Are there timeless theological truths present that will play their usual role also at the end? Is the passage inspirational because of its clear depiction of heavenly praise and worship? She does not say. A blank space is left, to be filled in by the reader.

One possibility lies in the mention of judgment both before and after the reference to chapter five. But this section of the address is neither an exegesis of Revelation 5, nor a theology of judgment.[23] The previous part of the statement associates judgment with the opening of the books, while in Revelation 5 a single book remains sealed until after the scene, so there is no explicit connection there. The later statement leads into the quotation of Revelation 6:12–17, where the Second Coming with its executive judgment is in view. Therefore, there is no explicit connection in her appeal to study Revelation 5 with these two references to judgment.

The soundest way to determine the reason for Ellen White's emphasis on the importance of Revelation 5 for those who live in the last days is to read all her statements regarding that chapter. I have learned from experience that it is unwise to say 'Ellen White says' until one has read every statement she made on a subject. When this procedure is followed, the reader is impressed by her repeated use of the chapter as an inspiring vision of heaven that can have a motivating effect on those who live on the earth, encouraging them to look above what their eyes can see and contemplate the glories of an eternal world, thus becoming inspired to want to be there themselves.

'Who can be trifling, who can engage in frivolous, common talk, while by faith he sees the Lamb that was slain pleading before the Father . . .' 'By faith let us look upon the rainbow round about the throne.'[24] 'Think of Jesus . . .'[25] 'In view of the

---

20. *Ibid*, 262–269.
21. *Ibid*, 262–264.
22. *Ibid*, 265–269.
23. *Ibid*.
24. See context in White, *Testimonies to Ministers, op cit*, 157.
25. See context in White, Letter 134, 1899 (quoted in Francis D Nichol editor, *SDA Bible Commen-*

revelation made to John on the Isle of Patmos . . . how can those who claim to see wondrous things out of the law of God, be found in the list of the impure, of the fornicators and adulterers . . .'[26]

After quoting portions of Revelation 5 she says:

> Will you catch the inspiration of the vision? Will you let your mind dwell upon the picture? Will you not be truly converted, and then go forth to labor in a spirit entirely different from the spirit in which you have labored in the past . . .[27]

and

> If we would permit our minds to dwell more upon Christ and the heavenly world, we should find a powerful stimulus and support in fighting the battles of the Lord. Pride and love of the world will lose their power as we contemplate the glories of that better land so soon to be our home. Beside the loveliness of Christ, all earthy attractions will seem of little worth.[28]

In these kinds of statements we find, perhaps, the best clue to the significance of Rev 5 in the last days. It is the clearest and most exciting depiction of heavenly worship in all of Scripture. Those who meditate upon this scene will find encouragement and motivation to remain faithful to the end, even as their spiritual forefathers in earlier times found encouragement and motivation in the same passage.

Did Ellen White associate the scene of Revelation 5 with any particular event in history? *Desire of Ages*, 833–835[29] ties the entire scene of Revelation 4 – 5 to the event of Christ's ascension and his subsequent enthronement in the heavenly sanctuary. There is no question that Ellen White has Revelation 4–5 in mind in this passage of DA, and that this scripture plays a central role in the segment. Her statement, found in one of her major books, is in harmony with the most natural understanding of the biblical text.

Although the events of Revelation 5 originally took place at a particular point in time, we should not insist that the three hymns of acclamation found in Revelation 5:9–14 were only sung once. No doubt they enter the repertoire of the ongoing worship services in the heavenly sanctuary. Thus, Ellen White can quote from this section in the context of what is happening in heaven now,[30] yet also quote

---

tary (Washington DC: Review & Herald), 7:933).
26. See context in White, *Testimonies to Ministers, op cit,* 433.
27. White, *Testimonies,* 8:44–45.
28. White, *Review and Herald,* 15 November 1887.
29. This statement is repeated more briefly in *Idem, Review and Herald,* July 29, 1890.
30. *SDA Bible Commentary,* edited by Nichol, *op cit,* 7:933; White, *Christ's Object Lessons, op cit,* 176;

verses 9–13 in the context of the experience of the redeemed as they enter the heavenly courts after the Second Coming.[31] This application is supported by the observation that the song of verse 13 presupposes the involvement of the entire creation; an event only fully realised after the destruction of sin and sinners at the close of the millennium.

Hauser, however, believes that a statement found in 7BC 967 suggests that Ellen White understood Christ's taking of the book to have occurred in 1844, not AD 31.[32] Let us examine this statement with some care.

> John writes, 'I beheld, and I heard the voice of many angels round about the throne'. Angels were united in the work of Him who had broken the seals and taken the book. Four mighty angels hold back the powers of this earth till the servants of God are sealed in their foreheads. The nations of the world are eager for conflict; but they are held in check by the angels. When this restraining power is removed, there will come a time of trouble and anguish.

The quotation in the initial sentence is clearly from Revelation 5:11. According to Hauser, Ellen White's statement sets Revelation 5:11 *after* the breaking of the seals. Since Revelation 5:11 contains an allusion to Daniel 7:9–10, Hauser argues that its location is in the Most Holy Place at the time of judgment. Thus, he argues that the taking of the book and the breaking of the seals take place in the Most Holy Place from 1844 on. When the Lamb 'came and took the book' in Revelation 5:7, he was moving from the Holy Place into the Most Holy.[33]

While Hauser's reasoning at this point seems strained, the statement he adduced is genuinely problematic and deserves investigation. It certainly associates Revelation 5:11 with the events of Revelation 7:1–3, which are end-time. However, her statement is a general description of the work of angels, and Ellen White repeatedly uses the language of Revelation 5:11 in general descriptions of the work of angels.[34] Therefore, if the primary function of the statement has to do with the

---

White, *Ministry of Healing, op cit*, 417. Note that in White, *Patriarchs and Prophets, op cit*, 36 she quotes Revelation 5:11 in a pre-creation context!

31. White, *Testimonies to Ministers, op cit*, 433; White, *Great Controversy, op cit*, 545, 647–648, 651–652, 671; *SDA Bible Commentary*, edited by White, *op cit*, 6:1083; White, *Testimonies, op cit*, 8:44. White, *Great Controversy, op cit*, 545 in particular appears exegetical with respect to Revelation 5:13.
32. Hauser, *Give Glory, op cit*, 31.
33. *Ibid*. Hauser has evidently overlooked the fact that the Lamb was already standing 'in the midst of the throne' (Rev 5:6) before he 'comes and takes the book'. To assume a change of apartments in Revelation 5:6–7 is to suggest that the 'throne' is a way of speaking for the entire sanctuary, something found in neither the Bible nor the writings of Ellen White.
34. Compare *SDA Bible Commentary*, edited by Nichol, 7:933; *Ibid*, 7:967–968; White, *Great Controversy, op cit*, 511–512; White, *Patriarchs and Prophets, op cit*, 36; White, *Counsels on Health*

work of angels in general, we should not overstate its significance for the exegesis of Revelation 5.

More problematic still is her second sentence: 'the work of Him who had broken the seals and taken the book.'[35] This reverses the order of the biblical text and seems to place the breaking of the seals in the past from her perspective.[36] The statement was taken from Letter 79, 1900, written on 10 May of that year. The letter is a rambling appeal to a William Kerr, calling for a fuller commitment to the gospel and to obedience to God's commandments. Ellen White's personal journal indicates she was extremely weak and weary from overwork and sleeplessness on that day. In fact she states that she had not slept significantly for three days, which would account for the rambling nature of the letter.[37] It nears its conclusion with a general description of the work of angels in helping God's people obey.[38] There is no reference to the investigative judgment.

The statement under examination is found nowhere else in Ellen White's writings. Nor, is it central to the point of the letter, which is quite homiletical in its thrust. Such an isolated statement in an unpublished letter should not be used to overturn the impact of careful exegesis and such major published statements as GC 414–415 and DA 833–835.[39] The fact that she was tired in the extreme that day may account for her confusion regarding the timing of the breaking of the seals and the order in which the breaking of the seals and the taking of the book took place.[40]

The sealed scroll of Revelation

Ellen White makes a handful of brief statements with regard to the sealed scroll of Revelation 5. TM 115 appears to suggest that the sealed scroll is the book of Daniel. After quoting Daniel 12:8–13 she says 'It was the Lion of the tribe of Judah who unsealed the book and gave to John the revelation of what should be in these last days'. After paraphrasing Daniel for some lines[41] she further states, 'The book

---

(Mountain View, CA: Pacific, 1951), 32, among others.
35. *SDA Bible Commentary*, op cit, 7: 967
36. The breaking of the seventh seal would appear to be at or after the Second Coming.
37. Although the letter is lengthy, there is little coherent flow of thought from one paragraph to another.
38. The section of the letter just previous to Nichol ed., *SDA Bible Commentary*, 7:967 is published in *ibid*, 7:922 (quoting Rev 1:6; 5:9,10; 12:11).
39. There is not a single statement in her writings that specifically interprets Hauser's key passage (Rev 5:7), so it should not be assumed that she saw a significant change there.
40. In the typewritten manuscript of the letter the original 'angels *are* united' was replaced with 'angels *were* united', as if she sensed a certain awkwardness in the statement.
41. See in context, White, *Testimonies to Ministers*, 115.

of Daniel is unsealed in the revelation to John, and carries us forward to the last scenes of this earth's history'.

Her statement in Christ's Object Lessons, 294, on the other hand, suggests she understood the scroll of Revelation 5 to contain much more than the book of Daniel:

> Thus the Jewish leaders made their choice. Their decision was registered in the book which John saw in the hand of Him that sat upon the throne, the bookwhich no man could open. In all its vindictiveness this decision will appear before them in the day when this book is unsealed by the Lion of the tribe of Judah.

The scroll contains both the history and the destiny of the world:

> The light we have received upon the third angel's message is the true light. Themark of the beast is exactly what it has been proclaimed to be. Not all in regardto this matter is yet understood, nor will it be understood until the unrolling of the scroll; but a most solemn work is to be accomplished in our world.[42]

Both statements suggest that Ellen White understood the full unrolling of the scroll as a matter for the future, not the past (such as 1844).

More recently, a letter has come to light, which contains a fairly clear statement on the identity of the scroll.[43] After quoting Revelation 5:1-3 she states:

> There in His open hand lay the book, the roll of the history of God's providences, the prophetic history of nations and the church. Herein was contained the divine utterances, His authority, His commandments, His laws, the whole symbolic counsel of the Eternal, and the history of all ruling powers in the nations. In symbolic language was contained in that roll the influence of every nation, tongue, and people from the beginning of earth's history to its close.

This roll was written within and without. John says: (Rev 5:4-5; 6:8-11; 8:1-4). This explicit statement about the scroll of Revelation 5 indicates that it contains the entire sum and substance of the Great Controversy as it pertains to the earth, including the acts of both God and His created beings throughout history. There are only two points in human history that sum up all things. One is in Christ at the cross,[44] the other is at the close of the millennium when all history is laid open

---

42. White, *Testimonies*, 6:17.
43. White, Letter 65, 1898. Manuscript release #667.
44. At the cross Christ embodied in Himself both the character of God and the sins of a fallen creation.

to view.⁴⁵ Since the judgment associated with the year 1844 is limited, in Ellen White's thinking, to those who have professed Christ,⁴⁶ this statement does not pinpoint the year 1844 as the time when the Lamb took the book.

The most likely reference point for this statement is Christ's enthronement in heaven in AD 31. Note that the scroll contains the 'roll of the history of God's providences',⁴⁷ an appropriate designation for the Old Testament, and 'the *prophetic* history of nations and the church', a statement most appropriate at the beginning of the Christian era, not near its close.

Combining all of the above, it appears that Ellen White understood the scroll of Revelation 5 to be the sum and substance of history, prophecy, and the entire plan and purpose of God. As such it contains that to which both Daniel and Revelation point and more. As such it is not fully opened to view until the end of history. It is truly the 'book of destiny'.

The breaking of the seals

There is a paucity of statements associated with the seals of Revelation 6. Most of Ellen White's scriptural allusions to the seals have to do with the souls under the altar in the fifth seal and the heavenly signs mentioned in the sixth seal. There is, however, one most interesting reference to the horsemen of Revelation 6:1–8.

> The same spirit is seen today that is represented in Rev 6:6–8. History is to be re-enacted. That which has been will be again. This spirit works to confuse and to perplex. Dissension will be seen in every nation, kindred, tongue and people, and those who have not had a spirit to follow the light that God has given through His living oracles, through His appointed agencies, will become confused. Their judgment will reveal weakness. Disorder and strife and confusion will be seen in the church.⁴⁸

This statement, in its context, is unquestionably a citation of the biblical text of the seals. The first two sentences imply that the third and fourth seals (Rev 6:6–8) refer to historical realities that are past, but the spirit of which continues in Ellen White's present and future. Her statement as a whole implies that the third and fourth seal represent spiritual confusion and perplexity in the church.

These seals have their primary historical fulfillment in the corrupted church of the Middle Ages, but the principle of confusion and apostasy is not limited to

---

45. White, *Great Controversy, op cit*, 666–671.
46. *Ibid*, 483.
47. White, Letter 65, 1898. Manuscript release #667.
48. White, Letter 65, 1898; Manuscript Release #667.

that period of history.⁴⁹ As exegesis has demonstrated the text of Revelation 6 – 7 points to an end-time consummation of the four horsemen in the four destroying winds of Revelation 7:1–3.⁵⁰

In *Testimonies for the Church*, Volume 6, 614 she alludes to the third seal:

> In view of the infinite price paid for man's redemption, how dare any professing the name of Christ treat with indifference one of His little ones? How carefully should brethren and sisters in the church guard every word and action lest they hurt the oil and the wine! How patiently, kindly, and affectionately should they deal with the purchase of the blood of Christ!

This echo of biblical language suggests that the oil and wine represent those who believe in Jesus. If so, the command of Revelation 6:6 not to hurt the oil and the wine symbolises God's protecting care for His 'little ones'.

Of the roughly half-dozen statements alluding to the souls under the altar in the fifth seal, one applies the cry of the martyrs to the persecutions of the Old Testament era!⁵¹ Two apply the cry of the martyrs in a general sense.⁵² The cry represents God's continuing awareness of the injustice in the world. Other statements clearly imply an end-time setting, although even here (with the possible exception of MS 39, 1906) the usage is primarily in a general sense rather than a specific exegetical interpretation.⁵³

This multiple focus and application is underscored by an exegesis of the passage.⁵⁴ The souls under the altar are the product of persecution throughout history leading up to the time of their cry. That cry is prior to the pre-advent judgment (*cf* Rev 6:10). The fact that the cry receives a partial response implies the judgment has begun within the seal subsequent to the time of the cry. The last part of the seal has entered into the time of judgment and anticipates the final persecution of earth's history. So, an end-time focus is not inappropriate within a broad historical perspective, but the seal as a whole covers a broader scope than just the end-time.

It is evident that Ellen White understands the fifth seal to be figurative. When she discusses the sixth seal, however, she sees it in literal terms. The earthquake of

---

49. See Jon Paulien, 'The Seven Seals', in *Symposium on Revelation: Book I*, Daniel and Revelation Committee Series 6, edited by FB Holbrook (Silver Spring, MD: Biblical Research Institute, 1992), 227–234.
50. *Ibid*, 233–234.
51. Ellen G White, *Review and Herald*, 17 July 1900.
52. 'The voices of those under the altar . . . are *still* saying . . . ' White, *Review and Herald*, 2 May 1893. *Cf* White, *Christ's Object Lessons, op cit*, 179–180.
53. *SDA Bible Commentary*, edited by Nichol, *op cit*, 6:1081 (White, *Review and Herald*, Dec 21, 1897); *SDA Bible Commentary, op cit*, 7:968 (Ellen G White, Manuscript 39, 1906); White, *Testimonies, op cit*, Volume 5, 451; *Idem*, *Review and Herald*, 15 June 1897.
54. Paulien, 'The Seven Seals', *op cit*, 234–236.

Revelation 6:12 is identified with the Lisbon earthquake of 1755. The signs in the sun, moon, and stars are tied to those predicted by Christ (Rev 6:12, 13; *cf* Matt 24:29; Luke 21:25). These are identified with the Dark Day, 19 May 1780, and the meteoric shower of November 13, 1833, both occurring in North America.[55] The dramatic events of Revelation 6:14, on the other hand, are associated with the return of Christ.[56] The despairing cry of the wicked asking to be hidden from the wrath of God and the Lamb is likewise understood to take place at Christ's Second Advent.[57]

Ellen White and the Trumpets

When it comes to the trumpets, unfortunately, Ellen White has very little to say. Only two statements are generally understood to offer meaningful comment on Revelation 8:7 through 9:21, they are found in Letter 109, 1890 and GC 334–335. One is often used to support an end-time scenario for the trumpets, the other to support Josiah Litch's historicist account. Each will be examined briefly in turn. Four other avenues will also be explored. Statements regarding Revelation 8:3–5 and 11:7 and 18 may shed some light on Revelation 8:7 – 9:21, and statements regarding the sealing of Revelation 7 are often understood to impact on the meaning of Revelation 9:4.

The trumpets and the end-time

Until recently Adventist interpreters have rejected any futurist understanding of the first six trumpets. In the last few years, however, some have suggested the seven trumpets have an end-time fulfillment, either in addition to, or in place of, the historical understandings of the past. This interpretation seeks support in Ellen White's statement in letter 109, 1890:

> Solemn events before us are yet to transpire. Trumpet after trumpet is to be sounded, vial after vial poured out one after another upon the inhabitants of the earth. Scenes of stupendous interest are right upon us.[58]

---

55. White, *Great Controversy,op cit*, 37, 304–308, 333–334.
56. White, *Signs of the Times, op cit*, 22 April 1913; White, *Story of Redemption,op cit*, 411; White, *Patriarchs and Prophets,op cit*, 340; White, *Review and Herald, op cit*, 22 September 1891; White, *Review and Herald, op cit*, 12 January 1886.
57. White, *Testimonies to Ministers, op cit*, 444; White, *Patriarchs and Prophets, op cit*, 340–341; White, *Story of Redemption, op cit*, 411; White, *Review and Herald*, 18 March 1880; White, *Review and Herald*, 12 January 1886; White, *Review and Herald*, 28 April 1891; White, *Review and Herald*, 18 June 1901 (*SDA Bible Commentary, op cit*, 6:1070); White, *Testimonies, op cit*, 2–41–42, etc.
58. Quoted in *SDA Bible Commentary, op cit*, 7:982.

The understanding of this statement, quoted in 7BC 982, is not aided by its context. The statement is very general and uses the term trumpet as part of a collection of statements concerning the terrors of the end. It is unlikely this statement offers any guide to the exegesis of the seven trumpets. The only connection to Revelation 8 – 11 is a single word 'trumpet'. There is no indication of an exegetical usage, and it is the lone reference in all of her writings. Since the comment is confined to a personal letter and is not intentionally included in her published works, she does not appear to be attaching any great significance to it.

Rather than attempting to advocate a future exegesis of the trumpets, therefore, Ellen White simply appears to be echoing the language of Revelation 8 – 11 to heighten her description of future calamity. There are too many uncertainties with regard to her intention here for the passage to offer any conclusive guidance to exegesis of the trumpets. If the trumpets are to be interpreted as future, it will have to be demonstrated by exegesis of Revelation, rather than required on the basis of this statement.

Ellen White and Litch's historicism

An entirely different approach seeks support from the statement in GC 334–335. In this statement Ellen White gives apparent support to the view proposed by Josiah Litch and published by Uriah Smith in *Daniel and the Revelation* that the fifth and sixth trumpets portray the activities of the Saracens and Turks over a 1,200 year period. While the SDA church holds the official view that doctrinal and exegetical positions should be based on the Bible, and not on the writings of Ellen White, most Seventh-day Adventists would be uncomfortable rejecting a view that she stated clearly and unequivocally. Her endorsement in a major published work would have an almost overwhelming effect on interpretation of the trumpets.

Many EG White scholars, however, including Arthur White and Robert Olson, do not consider her language to be an endorsement of the Islamic view.[59] She uses such neutral terms as 'according to his calculations', and 'the event exactly fulfilled the prediction'.[60] This leads one to suspect she was uncertain as to the true meaning of the passage and reported Litch's view because of its historical significance.[61] To compound the problem with the interpretation, Litch himself later repudiated that view because of, among other things, an error in calculating the supposed

---

59. I don't have a written reference for the above; however I am aware of it from multiple oral attestation.
60. *Great Controversy*, op cit, 334–335
61. She points out that as a result of the fulfilment of Litch's prediction multitudes were convinced of the correctness of the Millerite principles of prophetic interpretation, and many men of learning and position united with Miller.

time period of Revelation 9:15.[62] Since no one since has been able to salvage Litch's view in the form reported in GC 334-335, it is probably better to understand her account as a historical report and not a theological endorsement.[63]

The activity of Revelation 8:3–5

In the vision of Revelation 8:3-4 an angel stands before the golden altar ministering incense before God. In many statements Ellen White appears to equate the angel with Christ.[64] When she does so, she always speaks of the scene as a description of Christ's intercession.[65] At other times, however, she often describes the scene in terms of angels offering incense, but in those cases she never uses the term 'intercession', reserving it for Christ alone.[66] In her clearest allusions to Revelation 8:3-4, Ellen White relates this scene to the daily ministration in the first apartment of the heavenly sanctuary.[67] Early in her ministry, though, she alludes to portions of the imagery with reference to the second apartment.[68] In all allusions to Revelation 8:3-4, the ministration of incense is associated with Christ's work of intercession and not with the Investigative Judgment.[69] The incense represents the 'merits of Jesus'[70] or the 'blood of the atonement'.[71]

Earlier in this chapter we made an extensive analysis of her single echo of Revelation 8:5. She appears to understand the throwing down of the censer in terms of an end to intercession, but it is not clear if she understood that event as 'the' final close of probation.

---

62. He overlooked the effect of the calendar change in 1582 when he predicted that the supposed time period of Revelation 9:15 would wind up on 11 August 1840.
63. Assuming Litch was in error, it is not unlike God to preserve a threatened movement by providing the 'fulfilment' it so desperately looked for.
64. Ellen G White, *Early Writings* (Washington DC: Review & Herald, 1945), 32 (White, *Life Sketches of Ellen G White* [Mountain View, CA: Pacific, 1943], 252); White, Manuscript 142, 1899 (White, *Christ's Object Lessons, op cit,*156; *SDA Bible Commentary, op cit,* 7:931); Ellen G. White Manuscript 21, 1900 (White, *Sons and Daughters of God* [Washington DC: Review & Herald, 1955], 22); White, Manuscript 14, 1901 (*SDA Bible Commentary, op cit,* 6:1078).
65. Ellen G White, Manuscript 14, 1901 (*SDA Bible Commentary, op cit,* 6:1078); Ellen G White, Manuscript 142, 1899 (Nichol ed., *SDA Bible Commentary,* 7:931; White, *Christ's Object Lessons,* 156); White, *Sons and Daughters, op cit,* 22.
66. White, Manuscript 15, 1897 (*SDA Bible Commentary, op cit,* 7:971); Ellen G White, *Review and Herald,* 4 July 1893; White, *My Life Today* (Washington DC: Review & Herald), 29.
67. White, *Great Controversy, op cit,* 414–415; White, *Review and Herald,* 9 November 1905; White, *Patriarchs and Prophets, op cit,* 353.
68. White, *Early Writings, op cit,* 32 (White, *Life Sketches, op cit,* 100, 252, 256].
69. White, Manuscript 142, 1899 (White, *Christ's Object Lessons, op cit,* 156; *SDA Bible Commentary, op cit,* 7:931); Ellen G White, Manuscript 14, 1901 (*SDA Bible Commentary, op cit,* 6:1078).
70. White, *Review and Herald,* 4 July 1893.
71. White, Manuscript, 15, 1897 (*SDA Bible Commentary, op cit,* 7:971).

Her use of the language of Revelation 8:3–5 is remarkably compatible with the exegesis of the passage. The basic concept is the intercession of Christ. In some sense this is brought to an end by the act of throwing down the censer. Her writings make it unclear whether that act occurs before the blowing of the trumpets chronologically, repeatedly during the trumpets, or at a specific point toward the end. In other words, she respects the ambiguity of the text and does not go beyond what is reasonably evident there.

The sealing work and Revelation 9:4

A major issue in the Adventist interpretation of the trumpets is the significance of the sealing in Revelation 9:4. Is it the end-time sealing of Revelation 7? Or is it the ongoing sealing process of the New Testament? Does Ellen White have only one view of sealing in Revelation, or does she use the concept in the variety of ways in which New Testament writers used it? One thing is perfectly clear, she never discusses Revelation 9:4, not even in GC 334–335, the only place where she mentions the fifth trumpet at all. Consequently, her view of the matter is not explicit; it can only be inferred, if at all, from her view of the sealing in Revelaton 7.

It may be helpful to briefly review the variety of meanings that pertain to the New Testament concept of sealing.[72] When a seal is placed on a document, message, or tomb, its purpose is to conceal or to confine.[73] An alternative meaning is to certify that something or someone is reliable.[74] But the predominant meaning of sealing in connection with God's people is as an indication one has been accepted by God.[75] In this sense, it was a present reality already in the time of Abraham (Rom 4:11).

Ellen White has little to say about the New Testament passages that connect sealing to acceptance with God. Her primary interest is limited to the significance of Revelation 7, which clearly focuses on the end-time. In spite of this, however, she does not limit sealing to a purely end-time setting. She repeatedly refers to her time as the time when the four angels are holding the four winds,[76] and to the sealing time as a present reality.[77] Therefore, while she normally refers to the sealing

---

72. Jon Paulien, 'Seals and Trumpets: Some Current Discussions', in *Symposium on Revelation: Book I*, Daniel and Revelation Committee Series 6, edited by FB Holbrook (Silver Spring, MD: Biblical Research Institute, 1992), 197.
73. Matthew 27:66; Revelation 5:1,2,5,9; 6:1,3,5,7,9,12; 8:1; 10:4; 20:3; 22:10.
74. John 3:33; 6:27; Romans 15:28; 1 Corinthians 9:2.
75. 'God knows them that are His', 2 Timothy 2:19, *cf* 2 Corinthians 1:22; Ephesians 1:13; 4:30.
76. White, *Testimonies, op cit*, 5:717–718, 6:26, 61,426, and some 18 statements in the *Review and Herald* from 1885–1912.
77. White, *Early Writings, op cit*, 43–44; White, Letter 270, 1907, (*SDA Bible Commentary, op cit*, 7:969); Ellen G White, *Review and Herald*, 13 July 13 1897; White, *Selected Messages, op cit*, 166; White, *Testimonies, op cit*, 5:50.

as a future, end-time event[78] (in harmony with the exegesis of Rev 7) she does not limit the process to the very end of time.

In terms of the meaning of sealing, she once again is primarily interested in the meaning most appropriate to the situation of Revelation 7. The concept of the seal of God has special significance in the antitypical Day of Atonement.

> Only those who, in their attitude before God, are filling the position of those who are repenting and confessing their sins in the great antitypical day of atonement, will be recognised and marked as worthy of God's protection. The names of those who are steadfastly looking and waiting and watching for the appearing of their Saviour—more earnestly and wishfully than they who wait for the morning—will be numbered with those who are sealed.[79]

This end-time seal provides protection in the time of trouble.[80] It is placed upon those who prove loyal to the commandments of God[81] to the point of 'perfection of character',[82] 'the likeness of Christ's character',[83] and genuine, conscientious Sabbath-keeping (including rejection of Sunday-worship).[84] Such definitions, of course, are not appropriate to the more general New Testament understanding of sealing exhibited in passages such Ephesians 1:13; 4:30 and 2 Timothy 2:19. Was she unaware of the more general meanings common to the New Testament? Would she have considered it inappropriate to apply them to Revelation 9:4, for instance, a passage that she never quoted or discussed?

The reality is, in spite of her overwhelming interest in the end-time concept of the sealing, in places she is quite capable of using the concept of sealing in ways more reminiscent of Paul than of Revelation 7. In CT 459 the seal is a mark of God's approval of the message that Adventists were preaching:

---

78. See White, *Review and Herald*, 23 September 1873 and 28 May 1889 as examples.
79. White, *Testimonies to Ministers, op cit*, 445.
80. White, *Early Writings, op cit*, 67, 71.
81. White, *Great Controversy, op cit*, 613; White, Letter 76, 1900 (*SDA Bible Commentary, op cit*, 7:970); White, *Testimonies, op cit*, 2:468.
82. White, *Review and Herald*, 10 June 1902 (*SDA Bible Commentary, op cit*, 6:1118); White, *Testimonies, op cit*, 5:214, 216.
83. White, *Early Writings, op cit*, 71; Idem, *Review and Herald*, 21 May 1895 (*SDA Bible Commentary, op cit*, 7:970).
84. White, *Great Controversy,op cit*, 605; White, Letter 76, 1900 (*SDA Bible Commentary,op cit*, 7:970); Ellen G White, Manuscript 27, 1899 (*SDA Bible Commentary, op cit*, 7:970); Ellen G White, *Review and Herald*, 13 July 1897; White, *Review and Herald*, 23 April 1901; White, *Testimonies, op cit*, 5:213, cf (*SDA Bible Commentary, op cit*, 7:980); Ellen G White, *Historical Sketches of SDA Missions, op cit*, 213; White, *Great Controversy, op cit*, 640; White, *Patriarchs and Prophets, op cit*, 307.

> Who among our teachers are awake, and as faithful stewards of the grace of God are giving the trumpet a certain sound? Who are voicing the message of the third angel, calling upon the world to make ready for the great day of God? The message we bear has the seal of the living God.[85]

It appears that those who possess 'the sign of the cross of Calvary' and are wearing the wedding garment receive the seal of God.[86] The seal is a 'passport to the Holy City', which all must have in order to enter.[87] One is not saved without the seal.[88] It is placed on all who love God in the practice of everyday life.[89] The seal is placed on those who make their 'calling and election sure' (cf 2 Pet 1:10).[90]

This brief survey indicates that with regard to the sealing, as in so many areas, Ellen White demonstrates a sensitive awareness of the full richness of the biblical language she so readily adopts. Her grasp of the Scriptural intent seems far greater than that of most who quote her writings in relation to exegetical issues.

Wisdom would indicate that it is unwise to assume exactly how she would have exegeted Revelation 9:4 had she availed herself of the opportunity. Her lack of comment on Revelation 9:4 may rather indicate that it does *not* concern her primary interest in the concept of sealing—the end-time sealing so clearly portrayed in Revelation 7 and so oft quoted by her. To understand the seal of Revelation 9:4 in terms of the general New Testament usage is not contrary to her overall theology.

The beast from the abyss

In GC 265–288 Ellen White identifies the power which opposed the two witnesses as revolutionary France. She also believed that the ideological forces which shaped the revolution would have a powerful impact again at the end of time: the world-wide dissemination of the same teachings that led to the French Revolution—all are tending to involve the whole world in a struggle similar to that which convulsed France.[91]

Since the power who opposed the two witnesses in Revelation is identified as the 'beast which comes up out of the abyss' (Rev 11:7), it is intriguing to suspect that the fifth trumpet, which is concerned with the opening of the abyss and the tormenting powers thereby unleashed, may shed some light on the end-time

---

85. Compare with John 3:33; 6:27; Romans 15:28; 1 Corinthians 9:2.
86. Ellen G White, Letter 126, 1898, (*SDA Bible Commentary, op cit,* 7:968).
87. White, *Testimonies to Ministers, op cit,* 444–445.
88. White, Letter 80, 1898, (*SDA Bible Commentary, op cit,* 7:969).
89. Ellen G White, *Review and Herald,* 23 October 1888.
90. White, *Early Writings, op cit,* 58.
91. White, *Education, op cit,* 228.

manifestation of teachings that convulsed France some 200 years ago. While this pair of statements provided the intellectual stimulus for the historical application of the fifth trumpet I currently favor, I must admit that the connections are far too tenuous to argue that Ellen White held any such view.

The time of the seventh trumpet

At first glance, Ellen White's perspective on the seventh trumpet is problematic. In EW 36 she alludes to Revelation 11:18 as follows:

> I saw that the anger of the nations, the wrath of God, and the time to judge the dead were separate and distinct, one following the other, also that Michael had not stood up, and that the time of trouble, such as never was, had not yet commenced. The nations are now getting angry, but when our High Priest has finished His work in the sanctuary, He will stand up, put on the garments of vengeance, and then the seven last plagues will be poured out.

In this passage she 'saw' that the anger of the nations is a developing process climaxing at the close of probation. This is followed by the seven last plagues (wrath of God) and the judgment of the dead. This statement appears to reject equating the 'judgment of the dead' with the investigative judgment that begins in 1844. It is in harmony with her usual practice of placing the seventh trumpet in the future, from her perspective.[92] While the nations 'are getting angry' their angels are restrained by the four angels who hold the four winds in Revelation 7:1–3.[93]

Some fifty years later, however, she seems to suggest that the 'nations *are* angry, and the time of the dead *has come*, that they should be judged' (6T 14). Since the onset of the Investigative Judgment precedes both statements, they appear to be in tension with each other. The problem can be resolved, however, by a number of considerations. (1) The language of the first statement is more directly exegetical (she is unfolding the meaning of the text), while the latter is more an echo of the language of Revelation 11:18. (2) The former statement clearly harmonises with the close of probation language of Rev 10:7) The context of *6T 14* expresses her expectation of an imminent conclusion of history. She uses such statements as, 'We are standing upon the threshold of great and solemn events . . . Only a moment of time, as it were, yet remains.' Thus, an exegetical statement such as EW 36, describing events that are future in fulfillment, will naturally appear to be in tension with a statement of imminent expectation, such as in *6T 14*, where those events are described as 'at hand'.

---

92. *Cf* White, *Early Writings*, 85–86, 279–280.
93. *Ibid*, 85–86, Ellen G White, *Review and Herald*, 28 January 1909; White, *Review and Herald*, 17 November 1910; White, *Selected Messages,op cit*, 1–221–222; White, *Testimonies, op cit*, 6:14.

Conclusion regarding trumpets

The former statement clearly harmonises with the close of probation language of Rev 10:7). The context of *6T* 14 expresses her expectation of an imminent conclusion of history. She uses such statements as, 'We are standing upon the threshold of great and solemn events . . . Only a moment of time, as it were, yet remains.' Thus, an exegetical statement such as *EW* 36, describing events which are future in fulfillment, will naturally appear to be in tension with a statement of imminent expectation, where those events are described as 'at hand'.

The examination of these few avenues toward a clearer understanding of Ellen White's view of the trumpets well demonstrates the problem of ambiguity mentioned above. From our perspective it would have been extremely helpful had she clarified the issues regarding the timing and meaning of the trumpets that are of such interest today. But the Lord did not see fit to provide such information through her writings. If she had a view on those matters she has left no clear, unambiguous evidence of it. As has always been the case, revelation comes to a prophet within his/her time, place, circumstances, interests, and concerns.[94] When the questions of a later period are addressed to an inspired text, the text is often silent or ambiguous regarding those matters. At such times the soundest approach is to avoid the use of ambiguous texts as 'missiles' to confuse or confound the 'enemy' (those holding a different view). With regard to the meaning of the seven trumpets of Revelation, most relevant statements are less than crystal-clear. The meaning of the trumpets must be established on the basis of careful exegesis of the biblical text. Somehow I get the feeling Ellen White would have wanted it that way.

Conclusion

After a thorough study of the text of Revelation, it is helpful for an interpreter to examine Ellen White's use of Revelation for profitable insights. Her unparalleled grasp of the universal issues to which the book of Revelation points makes her statements about the book of enormous interest to Adventists. Nevertheless, her contribution to the discussion must not be expanded beyond her own intention. To do so would be to distort both her intention and John's, thus undermining the authority of inspiration. The above guidelines can help provide safeguards against such unintentional misuse.

---

94. Jon Paulien, 'Interpreting Revelation's Symbolism', in *Symposium on Revelation: Book I*, Daniel and Revelation Committee Series 6, edited by FB Holbrook (Silver Spring, MD: Biblical Research Institute, 1992), 74–76.

The Influence of Ellen White Towards an Adventist Understanding of Inspiration

Graeme S Bradford

Ellen White Under Attack

Ellen White's credentials as a prophet within the Adventist Church are under attack. Any search engine on the internet will find scores of anti-Ellen White sites. The trouble with this material is that a significant amount of it is true. Basically Adventists have three choices:

1. They can resist and ignore the material and go on with business as usual. This option would cost them many honest members who will feel the Church has betrayed them.
2. They can carry on with an attitude that 'we don't care'. This option would produce social Adventists with no sense of mission.
3. They can go back to the Bible and see if they have understood the gift correctly. Maybe Adventists and their critics alike have failed to dig deeply enough into the Word of God.

A few years ago I received a letter from a woman who had been shaken by some of the material presented to her. Here is part of the letter I received.

> Dear Pastor Bradford,
> I have left the Adventist Church for good. I cannot be a participant in the deception that is going on in regard to the church doctrines and Ellen White . . . I have never heard the church talk about the problems with Ellen White's unfulfilled visions in all the time I have been in it—that's because the church doesn't give a balanced view of her . . . There is only one reason that the church doesn't teach the full truth of Ellen White. It knows that, when armed with the full truth, people will reject her as a prophet . . .

A century ago there were some leaders in Adventism, like JH Kellogg and AT Jones, who rigidly held that everything Ellen White wrote had to be believed as fixed truth. On the other hand, there were leaders like Willie White, AG Daniels, and WW Prescott who had a more flexible approach to understanding her work. In their favor, they had worked with her in preparing her books for publication. Eventually Kellogg and Jones had to face the facts. The new information did not fit into their narrow views of her work. Instead of accommodating their views, they chose to leave Adventism. The other leaders stayed.[1]

Today we also have new information about how Ellen White worked. Some people go into a state of denial and become angry at any suggestion she could ever be wrong. Others find their faith in Adventism and even in Christ destroyed. A third way is to build upon the experientially based understanding of Willie White, AG Daniels and WW Prescott. This essay explores whether this understanding of the work of prophets is in harmony with that of Scripture itself.

In my search I feared being drawn more and more towards concepts on inspiration that were new to me. However, I remain a firm believer in the full inspiration of the Bible. I believe it has come to us in a trustworthy and reliable manner, and fulfils the claims for itself found in 2 Timothy 3:15–17. As such I believe in the inerrancy of its purpose. In the end what matters is what the Scriptures have to say on the subject, and not our own personal prejudices.

Steps to Understanding Biblical Inspiration

Biblical inspiration! How do you define it? Christianity has never done so in any of its creeds. Maybe the subject is best left in the too hard basket? We know God often puzzles us in the ways He works. He appears to be too hard on Uzzah and too kind to David. "'For my thoughts are not your thoughts, neither are your ways my ways', declares the Lord. "As the heavens are higher than the earth, so are my ways higher than your ways, and my thoughts than your thoughts.'" (Isa 55:8–9).[2]

Could it be that God gives sufficient evidence to believe; but never removes all cause for doubt? Could it be that God has so weighed the evidence that the honest in heart will know He is there; but those who do not want to believe will find hooks on which to hang their doubts? Different people look at the same evidence regarding Christianity; some believe while others doubt.[3] Finding God is not so much an intellectual pursuit as it is a heart experience. 'You will seek me and find me when you seek me with all your heart' (Jer 29:13). God respects human freedom.

---

1. Bert Haloviak and Gary Land, 'Ellen White and Doctrinal Conflict: Context of the 1919 Bible Conference', in *Spectrum* 12 (1982): 19–34.
2. All biblical quotations are from the NIV unless otherwise indicated.
3. An example of this is found in Acts 17: 16–34. Paul presented the claims of Christ only to be met with cynicism from some and belief from others.

There is need for a balanced view of the inspiration of the Bible. It is God's Word in human language. Just as Jesus is the Living Word of God and as such He is truly God and Man, so the Bible is truly divine and human. Liberals water down the miracles of the Bible and rob the Bible of the presence of God in its authorship. Fundamentalists virtually ignore some obviously human elements of the Bible.

Ellen White's contribution to an Adventist understanding of inspiration

A major reason I accept the inspiration of Ellen White is the harmony I find between her understanding of how inspiration worked through her ministry and the self-understandings of the Bible writers. Her ideas were not the prevailing views among her contemporaries. She herself wrote,

> The Bible is written by inspired men, but it is not God's mode of thought and expression. It is that of humanity. God as a writer, is not represented . . .
>
> It is not the words of the Bible that are inspired, but the men that were inspired. Inspiration acts not on the man's words or his expressions but on the man himself, who under the influence of the Holy Ghost, is imbued with thoughts. But the words receive the impress of the individual mind (1 SM 21).

Borrowing by Bible writers[4]

Of the New Testament writers, only Paul and John are known to have had visions. But Paul still felt the need to refer to the writings of others (2 Tim 4:13). Paul's quotations from pagan scholars are well known. In Acts 17:28 he quotes two: Epimendes, 'For in him we live and move and have our being" and Aratas, 'For we are also his offspring'.[5] In 1 Corinthians 15:33 he quotes Menander, without indicating he is quoting, 'Evil communications corrupt good manners'.[6]

Even some of the statements made by Christ sound similar to some statements previously made by Jewish rabbis. For example, 'What is hateful to you, do not do to your neighbours; that is the whole Torah, while the rest is the commentary thereof'.[7] This sounds much like the golden rule found in Matthew 7:12, yet it was said by Hillel, a famous Jewish teacher long before Jesus said it.[8] Ellen White's comment is significant:

---

4. The subsequent material is taken from my forthcoming book.
5. See *SDA Bible Commentary,* edited by Francis D Nichol (Washington DC: Review & Herald), 6:354.
6. *Ibid*, 6:808.
7. *Ibid*, 5:356.
8. For more examples see Tim Crosby 'Does Inspired Mean Original?', *Ministry* (February 1986): 4–7.

> Some of the truths that Christ spoke were familiar to the people. They had heard them from the lips of priests and rulers, and from men of thought; but for all that, they were distinctively the thoughts of Christ.
>
> He had given them to men in trust, to be communicated to the world . . . The work of Christ was to take the truth of which the people were in want, separate it from error, and present it free from the superstitions of the world, that the people might accept it on its own intrinsic and eternal merit. [9]

How much of the Bible would we abandon if we deleted all the allusions to pagan literature?

> Figures of speech in the Song of Solomon show similarities to the religious literature of ancient Sumer, a civilisation in existence three thousand years before Christ . . . Shall we abandon the Book of Proverbs because in places it follows the literary pattern of Egyptian and other ancient near eastern wisdom tradition, on occasion almost word for word? Must we cut the Psalter out of our Bibles because many of the psalms draw from imagery also used in Canaanite Baal hymns? [10]

God uses many diverse ways to convey His revelations to His prophets. Sometimes it is by supernatural events such as visions. Often it is as the prophet consults the works of others, or observes events. It seems there is an economy of miracles at work in the way God reveals His will. He never does supernaturally what can be done naturally. Regardless of the methods used, God still oversees the end product to make sure it reliably conveys His message to His people.

Literary assistance for inspired writers

Many Bible writers had help in putting their literary works together. Romans begins with greetings from Paul (Rom 1:1–7), but towards the end his secretary inserts a salutation of his own, 'I Tertius, who wrote down this letter, greet you in the Lord' (Rom 16:22). Leon Morris notes how Paul's literary style complicates study: 'He rushes on, often leaving out words he expected his readers to supply (and which they hope they are supplying correctly!). He is an original thinker, sometimes struggling with language to say things that no one had said before.' [11]

---

9. Ellen G White, *Review and Herald*, 7 January 1890, reprinted *Review and Herald*, 2 June 1983: 7.
10. Gerald Wheeler 'God Speaks with a Human Accent', in *Adventist Review*, 14 July 1983: 5.
11. Leon Morris, *New Testament Theology* (Academic Books, Zondervan, 1990), 21.

In response to scholars who reject the Pauline authorship of parts of the pastoral epistles, Morris notes that differences in style may be due to the influence of literary assistants.[12] Evidence of literary assistance has also been seen in the stylistic differences between 1st and 2nd Peter;[13] and between the Gospel of John and Revelation.[14] As for the Old Testament, the Book of Jeremiah shows signs of literary assistance.[15] The polished poetry of the prophets and of the Book of Job seems to reflect the same phenomenon.

How much do prophets know?

There is no single passage in the Bible telling us all we wish to know about the gift of prophecy. In Romans chapter 12, Paul writes regarding the operation of spiritual gifts and, as he mentions prophecy, he makes a remark that could have significant bearing on our understanding of this gift: 'We have different gifts, according to the grace given us. If a man's gift is prophesying, let him use it in proportion to his faith' (Rom 12:6).

Commentators have pondered the meaning of what Paul means 'let him use it in *proportion* to his faith'. How can a prophet prophesy in proportion to his faith? The word translated *proportion* is the Greek word *analogia*. This is the only place this word appears in the New Testament. Many commentators have suggested that *faith*, as mentioned here, is to be taken in a subjective manner tied in with *measure* mentioned in verse three. Paul here is probably referring to how a person should function.[16] David Hill offers the observation that,

> the person who exercises the gift of prophecy should speak only when conscious of his words as inspired and presumably only as long as he is confident that God is speaking through him.[17]

---

12. *Ibid.*
13. Michael Green, *The Second Epistle General of Peter and the General Epistle of Jude* (Leicester: Inter-Varsity Press, 1987), 16: 'The Greek of 1 Peter is polished, cultured, dignified; it is among the best in the New Testament. The Greek of 2 Peter is grandiose; it is rather like baroque art.'
14. 'It is not difficult to account for the linguistic and literary differences that exist between the Revelation, written probably when John was alone on Patmos, and the Gospel, written with the help of one or more fellow believers at Ephesus.' *SDA Bible Commentary, op cit*, 7:720.
15. Jeremiah dictated his message to Baruch, who wrote the words on a scroll and read them to the people in the temple (Jer 36:4–6). Baruch is accused of having undue influence over Jeremiah (Jer 43:3). According to Jeremiah 51:64, 'The words of Jeremiah end here'. What, then, is to be made of Jeremiah 52? This chapter has been taken out of 2 Kings 24:18 to 25:30 to show the fulfilment of Jeremiah's prophecies after his death. Perhaps it was put in by those we may well call 'The Jeremiah Estate'.
16. See CK Barrett, *The Epistle to the Romans* (New York, Harper and Row, 1957), 23. Also, AT Robertson, *Word Studies in the New Testament* (Nashville, Broadman, 1931), Volume 9, IV, 403.
17. David Hill, *New Testament Prophecy* (London: Marshall, Morgan and Scott, 1979), 119.

Hill's understanding of the text seems to be reflected in the New Living Translation, 'God has given each of us the ability to do certain things well. So if God has given you the ability to prophesy, speak out when you have faith that God is speaking through you' (Rom 12:6).

Cranfield offers the further insight that, 'It may be suggested that the simplest and most satisfactory interpretation... [is that prophets] are to be careful not to utter (under the impression that they are inspired) anything which is incompatible with their believing in Christ.'[18]

Recognising the fallibility of prophets

For those of us who have never received a revelation from God, it is difficult to understand what is taking place. What we do know is that there are three stages of the prophetic process:

1. The revelation,
2. The interpretation, and
3. The application.

Regarding the revelation, we would expect there would be no mistakes because God never offers anything imperfect or faulty. However, it is possible that mistakes could be made at stages 2 and 3, in the interpretation and application.[19]

Frederick Harder asks the following hard questions to help us gain some insights into the fallibility of prophets.

> How can personal prejudices and errors be distinguished from the divine word? How far were the prophet's natural faculties overruled or held in abeyance? On the other hand, to what extent were they heightened, sensitised, or strengthened in order to receive and understand the word revealed? How competent was the prophet to accurately communicate the message? Finally, and just as important,

---

18. CEB Cranfield, *The International Critical Commentary, A Critical and Exegetical Commentary on the Epistle to Romans* (Edinburgh: T&T Clark, 1979), 620–621.
19. Perhaps an example of this is to be seen in the prophetic activity of Agabus in Acts chapter 21. In verses 10–11 he prophesies that Paul will be bind him and hand him over to the Gentiles. When the prophecy is fulfilled [verses 30–33] there are two small mistakes. (1) It wasn't the Jews who bound Paul. They were trying to kill him. It was the Romans who bound him. (2) The Jews did not hand him over to the Gentiles; the Gentiles took him off them and rescued Paul. The general idea of Agabus is correct; but some of the details are wrong. Agabus is an experienced prophet; yet he seems to have some details incorrect. Could it be that God revealed to him the trouble ahead and Agabus had to fill in some of the details? We will never know the answer to this question; however the important point for us to bear in mind is that the looseness here does not seem to worry Luke. He does not apologise for it, nor does he see the need to touch things up to make them look better.

how competent am I to understand what he or she said? No simple, definitive answers exist. Certainly the prophet's mind did not become a typewriter or a recording tape used by the Spirit as an inanimate device. The prophet's personality was not absorbed in or merged with the Divine. Prophets sometimes even argued with God over the content of a message, as did Moses, Amos, and Habakkuk.[20]

That prophets do not always comprehend clearly what God is revealing is made clear by Peter's 'wondering about the meaning of the vision' (Acts 10:17). It was some time later that he understood that it meant Gentiles were to be accepted in the same way as the Jews (verses 34–35). Peter seems to indicate that this was a problem for Old Testament prophets as well as they pondered what God was revealing to them about Christ and His sufferings (1 Peter 1:10–11).

It seems that God corrects errors only when the prophet's mistake endangers the central message itself; that is, if the mistake would endanger spiritual welfare. Revelation 19:10 is such an example. John knelt before the angel. This is breaking the second commandment. Immediately the angel intervenes and corrects the error.

No doubt if you were a prophet it would take faith to believe that God had spoken, that you as a prophet had understood it correctly, and that you had delivered the message correctly to God's people. What a fearful responsibility! Think of the implications in the lives of the hearers if you got it wrong.[21]

Added to the statement Paul made in Romans is another statement that can be quite disturbing, particularly for those who always like to see things in black and white, and clear-cut. 'For we know in part and we prophesy in part, but when perfection comes, the imperfect disappears . . . Now we see but a poor reflection as in a mirror; then we shall see face to face. Now I know in part; then I shall know fully, even as I am known' (1 Cor 13:9–10, 12). Commenting on verse 9 the *SDA Bible Commentary* states, 'The gifts of knowledge and prophecy provide only partial glimpses of the inexhaustible treasures of divine knowledge. This limited knowledge will appear to be all but cancelled in the superior brightness of the eternal world, as the light of a candle loses its importance when placed in the bright light of the sun.'[22]

---

20. See *Creation Reconsidered*, edited by James L Hayward (Roseville Calif: Association of Adventist Forums, 2000), *Prophets: Infallible or Authoritative* (Frederick Harder), 226.
21. One cannot help getting the impression from Jeremiah's writings in Lamentations of how easy it would be for a prophet to have some self-doubts about their work. In Jeremiah 20:7–9 he seems to express anger at God as he lamented how he has been treated by others because he gave God's message to them.
22. *SDA Bible Commentary, op cit,* 6:784.

Allowing for human and cultural elements

It is important to remember that God meets people where they are to give them His life-giving messages about Jesus. In the Bible are some cultural statements that we may not think are accurate for us today. In fairness to the Bible, we must keep in mind that the language used was the popular language of the Ancient East and not that of the scientific world of the twenty-first century. The Bible is written for common people using the language of the market place and social gatherings. The language within the culture of the times was the medium God used to get across the spiritual truth He wished His people to understand. If the Bible had been written in the language of science today, it would not have been understood by the millions who have read it prior to our age.

God never offers anything faulty or imperfect, however He has to work with the best material He can find: humanity with all its strengths and weaknesses. No wonder Paul wrote, 'But we have this treasure in jars of clay . . . (2 Cor 4:7).

As God unfolds the life-giving message of His Son He uses the people's cultural concepts in order to speak to them in a meaningful way. He uses a star to guide the magi to the baby Jesus. The magi were eastern astrologers.[23] In the ancient world it was believed that the stars were gods who lived in the heavens above the clouds. The magi accepted that this star-god could move through the sky and guide them as they sought a specific house in Bethlehem.

Just preceding the return of Jesus the Bible describes the stars falling from heaven upon the earth (Rev 6:13, Matt 24:29). Today we know that stars do not fall to the earth. If one did we would be consumed. What they thought were shooting stars we now know to be meteors. This shows us how the Bible uses the language of the culture of the times in which it was written.

On some occasions when Jesus healed He used spittle. He spat on a blind man's eyes and put spittle on the tongue of a deaf man (Mark 7:32–33; Mark 8:22–23; John 9:1–6). Pliny the Elder explains that it was believed in the time of Christ that spittle had healing properties. Jesus used this thought pattern as He demonstrated His healing power.[24]

How then do we determine what is cultural and what is trans-cultural in the Bible? Bernard Ramm offers the following advice:

'1. Whatever in Scripture is in direct reference to natural things is most likely in terms of the prevailing cultural concepts';

---

23. There seems to be a general consensus on this point; for example, *The Illustrated Bible Dictionary* (Leicester: IVP, 1980), 2:930, article 'Magi', 'Both Daniel and Herodotus may contribute to the understanding of the Magi of Mt 2:1–12. Apparently the Magi were non-Jewish religious astrologers who, from astronomical observations, inferred the birth of a great Jewish King.'
24. Cited by William Barclay, *The Daily Study Bible*, revised edition (Edinburgh: The Saint Andrew Press, 1975), on John 9:6–12.

'2. Whatever is directly theological or didactic is most likely trans-cultural.'[25]

In other words, Ramm is telling us that the Bible is a book dealing with salvation through Jesus Christ, but it will do so frequently through the cultural concepts of the age in which it was written. The Bible is perfect for the purpose that God intended it to function.

Prophets do not have all knowledge

Just in case we are inclined to think that prophets used by God possessed the gift of omniscience, consider John the Baptist. Did he have a correct understanding of the nature of the kingdom to be set up by the Messiah? He was the greatest of the prophets. He was God's special messengerto herald the coming of the Messiah and yet when he was put in prison he almost lost his faith. He, along with the other disciples, believed that Christ would set up a kingdom on earth. When Christ did not do this he sent some of his followers to ask Christ is He really was the Messiah (Matt 11:3).

John the Baptist had some things to learn and some things to unlearn. Remember when he was asked what was required for eternal life he did not outline salvation by grace but rather told his inquirers to reform their lives (Luke 3:11–14). Later his converts had to be re-baptised when they grew in their understanding beyond what he had imparted (Acts 19:1–5).

In fact prophets may not even understand what the message God has given to them in vision really means. For the first decade the Christian Church that felt their message was just for the Jews. Even though Christ said the message was to go the ends of the earth, they did not see the openness of the gospel invitation clearly. So God gave Peter a vision on the rooftop at Joppa (Acts 10). Some unclean animals were paraded before Peter and he was told to arise, kill and eat. Coming out of the vision it says, 'Peter was wondering about the meaning of the vision . . .' (verse 17). He was not sure what God was trying to reveal to him. Later he said, 'God has shown me that I should not call any man impure or unclean' (verse 29). This is an excellent example of a prophet receiving a vision, not knowing what it was supposed to be teaching, but future experience helped him to understand.

Peter comments on the prophets of the Old Testament as having 'searched intently and with the greatest care, trying to find out the time and circumstances to which the Spirit of Christ in them was pointing when he predicted the sufferings of Christ and the glories that would follow' (1 Peter 1:10–11). No doubt Isaiah was one such prophet who struggled to understand the sufferings of the faithful servant passages found in his book.

---

25. Bernard Ramm, *The Christian View of Science and Scripture* (Exeter: Paternoster Press, 1965), 53.

Some may wonder if the prophets always had an open line to God. That is, whether on all occasions they will have God's answer to the situation. The evidence indicates that this is not correct. When challenged by Hananiah, Jeremiah has no answer but walks away. Later he receives the answer (Jer 28:10–11). Again, Jeremiah talks of how on one occasion he meditated for ten days to receive an answer from God (Jer 42:7). Elijah declares he is not under inspiration regarding the problems facing the Shunamite woman when he declares '… the Lord has hidden it from me and has not told me why' (2 Kgs 4:27). There is even evidence of a need for a type of spiritual 'tuning-in'. On one occasion Elisha called for a harpist to help him tune in and prophesy. Walter Kaiser Jr adds that '[Music] had the effect of quieting the disturbed thoughts and attitudes of the prophets, and of setting theology in the context of doxology'.[26]

King David inquired of his court prophet Nathan regarding the building of a temple. Should he do this? Nathan responded, yes God is with you. It seems that the prophet gave advice that was not from God. That night God told Nathan to go back and tell David he was not to build the temple because he was a man of blood. Solomon his son was to build the temple (1 Chron 17:1–4).

How Shall We Test True Prophets From False?

Not by prophecies coming to pass in isolation from other factors

Jeremiah 28:9 is often quoted regarding the need for prophecies to come to pass in order to tell a true prophet from a false prophet. Is this the right passage of Scripture to use? It deserves close consideration: 'The prophet who prophesies peace will be recognised as one truly sent by the Lord only if his prediction comes true'.

The context of this passage is of a prophetic contest between Jeremiah and Hananiah. Hananiah says there will be peace for Jerusalem and Judah; while Jeremiah says the Babylonians will come and destroy the city of Jerusalem, and the Kingdom of Judah will fall. Jeremiah responds by saying that if Hananiah's prophesy of peace comes to pass then they will know that God has spoken through him. In other words, this is a specific situation being addressed. It ought not to be used as a blanket test for evaluating prophets solely on a basis of whether what they say comes to pass.

Deuteronomy 13: 1–5 shows why this can be dangerous, and gives a more complete picture regarding fulfillment of predictions as a test,

> If a prophet, or one who foretells by dreams, appears among you and announces to you a miraculous sign or a wonder, and the sign or

---

26. Walter Kaiser, *Back Toward the Future: Hints for Interpreting Prophecy* (Grand Rapids, MI: Baker, 1989), 76.

> wonder of which he has spoken takes place, and he says, 'Let us follow other gods' (gods you have not known) and 'let us worship them,' you must not listen to the words of that prophet or dreamer ... That prophet or dreamer must be put to death, because he preached rebellion against the Lord your God ...

This passage warns that if a miraculous sign or wonder takes place as foretold by a prophet, this is not of itself sufficient to say that prophet is of God. False prophets, may, at times, predict events that come to pass. We see this through the powers operating within the occult. Evil angels can work through human agencies to foretell the future with greater accuracy than humans left to themselves. This passage tells us that the prophet must also teach us to worship the One True God and give obedience to Him. James Dunn comments that, 'The trouble was that sometimes the word of a false prophet did come true, and sometimes the word of a true prophet was not fulfilled; Yahweh could change his mind (2 Kgs 20:1–7).'[27] We must be careful in using fulfillment of prophecy to test a true prophet from a false prophet Do we consider Jonah to be a false prophet because Nineveh was not destroyed as he predicted? Obviously there are sometimes certain conditions to be met in the fulfillment of some prophecies even though the conditions may not be stated at the time the prophecy is given. Jonah did not state any conditions and yet in the mind of God there were conditions involved. When considering the fulfillment of prophecy for judging true and false prophets we must always keep in mind the following statement made through Jeremiah,

> If at any time I announce that a nation or kingdom is to be uprooted, torn down and destroyed, and if that nation I warned repents of its evil, then I will relent and not inflict on it the disaster I had planned. And if at another time I announce that a nation or kingdom is to be built up and planted, and if it does evil in my sight and does not obey me, then I will reconsider the good I had intended to do for it (Jer 18:7–10).

Sometimes when prophets predict the future they do so in order that something can be done about it, such as to bring about repentance and a right relationship with God, and so avoid the prophecy of judgment coming upon them. In Jeremiah 26:16–19 some of the elders argue that Jeremiah should not be put to death because Micah had also prophesied doom for Jerusalem and it did not happen because of a right response from Hezekiah.[28]

---

27. James DG Dunn, *The Christ and The Spirit, Volume 2 Pneumatology* (Grand Rapids, MI: Eerdmans, 1998), 29–30.
28. The prophecy was made in Micah 3:12 and avoided by Hezekiah in 2 Kings 18:3–6.

Think of the returning exiles from Babylon. Ezekiel had prophesied of the building of a glorious temple in the last chapters of his book. When they built Zerubbabel's temple some of them wept that it was not as glorious as Solomon's. It certainly was nothing like the glorious temple Ezekiel had predicted. Did this make Ezekiel a false prophet? Certainly not. Their poor response led to a poorer temple than God had promised. God had also promised a glorious future for the nation that was never realised.

Another reason why fulfillment must be limited as a test of a true prophet is that sometimes there may be a delay in the fulfillment. A whole generation may live and die and not see the prophecy come to pass as predicted. An example of this would be Ezekiel's prediction that Tyre would be destroyed and cast into the sea. It was destroyed by Nebuchadnezzar and then lay in ruins for many generations until Alexander the Great unwittingly fulfilled the prophecy. Think of all those who lived and died and never saw the complete fulfillment of what Ezekiel had prophesied.

Another reason why we must be careful in using fulfillment of prophecy as the means of judging true prophets from false is found in the nature of God. God is active and dynamic. If He chooses He may not limit Himself to fulfilling the prophecy the way in which it was originally given. It is possible that God may choose to exceed the original prediction and, because of this, the existing generation may fail to recognise that the prophecies are being fulfilled.

A good example of this is seen in how Jesus Christ fulfilled the prophecies concerning His coming as the long-awaited Messiah. The Jewish leaders made the point that He could not be the long-awaited one because He was a Galilean from Nazareth. They correctly pointed out that no prophet was predicted to come from Nazareth. They knew Bethlehem was predicted in Micah 5:2. However, the prophecy had been fulfilled when Christ was born in Bethlehem but later He went and lived in Galilee, and they did not expect this.

It is difficult for us to put ourselves in the mind-set of the Jews of Christ's day because we have the New Testament, which shows us the way in which Christ did fulfill the prophecies. But if we were able to put ourselves into the same situation as the Jews in Palestine in the 1st century with no New Testament to guide us would we have been any wiser?

Try this as an exercise some time: Can you find from the Old Testament prophecies alone the incarnation of Christ? That is, the fact that the Creator would Himself become a babe at Bethlehem. Can you find in the Old Testament the fact that He would die the death of crucifixion? Can you find from the Old Testament alone that the Messiah would be resurrected? Remember you are to do this without the help of the New Testament. At best, this is not an easy task, and yet these three events are pivotal in the ministry of Jesus. The fulfillment of prophecy can be full of surprises. God is not limited by what He has previously said. He is dynamic, ever moving forward, expanding the scope of His purposes and our understanding of them, and often giving more than what He has promised.

How Then Shall We Judge Prophets?

Regarding true and false prophets in the Old Testament, Craig Evans has some helpful advice,

> The difference lay in their hermeneutics. The false prophets and other 'official theologians' [that is, the priests and wise men] maintained a hermeneutic of continuity. That is, after reviewing Israel's sacred traditions, they were convinced that the God of Israel who had bought His people out of the land of slavery and into the land of promise would surely preserve His people in that land . . . Thus the official theologians attempted to limit, localise, and domesticate God for the immediate and short range interests of Israel. Such a hermeneutic sought to manipulate God: 'if we do this then He must do that.' The false prophet's messages of reassurance which were sweet to the ears . . . failed to inform Israel prophetically.
>
> The true prophet, likewise, appealed to these same Torah traditions. He agreed that Yahweh was indeed powerful enough to maintain His people in His land . . . but Yahweh was also powerful enough to take Israel out of the land and put her back into exile . . . The false prophet, by way of contrast was bound primarily with the interests of the people rather than with God.[29]

How could a king, sitting on his throne, with two sets of prophets speaking entirely different messages, determine who was speaking on behalf of God? The answer was to be found in the fact that the false prophets offered prosperity without repentance. They preached the gospel without the law. The writings of the true prophets are full of complaint against them.[30] True prophets stressed that God's people had to turn from their evil ways or face the consequences. They preached, 'repent or perish' (Ezek 14:6; 18:30). As such they were the guardians of the covenant God had made with Israel. They were there to remind Israel of the promised blessings that come from obedience and the curses that had been promised from disobedience. In New Testament times the classic test of a true prophet is the statement made by Jesus,

---

29. Craig A Evans, "ANIMADVERSIONES Paul and the Hermeneutics of 'True Prophecy': A Study of Romans 9-11", *Biblica* 65 (1984): 560-570.
30. For example, Jeremiah 6:13–14.

> Watch out for false prophets. They come to you in sheep's clothing, but inwardly they are ferocious wolves. By their fruit you will recognise them . . . Not everyone who says to me, 'Lord, Lord', will enter the kingdom of heaven, but only he who does the will of my Father who is in heaven. Many will say to me on that day, Lord, Lord, did we not prophesy in your name, and in your name drive out demons and perform miracles?' Then I will tell them plainly, 'I never knew you. Away from me, you evil-doers!' (Matt 7:15-23).

This passage of Scripture is of vital importance to testing prophets to identify the true from the false. Here Jesus Himself lays down clear criteria. It is not by claiming to working in the name of Jesus. It is not by miraculous manifestations whether they may be the physical manifestations accompanying the prophet's work. It is not by driving out demons.

The real test is that of obedience. Verse 23 says, literally, 'Depart from me the [ones] working lawlessness'. The word translated 'lawlessness' is *anomia*. *Nomia* means 'lawfulness' and an 'a' before a word in Greek means 'against'. It is the equivalent of 'un' in English and reverses the meaning of an adjective. So the word literally means 'against the law' or 'unlawfulness'.

True prophets will uphold obedience to God's law both in their lives and in the lives of others. Jesus illustrates this when He states in verses 24-27 that it was the wise man who built his house on the rock. He obeyed the words of Jesus. It was the foolish man who built his house on the sand and lost it. He was foolish because he did not obey the words of Christ.

When prophesying of the coming of the day of the Lord, Peter states another important work of prophets with the challenge to live holy lives, 'Since everything will be destroyed in this way, what kind of people ought you to be? You ought to live holy and godly lives as you look forward to the day of God and speed it's coming' (2 Peter 3:11-12).

Paul provides some additional ideas on how to test true prophecy from false when he addressed the church in Corinth. First, he says that people cannot be true prophets if they cried out, 'Jesus be cursed!' (1 Cor 12:3). Second, true prophecy will edify and build up the community of believers (1 Cor 14:4, 31). For John the test was that the prophet must acknowledge that Jesus Christ is come in the flesh (1 John 4:1-3). For both Paul and John the important test for a prophet can vary according to the local situation and the issues being faced.

The great test to be applied to prophets, to determine if they are true or false is, do they call us to worship the true God and obey His laws by living a holy life? If we have erred from the faith they will call us to repent and give obedience to God's Word. They will call us away from false worship. This is a test that is within the understanding of the educated and the uneducated alike.

New Testament Prophecy

New Testament prophecy commences with the appearance of John the Baptist. In his dress and solitary style of ministry he would have appealed to the populace as being a prophet after the tradition of the Old Testament. In addition he denounced immorality and wickedness and demanded repentance in view of the fact that God was about to send His long awaited Messiah, who would punish the ungodly. In doing this he met the Old Testament expectations of prophetic activity. This, with the power seen to attend his work, caused many to accept him as a true prophet.

In John 16:12–15, Jesus promised that the Holy Spirit would still speak to His followers after His departure. But when the followers of Christ say words caused by the prompting of the Holy Spirit it does not necessarily make them prophets. All the followers of Christ are able at times to say words prompted by the Spirit. (Perhaps we could label them 'prophetic statements'). This does not necessarily make a person a prophet. We will see that this term seems to be used in the biblical passages to describe those who are especially called and used by God for a prophetic ministry.

A useful way of defining prophecy in the New Testament context is by saying it is the Spirit of God revealing to believers what they need to know to meet specific situations. This is now a possibility for all believers, but there are some specially chosen individuals whom will receive the prophetic gift (1 Cor 12:29). As such they will be used more frequently and be recognised as having the prophetic gift.

In contrast to the Old Testament, the New Testament anticipates that the gift of prophecy will become more widespread. It will not be limited to the Hebrew race alone nor to a few select individuals as in the past. The opening of the Christian era was accompanied by a powerful manifestation of the Gift of Prophecy. Peter gave meaning to the outpouring of God's Spirit at Pentecost by saying,

> This is what was spoken by the prophet Joel: In the last days, God says, I will pour out my Spirit on all people. Your sons and daughters will prophesy, your young men will see visions, your old men will dream dreams. Even on my servants, both men and women, I will pour out my Spirit in those days and they will prophecy (Acts 2:17–18).

Peter is saying clearly that from now on God is going to pour out His Spirit upon all people regardless of race, gender, age or social standing. The Holy Spirit will now abide in every believer. The ministries of ancient prophets, priests and kings have now passed into the lives of ordinary people (Rev 1:6, 1 Peter 2:9–10, 1 Cor 14:1).

The Pentecost fulfillment indicates a wider number of people will now experience this gift. Paul in 1 Corinthians 14: 1 encourages all believers to 'eagerly desire spiritual gifts, especially the gift of prophecy'. At the same time he states that not all will have this gift (1 Cor 12:29). Paul does, however, rank the gift of prophecy over all the other gifts of grace. In 1 Corinthians 14:1 he admonishes them to desire spiritual gifts, especially prophecy. When he mentions the gifts he repeatedly lists prophecy after the apostles (1 Cor 12:28, Eph 2:20; 3:5; 4:11). Evangelists, pastors and teachers are always listed behind prophets. In Ephesians 2:20 the prophets are listed with the apostles as part of the foundation of the church. Ben Witherington III adds that,

> NT prophets did not have the same status, standing, or unquestioned authority as some of the OT prophets. Rather, there is evidence from Paul suggesting that the utterances of Christian prophets needed to be weighed, since it was possible for their prophecy, in the enthusiasm of the moment of revelation, to exceed the proportion of their faith and understanding . . . The prophet, it seems, did not have the highest honor rating in Paul's communities. Yet Paul clearly rated prophets as very important to the early church, placing them behind only the apostles in his lists of church roles and functionaries.[31]

Paul also clearly "pulls rank" on local prophets in 1 Cor 14:36–38 where he says, 'Did the word of God originate with you? Or are you the only people it has reached? If anybody thinks he is a prophet or spiritually gifted, let him acknowledge that what I am writing to you is the Lord's command. If he ignores this, he himself will be ignored.' Paul sees himself as one who passes on the words of Christ and calls for the local prophets to acknowledge what he says; if not they will be ignored. It does appear that there are different levels of the gift of prophecy operating in the New Testament.

Various manifestations of the gift of prophecy

It is to these diverse manifestations of the gift of prophecy we need to turn to understand the different functions and manifestations of the gift in the New Testament. Some are given a revelation, yet there is no record of them receiving another and they are not called prophets; for instance, there is a prophetic utterance by Mary (Luke 1:46–55); Zechariah the father of John the Baptist makes a prophetic speech about Jesus (Luke 1:67–79); Simeon makes a prophetic speech also about Jesus (Luke 2:25–35). Even Caiaphas the apostate high priest unwittingly makes a prophecy about the significance of the death of Christ (John 11:49–52). Ananias

---

31. Ben Witherington III, *Jesus The Seer* (Peabody, MA: Hendrickson, 1999), 316.

received a prophetic revelation regarding the life and work of Paul; yet he is not called a prophet. He is simply called 'a certain disciple' (Acts 9:10).

From these experiences we see that the gift of prophecy move upon a variety of individuals who may, consciously or unconsciously, make prophetic statements. This may or may not happen to them *again*. None of those mentioned here are ever called prophets. However, they gave prophetic messages.

All believers are encouraged by Paul to eagerly desire spiritual gifts especially the gift of prophecy (1 Cor 14:1). He also stated that not all will have this particular gift (1 Cor 12:29). According to the statement made by Peter at Pentecost (Acts 2:17–21) we can expect a widespread use of the gift now that we are in the age of the Spirit.

1 Corinthians 14 seems to be laying down the way in which the gift should operate at the local church level. Some would call this 'congregational prophecy'. The gift of prophecy is said to be for 'strengthening, encouragement, and comfort' (1 Cor 14:3). This gift includes a revelation (verse 30) and the prophet is in control of his/her mind (verse 32). They must also speak in harmony with what Paul has previously taught (verses 36–38). This form of prophecy operates when the congregation is assembled It may consists of personal encouragement or public testimonies;[32] however, it must be a revelation to be a prophecy, otherwise it simply a 'teaching.'[33] Chris Forbes comments on Christian prophecy and its relationship to preaching and teaching,

> Was Christian prophecy basically the same as preaching? Probably not. As far as I can tell it wasn't a matter of reading Scripture and expounding its meaning. The two examples in Acts certainly aren't exposition of Scripture and don't even quote it. In fact, you never find prophecy in the New Testament closely linked with expounding the Word of God. They were different things. Teachers and preachers expounded Scripture. Prophets passed on direct revelations from God . . . It was immediate, verbal, direct, about the congregational situation. It wasn't of long term relevance.[34]

Ephesians 5:19 admonishes local Christians to 'Speak to one another with psalms, hymns and spiritual songs. Sing and make music in your heart to the Lord . . .' Andrew Lincoln understands this as,

---

32. Michael Green, *To Corinth with Love: the vital relevance today of Paul's advice to the Corinthian Church* (London: Hodder and Stoughton, 1982), 75, speaks of this form of prophecy as follows, 'Prophecy is not the equivalent of Scripture. Prophecy is a particular word for a particular congregation (or person) at a particular time through a particular person. Scripture is for all Christians in all places at all times.'
33. 1 Corinthians 14:24, 30 seems to teach prophecy has to do with receiving revelations and making known secrets of people's hearts.
34. Chris Forbes, "Straight from God", in *On Being*, April (1991): 13.

> speaking to one another in psalms and hymns and songs inspired by the Spirit ... the songs which the believers sing to each other are spiritual because they are inspired by the Spirit ... Phil 2:6–11; Col 1:15–20; Eph 5:14; 1 Tim 3:16 may provide some examples which have found their way into the NT, to snatches of song freshly created in the assembly ...[35]

This singing would possibly be the same singing that Paul refers to when he says, 'So what shall I do? I will pray with my spirit, but I will also pray with my mind; I will sing with my spirit, but I will also sing with my mind' (1 Cor 14:15). No doubt the singing brought spiritual encouragement to the congregation in harmony with what prophecy was meant to do as outlined in 1 Corinthians 14:3. Paul also encourages the Thessalonians to treat this form of prophecy with respect (1 Thess 5:20).[36] For those used by God to prophesy on a regular basis, it would seem they are actually called prophets. This could include some at the local church level as pictured in 1 Corinthians 14 or even an itinerant prophet like Agabus (Acts 11:27). It seems that the early church had a good supply of people who were recognised as prophets (Acts 13:1).

At the higher level there were the Apostles, who were also called prophets (Eph 2:20). Paul exercises an authority unlike any other New Testament prophet. For instance, he writes, 'Shall I come to you with a whip, or in love and with a gentle spirit?' (1 Cor 4:21) and 'Among them are Hymenaeus and Alexander, whom I have handed over to Satan to be taught not to blaspheme' (1 Tim 1:20).

If we see the Apostles as the successors of the Old Testament prophets we should not expect to treat their messages with any less respect for they are the conveyers of Christ to us. They were instructed directly by Christ. Paul is conscious of this when he states, 'For I received from the Lord what I passed on to you ...' (1 Cor 11:23).

Paul zealously defends his authority, not on the basis that he is a prophet, but an apostle, 'Am I not free? Am I not an apostle? Have I not seen Jesus our Lord ..' (1 Cor 9:1). He writes, 'I want you to know, brothers, that the gospel I preached is not something that man made up. I did not receive it from any man, nor was I taught it; rather, I received it by revelation from Jesus Christ' (Gal 1:11–12). Paul's authority as an apostle means his writings have become an important part of the

---

35. Andrew Lincoln, *Word Biblical Commentary, Ephesians*, No. 42 (Dallas, Tex: Word Books, 1990), 345–346.
36. John Stott, *The Message of Thessalonians* (Inter-Varsity Press, 1991), 128. 'This form of prophecy was not considered to be a message which brought the very words of God to the people. It was rather a timely word of instruction, encouragement or rebuke which brought the general thrust of God's guidance to the church in each particular situation.'

Bible. To argue against his teachings would be in defiance of the fact that the apostles were men taught directly by Christ and commissioned by Christ.[37]

Peter understands that the authority of the Old Testament prophets has been passed on to the New Testament Apostles. Accordingly Peter writes, 'I want you to recall the words spoken *in the past by the holy prophets* and the command given by our Lord and Saviour *through your apostles*'.[38] In New Testament times the status of the Old Testament prophet was given to the Apostles who had seen Christ in the flesh and been taught by Him. They had also been witnesses to His resurrection (Acts 1:21-22; 1 Cor 9:1).

It is a mistake to consider the word 'prophet' in Old Testament times and equate its function with the word 'prophet' as it appears in the New Testament. However, it is true that certain functions of Christian prophets do remind us of Old Testament prophets:

1. They predict the future (Acts 11:28, 20:23).
2. They declare divine judgments (Acts 13:11; 28:25-28).
3. They use symbolic actions when prophesying (Acts 21:11).
4. They exhort and encourage God's people (Acts 15:32).

John who wrote the book of Revelation is in many ways like an Old Testament prophet.

Yet to equate prophets in both testaments as being essentially the same is to miss the importance of Acts 2:17-21, which implies that since Pentecost, the gift of prophecy will become more widespread and diverse. The New Testament says all God's people are potentially prophets. Not all will exercise this gift, yet they are all encouraged to seek it (1 Cor 14:1). Various individuals may be used as the Spirit selects them (1 Cor 12:29). They may be used once or many times, or may be so used in a way which enables them to be called prophets. The real successors of the classical prophets of the Old Testament are the Apostles in that they were taught directly by Christ and were used by God to give us the sacred canon.

It is difficult to classify where Ellen White's prophetic ministry fits within this scheme, because at times she appears like a classical prophet, while there are other times when she appears to function like a local prophet. She does no appear to fit into any one category.

The need for discernment

In the New Testament we are told to evaluate prophecies. Apart from the authority given to prophets in the Old Testament and the apostles in the New Testament, we

---

37. Apostles were men taught directly by Christ. Paul argues this way to defend his apostleship in Galatians 1:1,11,12. In Acts 1:21-22 it was seen as a necessary in finding a replacement for Judas.
38. 2 Peter 3:2, emphasis added.

have seen that prophecy is sometimes given a lower status in the New Testament. For instance, we can see the Thessalonians were inclined to treat it disrespectfully (1 Thess 5:20) and that Paul tries to advance it over the gift of tongues in the thinking of the Corinthians (1 Cor 14:5).

The New Testament does not picture prophets as taking over from the apostles after they died nor does it picture them as the ones who are in particular to guard the church against false teaching. Jude admonishes all church members 'to contend for the faith that was once for entrusted to the saints' (Jude 3). This does not mean that the gift does not have some doctrinal authority; however the authority that is to be used to protect the faithful from doctrinal error does not belong to the gift of prophecy alone but is also given to apostles, evangelists, pastors and teachers. (Eph 4:11–14)

In contrast to the authority given to the Apostles in the New Testament, prophets are to have their prophecies evaluated. Carson has this observation to offer as he contrasts Old and New Testament prophets,

> If a prophet speaking in the name of God was shown to be in error, the official sanction was death. But once a prophet is acknowledged as true, there is no trace of repeated checks on the content of his oracles. By contrast, New Testament prophets are to have their oracles carefully weighed (1 Cor 14:29; so also 1 Thess 5:19–21). Moreover, there is no hint of excommunication as the threatened sanction if the prophet occasionally does not live up to the mark.[39]

In his footnote Carson agrees with Grudem that the verb used in 1 Cor 14:29 which is *diakrino* translated "weigh carefully" bears "the meaning of sifting, separating, evaluating: whereas the simple form *krino* is used for judgments where there are clear cut options (guilty or innocent, true or false, right or wrong) and never for evaluative distinction."[40]

Scholarly consensus for evaluation

There is broad consensus among respected scholars for the need to evaluate Christian prophetic messages.[41] This is such an important point I will quote a few highly respected scholars. David Aune states,

---

39. DA Carson, *Showing the Spirit: A Theological Exposition of 1 Corinthians 12–14* (Homebush West, NSW: Anzea, 1988), 94–95.
40. *Ibid.*
41. Space forbids the inclusion of many of them; however a reader interested in this aspect of the subject should consult Thomas W Gillespie, *The First Theologians. A study in Early Christian Prophecy* (Grand Rapids, MI: Eerdmans, 1994), 33–63.

In several places within his letters Paul directly addresses the subject of evaluating Christian prophecy (1 Thess 5:19–22; 1 Cor 12:10; 14:29). These references are all-important since they constitute the earliest evidence that Christian prophecy was subject to some form of community control . . .[42]

Max Turner writes,

> Paul knows that congregational prophecy, by contrast, is sometimes so unprepossessing that prophecy as a whole is in danger of being despised (1 Thess 5:19, 20). Both at Thessalonica and at Corinth he demands that congregational prophecy be evaluated—not that it just be accepted totally as true prophecy or rejected totally as false prophecy (as in the Old Testament, according to Grudem).[43]

Turner then goes on to comment on the use of *diakrino* as being a word to imply evaluating and separating as opposed to *krino* being a word to say something is wholly true or false,

> It is a matter of deciding what is from God, and how it applies, and of separating this from what is merely human interference. Indeed the human element and human error appears to have been so apparent that in 1 Thessalonians 5:19, 20 Paul has to warn the congregation, 'Do not despise prophecies, but test everything hold fast to what is good'. Arguably, then, prophecy in the New Testament is thus a mixed phenomenon.[44]

Commenting on 1 Corinthians 14:29, Anthony Thiselton says,

> The authentic is to be *sifted* from the inauthentic or spurious, in the light of the OT scriptures, the gospel of Christ, the traditions of all the churches, and critical reflections. Nowhere does Paul hint that preaching or 'prophecy' achieves a privileged status which places them above critical reflection in the light of the gospel, the Spirit, and the scriptures. *It is never infallible.*[45]

---

42. David E Aune, *Prophecy in Early Christianity and the Ancient Near Eastern World* (Grand Rapids, MI: Eerdmans, 1983), 219.
43. Max Turner, *The Holy Spirit and Spiritual Gifts Then and Now* (Cumbria, CA: Paternoster 1996), 213–214.
44. *Ibid*, 214.
45. Anthony C Thiselton, *The First Epistle to the Corinthians: A Commentary on the Greek Text*

The NEB translates 1 Thessalonians 5:19-22 in the following way, 'Do not stifle inspiration, and do not despise prophetic utterances, but bring them all to the test and then keep what is good in them and avoid the bad of whatever kind'. It is important to note that neither the passage in 1 Corinthians 14:29 nor 1 Thessalonians 5:19-21 are talking about testing true prophets from false prophets. Both statements are made in the context of worship services where regular, accepted prophets are operating. The evaluation is not of the prophet who has already been accepted by the congregation, but the message itself, which may be of mixed quality. There can be no doubt that 1 Corinthians 14 is dealing with a worship service.

Cranfield offers this helpful advice when commenting on Romans 12:6,

> While any Christian might from time to time be inspired to prophesy, there were some who were so frequently inspired that they were regarded as being prophets and forming a distinct group of persons . . . But Paul recognised the need for prophetic utterances to be received with discrimination. He gives instruction in 1 Cor 14:29 that, while the prophets are prophesying, the rest of the congregation is to 'discern' . . . And in 1 Cor 12:10 the gift of discerning of spirits . . . is significantly mentioned immediately after the gift of prophecy.[46]

Witherington comments on Romans 12:6 that:

> Grudem is likely right that Paul sees the prophecy of the Gentile churches as not having the same degree of inspiration or authority as either OT prophecy or his own teaching or, for that matter, Jesus' prophecy and teaching, none of which is said to need weighing or sifting (cf 1 Cor 12:10; 14:29).[47]

An important point coming out of Paul's counsel regarding prophecy is for us not to make the same mistake (as was made in Corinth) of overvaluing prophecy by thinking of prophecies as always being the very words of God. For Paul the test of prophecy was that it exalted Jesus (1 Cor 12:3), manifested love (1 Cor 13:4-7) and built up the body (1 Cor 14:3). Aune agrees with Cranfield on the intent of the gift 'discerning of spirits' being mentioned after the gift of prophecy.

> The close relationship between prophesying and the evaluation of prophetic utterances in 1 Cor 14:29 indicates that there is a connec-

---

(Grand Rapids, MI: Eerdmans, 2000), 1140.
46. Cranfield, *The International Critical Commentary*, op cit, 620.
47. Witherington, *Jesus the Seer*, op cit, 326. The following statement from Witherington is also worth noting: 'Although prophecy is alive and well in the Pauline churches . . . Texts in both 1 Corinthians 14 and Romans 12 suggest that Paul thought that it was possible to prophesy beyond the extent of one's inspiration and faith, and so such prophecy had to be sifted or weighed." *Ibid*, 328.

tion between the gift of prophecy and the gift of 'discerning of spirits,' just as there is between the gift of tongues and the gift of interpreting tongues (1 Cor 12:10) . . . This evaluative process or procedure may lie behind such enigmatical expressions as 'it seemed good to the Holy Spirit and to us' (Acts 15:28).[48]

An evaluation of prophetic utterances

Aune's reference to Paul's decision to still head towards Jerusalem as recorded in Acts 21 is an excellent example of what Paul means when he states we are to evaluate prophesy. Acts 21 has New Testament prophecy operating at the different levels already referred to. First, Paul, an apostle who is also a prophet, feels 'compelled by the Spirit to go to Jerusalem' (Acts 20:22). On the way he is met by some disciples at Tyre who 'through the Spirit'[49] urge him not to go up to Jerusalem. It appears that Paul evaluates their message and still decides to press on. These disciples were not established prophets; they are called 'disciples'. Probably they are operating at the 1 Corinthians 14 level. It is possible they were given an insight, by the Spirit, of trouble ahead for Paul. They put their interpretation on it to warn him not to go. They probably had a wrong interpretation because Paul previously said he was being compelled by the Spirit to go to Jerusalem. Paul therefore exercises his right to do some sifting of the message in harmony with 1 Cor 14:29.

Paul stays at the home of Phillip who has four daughters who prophesy (verse 8). We are not told the content of their prophecies, however they are probably once again operating at the 1 Corinthians 14 level. The present tense expressed by the word *propheteuousai* would seem to suggest that they exercised the gift regularly. While he is there, Agabus comes and warns of the dangers ahead (verses 10–14). It appears that the Holy Spirit has spoken to Agabus and given him an insight into the troubles Paul can expect. He states that the Jews will bind Paul and hand him over to the Gentiles.

Notice that Agabus does not put his own interpretation on the prophecy by saying Paul should not go. He merely states what will happen. It is those listening who put their interpretation on the matter and plead with him not to go. Paul overrides their interpretation as he did with the disciples from Tyre. Agabus is a man used so often by God through the gift of prophecy that he is called a 'prophet'; yet, even though he was an experienced prophet, his prediction did not quite work out exactly as he stated. Compare verse 11, where Agabus states that Paul will be taken by the Jews and handed over to the Gentiles; with the fulfillment in verses 30–33, which shows that what actually happens is that the Jews took Paul

---

48. Aune, *Prophecy in Early Christianity and the Ancient Near Eastern World*, op cit, 220–222.
49. A term usually considered to mean the gift of prophecy at work. Compare the expression as it is used when Agabus prophesies in Acts 11:28.

and tried to kill him. They did not hand him over to the Gentiles; rather, it was the Gentiles who rescued him and took him away from the Jews.

It did not work out exactly as Agabus had stated. Perhaps Agabus had a revelation of trouble ahead. Maybe he did a little filling in himself. All we know is that there is a lack of precise detail here in a true prophecy, made by an experienced prophet. Acts 21 is an important passage to study to understand more fully the nature of New Testament prophecy.[50]

Gillespie sees in 1 Corinthians 15 an example of what Paul has been stating about the need to evaluate prophecy in the previous chapter. It seems that some were saying that there was no resurrection of the dead, and Paul is using his prophetic revelation in verses 51–55 as a critique of what other prophets were saying. In other words when he states in 14:37 that the other prophets must acknowledge what he is saying as the Word of God or they will be ignored, he is demonstrating what he means in the next chapter.[51] Alistar Stewart-Sykes quotes Gillespie and supports him in this concept,

> In the description of Corinthian worship which precedes this chapter we are told that prophecies which are given are to be subjected to prophetic judgement [sic] and interpretation. In what follows we may have such a prophetic judgement [sic] of a prophecy ... a transition from a prophecy to a judgement [sic] of a prophecy in the way that was normal in worship.[52]

Stewart-Sykes adds that the book of Revelation offers another example of a hierarchy of prophets.[53] He sees John as a 'visionary prophet'; in other words, that 'his means of inspiration are visions revived outside of the context of worship, the contents of which are subsequently reported to the community'.[54] He also sees John as a 'free prophet of the Old Testament type' in that, unlike the prophets described in 1 Corinthians, he is not subjected to evaluation,

---

50. Graeme S Bradford, *Was Paul resisting the Spirit of Prophecy on his way to Jerusalem?* (Unpublished MA paper, December 1993). In this paper I suggest that Paul was indeed following the procedure of evaluating prophecy when he still followed his own convictions that God wanted him to witness to his faith in Jerusalem. He still continued on his journey despite warnings given to him through Christian prophecy. Witherington expresses a similar view when he makes the following comment regarding Paul's attitude towards Agabus in Acts 21. Witherington, *Jesus the Seer, op cit*, 342.
51. Gillespie, *The First Theologians, op cit*, 220–221.
52. Alistar Stewart-Sykes, *From Prophecy to Preaching: A Search For The Origins Of The Christian Homily* (Leiden, The Netherlands: Brill, 2001), 102–3.
53. *Ibid*, 118.
54. *Ibid*, 126.

Aune picks up hints of opposition to John among the churches at 2:14 and 2:20–23, where other (presumably local) prophets are tarred with the brush of false prophecy under biblical pseudonyms. The fact that John needs to oppose prophecy with prophecy is an indication that only a prophetic message carried authority in these communities . . . Quite regardless of its date, the Johannine apocalypse thus enables us to see the church functioning at its most primitive level in terms of how the word of God was communicated to the community.[55]

Stewart-Sykes summarises his arguments as follows,

Herein lies one of the origins of Christian preaching: for when prophecy was delivered it was necessary that the prophecy be judged, interpreted and expounded. Thus it is in this process, it is suggested, that the origins of the homily lie . . . The theological development of a growing respect paid to the written canon . . . [had] the eventual result that Scripture comes to dominate prophecy to such an extent that the prophetic voice disappears altogether.[56]

The evidence from the New Testament is that prophecy was being as much looked down upon and despised as it was being abused. The danger the church faced was that they would not hear the genuine messages coming from authentic prophets. Paul counseled the church not to despise prophecies, but to test them. However, even with the genuine prophet there appears to be an expectation at times of a mixture of 'wheat and chaff', as we see the human element surfacing. We should not therefore necessarily reject as false prophets those who at the lower level of prophecy do not demonstrate infallibility in conveying their messages. This judging of Christian prophets should not be confused with the Old Testament rules about judging false prophets. The New Testament passages deal with judging the prophecies being delivered, and not the prophet themselves.

Adventism After the Death of Ellen White

The 1919 Bible Conference

Little was known of the 1919 Bible Conference until December 6, 1974, when Donald Yost, the senior archivist at the General Conference headquarters in Washington, DC was setting up the newly formed archives. He accidentally discovered two

---

55. *Ibid*, 131.
56. *Ibid*, 270–271.

packets of papers containing some 2400 pages of typewritten material that were stenographic notes taken at the Bible Conference held in Takoma Park, Maryland, in July 1919. The subsequent publication of those minutes in *Spectrum* gave Adventists a unique opportunity to see how some of the contemporaries of Ellen White viewed her function and authority. This was a world of thought that few, if any, of even the best-informed Seventh-day Adventists knew existed.

We will not focus on the conference itself, but on a smaller after meeting called The Bible and History Teachers Council attended by twenty-two delegates, some of them prominent church leaders. In the after-meeting of the 1919 Bible Conference, AG Daniells[57] could speak with authority. He had on many occasions, along with WW Prescott, been part of the team that worked with her in the putting together of some of her books. During the course of the after-meeting he made this observation,

> Well, now, as I understand it, Sister White never claimed to be an authority on history, and never claimed to be a dogmatic teacher on theology. She never outlined a course of theology, like Mrs Eddy's book on teaching . . . She never claimed to be an authority on history . . . she was ready to correct in revision such statements as she thought should be corrected. I have never gone to her writings, and taken the history that I found in her writings, as the positive statement of history regarding the fulfilment of prophecy.[58]

It would seem that the leaders of the church, along with the Bible teachers present, did not feel quite comfortable in presenting what they knew to be the truth regarding the subject of the inspiration of Ellen White's writings to the laity of the church. Although most present at the conference were pleased with the open and frank discussion about some sensitive issues regarding inspiration, the subsequent reaction by some who were also present shows that not all were in agreement with presenters like Daniells, Prescott and Lacey. Serious trouble lay ahead, culminating in the dismissal of Daniells as General Conference President in the 1922 General Conference session.

The death of the founder of any movement is often of great significance. This was certainly true for the Seventh-day Adventist Church with the death of Ellen White in 1915. History shows that when this has happened to other movements

---

57. The 1919 after-meeting was held with church administrators and Bible teachers to try and sort out some of the wrong views that were coming to the fore regarding the use of Ellen White's writings. This meeting was held just four years after her death.
58. 1919 Bible Conference Minutes printed in 'The Bible Conference of 1919', in *Spectrum* 1 34. See similar statements in *ibid*, 34. AG Daniels; *ibid*, 38. HC Lacey to AG Daniels; *ibid*, 38. HC Lacey; *ibid*, 40. WG Wirth; *ibid*, 46. JN Anderson; *ibid*, 49. GB Thompson.

of the past the tendency is for the next generation to 'pull down the shutters' and strive towards conserving rather than exploring. Bull and Lockhart maintain that this also happened to the Seventh-day Adventist Church,

> [When] Ellen White died . . . the church was robbed of its chief means of authorising innovation. The liveliness and flexibility that had characterised the Adventist theological debate in the nineteenth century evaporated . . . The intellectually disciplined theological debates that had filled the pages of *The Review* now disappeared . . . The writings of Ellen White and the Bible now functioned not as a source of new ideas but as a compendium of truths to be expounded and memorised . . . Adventist theology has developed in parallel with that of the mainstream. It was at its most distinctive during a period of great diversity; *it became fundamentalist in the era of fundamentalism; and softened with the rise of evangelicalism*[59]

The history of the Seventh-day Adventist Church reflects many eras of change. Bull and Lockhart have correctly observed that after the death of Ellen White there were forces at work in society that pushed the movement into an unnatural fundamentalist stance. Later, the forces in society would also push it back toward what many would claim to be its more natural position. Mostly this was caused by Ellen White's legacy to the Church that it should pursue higher education. However, these same forces were also at work in the Protestant world and affected other denominations in a similar way.

It was only in 1958 that her material on inspiration was printed in *Selected Messages* volume one, and it was not until 1980 that more material was made available in *Selected Messages* volume three. If the material found in these volumes had been more readily available, and if it had been understood, it may have spared the Church many divisive problems.

For us today it is important to notice that those who associated with her, and who reflected on her ministry in the 1919 Conference, appear to have a firm understanding of what to expect from a prophet. They understood this not so much from the Bible as from their association with a genuine prophet. Today we can see the recent scholarship on prophecy has given us a clearer understanding from the Bible. We can get it from the Bible; they got it from their association with a prophet. Surely this must be seen as convincing evidence that they were associating with a genuine prophet who met every biblical expectation.

---

59. Malcolm Bull and Keith Lockhart, *Seeking A Sanctuary: Seventh-day Adventism and the American Dream* (New York: Harper and Row, 1989), 88–89. Emphasis added.

PART FIVE

Other Studies

A Feast of Reason—The Legacy of William Miller on Seventh-day Adventist Hermeneutics

Jeff Crocombe

In his historical survey of Seventh-day Adventist views on inspiration, Alberto Timm makes the following observation: 'Seventh-dayAdventists inherited their early views of scripture from their former denominations and the Millerites.'[1] This essay will test the validity of this assertion, particularly the important role attributed to Millerite views. It will consider the sources of Miller's hermeneutics, and then explore their impact on contemporary Seventh-day Adventist approaches.

Miller's Hermeneutics

William Miller stated that his beliefs were founded upon a systematic reading of the Bible, verse by verse, from beginning to end with a commitment not to proceed until the passage made sense and was without, 'any mysticism or contradictions.'[2] Miller's methodical Bible study soon developed into a systematic process with a series of *Rules of Interpretation*. He believed that the application of these rules to any biblical passage would result in its correct understanding. Accompanying each of Miller's rules was a list of 'proofs'—biblical texts that were given as proof of the validity of each of his rules.

The exact number of Miller's rules varies—thirteen, fourteen, sixteen, nineteen—according to when and where they were published. I am using the list of fourteen *Rules of Interpretation* found in Miller's article in *The Midnight Cry*, 17 November 1842.[3] The list may be divided into three sections: the first five rules deal with general principles of interpretation applicable to the entire Bible, while the next eight deal specifically with the interpretation of Bible prophecy. Miller's final rule, #14, outlines the importance of having faith, of approaching the Bible

---

1. Alberto R. Timm, 'A History of Seventh-day Adventist Views on Biblical and Prophetic Inspiration (1844–2000)', in *Journal of the Adventist Theological Society*, Volume 10, No. 1/2 (1999): 487.
2. William Miller, *Wm Miller's Apology and Defence* (Boston, MT: Joshua V Himes, 1845), 6.
3. William Miller, 'Rules of Interpretation', *The Midnight Cry*, 17 November 1842, 4.

with the correct—believing—mind-set: 'The most important rule of all is, that you must have *faith*.'[4]

Miller of course, did not develop either his methods of interpretation, or the interpretations themselves in isolation. Accordingly, it is worth considering what Miller's sources were.

Miller's Sources

Influential theologians & Bible commentators

Popular Seventh-day Adventist perception focuses on Miller's claim that he, 'laid by all commentaries, former views and prepossessions, and determined to read and try to understand for [himself]'.[5] Generally unrecognised however, is that implicit in this statement, of course, is the idea that Miller had at one time, done at least some reading in this area—otherwise he would have nothing to 'lay aside'. As Knight states, 'In a world in which much of the published literature was theological and biblical, it seems quite reasonable to assume that he had examined various religious and biblical works before he began his intense study of the Bible in 1816'.[6] Further evidence of Miller's study comes from a contemporary, N Southard, who wrote in 1843 that Miller 'never had a commentary in his house, and did not remember reading any work upon the prophecies except Newton and Faber, about thirty years ago'.[7] Knight refers to a statement by one of Miller's daughters who is said to have remarked in 1843, 'two authors on the prophecies that he [Miller] distinctly remembered having read prior to 1816 were Newton and Faber'.[8]

Thomas Newton was an Anglican Bishop & dean of St Paul's Cathedral in London.[9] His *Dissertations on the Prophecies* was first published in 1754 and became 'immensely popular'.[10] Like most of his contemporaries, Newton was an historicist. His fundamental idea was that the Bible presented a harmonious chain of prophecy on Christ's first and second advents. Kai Arasola sees his influence on

---

4. Miller, 'Rules of Interpretation', *op cit*, 4.
5. William Miller, *The Midnight Cry*, 11 April 1844, 88. See also Miller's 1845statement, 'I determined to lay aside all my prepossessions, to thoroughly compare scripture with scripture, and to pursue its study in a regular and methodical manner.' Miller, *Apology and Defence, op cit*, 6. Bliss also emphasised this point, noting that Miller 'laid aside all commentaries, and used the marginal references and his Concordance as his only helps'. Sylvester Bliss, *Memoirs of William Miller* (Boston: Joshua V Himes, 1853), 69.
6. George R Knight, *Millennial Fever and the End of the World* (Boise, ID: Pacific Press, 1993), 40.
7. Quoted in Bliss, *Memoirs of William Miller*, 246.
8. Knight, *Millennial Fever, op cit*, 40. Knight does not however, provide a reference for this comment and it seems likely that this is a misreading of the Southard document quoted previously.
9. Kai Arasola, *The End of Historicism: Millerite Hermeneutic of Time Prophecies in the Old Testament* (Uppsala: University of Uppsala, 1990), 37.
10. Arasola, *The End of Historicism, op cit*, 37.

Miller as considerable, stating, 'It would not be surprising if the 'Newton' Miller had in his library was Thomas Newton's book and that it inspired William Miller to try harmonising all time prophecies of the Bible'.[11]

Amongst Miller's contemporaries the most productive exegete of biblical prophecy was George Stanley Faber; according to Leroy L Froom, he was the most voluminous religious writer of his generation.[12] As Miller's daughter does not elaborate further, it is impossible to determine which of Faber's many works Miller had consulted. Kai Arasola states that "It is likely that it was *Dissertation on the Prophecies* ... distributed in America in 1808."[13] Again, Faber is an historicist.

John Gill was a Baptist scholar who wrote multi-volume commentaries on the Old and New Testaments, which like Faber and Newton's works, followed the historicist method of prophetic interpretation. Miller's *Evidences From Scripture and History of the Second Coming of Christ About the Year 1843* contains a quote from Gill.

All three of these writers rely heavily on the work of Joseph Mede, a British pioneer of Historicism, whose works although written in the seventeenth century, remained in print in the nineteenth. Mede's methodology included three important elements that were utilised by Newton, Faber and Gill, and through their works, by William Miller himself:

1. The use of the year-day principle to interpret prophecy.
2. The consistent and comprehensive relation of historical events to biblical prophecy.
3. The synchronisation of different prophecies into a coherent system.[14]

Miller's Culture

Rationalist thought

It is important to note that Miller developed his system of interpretation to answer specific questions that arose out of his spiritual/philosophical journey. While raised a Baptist, under the influence of rationalist friends with, as Miller puts it, 'their sceptical principles and deistical theories',[15] Miller turned to deism in his

---

11. *Ibid*, 38.
12. Le Roy Edwin Froom, *The Prophetic Faith of Our Fathers Volume III*, 4 volumes (Washington, DC: Review and Herald, 1946), 339.
13. Arasola, *The End of Historicism, op cit*, 40.
14. Anne Freed, "'A Feast of Reason" The Appeal of William Miller's Way of Reading the Bible', *Adventist Heritage: A Magazine of Adventist History*, Volume 16, No. 3 (1995): 16.
15. Bliss, *Memoirs of William Miller, op cit*, 24–25.

early twenties. In 1816, after some years of increasing discomfort with his deistic beliefs, Miller converted to Christianity.[16]

Needing then, to answer the taunts of his deist friends and their accusations about 'blind faith', Miller turned to the Bible, and he turned to the Bible using a particular method. As David Rowe puts it:

> [Miller] searched for an empirical verification for faith, and he found it through hermeneutics... Miller decided that the scriptures themselves held the key to their validity and that by studying the Bible in a scientific way, he could provide evidence of its divine origin.[17]

Miller's elevation of reason was both the legacy of the Enlightenment skeptics that he read as a deist, and a reflection of the dominant philosophy of his time.[18] His hermeneutics were not new, nor were they unique. Miller utilised the methods he did because they offered the best answers to his questions. As Anne Freed states:

> Miller defended his Biblical interpretations by appealing to the rationality of his listeners. His method of prophetic interpretation shared the language and categories of the scientific method during a time when this method seemed to offer direct access to 'facts' or 'truth'.[19]

Miller himself stated that to him, the Bible was a 'feast of reason'[20] and his *Rules of Interpretation* reflect this viewpoint, appealing to the interpreter's use of reason. The foundation of Miller's rules is that any interpretation has to make 'good sense' to the interpreter. This phraseology is found in Miller's rule #10: 'If you put on the right construction, it will harmonise with the Bible and *make good sense*, otherwise it will not.'[21] In his rule #11: If it *makes good sense* as it stands... then it must be understood literally, if not, figuratively.'[22] And in rule #12: 'To learn the true meaning of figures... if it *makes good sense* you need look no further.'[23]

Not only does Miller emphasise a rational approach through the use of this terminology, but even a cursory survey of his rules reveals his emphasis on reason and logic, admittedly tempered with his emphasis on the need for searching in 'faith'.

---

16. Knight, *Search for Identity*, op cit, 39.
17. David L Rowe, *Thunder and Trumpets: Millerites and Dissenting Religion in Upstate New York, 1800–1850* (Chico, CA: Scholars Press, 1985), 10.
18. Malcolm Bull and Keith Lockhart, *Seeking a Sanctuary: Seventh-Day Adventism and the American Dream* (San Francisco, CA: Harper & Row, 1989), 23.
19. Freed, '"A Feast of Reason' The Appeal of William Miller's Way of Reading the Bible', op cit, 14.
20. Miller, *Apology and Defence*, op cit, 12.
21. *Ibid*, Emphasis mine.
22. *Ibid*, 4. Emphasis mine.
23. *Ibid*, 4. Emphasis mine.

After listing his rules, Miller goes on to state,

> These are some of the most important rules which I find the word of God warrants me to adopt and follow, in order for system and regularity. And if I am not greatly deceived, in so doing, *I have found the Bible, as a whole, one of the most simple, plain, and intelligible books ever written.*[24]

The influence of Bible popularism

That Miller's approach reduced a text with thousands of years of history behind it to a simple, plain and easily understood book was one of the strongest appeals of his system. His literalist method gave power to the ordinary person—a key theme in Jacksonian America. James E Miller refers to this literalist approach as,

> a popularist protest against the power of oligarchies seeking to control our lives, and against the traditions that warp the plain meaning of foundation documents. The literalist ideal is direct access to the text. The Bible is not to be interpreted only by church prelates and theologians, but by every layman.[25]

Rowe echoes this when he states that Miller's appeal lay in the fact that,

> Instead of claiming to be a prophet or to have received a new revelation, he explained how each person could discover the 'truth' he had found, thus making the secrets of revelation accessible to any believer. In this regard his views were the religious counterpart of the political antinomianism and popular democracy of the age of the common American.[26]

Not only was this part of Miller's appeal, but it was also part of Miller's personal hermeneutical approach: Miller specifically, 'laid by all commentaries, former views and prepossessions, and determined to read and try to understand for [himself]'.[27] Essentially, he put away (in his mind at least) the experts and relied on his own intelligence and common sense as an ordinary person.

---

24. *Ibid*, 4. Emphasis mine.
25. James E. Miller, 'Review of Vincent Capanzano, *Serving the Word? Literalism in America From the Pulpit to the Bench*', in *Andrews University Seminary Studies* Volume 40, No. 1 (2002): 139–140.
26. David L Rowe, 'Millerites: A Shadow Portrait', in *The Disappointed: Millerism and Millenarianism in the Nineteenth Century*, edited by Ronald L Numbers and Jonathan M Butler (Knoxville, TN: University of Tennessee Press, 1993), 13.
27. See *Miller's Works Volume 1: Views of the Prophecies and Prophetic Chronology, Selected From the Manuscripts of William Miller With a Memoir of his Life*, edited by Joshua V Himes (Boston, MT: 1841), 11.

Miller's biblicism

Millerism was a Bible-centered religion, offering an alternative to deism & universalism. The prophecies demonstrated that not only was there a God, but that God had revealed Himself in the Bible. As Miller stated: 'You must preach *Bible* you must prove all things by *Bible* you must talk B*ible*, you must exhort *Bible*, you must pray *Bible*, and Love *Bible*, and do all in your power to make others Love *Bible* too.'[28] The Millerites even made the claim that 'Millerism equalled biblicism'.[29]

Biblicism may be simply defined as 'the principle that the Bible is to be considered wholly homogenous and that any passage can be used to clarify the significance of any other, irrespective of context'.[30] 'This method—Biblicism . . . was a method of biblical interpretation commonly used by Miller's Protestant contemporaries.'[31] Evidence of this approach is not only found in statements like those already mentioned, but can be found when Miller's *Rules of Interpretation* are themselves examined. Each rule (other than the final) is followed by at least one Bible reference as the 'evidence' of its validity. Most rules have multiple references: rule five has seven texts, rule thirteen, has five. None of the references are explained or expanded; the texts themselves were apparently viewed by Miller as being overwhelming evidence that needed no further comment.

The Impact Of Miller's Methods

Sabbatarian Adventists retained Miller's view of the Bible

Miller's methods of biblical interpretation remained the standard for the early Adventists. In 1854, the following note was published in the April 18 *Advent Review and Sabbath Herald*: 'The following we take from a small work entitled *Wm Miller's Apology and Defense*, published in Boston, 1845. It gives a brief sketch of the experience of this servant of God, and the manner in which he studied the holy Scriptures which will be deeply interesting to many, at least of the readers of the REVIEW.'[32] Following this was the promised extract that outlined Miller's life and hermeneutics.

---

28. William Miller to Truman Hendryx, 26 March 1832. Original emphasis. Original capitalisation of Bible/bible and Love.
29. *Signs of the Times*, 20 May 1846, 117.
30. Ingemar Lindén, *The Last Trump* (Frankfurt: Peter Lang, 1978), 28.
31. Laura L Vance, *Seventh-day Adventism in Crisis: Gender and Sectarian Change in an Emerging Religion* (Chicago, IL: University of Illinois Press, 1999), 15.
32. 'William Miller', in *The Advent Review and Sabbath Herald*, 18 April 1854, 97.

Early Seventh-day Adventists echoed Miller's hermeneutics

In January 1887 JH Waggoner published two articles on his principles of interpretation in the *Signs of the Times*. This list is the first Seventh-day Adventist presentation of hermeneutical principles. In his introduction he stated:

> The Signs of the Times was established to present Scripture truth in the simplest and clearest manner possible ... we wish to lay down for our readers a few of the principles which we shall invariably follow in our interpretation, and which, if followed, in a prayerful and candid spirit, cannot fail to lead a person to a proper understanding of the sacred word.[33]

The principles that Waggoner listed in his two articles included:

1. Scripture must interpret Scripture.
2. There is no book of the Bible upon which light is not shed by every other book.
3. Symbols always have the same meaning, provided the same subject is under consideration.

In an earlier *Advent Review and Sabbath Herald* article, he expressed his support of Miller's method: 'We leave with such the good old rule of Scripture interpretation as follows: "All scripture should be literally interpreted, unless there be good reasons why it should be topically or figuratively understood."'[34]

In 1884 Ellen G White wrote,

> Those who are engaged in proclaiming the third angel's message are searching the Scriptures under the same plan that Father Miller adopted. In the little book entitled 'Views of the Prophecies and Prophetic Chronology,' Father Miller gives the following simple but intelligent and important rules for Bible Study and Interpretation:
> '1. Every word must have its proper bearing on the subject presented in the Bible;
> 2. All scripture is necessary, and may be understood by diligent application and study;
> 3. Nothing revealed in scripture can or will be hid from those who ask in faith, not wavering;
> 4. To understand doctrine, bring all the scriptures together on the

---

33. JH Waggoner, 'A Few Principles of Interpretation', in *Signs of the Times*, 6 January 1887, 8.
34. JH Waggoner, 'Revelation XVIII–XXI', in *The Advent Review and Sabbath Herald*, 5 March 1857, 141.

subject you wish to know, then let every word have its proper influence; and if you can form your theory without contradiction, you cannot be in error;

5. Scripture must be its own expositor, since it is a rule of itself. If I depend on a teacher to expound it to me, and he should guess at its meaning, or desire to have it so on account of his sectarian creed, or to be thought wise, then his guessing, desire, creed, or wisdom is my rule, and not the Bible.'

The above is a portion of these rules; and in our study of the Bible we shall all do well to heed the principles set forth.[35]

Ellen White is a seminal figure in Seventh-day Adventist history with her voluminous writings remaining very influential within the church. White's hermeneutics are particularly important to examine, not because of their originality—essentially she follows Miller's ideas—but because of her prophetic role within the Seventh-day Adventist Church. In her role as a prophet, by repeating Miller's views, White validated them so that they became authoritative for members of the Seventh-day Adventist church.

Adventist hermeneutics and the Modernist/Fundamentalist controversy

During the 1920s and 1930s Seventh-day Adventists supported fundamentalism in upholding the trustworthiness of the Bible in response to the inroads of the higher critics, or 'infidels' as Seventh-day Adventist publications of the time often labeled them. It is important to note that there were no major changes to Seventh-day Adventist hermeneutics at this time. Essentially the church still fought the scientists on their terms: their rationalistic, scientific perspective. The Seventh-day Adventist Church did not spiritualise or allegorise the biblical text, but continued to appeal to historical, scientific and logical evidence to support our case for reading the Bible in this way.

Seventh-day Adventist hermeneutics—the 1950s

The 1954 publication, *Problems in Bible Translation* in a chapter entitled 'Principles of Biblical Interpretation' mentions a number of points that echo Miller's approach 120 years before. Unlike Miller's *Rules of interpretation* however, these points were backed not by Bible verses like Miller's rules, but entirely by quotes from the works of Ellen G White. The points include:

---

35. Ellen G White, 'Notes of Travel', in *The Advent Review and Sabbath Herald*, 25 November 1884, 4.

1. Apply sound principles.
2. Make the Bible its own expositor.
3. Adhere closely to the literal interpretation of Scripture.
4. Give discriminating study to the words of Scripture.[36]

Seventh-day Adventist hermeneutics—the 1970s

The 1974 Bible Conferences and the publication of a collection of resource papers under the title, *A Symposium on Biblical Hermeneutics* again parallels Miller's rules. Gerhard F Hasel's chapter, 'General Principles of Interpretation' contains the following points of interest:

1. The Bible as its own interpreter.
2. An objective interpretation is the interpreter's goal.
3. The literal meaning of words (on which nearly five pages are spent.).
4. The unity of the Bible.[37]

Seventh-day Adventist hermeneutics—the 1980's

Perhaps the most recent—and certainly the most 'official' guidelines for Seventh-day Adventist hermeneutics are found in the document entitled 'Methods of Bible Study', and passed by the Executive Committee of the General Conference in 1986. Among the points listed are:

1. Choose a definite plan of study, avoiding haphazard and aimless approaches.
2. Seek to grasp the simple, most obvious meaning of the biblical passage being studied.
3. Recognise that the Bible is its own interpreter.
4. Recognise that the meaning of words, texts, and passages is best determined by diligently comparing Scripture with Scripture.

Contemporary Seventh-day Adventist hermeneutics

Finally, a look at the chapter entitled 'Biblical interpretation' by Richard M Davidson in the twelfth volume of the Bible Commentary series, *Handbook of Seventh-day Adventist Theology*, is also instructive. Among the points raised by Davidson are the following:

---

36. *Problems in Bible Translation* (Washington DC: Committee on Problems in Bible Translation, 1954), 79–127.
37. Gerhard F Hasel, 'General Principles of Interpretation', in *A Symposium on Biblical Hermeneutics*, edited by Gordon M Hyde (Washington: General Conference of Seventh-day Adventists, 1974), 163–193.

1. 'Scripture is its own interpreter'.
2. The Bible is consistent, without contradiction or misinterpretation.
3. 'The meaning of Scripture is clear and straightforward'.
4. 'The Scriptures are to be taken in their plain, literal sense, unless a clear and obvious figure is intended'.[38]

It is important to state at this point that the above extracts do not by any means exhaust the guidelines of each of the above authors; but give insight into a common thread running from William Miller to the present day.

Conclusions

The influence of rationalist thought on Miller's hermeneutics has not generally been recognised by Seventh-day Adventists. Most seem to simply take Miller's methods for granted without enquiring further into their origins. Others like Richard M Davidson seem to view Seventh-day Adventists as solely 'the hermeneutical heirs of the Reformation,'[39] completely ignoring any effect that nineteenth century American culture exerted on Miller. Another view is that taken by P Gerard Damsteegt in his 1977 book, *Foundations of the Seventh-day Adventist Message and Mission*, where he is content to state, 'In general Miller's hermeneutical principles were a part of the Protestant hermeneutical tradition which can be traced back to the primitive church'.[40] Similarly Don F Neufeld in his essay 'Biblical Interpretation in the Advent Movement' presented at the 1974 Bible Conference, states, 'In general principles the Millerites represented the various churches out of which they came, which usually followed the Protestant hermeneutic'.[41]

Exceptions to this superficial view include Kai Arasola's ground-breaking study entitled *The End of Historicism*, and the work of Malcolm Bull and Keith Lockhart entitled *Seeking a Sanctuary: Seventh-Day Adventism and the American Dream*. Another exception is Arthur Patrick's exploration of Miller's Christology in which he recognises that:

> The era of William Miller was markedly influenced by the rationalism which has either molded or threatened religious attitudes since

---

38. Richard M Davidson, 'Biblical Interpretation', in *Handbook of Seventh-day Adventist Theology* (Hagerstown, MD: Review and Herald, 2000), 58–104.
39. Davidson, 'Biblical Interpretation', *op cit*, 97.
40. P Gerard Damsteegt, *Foundations of the Seventh-day Adventist Message and Mission* (Grand Rapids, MI: Eerdmans, 1977), 16.
41. Don F Neufeld, 'Biblical Interpretation in the Advent Movement', in *A Symposium on Biblical Hermeneutics*, edited by Gordon M Hyde (Washington, DC: General Conference of Seventh-day Adventists, 1974), 117.

the Enlightenment. Miller's Christology had to be formed and stated with an acute consciousness of deism. Further, his letters reveal that his public proclamation was preceded by almost two decades of conflict with universalism. His thought was formed by diligent historical enquiry, and by reformed teaching as expressed by John Calvin.[42]

George R Knight's aptly titled chapter, 'Adventism wasn't Born in a Vacuum', contains an excellent overview of the theological roots of Adventism, and particularly the impact of the restorationist movement; however he covers the influence of deism and rationalism only superficially.[43]

Miller's rules have had a profound effect in shaping how the Seventh-day Adventist Church has approached the biblical text throughout its history, and their underlying rationalistic focus still impacts how many Seventh-day Adventists interpret the biblical text in the twenty-first Century. As Steen Rasmussen states, 'Miller's basic attitude towards the Bible—that to be the word of God it must be wholly clear, consistent, and without contradictions—never changed from his childhood till his death'.[44] It seems to me that this statement still holds true for many Seventh-day Adventists today. Furthermore, I believe that it underlies much of our discomfort with less rational methods like reader response theory, poststructuralism, and the hermeneutics of interest groups like feminism, liberation theology, gay and lesbian readings and others. Miller's approach was a product of his time, both grounded in and responding to, the rationalism of 1800's America. Further, it is essential that this legacy be recognised and understood when methods of biblical interpretation are being debated in Seventh-day Adventist Church today.

Recognition of Miller's heritage does not of course, invalidate his hermeneutical approach. It does, however, remind us that any biblical hermeneutic is inescapably grounded in the culture and times of the interpreter. Miller did not choose a hermeneutical method that was unrelated to his culture and to the dominant philosophical paradigms of his time. Perhaps we should be asking ourselves if we should not do likewise?

---

42. Arthur N Patrick, 'The Christology of William Miller, 1972', Selected Manuscripts, Cooranbong, NSW, 8.
43. Knight, *Search for Identity*, op cit, 29–37.
44. Steen R Rasmussen, 'Roots of the Prophetic Hermeneutic of William Miller' (MA thesis, Andrews University, 1983), 20.

Where Did Satan Come From?

Andrew Skeggs

Introduction
One of the most important parts of appreciating a story is identifying and understanding the main characters, including their origin and background. The key characters in the Christian story are God, Satan, and the human race. The Bible reveals the origin of humanity and teaches us that the eternal God has no origin. But where does Satan come from? This study will examine what the Bible actually tells us about the origin of Satan, namely about his origin, and his fall.

This is a particularly enlightening topic for study because it illustrates the development of theological ideas during the biblical period. It leads us to consider how we read the Old Testament in the light of the New Testament, how the New Testament uses and builds on the Old Testament material, and how the intertestamental period affects the thinking of the New Testament. Furthermore, this will be considered within the context of how Seventh-day Adventists use the writings of Ellen G White with regard to this topic.

First we will consider the significance of Satan to both the New Testament and the Seventh-day Adventist worldviews, and then we will examine the Old Testament and New Testament texts that have been thought to teach the origin of Satan. We will next consider the influence of the intertestamental literature on the New Testament, and then the place that the thoughts of Ellen G White should take in Adventist deliberations. We will finally consider what all this tells us about inspiration and hermeneutics.

The Importance of Satan to the New Testament Worldview
The New Testament is permeated with the apocalyptic worldview that has human beings caught in the middle of a cosmic spiritual battle between God and Satan. Angels and demons fight for their respective side. Satan ('the devil') is the great adversary of God and humankind. He seeks to oppose God, and to seduce and enslave human beings:

> Your enemy the devil prowls around like a roaring lion looking for someone to devour. (1 Pet 5:8)[1]
>
> Put on the full armour of God so that you can take your stand against the devil's schemes. For our struggle is not against flesh and blood, but against the rulers, against the authorities, against the powers of this dark world and against the spiritual forces of evil in the heavenly realms. (Eph 6:11, 12)

Christ personally faces the onslaughts of the Devil (Matt 4:1-11), and a major part of His ministry consists in delivering people from the oppression of demons (Mark 1:32-34). Gregory A Boyd says, 'The reason that the Son of God appeared was to destroy the devil's work' (1 John 3:8).[2]

The Importance of Satan to the Seventh-day Adventist Worldview

Satan clearly plays a very important role in the New Testament worldview and therefore the theological understanding of most Christians. The cosmic conflict between Christ and Satan is of special significance to the Seventh-day Adventist worldview. Since their earliest days Adventists have seen the 'great controversy' between Christ and Satan as a key factor in their understanding of history, salvation, Christian living and eschatology.[3] In Adventist theology, the great controversy finds its origin in the rebellion of Satan:

> Lucifer, a high-ranking being in the angelic world, became proud. Dissatisfied with his position in God's government, he began to covet God's own place. In an attempt to take control of the universe, this fallen angel sowed seeds of discontent among his fellow angels, and won the allegiance of many. The resulting heavenly conflict ended when Lucifer, now known as Satan, the adversary, and his angels were expelled from heaven. Undeterred by his expulsion from heaven, Satan determined to entice others to join his rebellion against God's government. His attention was drawn to the human race . . .[4]

---

1. All Bible references are from the NIV, unless otherwise indicated.
2. Gregory A Boyd, *God At War* (Downers Grove, IL: InterVarsity, 1997), 55, and *passim*.
3. George R Knight, *A Search for Identity: The Development of Seventh-day Adventist Beliefs* (Hagerstown, MD: Review & Herald, 2000), 68–71; Richard Rice, *The Reign of God: An Introduction to Christian Theology from a Seventh-day Adventist Perspective* (Berrien Springs, MI: Andrew University Press, 1985), 128–30; John M Fowler, *The Cosmic Conflict Between Christ and Satan* (Nampa, ID: Pacific, 2001). 'It should be noted that Ellen White . . . integrated a warfare perspective into the problem of evil and the doctrine of God perhaps more thoroughly than anyone else in church history.' Boyd, *God at War, op cit*, 307, n. 44.
4. Ministerial Association, General Conference of Seventh-day Adventists, *Seventh-day Adventists Believe . . .* , (Hagerstown, MD: Review & Herald, 1988), 87. I have removed textual references

Thus Satan, the rebellious angel, is a key figure in the New Testament worldview and has a special significance at the highest levels of Seventh-day Adventist theology. But where did the New Testament position come from, and what biblical evidence is the Adventist position based on?

Satan's Low Profile in the Old Testament

Somewhat surprisingly, given the New Testament's outlook, Satan is rarely mentioned explicitly in the Old Testament. Of course, it is possible to deduce the role of Satan behind the scenes in the Old Testament based on the information of the New Testament. But taking the Old Testament on its own terms, Satan has a very low profile.

When thinking about Satan, Christians readily recall the temptation of Adam and Eve in the Garden of Eden. However, Genesis 3 never identifies the serpent as Satan; this identification is based on the teaching of the New Testament (for example, Rev 12:9). Such an identification does fit with the association of snakes with demons in the Ancient Near East and some of the textual clues about the serpent and his fate.[5] Genesis 3 doesn't explicitly mention Satan, nor tell of his fall.

There is also mention of evil spirits in the Old Testament, and from a New Testament perspective, we would identify them as Satan's demons. But again, there is no explicit mention of Satan in these texts themselves.[6]

Satan is only mentioned by name in the Old Testament in 1 Chronicles 21:1; Job 1-2; and Zechariah 3:1-2. Even here there are significant differences with the New Testament picture of Satan, and many commentators feel that Satan is only used as a proper name in 1 Chronicles, with Job and Zechariah merely picturing an adversary.[7] All three references to Satan are in books written or canonised late in the Old Testament period, a fact that situates them during the fruitful development in angelology and demonology of the exilic and postexilic periods.[8] 'All

---

and subheadings from the quote. *Cf* Frank B Holbrook, 'The Great Controversy', in *Handbook of Seventh-day Adventist Theology*, edited by Raoul Dederen, (Hagerstown, MD: Review & Herald, 2000), 969-1009.

5. Boyd, *God at War, op cit,* 155-57; Richard M Davidson, 'Revelation/Inspiration in the Old Testament: A Critique of Alden Thompson's "Incarnational" Model', in *Issues in Revelation and Inspiration*, edited by Frank Holbrook and Leo Van Dolson (Berrien Springs, MI: Adventist Theological Society, 1992), 117-118.
6. Sydney HT Page, *Powers of Evil: A Biblical Study of Satan and Demons* (Grand Rapids, MI: Baker, 1995), 43-86; Boyd, *God at War, op cit,* 79-83. The figure of Azazel in Leviticus 16 similarly hints of Satan. See Alden Thompson, *Inspiration: Hard Questions, Honest Answers* (Hagerstown, MD: Review & Herald, 1991), 182.
7. Daniel P Fuller, 'Satan', in *International Standard Bible Encyclopedia* (Grand Rapids, MI: Eerdmans, 1988), 4:341.
8. Page, *Powers of Evil, op cit,* 37; Alden Thompson, *Who's Afraid of the Old Testament God?* (Grand

three passages presume some familiarity with the concept of Satan on the part of the original readers, but it is difficult to be sure what was believed about him.'[9]

So Satan is a somewhat shadowy figure in Old Testament thinking. What do we learn about him from explicit Old Testament references? Satan is a supernatural being with access to heaven; an opponent of God and humanity; an accuser, persecutor and tempter (but under God's sovereignty); and is presumably a rebel from the heavenly court.[10] But we are given no details about the actual fall of Satan.

The Fall of Satan in the Old Testament?

The idea that Satan has fallen into sin is a logical deduction from the overall biblical story. The Bible says that God has created a good universe (Gen 1) and that Satan is a rebel and the father of rebellion. (Jn 8:44). It seems likely that there has been a fall of Satan parallel to the fall of man (Gen 3). But does the Bible actually describe such a fall? Since intertestamental times, two Old Testament passages have been thought by many to provide information on Satan's original rebellion: Isaiah 14:12-15 and Ezekiel 28:12-19.

Isaiah 14:12-15 is part of a larger passage that is a taunt song against the king of Babylon (13:1 – 14:23). However, 14:12-15 has striking mythological[11] language that speaks of a being called 'Morning Star, son of the dawn' who has decided to ascend to heaven and be enthroned there and to make himself like the Most High, but who in the end falls from heaven, being cast down to the earth. This is a stark contrast for one who 'once laid low the nations'.

It is easy to see how such a passage has been interpreted as describing the fall of Satan, but such an interpretation raises a number of questions. Isaiah 14:12-15 is a distinct unit within the chapter, but verses 9-11 and verses 16, 17, seem to be part of the same narrative but and use imagery about the underworld that does not fit the Satan story. Nonetheless, are verses 12-15 specifically comparing the arrogance of the king to the arrogance of Satan? Or is the prophet here giving a glimpse of the evil spiritual power behind the evil political power of Babylon?[12]

A careful reading shows that the actual details of the myth of Isaiah 14:12-15 fit the fall of Satan in some ways, but not in others. Aspects that fit Satan are the

---

Rapids, MI: Zondervan, 1989), 48-54. Davidson, 'Revelation/Inspiration', *op cit*, 117, disputes the late date of the Book of Job.

9. Page, *Powers of Evil, op cit*, 37.
10. Alden Thompson speculates that God intentionally keeps Satan's profile low in Old Testament to discourage Israelites worshipping Satan. Thompson, *Who's Afraid?, op cit*, 47-48.
11. 'Mythological' is not used here in the sense of something that is untrue, but in the sense of the language of ancient times to do with the supernatural, whether speaking of real or imaginary events'
12. Holbrook, 'The Great Controversy', *op cit*, 974.

description of a powerful being with access to heaven, who seeks to exalt himself to the place of God, who lays low the nations, and who is cast down out of heaven to earth. But aspects of the myth that don't fit Satan are that the being desires to ascend to heaven rather than starting a rebellion from within heaven where he already dwells), the being lays low the nations before he is cast out of heaven, and his casting down to earth seems to involve his death. Verses 14, 15 picture his ascent to heaven followed by a descent into Sheol, the grave. It seems arbitrary to literalise some aspects of the myth and not others in applying it to Satan.[13]

Which myth is in view in Isaiah 14:12-15? It could be the story of the fall of Satan, but it could be another story/stories. The imagery of Isaiah's passage is found in other Ancient Near Eastern mythology, particularly Ugaritic.[14] There is no one myth that exactly parallels the biblical passage.[15]

It is just as likely that Isaiah is drawing on the imagery of Venus, the morning star,[16] and other mythological imagery of the day as he is drawing on a story of the fall of Satan. Even then, the use imagery gives us no indication about the literalness or historicity of the imagery itself.[17] So we really have no way of knowing what imagery Isaiah is drawing on, nor whether the imagery comes from a real or imaginary event.

It has also been thought that Ezekiel 28:12-19 provides information on the origin of Satan's rebellion. This passage is a mocking lament against the king of Tyre. It uses the imagery of an inhabitant of paradise originally characterised by exceptional beauty, wisdom, and purity until pride leads him into sin and he was expelled from paradise. The being is described as having been a perfect and

---

13. BJ Oropeza, *Ninety-nine Answers to Questions about Angels, Demons and Spiritual Warfare* (Downers Grove, IL: InterVarsity, 1997), 81-82.
14. Jose M Bertoluci, 'The Son of the Morning and The Guardian Cherub in the Context of the Great Controversy Between Good and Evil' (ThD thesis, Andrews University, 1985), 57-97, especially 95-96.
15. *Ibid*, 109; John N Oswalt, *Isaiah 1-39*, New International Commentary on the Old Testament (Grand Rapids, MI: Eerdmans, 1986), 321.
16. Bertoluci, 'Son of the Morning', 198-199. The Vulgate translation of morning star as 'Lucifer' is a poor basis for declaring Satan's pre-fall name. Interestingly, the eighth Fundamental Belief of Seventh-day Adventists, 'The Great Controversy', avoids using Lucifer as a proper name for Satan.
17. The traditional interpretation 'ignores the metaphorical context of both passages, however. The king of Tyre is no more literally the first creature, the cherub of the garden, than Tyre itself is literally a merchant ship in Ezekiel 27 ... In each case, the perfection of the initial state is magnified to hyperbolic proportions in order to underscore the calamity when it comes. This means that just as there was never a literal ship that fit the description of the ship Tyre that actually sank ... so there need not here be reference to an actual perfect creature exactly matching the description of the guardian cherub, who was cast down to earth.' A point strongly supported by Iain Duguid when commenting on Isaiah 14 and Ezekiel 28 in *Ezekiel*, New International Version Application Commentary (Grand Rapids, MI: Zondervan, 1999), 348.

blameless guardian cherub who dwelt on the 'mount of God' and was thrown to the earth. Some interpreters have posited that Ezekiel is either drawing on the story of the fall of Satan to comment on the career of the king of Tyre, or is giving a glimpse of the evil spiritual power behind the political ruler of Tyre.

The imagery of the fall of the perfect being from heaven to earth does fit the story of the fall of Satan in notable ways. However, this method of interpretation takes an arbitrary approach to how the imagery is applied. The perfection of the being, his status as a cherub, his sin of pride and his fall from heaven are all taken literally. The images of Eden, the mount of God, the fiery stones, and presumably the adorning precious stones are all taken symbolically. The sin of dishonest trade clearly fits Tyre and not Satan, although this could be a case where the application intrudes into the myth.

And as in the Isaiah passage, there also seems to be a close link between the casting down of the being and his destruction (verses 17–19), which does not fit the fall of Satan. Once again we must ask what myth(s) the prophet is drawing on. It might or might not be the fall of Satan.

While allowing for extra biblical sources, Daniel Block comments that 'most of the features in the present oracle can be accounted for within the biblical tradition'.[18] On the other hand, Gowan points out that 'most elements from which Ezekiel 28:1–19 was composed appear to have been well known to the people of the Ancient Near East',[19] including shining heroes, gardens of the gods, mountains of the gods, precious stones and cherubs.[20] How can we be dogmatic about which myth(s) Ezekiel is drawing from when the imagery is not specific to any one myth? Ezekiel 28:12–19 seems to be draw on Genesis 1 – 3,[21] and many commentators agree with the Septuagint rendering of the text which associates the fallen hero *with* a cherub rather than *being* a cherub.[22] So to say that Ezekiel is definitely alluding to the story of the fall of Satan is to oversimplify the possible

---

18. Daniel Block, *Ezekiel 25–48*, New International Commentary on the Old Testament (Grand Rapids, MI: Eerdmans, 1998), 120. *Cf* Bertoluci, 'Son of the Morning', *op cit*, 144.
19. Bertoluci, 'Son of the Morning', *op cit*, 129, citing Donald E Gowan, *When Man Becomes God* (Pittsburgh: Pickwick Press, 1975), 88, 90.
20. Bertoluci, 'Son of the Morning', *op cit*, 124–134.
21. See Block, *Ezekiel 25–48, op cit,* 117–118, but note Bertoluci, 'Son of the Morning', *op cit*, 134–139.
22. Leslie C Allen, *Ezekiel 20–48, op cit,* Word Biblical Commentary (Dallas, TX: Word, 1990), 29:90–91; John B Taylor, *Ezekiel,* Tyndale Old Testament Commentaries (Downers Grove, IL: InterVarsity, 1969), 196, 197; Walther Zimmerli, *Ezekiel 2*, translated by JD Martin (Hermeneia; Philadelphia, PA: Fortress, 1983), 85, 86; Walter Eichrodt, *Ezekiel: A Commentary*, translated by C Quin (Philadelphia, PA: Fortress, 1970), 389, 393; Kalman Yaron, 'The Dirge Over the King of Tyre', in *Annual of the Swedish Theological Institute,* 3 (1964):28–31. Block, *Ezekiel 25–48, op cit,* 114–118, and Bertoluci, 'Son of the Morning', *op cit*, 138–139, 262–264, follow the Masoretic reading.

sources of his imagery, and to falsely assume that his use of imagery makes a statement about the historicity of that imagery.

Both Jose Bertoluci (an Adventist scholar) and Gregory Boyd have attempted to interpret Isaiah 14 and Ezekiel 28 from fresh perspectives that still see the passages speaking about Satan, but avoid some of the pitfalls of traditional approaches.[23] Bertoluci points out that both Isaiah 14:4b–21 and Ezekiel 28:12–19 are set in heaven and contain chiasms whose apex is the sin of the cosmic rebel.[24] He also contrasts the pride-filled rebel of Isaiah 14 with the humble servant of Isaiah 53, and detects an eschatological dimension in these and other sections of Isaiah, which he argues takes the relevance of Isaiah 14 into the cosmic zone.[25] He says that the Old Testament has a larger context hinting of rebel angels (Gen 6:1–4; Ps 82; Isa 24:21, 22).[26] He sees a distinction between the (political) prince/ruler of Tyre (Ezek 28:2) and the (spiritual) king of Tyre (Ezek 28:12), and recommends typology as a way of linking historical applications and cosmic applications of the texts in question.[27]

What are we to make of these lines of reasoning? Bertoluci's attempt to distinguish between the prince and the king of Tyre seems to run into problems with other uses of these terms in Ezekiel.[28] His observations do force us to grapple with the significance of the passages in question, in terms of their chiasms and the powerful imagery they employ. However, despite his careful exegesis and the insights of his wider perspectives, Bertoluci makes two fundamental errors in assuming: (1) that because the vivid imagery of the passages is not drawn from a single extra biblical myth, it must be describing the actual history of an cosmic being;[29] and (2) that evidence of eschatological undertones, rebel angels and typology proves that the passages *are* referring to Satan rather than *might be*.

In fact the eschatological dimensions and typological potential of the passages are debatable. So is the tradition of rebel angels in the Old Testament and its relevance to the passages in question. Such the evidence is significant enough to be

---

23. Bertoluci, 'Son of the Morning', *op cit*; Boyd, *God at War, op cit,* 157–164.
24. Bertoluci, 'Son of the Morning', *op cit*, 136–137, 208, 229.
25. *Ibid*, 208–220, 229, 287. *Ibid*, 160–166, also claims the fact that the genre of Isaiah 14 is a *mashal* (14:4b) is significant. *Mashal*, though translated 'taunt,' has the connotation of a poetic comparison or parable, designed to serve as a provocative example to the reader. Bertoluci claims that the passage's use of the Babel/Babylon tradition coupled with the eschatological context of Isaiah 24 means that central figure of the passage is being presented as the ultimate paradigm of pride, arrogance, and evil. However, it seems simpler to see the *mashal* as using the king of Babylon as a negative example. See Oswalt, *Isaiah 1-39, op cit,* 311.
26. Bertoluci, 'Son of the Morning', *op cit*, 98–105, 165, 192, 216.
27. *Ibid*, 248–250, 253–256, 288–293.
28. Ezekiel 17:12; 19:9; 27:33; 28:17; 29:2–3. See the discussion in Block, *Ezekiel 25-48, op cit,*103.
29. Bertoluci, 'Son of the Morning', *op cit*, 187, 192, 197, 214, 277–78, 282, 286. Contrast G Boyd, *God at War, op cit,*158; Duguid, *Ezekiel, op cit,* 348.

thought-provoking, but not powerful enough to be decisive. And the imagery, however vivid, may just be imagery. To be accepted as more, there must be some clear indication in the text that one is employing images drawn from real events. Such an indication is what is lacking in Isaiah 14 and Ezekiel 28.

Boyd is aware of such problems in interpreting the imagery of these passages. He maintains that nothing in the text requires that the prophet's poetic language should be taken literally.[30] He also thinks it most likely that Isaiah and Ezekiel are appropriating aspects of Ancient Near Eastern cosmic combat myths. However, he argues that the Old Testament's general use of the combat myths is intended to show that there is a cosmic rebellion and a cosmic rebel, whose full identity is revealed at the end of the Old Testament period and in the New Testament as Satan. Boyd sees Isaiah 14 and Ezekiel 28 as instructive about the fall of Satan, although he concedes 'we are told virtually nothing about the time and circumstances of this cosmic fall'.[31] He makes a strong case and seems to overstep in only one regard. The combat myth imagery in the Old Testament suggests a cosmic rebellion, but to see in it also a cosmic rebel (that is, Satan) is to risk over-literalising poetic language. We may want to see Isaiah 14 and Ezekiel 28 as proving the existence of Satan, but does not such an approach force us to see Psalm 74:14 or Isaiah 27:1 as proving the actual existence of Leviathan the sea monster?[32] Yet, with this qualification, Boyd's overall approach is the most fruitful and exegetically supportable of any in regard to Satan in the Old Testament.

Tellingly, because of the sort of concerns we have been raising, no modern evangelical commentary on Isaiah or Ezekiel sees Isaiah 14 or Ezekiel 28 as providing information about the fall of Satan.[33] In fact, many of them strongly speak against such an approach.[34] Furthermore, systematic theologies written by evangelicals ignore Ezekiel 28 and at best cautiously use Isaiah 14 in referring to the history of Satan.[35] Even some Adventist writers also show reservations.

---

30. Boyd, *God at War, op cit*, 158.
31. *Ibid*, 157-164; quote from 164.
32. Boyd seems unresolved on this dilemma in his methodology. See his comments on Leviathan in Boyd, *God at War, op cit*, 89, 92.
33. Cf Alec Motyer, *Isaiah*, Tyndale Old Testament Commentaries (Leicester, Eng.: InterVarsity, 1999), 119-120; John DW Watts, *Isaiah 1-33*, Word Biblical Commentary (Waco, TX: Word, 1985), 24:204-212; Oswalt, *Isaiah 1-39, op cit*, 319-323; Taylor, *Ezekiel, op cit*, 196, 197; Allen, *Ezekiel 20-48, op cit*, 89-96; Block, *Ezekiel 25-48, op cit*, 99-121; Douglas Stuart, *Ezekiel*, Communicator's Commentary (Dallas, TX: Word, 1989), 271-274; Duguid, *Ezekiel, op cit*, 344-349; Christopher JH Wright, *The Message of Ezekiel*, The Bible Speaks Today (Leicester, England: InterVarsity, 2001), 244-246.
34. Oswalt, *Isaiah 1-39, op cit*, 320; Allen, *Ezekiel 20-48, op cit*, 95; Block, *Ezekiel 25-48, op cit*, 118-119; Duguid, *Ezekiel, op cit*, 348; Wright, *The Message of Ezekiel, op cit*, 244.
35. Stanley J Grenz, *Theology for the Community of God* (Carlisle, UK: Paternoster, 1994), 292-296; Erickson, *Christian Theology* (Grand Rapids, MI: Baker, 1985), 447-449, 586; Wayne Grudem, *Systematic Theology: An Introduction to Biblical Doctrine* (Grand Rapids, MI: Zondervan, 1994),

Robert McIver states how Ezekiel 28 compares the fall of the king of Tyre to 'the fall of the one who was anointed as the guardian cherub, who was created blameless'. Yet he goes on to mention only 'parallels' between the beauty and pride of the king of Tyre and of 'the angel of light who turned into the devil'.[36] McIver seems to be insinuating a connection between the story of the guardian cherub and the story of Satan, but makes less of it than Adventists traditionally do. Alden Thompson states that 'the original intent of Isaiah 14:12-15 and Ezekiel 28:11-19 was probably not to outline the history of Satan', although he does speculate that perhaps the knowledge of Satan's fall has come down from ancient times into the pagan myths.[37] Thompson believes that God deliberately keeps knowledge of Satan sketchy in OT times to discourage polytheism and encourage monotheism.[38]

To summarise, on the subject of the fall of Satan in the Old Testament, Gregory Boyd offers some good general points, and Alden Thompson offers some plausible though ultimately unprovable suggestions. Yet if the best in evangelical scholarship is saying that the Old Testament has virtually nothing clear to say on the fall of Satan, it is time that all evangelicals, and particularly Adventists, make sure they are listening.

The Fall of Satan in the New Testament?

Turning from the debated texts of the Old Testament, let us consider what the New Testament has to offer on the fall of Satan. There are six texts that should be examined: John 8:44; 1 Timothy 3:6; Luke 10:18; Revelation 12:4, 7-9; and 2 Peter 2:4 (paralleled by Jude 6).

John 8:44 records Jesus saying that the devil was a 'murderer from the beginning . . . a liar and the father of lies'. This states that Satan was the originator of sin from the beginning of human history, and may be pointing to a time even before that. Yet though it shows how ancient Satan's rebellion is, the text does not say much more than that there was a rebellion. Presumably Jesus is drawing on a tradition here, but the question is, which tradition? What Old Testament and/or intertestamental texts does He have in mind?

1 Timothy 3:6 states: '[An overseer] must not be a recent convert, or he may become conceited and fall under the same judgment as the devil.' The last phrase is literally, 'fall into (the) judgment of the devil'. It could mean, 'fall into same type

---

412-415. *Cf* Page, *Powers of Evil, op cit*, 37-42; Oropeza, *Answers,op cit*, 80-88; Stephen F Noll, *Angels of Light, Powers of Darkness: Thinking Biblically About Angels, Satan and Principalities* (Downers Grove, IL: InterVarsity, 1998), 109, 120, 121.
36. Robert K McIver, *Ezekiel: Through Crisis to Glory*, Abundant Life Bible Amplifier Series (Boise, ID: Pacific Press, 1997), 153.
37. Alden Thompson, *Who's Afraid?, op cit*, 57, 58.
38. *Ibid*, 47, 48; *cf* Boyd, *God at War, op cit*, 83.

of judgment the devil experienced', as the NIV translates it, or 'fall into the judgment the devil causes/executes'. If the latter reading is correct, this text is not even talking about the fall of Satan. Most commentators do take the former reading.[39] However, even in this reading the judgment in question may be Christ's victory over Satan, realised through His life, death and resurrection and consummated at the end of time.[40] The text does seem to indicate that whenever it is conceptualised in time, Satan's judgment is as a result of pride. Of course, pride is a key theme in Isaiah 14 and Ezekiel 28. If there is a link, to what degree should 1 Timothy 3:6 determine our reading of the Old Testament texts? We will return to this issue in due course.

Luke 10:18 records Jesus saying, 'I saw Satan fall like lightning from heaven'. When is this fall? Although there could be an allusion to Isaiah 14 here,[41] the context of the success of the mission of the seventy-two disciples is determinative for the focus of the text. Jesus is declaring that the anticipated future defeat of Satan is already being realised in the work of his disciples, who exclaim, 'even the demons submit to us in your name' (Luke 10:17). It seems unlikely Luke 10:17 refers to Satan's original rebellion.[42]

The great vision of war in heaven found in Revelation 12:7–9 has been thought to refer to Satan's original rebellion and casting down to earth. To interpret the text this way, one must argue that verses 7–12 constitute a flashback that disrupts the chronological flow of the vision, in an attempt to explain the prehistory of Satan's war against the church. However, there are good exegetical reasons to read verses 7–12 as the heavenly counterpart to Christ's victory over the Devil in his death and resurrection (verses 5, 6). First, Satan persecutes the church (1) after he has been cast down and (2) after the birth of Jesus (verse 7). The failure of his attack on the Christ child results in his being cast down to earth and in his attack on the church. In other words, 'the dragon's [that is, Satan's] failure to destroy the Christ child seems to be equated with its defeat in the heavenly warfare of verses 7–9'.[43] Second, Satan's activities in verse 13 follow directly on from verse 9.[44] Third, verse 10 lists what is achieved at the casting down of Satan: salvation,

---

39. See the discussion in William D Mounce, *Pastoral Epistles*, Word Biblical Commentary (Nashville, TN: Thomas Nelson, 2000), op cit, 46:180–182; cf Oropeza, *Answers*, 86.
40. Gordon D Fee, *1 and 2 Timothy, Titus*, New International Bible Commentary (Peabody, MA: Hendrickson, 1988), 83.
41. Joel B Green, *Luke*, New International Commentary on the New Testament (Grand Rapids, MI: Eerdmans, 1997), 418.
42. *Ibid*, 418, 419; John Nolland, *Luke 9:21–18:34*, Word Biblical Commentary (Dallas, TX: Word, 1993), 35a:563–564; Page, *Powers of Evil, op cit*, 109, 111.
43. William Johnsson, 'The Saints End-Time Victory Over the Forces of Evil', in *Symposium on Revelation, Book II*, edited by Frank B Holbrook (Silver Spring, MD: Biblical Research Institute, General Conference of Seventh-day Adventists, 1992), 19.
44. Verses. 10–12 are simply an interlude commenting on the impact of the events in vs. 9.

power, God's kingdom, and the authority of Christ—all things that are achieved at the cross. Most evangelical commentators today therefore take the war in heaven in Revelation 12 as a picture of Christ's defeat of Satan at the cross.[45] Interestingly, so do many Adventist interpreters, including the Adventist Bible Commentary, Roy Naden, Jon Paulien, Hans K LaRondelle, William Johnsson, and Ranko Stefanovic.[46]

If it is doubtful that Revelation 12:7–9 refers to Satan's original fall from heaven, what about Revelation 12:4? That the Dragon's tail 'swept a third of the stars out of the sky and flung them to the earth' has been interpreted as a reference to the original fall of the angels who follow Satan.[47] Although Satan might be said to have 'dragged' the fallen angels down with him, the actual expulsion from heaven is presumably executed by God. However, the text pictures the dragon sweeping the 'stars' from heaven before he himself is 'cast down'. We may be stretching the details of the imagery too far here, but there are other considerations that muddy the waters. Some commentators read the image of the falling stars as a symbol of the dragon's power to create a cosmic catastrophe,[48] and/or as building on Daniel 8:10 to symbolise persecution of God's people.[49] Other commentators do see a place for the stars as fallen angels, particularly in the light of intertestamental literature.[50] If Revelation 12:4 is referring to the primordial fall of Satan, it doesn't do so clearly, and the basis is in intertestamental rather than Old Testament literature.

The influence of the intertestamental period can also be seen in our last New Testament texts: 2 Peter 2:4 and its parallel in Jude 6. 2 Peter 2:4 says: 'God did not spare angels when they sinned, but sent them to hell, putting them into gloomy dungeons to be held for judgment.' Jude 6 says: 'And the angels who did not keep their positions of authority but abandoned their own home—these he has kept

---

45. Robert H Mounce, *Revelation*, New International Commentary on the New Testament, revised edition (Grand Rapids, MI: Eerdmans, 1998), 235; GK Beale, *Revelation*, New International Greek Testament Commentary (Grand Rapids, MI: Eerdmans, 1999), 650, 658–661; Craig S Keener, *Revelation*, New International Version Application Commentary (Grand Rapids, MI: Zondervan, 2000), 321; Alan F Johnson, 'Revelation', in *The Expositor's Bible Commentary* (Grand Rapids, MI: Zondervan, 1981), 12:516; Richard Bauckham, *The Climax of Prophecy* (Edinburgh: T&T Clark, 1993), 186.
46. *The SDA Bible Commentary*, second edition, edited by FD Nichol (Washington, DC: Review & Herald, 1980), 7:809–10; Roy C. Naden, *The Lamb Among the Beasts* (Hagerstown, MD: Review & Herald, 1996), 187; Jon Paulien, 'Revelation', in *The Bible Explorer Cassette Series* (Harrisburg, PA: TAG, 1996, 5 volumes.); Hans K LaRondelle, *Light for the Last Days* (Nampa, ID: Pacific, 1999), 65; Johnsson, 'The Saints', op cit, 19; Ranko Stefanovic, *Revelation of Jesus Christ* (Berrien Springs, MI: Andrews Univ Press, 2002), 387–388.
47. Stefanovic, *Revelation, op cit*, 382.
48. Johnsson, 'The Saints', *op cit*, 515; Mounce, *Revelation, op cit*, 233.
49. Beale, *Revelation,op cit*, 635-637, sees a secondary application to angels.
50. David Aune, *Revelation 6-16*, Word Biblical Commentary (Nashville, TN: Thomas Nelson, 1998), 52b:686; Keener, *Revelation, op cit*, 317.

in darkness, bound with everlasting chains for judgment on the great Day.' These are illustrations used by the writers to show how God judges the unrighteous. The illustrations are drawn from *1 Enoch* and its intertestamental stories about rebel angels; stories that in turn were elaborations of Genesis 6:1–4.[51] Does the use of these stories as illustrations mean that we must assume the writers are necessarily endorsing the reality of the stories themselves? The details of such texts are different from those of the story of the fall of Satan and his angels; the angels of *1 Enoch* are not banished to earth and free to tempt mankind, but imprisoned in gloomy dark dungeons awaiting judgment day.

So the New Testament texts thought to refer to the primordial fall of Satan are in two categories: (1) texts that do not actually refer to the original fall; and (2) texts that give us the barest of information, are somewhat debatable, and are to varying degrees influenced by intertestamental thinking. We will briefly consider this last factor further.

The Influence of Intertestamental Literature on the New Testament

The Christian Bible consists of the Old and New Testaments, whose witness Christians combine into an integrated whole. We therefore do not always consider the differences between the testaments and how much these differences have to do with the developments of the intertestamental period. This fact is particularly significant in relation to the topic of the origin of Satan:

> Many NT readers are unaware of doctrinal developments that may be traced to Jewish sources other than the OT. Yet a cursory reading of the NT demonstrates that certain ideas and assumptions about reality do not stem directly from the OT but are mediated by the literature between the Testaments. One such area is angelology, the branch of theology having to do with angels and demons.[52]

Such doctrinal and philosophical developments are not necessarily an unwarranted departure from the Old Testament foundation. Whatever external influences one allows for, the apocalyptic worldview and the demonology that go with it has its roots and its earliest examples in the Old Testament.[53] However, the in-

---

51. Richard J Bauckham, *Jude, 2 Peter*, Word Biblical Commentary (Waco, TX: Word, 1983), 50:51–53, 248–49.
52. Larry R Helyer, *Exploring Jewish Literature of the Second Temple Period: A Guide for New Testament Students* (Downers Grove, IL: InterVarsity, 2002), 68–69.
53. Fuller, 'Satan', *op cit*, 341, 342; John N Oswalt, 'Recent Studies in Old Testament Apocalyptic', in *The Face of Old Testament Studies*, edited by DW Baker and BT Arnold (Grand Rapids, MI: Baker, 1999), *op cit*, 374–90; Boyd, *God At War*, *op cit*, 172–176. *Cf* Helyer, *Exploring Jewish Literature, op cit*, 501.

tertestamental developments go beyond the Old Testament to such a significant degree that to ignore them is to lose a critical component for understanding the New Testament worldview.[54] Theologians cannot proceed as if the New Testament worldview is based on biblical revelation alone; they must take the intertestamental influences into account.

However, the fact remains that as we try to put together a biblical picture of the fall of Satan, the intertestamental factor leads to some thorny hermeneutical issues. First, how do we read the Old Testament in the light of the New Testament's adoption of some intertestamental ideas? For example, if an intertestamental tradition of fallen angels affected how New Testament writers read Isaiah 14 and Ezekiel 28, how obliged are we to follow that tradition in our reading of the texts? How much should 1 Timothy 3:6 affect our understanding of Isaiah 14 and Ezekiel 28, particularly if intertestamental thinking could be a big factor behind 1 Timothy 3:6 anyway? How do we understand New Testament demonological concepts that have some Old Testament base, but are heavily indebted to intertestamental thinking? How are we to interpret Revelation 12:4 in the light of its strong intertestamental parallels? What place do we give the illustrations in 2 Peter 2:4 and Jude 6 in our considerations?

This is not to suggest that an inspired text cannot make use of uninspired material or draw on the cultural thinking of its time and still be inspired; it can! However, we need to analyse carefully how inspiration is working in such instances, and how that knowledge affects our interpretation.

What About Ellen White's Views on the Fall of Satan?

There is one more factor in this theological equation that we need to address before attempting a solution. Adventists believe Ellen White wrote under inspiration, and she has written extensive narratives on the fall of Satan.[55] These narratives match up with the traditional picture of the fall, extending back to the Church Fathers and in line with such works as John Milton's *'Paradise Lost'*. Ellen White's views raise two issues in the light of the present study: (1) The biblical basis for her views are readings of Isaiah 14 and Ezekiel 28 that see both passages as referring to the fall of Satan, and (2) Some of her narrative detail goes beyond what is found in these or any other Bible passages.

So does a belief in Ellen White's inspired gift mean that we are bound to affirm her exegetical positions and extra biblical details? The Adventist Church has

---

54. Boyd, *God at War, op cit,* 176; Elaine Pagels, *The Origin of Satan* (London: Penguin, 1995), 35–62.
55. Ellen G White, *Patriarchs and Prophets* (Mountain View, CA: Pacific, 1890), 33–43; White, *The Great Controversy Between Christ and Satan* (Mountain View, CA: Pacific, 1911), 492–504.

been wrestling with such issues since Ellen White's day, and in earnest since the 1970's.[56] Adventists say Ellen White's gift means her writings are 'authoritative', but insist the Bible is 'the final authority in all matters of doctrine and practice'.[57] This insistence lines up with Ellen White's own views on the relation of her gift to the Bible.[58] If Adventists adhere to *sola Scriptura*, says Adventist scholar Richard Rice, 'they will not treat Ellen White as the infallible interpreter of the Bible'.[59] Nevertheless, in practice, Adventists find it difficult to disagree with Ellen White and still uphold her inspiration.

But perhaps a better understanding of how inspiration works can help here. Adventists believe in thought-inspiration; that is, they believe that God inspires the thoughts of a writer who then expresses them in his/her own words.[60] What if God has inspired the thoughts of Ellen White regarding the general outline of the great controversy story, but and Ellen White has then filled in the details? We should then approach her as we would a historical novelist, confident in the basic historicity of the narrative, but not bound to agree with all the detail.

In such a model, Ellen White's general picture of the fall of Satan becomes a plausible reconstruction of events, but we are not bound to agree with her biblical interpretations or to affirm all the details of her narratives.[61]

The Fall of Satan, the Bible, Inspiration, and Hermeneutics

It is extremely difficult to be a Christian and not believe in the fall of Satan. The affirmations of Jesus, the New Testament, and the general biblical picture mean that to believe in Jesus is usually also to believe in the New Testament picture of a

---

56. Arthur N Patrick, 'Does Our Past Embarrass Us?', in *Ministry*, 64 (April 1991): 7–10.
57. From the statement 'The Inspiration and Authority of the Ellen G. White Writings: Affirmations and Denials', prepared by an ad hoc committee of the General Conference of Seventh-day Adventists in 1982 and published in *Adventist Review*, 15 July 1982: 659; *cf* 'Fundamental Beliefs of Seventh-day Adventists', No.1 and No. 7.
58. See the compendium of her statements in George R Knight, *Reading Ellen White: How to Understand and Apply Her Writings* (Hagerstown, MD: Review & Herald, 1997), 21–29.
59. Richard Rice, *The Reign of God: An Introduction to Christian Theology from a Seventh-day Adventist Perspective* (Berrien Springs, MI: Andrew University Press, 1985), 201; *cf* Fritz Guy, *Thinking Theologically: Adventist Christianity and the Interpretation of Faith* (Berrien Springs, MI: Andrews University Press, 1999), 122–126.
60. '*Seventh-day Adventists Believe . . .*', *op cit*, 8–9; William Johnsson, 'How Does God Speak?', in *Ministry*, 54 (October 1981): 4–6.
61. Some useful resources in understanding the role of Ellen White in Adventist theology include Donald R McAdams, 'The Scope of Ellen G White's Authority', in *Spectrum*, 16 (August 1985): 2–7; Herold Weiss, 'Formative Authority, Yes; Canonisation, No', in *Spectrum*, 16 (August 1985): 8–13; Walter M Booth, 'Ellen White, Theologian?', in *Ministry* 73 (October 2000): 5–7; and Knight, *Search for Identity*, *op cit*.

fallen rebellious angel called Satan. Yet the actual biblical information about the fall of Satan needs to be handled carefully.

The Old Testament evidences a developing understanding of the role of Satan.[62] The only Old Testament texts that can be seen as about Satan's fall must be re-examined. One cannot be certain either about the origins of the mythological imagery of Isaiah 14 and Ezekiel 28, or confident that it is drawn from real events rather than imaginary ones. The arbitrary nature of literal and symbolic applications of the imagery to Satan further weakens such an approach. The Old Testament teaches that there are cosmic forces opposed to God, and moves toward centering them in a rebel being called Satan, but it seems very uncertain that the Old Testament contains a description of Satan's rebellion.

The New Testament has a much more developed view of Satan, but contains only the barest of information about his fall. Luke 10:18 and Rev 12:7-9 do not seem to be referring to the original fall of Satan. 2 Pet 2:4 and Jude 6 refer to fallen angels as illustrations, but their sources are intertestamental works. It seems better to affirm the main point the biblical writers are making, while not necessarily also being compelled to affirm the logic or historicity of their illustrations. 1 Timothy 3:6 is instructive regarding the fall of Satan, but raises the issue of how to what degree we are bound to exegete the Old Testament as the New Testament does, particularly when the Old Testament reference may be an illustration to a larger point, and when intertestamental thinking may play a factor. John 8:44 and possibly Revelation 12:4 speak of the rebellion of Satan, but not with much detail and again we must wonder how much they draw on intertestamental thinking.

It appears, then, that one of the most significant events in the history of the universe, the fall of Satan, receives scant attention in the Word of God. Although there are key moments in salvation history when God, Christ, the Spirit, creation, and salvation are revealed to human beings, there is no revelation of Satan, or of the fall of Satan. Satan appears in the biblical narratives with an assumed history that is only alluded to in passing. Some of this history, although rooted in the Old Testament, appears to be substantially based on the ideas and influence of the non-canonical intertestamental literature. The fact that the New Testament takes on board such ideas is both reassuring and perplexing: reassuring: as the New Testament as an inspired source can affirm the ideas developed in uninspired sources; but perplexing, because the New Testament seems to do so in unreflective ways, raising hermeneutical questions. We end up affirming some of the ways the New Testament uses the intertestamental literature, but not others.

Such dynamics lead Richard Rice to call biblical interpreters to distinguish between beliefs that are essential to the biblical message and those that are as-

---

62. Bernard McGinn, *Antichrist: Two Thousand Years of the Human Fascination with Evil* (San Francisco: Harper, 1994), 22–26; Boyd, *God at War, op cit,* 83.

sumed unconsciously by the Bible writers as 'part of the intellectual atmosphere of ancient times', 'the intellectual apparatus ... of their cultural heritage'.[63] Such a realisation will result in a more nuanced understanding of what the Bible teaches, including on the history of Satan. In the same vein, it is time that Seventh-day Adventists seriously considered more nuanced presentations of Bible teaching on the fall of Satan in their Bible studies, evangelistic materials, and works of popular theology.

When we look at the way the Bible deals with the fall of Satan we are led to some interesting conclusions about how inspiration works. Inspiration can leave some crucial details about the supernatural world and salvation history on the periphery of its focus, encompass theological development, and take on board a good deal of uninspired human thinking about essential theological topics, all seemingly without much reflection by the human writers. A good hermeneutical method needs to be aware of these dynamics, and while searching for a biblical theology, be sensitive to intertestamental factors and reflect on their significance. We need to be aware of the human and the temporal while listening for the divine and the eternal. Such awareness makes biblical interpretation more complicated, but doesn't lessen our appreciation of biblical inspiration, because a proper understanding of thought-inspiration acknowledges that the Bible has a human side, using the words of men to express the word of God.

---

63. Richard Rice, *Reason and the Contours of Faith* (Riverside, CA: La Sierra University Press, 1991), 83–84.

Historicism in the Twenty-First Century

Donna Worley

Introduction

Adventism at the beginning of the twenty-first century is being challenged by an increasing diversity in apocalyptic prophetic interpretation.[1] For over a hundred years there was little variation in the standard Adventist interpretation of Daniel and Revelation, but that started changing around fifty years ago.[2]

On one hand, the danger is expressed by denominational scholars and leaders by noting that counter-reformation approaches are 'knocking at the Adventist door' in the form of preterism and futurism.[3] On the other hand, there is a wide range of responses from those who are uncomfortable with historicism or at least some aspects of it. Historicism is downplayed by classifying it as one of the four major approaches that make a contribution to apocalyptic interpretation but are inadequate alone and worthy of criticism.[4] Furthermore, thousands are ignoring prophecy or are losing interest in it, and many thousands of new members have 'only the barest knowledge' of prophetic interpretation.[5]

---

1. The diversity has been indicated by numerous articles and books published in the last twenty-five years. However, prophetic interpretation issues are minimal and/or different in many world regions.
2. Biblical Research Institute [BRI], 'Ellen G White and the Interpretation of Daniel and Revelation' (online article) http://biblicalresearch.gc.adventist.org/documents/WhiteInterDaniel&Rev.htm, 2001). For an overview of how Adventist doctrinal positions have developed and changed, see Chapter IV in a dissertation by Rolf J Pohler, *Change in Seventh-day Adventist Theology: A Study of the Problem of Doctrinal Development* (Andrews University, 1995), 147–305.
3. Gerhard F Hasel, 'Crossroads in Prophetic Interpretation: Historicism versus Futurism, Part 1' (paper presented to the 1990 World Ministers' Council, 3 July 1990, in Indianapolis, Indiana, online: (http://www.e-historicist.com/GFHasel/gfhcrossroads1.html).Other references include the BRI article cited above.
4. Ranko Stefanovic, *Revelation of Jesus Christ: Commentary on the Book of Revelation* (Berrien Springs, MI: Andrews University Press, 2002), 9–12. Stefanovic commends exegesis. Some expositors recognise problems with certain historicist interpretations but do not feel limited by them. For example, Hans K LaRondelle in *How to Understand the End-Time Prophecies of the Bible* (Sarasota, FL: First Impressions, 1997) tends to focus on the text, sometimes affirming the historicist approach and other times interpreting beyond it.
5. Alden Thompson, 'Daniel 9: Putting the Focus on Jesus', in *Spectrum*, 29 (April 2002). Thomp-

Diversity of belief arises from a complex intermix of factors present in our world. It can be driven by philosophical and sociological change as the prevailing worldview moves from modern to post-modern and beyond, and as the world becomes a global village. Even the exploding changes in knowledge, communications, transportation, media, and tech-nology which impact political, economic, and religious realities contribute to the diversity in regards to interpretation. Truly, our world today is vastly different from the world of the early church, the reformers, or the pioneers of the Adventist Church.

The impact of challenge and diversity is not necessarily negative.[6] In fact, it is a normal part of life and a requisite to progress and change. Diversity has been present throughout interpretation history and is inevitable in the process of arriving at an understanding of prophecy. Yet, the current diversity and disinterest in prophetic interpretation are significant developments for the church because, even though there has never been unanimity in the interpretation of minor prophetic details, there has usually been substantial agreement on major details and approach whenever a fulfillment was forthcoming. Even more significant is the way they strike at the heart of Adventist identity and mission.[7] Founded and shaped by a historicist-driven apocalyptic movement, Adventism has much to lose by rejecting, ignoring or abandoning its unique understanding of apocalyptic prophecy.

The current challenge is important for many other reasons. First of all, truth is valuable for truth's sake; who really wants to believe error when destiny is at stake![8] Contrary to the postmodern climate, logic reminds Adventists that there is only one possible scenario for the destiny of the world and its peoples. And when inspired Scripture is the one dependable and primary source for truth, they tend to expect a large degree of harmony among those who base their hermeneutics and interpretations on it. When serious disagreements arise, some of the solutions may compromise biblical truth. Besides, the mission that was understood by the pioneers of the Adventist Church, to prepare the world for the Second Coming, has not yet been completed, and if the Adventist Church is unable to 'give the trumpet a certain sound' it may not be heard at all. But most importantly, 'historicism—though sometimes marred by diverse, sensational, speculative, and

---

son's remarks are made in specific reference to the prophecies of Daniel 8 and 9.
6. Pohler, *Change, op cit,* 440, stresses the importance of balance by quoting David Thiele in 'Is Conservatism a Heresy?', in *Spectrum,* 23 (1994): 14. Thiele likens the struggle for balance to a ship's keel and sail.
7. Pohler states that challenges in Adventism usually involve identity, theology and authority issues, *Change, op cit,* 2–3.
8. James Sire defends truth for our post-modern world by using philosophy as a tool to support the claims of Christianity in his book *Why Shouldn't I Believe Anything at All* (Downers Grove, IL: InterVarsity Press, 1994).

contradictory approaches—appears as the most valid hermeneutical approach to the biblical apocalypses'.[9]

This essay is not intended to fully address the current diversity and disinterest in prophecy or what the future holds for historicism in the new century. However, a look at the past helps explain the present and define the future because history is like a 'seamless garment,' 'a continuous stream of events within the framework of time and space'.[10] And, the 'present-day problems of the church are often illuminated by study of the past because patterns or parallels exist in history'.[11] As one Adventist put it, 'Too often we fail to forget the ups and downs of the past . . . [and] this failure to perceive the nature and extent of historical development of faith, doctrine, and practice in the Seventh-Day Adventist Church has caused a chasm of misunderstanding between the faith of many Adventists and the realities of their heritage.'[12]

Therefore, this essay will briefly discuss thoughts generated by an informal examination of historicism's history in four perspectives: progressive revelation, the origin and nature of historicism, comparison of interpretations, and the pattern of transitions. It is designed to propose preliminary concepts relating to aspects of diversity and to the future of historicism, as well as suggest ways of revitalising historicism to be a relevant voice in the 21st Century. Although it does not explain the complex interrelationship of dynamic factors typical of historical research, the study does support the premise that a better understanding a changing historicism can provide some guidance for our times as we work and wait for the soon return of Jesus.

Perspectives from History

Historicism is one of the four main Bible-based approaches for interpreting apocalyptic prophecy.[13] All have roots going back around 2,000 years, but historicism

---

9. William Johnsson, 'Biblical Apocalyptic', in *Handbook of Seventh-day Adventist Theology*, Commentary Reference Series 12, edited by Raoul Dederen (Hagerstown, MD: Review & Herald, 2002), 797. Gerhard Hasel states that, although all four schools have weaknesses, historicism has fewer difficulties and is the 'most adequate of all major current interpretations', Gerhard F Hasel in 'Interpretations of the Chronology of the Seventy Weeks', in *Seventy Weeks, Leviticus, and the Nature of Prophecy*, Daniel and Revelation Committee Series 3, edited by FB Holbrook (Washington DC: Biblical Research Institute, 1986), 63.
10. A term and concept of Maitland described by Earle E. Cairns in *Christianity Through the Centuries*, third edition (Grand Rapids, MI: Zondervan Publishing House, 1996), 24.
11. Cairns, *Christianity, op cit,* 21.
12. Arthur N Patrick, 'Does Our Past Embarrass Us?', in *Ministry* (April 1991): 8.
13. Preterism focuses on the literal details of a prophet's context and places the fulfillments in the past up to around 400 AD. Futurism interprets prophecy very literally, but places the majority of prophetic events in a seven-year period in the future. Idealism emphasises the spiritual meaning

is apparently the original.[14] Of these approaches, preterism and futurism are most commonly held within Christianity today, but there is wide variation among their proponents.

The historicist approach sees apocalyptic prophecy as a continuous and progressively unfolding outline of the struggle for control over the world from the prophet's time until God's victory is complete. It recognises that history is one of God's avenues of disclosure. Historicist interpreters have generally sought to be faithful to the principles and content found in the Scriptures, as they understood them, and as they searched for meaning in history contemporary to them. Historicism weds prophecy and history in such a way that it may be the only approach that truly 'respects the historical intention of the biblical author', even though historicist interpreters have 'often overlooked the reality of the biblical text' in their attempt to corroborate prophecy with history.[15] The current trend is emphasising the pre-eminence of the text in relationship to history.[16]

Progressive Revelation

Progressive revelation provides a backdrop for interpreting apocalyptic. Perhaps it is the most foundational, yet dynamic and challenging hermeneutic principle for historicism. Progressive or cumulative[17] revelation does not mean the *discovery* of truth but its *revealing* by God according to His timetable, and the *understanding* by His people as they become prepared to receive more light.[18] Further, because 'prophecy has been progressively understood just as fast as history has fulfilled it, step by step, down through the passing centuries',[19] we have come to expect improved understanding as history gradually unfolds and fulfillments take place.

Several other aspects of progressive revelation are important to comprehend. God initiates His revelation by always speaking 'to people in terms appropriate to their own time, place, and circumstances'.[20] God provides only that information He sees people need and can bear, 'never expecting them to grasp more than

---

of the prophecies, so is not concerned with literal details rooted in history.
14. Jacques B Doukhan, *Daniel: The Vision of the End*, revised edition (Berrien Springs, MI: Andrews University Press 1989), 8.
15. *Ibid, Daniel*, 8.
16. See also Jon Paulien, *What the Bible Says About the Endtime* (Hagerstown, MD: Review and Herald Pub, 1998), 111, and Stefanovic, *Revelation of Jesus Christ, op cit*, 12.
17. Clark H Pinnock, *Biblical Revelation: The Foundation of Christian Theology* (Phillipsburg, NJ: Presbyterian & Reformed, 1971), 214.
18. LeRoy Edwin Froom, *The Prophetic Faith of Our Fathers* (Washington, DC: Hagerstown MD: Review & Herald, 1978), 4 volumses; *Ibid*, 1:161, quotes Samuel A Cartledge, *A Conservative Introduction to the Old Testament* (Grand Rapids, MI: Zondervan, 1943), 110.
19. Froom, *Prophetic Faith*, 1:15.
20. Paulien, *Endtime*, 34.

is genuinely possible at any stage.'[21] He discloses when His eternal omniscience requires it, and adds to people's understanding by giving later revelations to provide an ever clearer picture.[22] The ambiguity found in biblical apocalyptic is Divinely intended and its understanding is divinely superintended. Moreover, because the possibility of misinterpreting any passage of Scripture is always present, 'God has placed within the Bible as a whole the capacity for self-correction of understanding.'[23]

Benefits and challenges accompany the principle of progressive revelation. Scripture is one of God's means of speaking to all people of all times, even though it was written from the perspective of the writer's context of time, place and worldview. But how can a generation hundreds of years removed from the original context interpret the apocalyptic prophecies accurately? We recognise that no two generations' perspectives are exactly the same because they do not live in exactly the same context. Moreover, the challenge becomes greater as the distance between the contexts of the writer and interpreter increases. A gap presupposes a degree of misunderstanding, subjectivity, and consequent misinterpretation. But interpreters sometimes find it impossible to comprehend or accept a previous generation's explanation of the future even when they acknowledge that no generation can be expected to understand clearly those details beyond their time and place or the Holy Spirit's disclosure.

However, God is not limited by clashing interpretations, but rather weaves all human limitations and misconceptions into His omniscient plan. History is replete with examples of those with misinterpretations and human weaknesses through which God has worked to achieve His will. One interesting example is the mystic Joachim of Floris (twelfth century) whose contribution 'lay more in the forces he set in motion' than in accurate understanding.[24] He is credited with rescuing historicism from a millennium of a Trichonian allegorical hermeneutic, but his voluminous writings were laced with errors and he frequently developed the biblical text in a fanciful way. Joachim also paved the way for the year-day principle even though he believed the 1260 day-years were soon to be fulfilled, and, he contributed to the concept of progressive revelation in spite of his elaborate charts and forced timeframes. Even the longing for spiritual renewal that motivated his study of the Scriptures, and was expressed in his life and writings, was motivated by a love for the church and its pope that were labeled 'antichrist' within three years of his death.

---

21. *Ibid*, 58.
22. *Ibid*, 57.
23. *Ibid*, 57.
24. Froom, *Prophetic Faith, op cit,* 1:903. A discussion of Joachim is found in Ibid., 1:683-716.

Ellen White provided an inspired perspective when she advised students of prophecy against criticising earlier witnesses:

> These men were God's noblemen, his living agencies, through whom he wrought in a wonderful manner. They were depositaries of divine truth to the extent that the Lord saw fit to reveal the truth that the world could bear to hear . . . I could wish that the curtain could be rolled back, and that those who have not spiritual eyesight might see these men as they appear in the sight of God . . . Living down in our own generation, we may not pronounce judgment upon the men whom God raised up to do a special work, according to the light given to them in their day.[25]

It is essential to remember that security and assurance in progressive revelation come from God who is sovereign and omniscient. He knows the future, and how to guide history and interpretation to fulfill His plan in a way that fully represents His character of love and justice. He appears to be less concerned about the potential dangers of mistakes and misunderstandings than we are. To accomplish His purposes, God speaks in the 'language' of the world's needs. Truth comes when truth is needed; prophecy 'shines more and more' unto the day of His intended fulfillment (Proverbs 4:18, 2 Peter 1:19). God warns in anticipation of fulfillment, then convicts that a fulfillment is taking place, and finally confirms that it has taken place.

With this backdrop in mind, we will now focus on a few selected details and conditions in three areas of historicism's development: (1) varying perceptions of the origin, concept and nature of historicism; (2) contrasting interpretations relating to historicist principles, methods, and interpretations; and (3) the pattern of events and conditions that characterises the transition process of prophetic interpretation.

Concept and Nature of Historicism

How people respond to historicism's difficulties is affected by what they believe historicism is. Progressive revelation suggests that the understanding of historicism's nature and its methods would change over time, but some changes have been a result of careless or faulty use. To begin with, the term 'historicism' has not been used in a consistent manner, even though clarity of terms is important for reliable interpretation. Like 'philosophy', historicism can be used in two major

---

25. *Ibid*, 4:1149, quotes Ellen White, 'Exposing of the Brethren's Mistakes Reproved', in *Review and Herald*, 30 November 1897: 753; (See his footnote nos 66, 67).

ways: as a tool or method, and as the content that results from its use. In practice, the term has been variously used to refer to a set of principles, a method, a school of interpretation, an approach, as well as the content of interpretation, but each reference has a different connotation.

For example, we might ask if historicism is a set of principles, a method or content. These words are not equivalent, though often used interchangeably. *Content* continues to be posited, discarded, and refined as time passes and methods become more relevant and perspectives clearer. *Methods* are derived from biblical principles, but will change as time perspectives shift and improved interpretive tools for exegetical and theological analysis are devised. However, *principles*, though subject to God's progressive disclosures, are fairly stable. Thus, interpretive content should be formed by the use of methods that are derived from principles. The notation 'year-day principle' illustrates the confusion between principle and method. It would be more accurate to call the calculation of time using year-for-a-day a 'method' since time was figured in literal terms until the twelfth century,[26] and because the Bible does not explicitly indicate that prophetic time should be figured by translating the days into years.

Furthermore, there is an inconsistent understanding of historicism's origins and development. 'Historical-biblical', the first term used for what we commonly call historicism,[27] was the label attached during the reformation to indicate that its interpretation of prophecy combined both history and Bible. At that time, the major elements added to the basic outline of Daniel 2 included the several symbolic designations for the papacy, the year-day method of reckoning time periods, an emphasis on chronological sequencing of events, and a synchronisation of prophecies and their symbols. But historicism, as an interpretive approach, did not begin during that period. Even though some may argue against applying the 'historicism' label prior to the reformation,[28] most still recognise that the elements comprising the historicist approach grew up over a millennium prior to it. The reformers did combine and systematise these accumulated elements and formalised them into a school of interpretation, but the standard Adventist position reminds us that the concept of historicism was initiated by the angelic interpretations in

---

26. See *SDA Bible Commentary*, edited by Francis D Nichol (Washington DC: Review & Herald, 1955, 1977), 4:50.
27. Historicism as an approach has also been referred to as historical, grammatical-historical, continuous historical, Protestant, and historical messianic.
28. Kai J Arasola, *The End of Historicism: Millerite Hermeneutic of Time Prophecies in the Old Testament*, dissertation (Uppsala, Sweden: Uppsala University [Datem Pub], 1989), 32. Arasola believes that Froom's identification of patristic exegesis with historicism is a mistake because there is no synchronisation of prophecies, no papal Little Horn, and no strong emphasis on chronology prior to the Reformation era. However, he recognises the evolution of elements over time before the Reformation, *ibid*, 47.

the visions given Daniel, was expanded by Jesus, added to by Paul, and enlarged by John.[29]

Progressive revelation indicates that historicism should be dynamic rather than become fossilised or limited in scope to any particular period. Reformation historicism was revived during the Millerite era when historicist expositors around the world extended the reformers' focus to include the prophecy of Daniel 8.[30] The pioneers of Adventism continued the work of Miller's advent movement by adding their understanding of the sanctuary, its cleansing, and the investigative judgment. However, over the 160-year history of prophetic understanding that arose from the ashes of the Great Disappointment, many have struggled over the interpretations of our forefathers.[31]

The concept of historicism may be limited by the human tendency to distance ourselves from that which cannot be supported by a later perspective. The author of a 1989 dissertation entitled *The End of Historicism* referred to historicism as 'Miller's hermeneutic'.[32] Although the research highlighted the decline of historicism as the primary interpretive approach after the Great Disappointment,[33] its focus was on Miller's principles of interpretation for Daniel 8:14. Even characterising historicism narrowly as Miller's hermeneutic is unfortunate because it has a tendency to distort its true nature. To limit historicism to any of the proponents, movements, or periods of dominance is tantamount to ignoring the biblical basis of God-ordained interpretation and His sovereign guidance over all approaches through the centuries. It leads to a misunderstanding of both historicism and the principle of progressive revelation.

The danger of a narrow concept is also illustrated by the response to this dissertation. Shortly after publication, some used the research to support the doubts and views they had already entertained. One summed up the sentiments of several: 'The whole system of Adventist prophetic interpretation is defective because it is built on a very restricted view of prophecy . . . [In] many instances it has neglected much of biblical reality and perverted some of the rest . . . It can not en-

---

29. See *Seventh-day Adventist Encyclopedia,* Commentary Reference Series, second revised edition, edited by Don F Neufeld (Hagerstown, MD: Review and Herald, 1996), 10: 698–699.
30. Nichol, *SDA Bible Commentary, op cit,* 4:59–60. Most Protestant Old and New World expositors in the nineteenth century focused on Daniel 8 and the cleansing of the sanctuary, but differed in explaining the meaning of the cleansing of the sanctuary. Miller's interpretation of the sanctuary as being the earth that was to be cleansed by fire was somewhat unique. Others thought the sanctuary was the church or individual Christians.
31. One of the most recent discussions includes a lengthy paper by Raymond Cottrell presented in 2001 and 2002 to the Association of Adventist Forums in San Diego, CA. It is posted on the Jesus Institute Forum symposium website: http://www.jesusinstituteforum.org/AssetOrLiability.html.
32. . Arasola, *End of Historicism, op cit,* 17.
33. *Ibid,* 1–2.

dure a careful biblical investigation.'[34] These charges not only classify Millerite historicism too narrowly, but also seem to be an attempt to discredit historicism as a valid approach. This same writer also predicted that Adventist scholars would 'repudiate such teaching (except for some few dedicated to upholding the traditional positions for reasons other than scholarship)'.[35] Although this prediction has not come to pass,[36] the debate has made support for historicism more tentative. These responses do illustrate the need to keep a broad, dynamic view of historicism to avoid discarding it during a time of apparent decline. They also point up the danger of judging previous interpretations out of context, measuring their validity on the basis of our contemporary context, tools, and experience. To reject historicism on such shaky grounds means to limit and misconstrue its true nature, to abandon the most biblically accurate approach to understanding prophecy,[37] and to deny divine providence in the reformation and advent movement.

Several other factors may promote a limited view of historicism. One is an over-emphasis on differentiating it from competing views. When the counter-reformation created a pair of incompatible approaches to biblical-historical interpretation, it placed apocalyptic prophecies largely in the past or future. Preterism and futurism were designed to deflect the identification of antichrist as the papacy and Babylon as the Roman church. Certain of their elements have prompted an attempt in Adventist writing over the last three decades to distance historicism from these views by pointing out the differences while reaffirming and defending historicism. While comparison and contrast are necessary, to focus on them may fail to deal with larger issues. Another factor is the call to sustain our pioneers' heritage. Such a call resounds in the 'knocking at the door' phrase that has surfaced in articles for more than a decade. While Adventists should be called to stand for truth, subtle emotive language may discourage a serious study of unresolved issues that have been raised by Adventists who remain loyal to historicism's divinely appointed role despite their questions. Pointing out the major points of dispute between historicism and futurism, for example, does not contribute to the understanding of those who are not tempted by literalism, dispensationalism and rapturism.

God's long-range plan is more obscure to a contemporary generation that is not unfamiliar with its history. One Adventist scholar shows how the concept of 'the end', as revealed in Scripture, went through several transitions, unfold-

---

34. Ford, 'Foundation'.
35. Ford, 'J'Accuse', online: http://www.goodnewsforadventists.com/williammiller/. Accessed 14 September 2010.
36. Gerhard Pfandl, 'Is Historicism Dead?', in South Pacific Division *Record*, 22 August 1998: 8. Pfandl affirms the vitality of Adventist historicism by noting that more than 200 Bible scholars from around the world attended a 1998 Bible Conference in Jerusalem.
37. Johnsson, 'Biblical Apocalyptic', *op cit*, 797; Hasel, 'Crossroads', *op cit*, 63.

ing stages of development, from Noah through Abraham, Moses, Old Testament prophets, intertestamental writings, to the New Testament prophets.[38] A valid eschatological picture would be impossible if it left out or was limited to any stage. Likewise, the best way to understand historicism is to keep all of its past development in view. Historicism must be seen for what it is: a progressively developing systematic approach to the interpretation of apocalyptic prophecy that is biblically faithful, flexible, dynamic, and valid, while being open to God's continuing disclosures.

Contrasting Historicist Interpretations

The principle of progressive revelation requires a solid foundation of biblical presuppositions and hermeneutics to guide interpretation in order to avoid speculation and misinterpretations. Generally, Adventists believe that historicist principles and methods should be derived from, be compatible with, or serve as extensions of, a sound biblical foundation that directs the understanding of inspiration and revelation. Thus, it is vital for an interpreter to reflect this foundation in their interpretation of apocalyptic. It also is axiomatic that consensus in key interpretations is only possible when the same presuppositions and hermeneutics are shared.[39]

Confusion concerning the Adventist hermeneutical foundation is a source of diversity.[40] Historical-critical methodologies, along with post-modern values and practices, have helped destabilise this foundation. Prior to 1950 there was 'substantial unity' concerning the validity, authenticity, authority and pre-eminence of Scripture[41] within the Adventist Church. Scripture was understood "quite literally unless coercive evidence suggested otherwise," theology predominated over the social sciences and critical studies, and Adventists held a 'high view' of Scripture. Ellen White's influence significantly impacted interpretation, but was not intended to be definitive nor determinative.[42] Today, however, certain of these principles and foundations are thought to be naive by some scholars, and when scholars disagree, the leaders and members become confused. In spite of the books and articles written on the topic over the last decade, the debate has not been resolved.[43]

---

38. Paulien, *Endtime, op cit*, 43–83.
39. George W Reid, 'Another Look at Adventist Hermeneutics', an online article posted by the Biblical Research Institute, 2001: http://biblicalresearch.gc.adventist.org/documents/Adventist%20 Hermeneutics.htm.
40. *Ibid*.
41. *Ibid*.
42. *Ibid*.
43. Three books to note are: Alden Thompson, *Inspiration: Hard Questions, Honest Answers* (Hagerstown, MD: Review & Herald, 1991); Frank Holbrook and Leo Van Dolson, ed., *Issues in Revelation and Inspiration*, Adventist Theological Society Occasional Papers 1 (Berrien Springs,

The hermeneutic foundation determines the approach to interpretation. Each of the four approaches operates under a different set of principles and methods. With the debate in historicism has come disagreement among Adventist scholars over how to relate to the other approaches. Some Adventist scholars appear to view preterism and futurism as sinister plots to derail historicism, others acknowledge that the counter-views contain 'elements of truth', but believe their approach cannot be sustained biblically.[44] A third view suggests that interpreters should 'combine the strongest elements of two or more of the traditional approaches in their exposition . . .' to adequately understand apocalyptic.[45] A fourth commends the use of exegesis, letting the text govern the interpretation according to the intention of the prophet, along with the use of all four approaches: 'If the message of the studied text was primarily for John's day, then it calls for the preterist or idealist approach. On the other hand, if it discusses the very end times, then its interpretation calls for a futurist approach. If the studied text presents the events occurring throughout the course of history, however, a sound interpretation calls for a historicist approach to the text.'[46]

The author commending exegesis supports his view by stating 'the method of interpretation an author chooses normally governs the way he or she reads and interprets the text. It usually results in forcing an interpretation into the framework of a predetermined idea, regardless of whether or not it fits the context. Such interpretation is often used to prove a point rather than to find the meaning of the text.'[47] While exegesis may not be as definitive for interpreting apocalyptic,[48] the problem of bias is real and its avoidance critical. Perhaps exegesis is freer from bias than is inherent in the four approaches, but an eclectic approach, even if governed by exegesis, may not really be possible with incompatible hermeneutics. Furthermore, both theological and exegetical methods are necessary.[49] Historicism must embrace exegesis and theology more responsibly. It must be re-examined, and a serious attempt be made to bring its principles, methods, and interpretations into correspondence with biblical hermeneutics.

MI: Adventist Theological Society, 1992); Samuel Koranteng-Pipim, *Receiving the Word* (Ann Arbor, MI: Berean Books, 1996).
44. Doukhan, *Daniel*, 8.
45. Stefanovic, *Revelation of Jesus Christ*, 9. Although the author is not necessarily referring to Adventist scholars, this approach can be found in Adventist circles.
46. *Ibid*, 12. The author's comments are directed primarily to the book of Revelation.
47. *Ibid*, 11-12.
48. The role of the prophet's intention and his contextual perspective is not as definitive for biblical apocalyptic as for other Scriptures because he is a recipient of the visions and explanations rather than the creator.
49. Kenneth A Strand, 'Foundational Principles of Interpretation', Volume 6 (*Symposium on Revelation: Introductory and Exegetical Studies—Book 1*, 1992), Silver Spring MA: BRI, 7-8.

Another difficult question is how to relate to repeated historical applications. Classical prophecy's conditionality and dual applications are seen as rather distinct from apocalyptic,[50] but there has been variation about whether apocalyptic prophecies can have more than one fulfillment. A comparison of the *Seventh-day Adventist Commentary* and the Daniel and Revelation Committee Series illustrates the difficulty. Volume 4 of the Commentary (both 1955 and 1977 editions) refers to dual or double applications or fulfillments to explain the apparent repetition of historical events or entities that are described by the same prophecy or symbol in Daniel 8 – 9 and 11.[51] The commentary identifies the symbolic horn of Daniel 8 as both pagan and papal Rome and calls it a 'double application'.[52] This means the *tamid* (continual) would refer to both paganism and the papacy, or to Christ's ministry in both the earthy temple that Rome destroyed in AD 70 and His continual heavenly ministry after ascension.[53] To explain the three references to the desolation and abomination (8:11–13, 9:27, and 11:31), the commentary again refers to pagan and papal Rome, but calls Daniel 8:11–13 a 'blended prophecy' like that in Matthew 24, with some elements applying to both AD 70 and the Middle Ages, but some only to one or the other (Daniel 11:31 can only refer to the papacy). Volume 1 of the commentaries supports the concept of dual application: if we are 'to be consistent', we must acknowledge that prophecies in the Old Testament that are applied or reapplied by a later inspired writer 'have a dual application' because we believe all the prophets were fully inspired.[54] And just because 'the prophets themselves may not have been aware that their inspired utterances had, at times, a dual application in no way impairs the validity of such an application. Rather, it testifies to the more than human wisdom that inspired the utterance.'[55]

Twenty-five years later, however, additional study and the incursions of preterism and futurism encouraged expositors to not only avoid the terms 'double' or 'dual', but to deny the possibility of such. In the Daniel and Revelation Committee (DARCOM)series published largely in the 1980s, several articles state categorically that there can be only one single application or fulfillment possible for each symbol, entity or time period in apocalyptic prophecy,[56] although one scholar

---

50. *Ibid*, 16–22; Johnsson, 'Biblical Apocalyptic', *op cit*, 12:789–795.
51. *SDA Bible Commentary*, edited by Nicol, *op cit*, 4:841, 843, 845.
52. *Ibid*, 4:841.
53. *Ibid*, 4:843.
54. *Ibid*, 1:1019.
55. *Ibid*, 1:1019. Conditionality is an issue that relates to dual fulfilments because apocalyptic recognises God's sovereignty and requires certainty. See William G Johnsson, 'Conditionality in Biblical Prophecy with Particular Reference to Apocalyptic', in Daniel and Revelation Committee 3, 259–287.
56. Gerhard F Hasel, 'Fulfilments of Prophecy', in *The Seventy Weeks, Leviticus, and the Nature of Prophecy*, edited by Frank B Holbrook, Daniel and Revelation Committee Series, Volume 3 (Washington DC: Biblical Research Institute, 1986), 288–322; Strand, 'Interpretation', *op cit*,

would allow for two if 'every point of identification and every detail' were met in both fulfillments.[57] The series itself was commissioned partly by a perceived need to protect prophecies that have already been fulfilled from being applied to the distant past or the future. Since this series was written at a later date, can we assume that it represents a refinement in understanding and therefore a more correct view?

So how should the phenomenon of repetition be labeled or described? A Biblical Research Institute article posted on their internet site in 2001 that strongly denies any possibility of dualism explains the phenomenon in Matthew 24 as a 'two-fold prophecy' in a kind of type-antitype relationship.[58] Another solution posited is a 'philosophy-of-history' perspective, a certain kind of recurring application of pattern or characterisation because 'history repeats itself', though a real application or fulfillment does not.[59] A third suggests that prophecies pointing to different historical times should simply be '"seen" as in the same perspective—following the linear Hebrew conception of time'.[60] Or perhaps the solution is a blending as mentioned earlier, or a recognition that a single prophecy can refer to more than one event or period of history. Clearly there are subtle differences in the designations and the explanations that support them which have not been resolved.

On the practical level, however, the single fulfillment principle appears to be shifting under the pressure of a closer scrutiny of Scripture, improved exegetical tools, and a perspective that comes from a later point in time. Examples from recent books by well known Adventist scholars include a biblically based future scenario for Revelation 13 without addressing how to resolve the contrasts with our pioneers' interpretation,[61] a two-fold interpretation for 2 Thessalonians,[62] and a rejection of the traditional positions regarding the French Revolution.[63]

Other traditional practices in interpretation are in transition. Examples include:

1. Whether a word in apocalyptic prophecy should be understood literally or symbolically. It was common, for centuries, to interpret a symbol literally unless doing so would not make sense, but today it is becoming

---

3-34, and 'Ellen G White's Use of Daniel and Revelation', George E Rice, *op cit*, 145-161; W Richard Lesher and Frank B Holbrook, Appendix C, 'Daniel and Revelation Committee: Final Report', (*Symposium on Revelation: Exegetical and General Studies—Book II*, 1992), 7:451-460.
57. Hasel, 'Fulfilments of Prophecy', *op cit*, 3:316.
58. BRI.
59. Strand, 'Interpretation', 3:19-20.
60. Doukhan, *Daniel*, 9, citing Oscar Cullman, *Christ and Time*, 1962, 50ff.
61. Chapter 10 of Paulien, *Endtime*, 109-119; LaRondelle, *How to Understand*, 300-307.
62. See Chapter 8 of Paulien, *Endtime*, 95-101. He believes Ellen White's writings support a two-fold approach (see footnote 2, 101).
63. LaRondelle, *How to Understand*, 232.

more common for an apocalyptic symbol to be interpreted symbolically unless there is some reason to interpret it literally.[64]
2. How strictly an apocalyptic time period should be interpreted. For centuries interpreters have struggled to line up meaningful historical dates for the time periods in prophecy. However, in a very recent commentary on Revelation by an Adventist scholar, the 1260 prophetic years are interpreted to mean 'around 1200 years'.[65]
3. Whether a prophecy has been fulfilled before all of its details have been fulfilled.[66] If all details must be fulfilled, how can we explain a partial 'fulfillment' that was believed to be, and experienced as, a fulfillment by those who applied the prophecy loosely? Was it an application, or a false interpretation? Shall we deny a previous generation's recognition of prophetic fulfillment even when its impact for God's kingdom can be documented and His involvement evidenced? The dangers of misapplication, non-certainty and diffusion of fulfillments, nonetheless however, are real.

None deny that interpretations of prophetic details and symbols have changed. Each generation has interpreted prophetic symbols in the way that made the most sense to them. Perhaps this is one way God has kept His coming 'soon' for 2000 years. So, the antichrist who was an individual for the early church became an apostate system for the protesters who saw the Roman church as Babylon. And the time prophecies that were in literal time during the first three or four centuries AD became viewed as prophetic time. As centuries passed and the early church gradually lost hope in an imminent return, the stage was set for a major shift to a spiritualisation of apocalyptic prophecies and the view that the church was God's kingdom on earth already experiencing the millennium. This shift impacted interpretation for nearly a millennium. Towards the end of that time, Bible students who restudied the prophecies could only make sense of time prophecies by using the year-day method of calculation. Over the next 500 years, this method was applied first to the 1260 days of Revelation 13:13, and then gradually to each of the remaining time elements in prophecy.

As generations interpreted apocalyptic from their perspectives, contexts, needs, and circumstances, their interpretations impacted their worldviews and directed their behavior. Some of the interpretations based on historicist principles or methods appear faulty or have failed at least partially from our perspective, yet they made a positive impact in the lives of people and in the growth and progress of God's kingdom. Perhaps all historicist expositors have held some beliefs

---

64. Stefanovic, *Revelation of Jesus Christ*, 17.
65. *Ibid*, 338, 342, 347, 379, 384.
66. Hasel, 'Fulfilments,' *op cit*, 290.

that are unbiblical. Even the inspired prophets 'misunderstood' or questioned the meaning of some aspects of their prophecies. In spite of these limitations, however, God used, replaced, or redirected interpretations in His time. We must be cautious in judging interpreters and their views because we are unable to know how God disclosed to them or how the Holy Spirit used their misperceptions. Further, Ellen White admonishes us to be open to growth rather than to 'become static and rigid in our concepts. We are to think for ourselves . . . not taking traditional positions for granted' because 'increasing light is to shine' as we seek to understand prophecy.[67]

Transitions in Interpretation

Uncertainty tends to encourage diversity, but the anticipation of a fulfillment helps to mobilise believers around the expectation. Although transitions can be partially explained as sociological rhythms in the cycles of human existence,[68] they are governed by a complex set of interrelated factors, conditions, and patterns. Patterns in history help us identify our current status and what to expect in the future. They are another way by which God reveals and involves Himself with humanity. Historicism has been dominant three times in the 2,600 years since Daniel wrote his amazing book: the apostolic-early Church, reformation, and Millerite-pioneer eras. The periodic rise and decline of historicism over the centuries seems to have followed a progressive pattern that can be described in the following overlapping and cyclic phases of indeterminate length.

Awareness

The process starts with an awareness of relevant prophecy that becomes associated with current history and raises a fulfillment expectation. As the time approaches, a new vision, goal, message and mission driven by the expected fulfillment become increasingly clear and focused. These become shaped and shared by a few prominent proponents, accepted by others, and supported by some form of structure. A rise in historicism has often been accompanied by an awareness of spiritual need and longing for revival which may also prompt a greater dependence on Scripture. Perhaps the clearest example is the disgust provoked by the non-spiritual condition of the medieval church with its glaring and blatant corruption of the leadership, a condition that drove the faithful to the Bible and answers found in the prophecies. Awareness has often been accompanied by such

---

67. Froom paraphrases and quotes Ellen White from *Review and Herald,* June 18, 1889, 385, and May 27, 1890, 321. See particularly his footnotes 57 and 58 in Froom, *Prophetic Faith,* 1147.
68. Pohler develops this concept in *Change, op cit,* 442, no. 2

means as the printing press, vernacular translations, media, and cultural movements like the Enlightenment and Renaissance.

Mobilisation

Awareness becomes mobilised. As the expected fulfillment draws near it becomes crystallised by some event or set of circumstances that heightens an issue or creates a crisis. Sometimes the fulfilling of minor prophetic details or conditions that are a part of a larger fulfillment brings mobilisation. The attention of a critical mass of people is captured, and they join the expectation of fulfillment while others become more confirmed in their denial. In a climate of crisis, historicism has often gained strength amidst debate, conflict, and even persecution, partly because these conditions encouraged separation from the careless world and deeper spirituality with a closer study and exposition of Scripture. When non-biblical philosophies and theories such as Gnosticism, humanism, and post-modernism have crept in, they have both strengthened believers and encouraged diversity and decline as they challenged spiritual strength and deflected interest from the historicity and dependability of the Bible.

Expectation is one of the most crucial factors in maintaining a historicist perspective because it is rooted in the unfolding of history. A sense of imminence, or movement towards the fulfillment of prophecy provides direction and identity. If time continues too long without the realisation of fulfillment, or sense of movement towards it, or even a mere anticipation of some aspect, negative results occur. These may be a loss of hope, drift in direction, diminished spirituality and/or decline in Bible study, and perhaps a shift in belief result.[69] A lost sense of imminent fulfillment encourages apathy, dissatisfaction, abandonment, or even rejection of the current approach. Significant changes in prophetic interpretation can occur at this time.

The pre-incarnation Jews lost their eschatological sense in part as prophetism died out. The new focus prompted them to materialise, localise, and literalise prophecies that distracted them from recognising or accepting Jesus as Messiah because He didn't fit their apocalyptic expectations.[70] The apostolic generation who lived in the expectation of Jesus' soon return spread the gospel to the then-known world in two or three decades (Col 1:23). This same expectation 'nerved the early Christians to endure persecution' and prompted them to pray earnestly for the continuance of Rome to defer the rise of the dreaded antichrist. But, as the centuries passed and hope waned, even the long-expected break-up of the Roman Empire by the barbarian invasions could not overcome the inertia of apathy.[71]

---

69. For examples see Pohler, *Change, op cit*, 228–233.
70. Froom, *Prophetic Faith, op cit*, 1:113.
71. *Ibid*, 1:473–475.

Fulfillment

When time for the fulfillment arrives, the fulfillment either fails or is confirmed. If it fails, discouragement, disillusionment, or abandonment will result for the majority unless an adjustment is made or an explanation found. If the prophecy is confirmed, faith is strengthened. But after the fulfillment, a decline in relevance and enthusiasm will inevitably set in until awareness of a new expectation starts this process anew. Even though people cannot live in a continual sense of urgency, a sense of direction and movement toward destiny is essential for maintaining fervent expectation and anticipation.

Thus, the movement of apocalyptic expectation rises and declines. For Adventists, however, the most important 'factor' to explain transition is God's activity. Adventists affirm Divine involvement in the rise and fall of every approach to prophetic interpretation because we believe in a God who knows the future and is sovereign over history and world affairs. So, instead of being limited or bound by world events and conditions, He controls and works through them for His omniscient purposes; He is not caught by surprise.

The Future of Historicism

Diversity among Adventists will continue to grow until an expectation is fulfilled, or a major fulfillment is perceived to be imminent. The second coming is the climactic prophetic event for Christians. Each time an expected fulfillment raised the hope of Christ's return, time passed without the realisation. One major difference between the strength of the Reformation interpretations and the difficulties following 1844 may be partially explained by the latter's lack of intersection with concrete history. It required faith without historical evidence to believe that Jesus had moved from one phase of ministry to another. Since then, no significant person or event that came to be identified in prophecy has been verified in history. Although faith is the evidence of things not seen, and the heavenly reality is no less valid than visible historical evidence, the fulfillment tied to 1844 is not the same kind of evidence as the crucifixion, destruction of Jerusalem, or identification of the antichrist.

God will use the diversity to prepare the church for the journey ahead. The diversity that is a part of current Adventist prophetic understanding is an essential climate for God to prepare His people for their future mission. It clarifies, motivates, and builds faith among seekers. Diversity has raised new issues that have challenged us to a deeper spirituality and study of the Scriptures. During this waiting time, we should:

1. continue to search for a more complete understanding of how progressive revelation functions as a framework for interpreting apocalyptic prophecy;
2. begin to view historicism from a more consistent, holistic, broad, unbiased, and non-defensive perspective which is essential for keeping our biblical focus on prophetic interpretation alive; and
3. make sure that our interpretation of prophecy uses all available methods that are consistent with valid Adventist biblical presuppositions and hermeneutics.

Adventists will continue to strengthen their apocalyptic focus in traditional and non-traditional ways. Since 1844, hope has been kept alive through reaffirming already-fulfilled prophecies, studying the Scriptures and Ellen White's writings, and seeking historical confirmation of the signs recorded in Matthew. Generations of Adventists have attempted to use the signs Christ gave in His apocalyptic sermon as historical indicators for an imminent return. Contemporary Adventists recognise that those signs are not the kind of prophetic details whose fulfillment can provide that kind of certainty. We may believe that the second coming is imminent, but we have not been able to point to any concrete prophetic details that have been fulfilled in history for more than one hundred years.

A transformed and biblically faithful historicism will become dominant a fourth and final time. The prophecies relating to gospel closure have yet to be fulfilled. God's Word will be the only valid source for unfolding the end times, and the prophetic details found there will be identifiable in events and entities. Other interpretations to explain final events will continue to proliferate, and perhaps integrate into a single alternative explanation to compete with the biblical scenario. The elements of truth found in each of the other approaches to interpretation will connect sincere seekers to the final biblical view of prophecy. Disinterest in historicism will evaporate for many as their attention is riveted on fulfilling prophecy. It will revitalise the Adventist identity and renew the mission. God will superintend the final process in such a way that His people will be made ready and will fulfill their opportunity.

The final historicism will be compatible with, but different from, traditional historicism. Expositors and believers during each of historicism's previous dominant periods would not have been able to project or recognise the shape of a historicism future to them. So it is with us. Although the general process and major themes of the final unfolding are clear, the fulfilling of many ambiguous details of prophecy will undoubtedly be surprising. Trends reveal that Adventists are currently moving away from the same type of rationalistic and temporal-focus that characterised the reformers and advent pioneers. The final apocalyptic message to the world will be a remarkably simple one, clear enough for every person to understand. But, as Ellen White admonished, God has much more to teach us about closing events. We should set aside all but the Bible and sound biblical methods to study apocalyptic until we see the complete picture of what God plans for our generation to see. He will enlighten our understanding in His time and way, confirm through Scripture both prophecy and events as they unfold, and provide confidence and security through the final days for all who will be a part of His eternal kingdom.

To revitalise historicism we should continue to follow the direction of God's leading. The forces of materialism, secularism, and post-modernism—the new Gnosticism[72]—are engrossing the attention of our generation and bringing apathy towards concerns of eternal consequence. As these forces impact the church, the resulting formalism, that takes over when the spirit dies, becomes so unsatisfying that it either drives people from church or brings a return to the gospel. I believe we are in the midst of a timely renewal of the gospel in our community of faith evidenced by a rising interest in authentic and meaningful relationships along with a passion for the lost and less fortunate. Although spirituality in some sectors is declining, the numbers getting involved in evangelism, mission outreach, church planting, service, and humanitarian programs are accelerating at a rate unknown for many decades. The gospel focus is an essential foundation for a return to spirituality and the study of Scripture and ultimately to be able to proclaim the imminent return.

To revitalise historicism we should continue to encourage global gospel oriented, dynamic, and deep study of apocalyptic Scriptures. Contemporary Adventism should emulate its pioneers in commitment to truth and faithfulness rather than their apocalyptic beliefs alone. Their unwavering security in God's love for them and His trustworthiness enabled them to explore and debate the Scriptures freely and to tolerate differences of view. Their biblical findings were shared in church publications and encouraged dialogue among the rank and file, resulting in improved understanding and commitment. Now is the time to prepare our church to understand how to reach the world in new and creative ways for what lies ahead. Members worldwide should contribute to initiatives designed to make the prophecies meaningful but simple for each cultural group in a diverse, multi-cultural world, by using the best, most biblical, and accessible methods and tools that are compatible with Scripture.

To revitalise historicism we should continue to search for new ways to prepare the world for events that may soon come upon us all. The advent movement was made up of people from many denominations who were committed to the truth as it is found in Scripture. The final movement will also gather people from all

---

72. Peter Jones, *The Gnostic Empire Strikes Back: An Old Heresy for the New Age* (Phillipsburg, NJ: P&R, 1992).

persuasions and religions. In addition to satellite and friendship evangelism, other twenty-first century methods to prepare the world for the second coming should be devised. The church could set up new kinds of web sites, begin dialoguing with other historicist organisations, and organise interdenominational prophecy conferences where scholars, theologians, leaders and laity share insights together. The world will not be convinced by lengthy exegetical or theological explanations of the prophecies as much as by the Holy Spirit's empowerment of the simple biblical record made visible in prophetic fulfillment.

To summarise, a review of historicism's pattern of rise and decline encourages us by reminding us that God has been present throughout its history and continues to work within each generation's historical context and time frame. He has silently allowed and worked through persons, events, and conditions that may seem to have been disastrous from a human perspective to move the world closer to its final destiny and His eternal reign. He guides the world's human rhythm of ebb and flow, not expecting His people to live in a continual sense of urgency, but to balance watching, working, and waiting. For historicism to predominate in our church again may require a crisis that drives us to Christ and a searching of Scripture. However, it will certainly require a strong sense of impending fulfillment to provide a new or renewed vision, goal, message, and mission, and a people to spread the good news with certainty. As Froom says: There's nothing more powerful than a prophecy whose time has come.[73]

---

73. Froom, *Prophetic Faith, op cit*, 3:741.

The Fatherhood of God

David Tasker

Introduction

The Christian religion, like every other religion, stands or falls by its conception of God, and to that conception of God the idea of the Fatherhood of God is integral.[1]

How do we understand the concept of God? Where do we draw our ideas from? This essay takes up the challenge of Selbie's perceptive and provocative statement in three steps: first, through an historical overview of Christian theology; second, through an examination of ideas from the ancient Near East (ANE); and third, through an exploration of Old Testament theology.

Historical-Theological Overview

Origen recognises that the fatherhood of God lies at the heart of the Christian faith. However, he takes it somewhat for granted, and often uses the word 'Father' merely as a synonym for God.[2] Nevertheless, he links middle Platonist thought and biblical ideas in his attempts to define God and the world,[3] and is thus the first theologian to attempt any analysis of the idea of God as Father. Basically, he presents a caricature of God formed by combining Hebrew Scriptures and Greek philosophy, and then contrasts this caricature with the Christian Father-God, before whom humans stand in love rather than fear.[4]

It is not until Athanasius in the fourth century that the fatherhood of God becomes an issue of sustained discussion, more for the purpose of trinitarian debate and as a polemic against Arius and the Alexandrian school than as an investigation of the fatherhood of God, *per se*.[5] His position becomes orthodoxy in the hands of his successors, the Cappadocian fathers and Augustine.[6]

---

1. William Boothby Selbie, *The Fatherhood of God* (New York: Scribners, 1936), 11.
2. Peter Widdicombe, *The Fatherhood of God from Origen to Athanasius*, Oxford Theological Monographs, edited by J Day et al (Oxford: Clarendon Press, 1994), 7.
3. *Ibid*, 9.
4. *Ibid*, 253.
5. *Ibid*, 1, 136, 159–160.
6. *Ibid*, 255.

In other words, from the time of Origen on, discussion on the fatherhood of God serves mainly to explain the metaphysics of the Godhead. Under Gnostic influence and with the tools of Greco-oriental theology, a great gulf is fixed between God and His Creation,[7] with an impact on the understanding of the Fatherhood of God that is maintained by the Protestant Reformers centuries later. For example, Luther portrays God as a 'consuming fire',[8] inflicting punishment in a 'fatherly spirit',[9] and as an 'iron wall, against which we cannot bump without destroying ourselves'.[10] Similarly, Calvin declares that no 'ruined' man 'will ever perceive God to be a Father',[11] and that humans may only call God 'Father' because He is Christ's Father.[12] Calvin's systematised theological structure is founded on the contrast between God's sovereignty and human remoteness,[13] and the ideas of atonement and God's fatherhood are considered forensically incompatible.[14]

In a late-nineteenth-century reaction to the autocratic theism of Calvinism, Clarke, Peabody, and Rauschenbusch formulate a 'social gospel'.[15] For them, God is Father of all humanity and all men are brothers. These new 'liberal' ideas about God are the culmination of a universalistic perspective evolving over centuries.[16] Reverend Dr Rob S Candlish and Professor Thomas J Crawford vigorously debate whether

---

7. Selbie, *Fatherhood of God, op cit*, 66.
8. Martin Luther, 'Lectures on Isaiah, Chapters 1–39', in *Luther's Works*, translated by Herbert JA Bouman, edited by Jaroslav Pelikan (Saint Louis: Concordia, 1969), 16:55.
9. *Ibid*, 54.
10. Martin Luther, 'Selected Psalms I' in *Luther's Works*, translated by LW Spitz Jr, edited by Jaroslav Pelikan (Saint Louis: Concordia, 1955), 12:312. Luther describes the impossibility of humans approaching God 'naked', that is, unclothed without Christ. Luther, 'First Lectures on the Psalms II, Psalms 76–126', in *Luther's Works*, translated by Herbert JA Bouman, edited by Hilton C Oswald (Saint Louis: Concordia, 1976), 11:208–209.
11. John Calvin, *Institutes of the Christian Religion*, translated by John Allen; (Philadelphia: Presbyterian Board of Christian Education, 1936), 1:51.
12. John Calvin, *Tracts and Treatises on the Doctrine and Worship of the Church*, translated by Henry Beveridge (Grand Rapids, MI: Eerdmans, 1958), 2:40.
13. Selbie, *Fatherhood of God, op cit*, 75.
14. *Ibid*, 72.
15. Janet Forsythe Fishburn, *The Fatherhood of God and the Victorian Family: The Social Gospel in America* (Philadelphia, PA: Fortress, 1982), 136–139. This emphasis is based exclusively on the parable of the prodigal son, focussing on God's patience, pity, and willingness to forgive. *Ibid*, 140.
16. Washington Gladden, *How Much Is Left of the Old Doctrines? A Book for the People* (Boston: Houghton Mifflin, 1899), 23. Gladden speaks of the universal hunger for a God whom people can know and love. Walter Lippmann observes that the God of medieval Christianity is like a great feudal lord, duty-bound to treat his vassals well; the God of the Enlightenment is like a constitutional monarch, who reigns but does not govern; and the God of Modernism is the sum total of the laws of nature, or an expression of some kind of deified constitutionalism. Walter Lippmann, *Preface to Morals* (New York, NY: Macmillan, 1929), 54–55, cited by Harriet Crabtree, *The Christian Life: Traditional Metaphors and Contemporary Theologies*, Harvard Dissertations in Religion 29, edited by MR Miles and BJ Brooten (Minneapolis, MN: Fortress, 1991), 6.

God's fatherhood is universal, or whether He can only be called 'Father' in Christ.[17] The final death of the wicked at the *eschaton* is offered as proof that God's fatherhood does not apply to all.[18] Rather, one must be 'blameless and harmless' before he can be called a child of God.[19] This is a revival of Origen's idea that only a person free from sin has the right to call God 'Father.'[20]

From these debates an anthropocentric approach to God's father-hood develops, with an emphasis on understanding it from the perspective of human experience. To some extent, Sigmund Freud systematises and popularises this approach. He largely draws his inspiration from Greek mythology, to develop a paradigm that holds fatherhood responsible for a range of guilt neuroses experienced throughout the lifespan.[21] It is not surprising, then, that the motif of the fatherhood of God has been labeled as the '"Achilles" heel'[22] of the Judeo-Christian religion.

The fatherhood of God motif attracts little attention in twentieth century biblical studies until feminist theology, which draws heavily upon, and expands, the work of Freud.[23] The most prominent feminist theologian to tackle the motif of

---

17. For example, see Professor Thomas J Crawford, *The Fatherhood of God: Considered in Its General and Special Aspects and Particularly in Relation to the Atonement, with a Review of Recent Speculations on the Subject, and a Reply to the Strictures of Dr Candlish* (Edinburgh: William Blackwood and Sons, 1868), 275; and Reverend Dr Rob S Candlish, *The Fatherhood of God: Being the First Course of the Cunningham Lectures* (Edinburgh: Adam and Charles Black, 1867), 117.
18. Charles IIII Wright, *The Fatherhood of God and Its Relation to the Person and Work of Christ, and the Operations of the Holy Spirit* (Edinburgh: T&T Clark, 1867), 79-97.
19. *Ibid*, 193-194.
20. Widdicombe, *Fatherhood of God, op cit*, 109. For Origen, such a person assumes a new ontological condition that makes him/her constitutionally incapable of sinning. *Ibid*, 103.
21. Sigmund Freud, *Moses and Monotheism*, International Psycho-Analytical Library 33, translated by Katherine Jones (London: Hogarth, 1951), 187-189. His hypothesis that all moral authority springs from the father impugns God with the responsibility for human dysfunction. Annemarie Ohler observes that 'The broad aftereffect of the Freudian Hypothesis about the "Oedipus Complex" has contributed in no small measure to the darkening of the image of the father.' Annemarie Ohler, *The Bible Looks at Fathers*, translated by Omar Kaste (Collegeville, MN: Liturgical Press, 1999), xix. The son can only succeed if he 'kills' his father, a 'law of nature' that suggests a son cannot succeed without first disposing of his father in some way. In response, Ohler suggests that Freud should have visited America. As early as 1830, the aristocratic Frenchman Alexis de Tocqueville notes that there fathers actively encourage sons to strike out on their own, in contrast to the continental practice of fathers tightly reining in their sons until after their own retirement. Ibid.
22. Robert Hamerton-Kelly, *God the Father: Theology and Patriarchy in the Teaching of Jesus* (Philadelphia, PA: Fortress, 1979), 5-7.
23. With the possible exception of liberation theology, which uses the concept of God as Father in an attempt to avoid 'speculative philosophical language', portraying Him rather as 'the merciful Father who is revealed to the simple' and as 'our solicitous, infinitely able Parent'. Ronaldo Muñoz, 'God the Father', in *Mysterium Liberationis: Fundamental Concepts of Liberation Theology*, translated by Robert R Barr, edited by Ignacio Allacuria and Jon Sobrino (Maryknoll, NY: Orbis, 1993), 406, 413.

God's fatherhood is Mary Daly, who takes Freud's theories to their logical conclusion and blames fatherhood for a self-alienation that produces rape, genocide, and war.[24] As Catherina Halkes observes, 'it is hardly possible to call to mind a single feminist theologian, whatever her phase of development may be, who does not find the image of the Father-God a challenge and a direct confrontation'.[25]

One final issue concerning God's fatherhood is the popular misconception that "the idea of God as Father is essentially a New Testament concept."[26] In modern times, this opinion can be traced to the influential Wilhelm Bousset,[27] who lays the foundations on which his student Rudolf Bultmann builds.[28] Bultmann, in turn, influences a generation of New Testament scholars, including Joachim Jeremias,[29] the scholar most responsible for the current popular view.[30] The general contemporary understanding is that the fatherhood of God has particular significance in the New Testament,[31] but is 'thin and underdeveloped' in the Old Testament.[32] Underlying this misconception is a presupposition, based largely on the writings of Paul but reflecting Origen's conclusions, that the benevolent Father

---

24. Mary Daly, *Beyond God the Father: Toward a Philosophy of Women's Liberation* (Boston: Beacon, 1973), 114–122. She could have made a much stronger case if she had not appealed to Greek mythology, for in so doing she legitimises Augustine's use of Plato to arrive at the conclusion of the woman only being complete in the man.
25. Catherina Halkes, 'The Themes of Protest in Feminist Theology against God the Father', in *Concilium: An International Review of Theology*, 143 (1981): 103–110 This antipathy against God arises from a perceived hierarchical and patriarchal authoritarian structure based on the Lord-God, father of all, who directs the 'Holy Father', the ecclesiastical head of pastoral rulers and spiritual 'fathers', and then on down to the prince, 'father of his country' (that is, ruler over the fatherland), finally to the father over a family, head over his wife, and owner of his children. Thus 'Authority and right come from above; obedience, dependence and reliance operate below'. Jürgen Moltmann, 'The Motherly Father: Is Trinitarian Patripassianism Replacing Theological Patriarchalism?', translated by GWS Knowles, *God as Father?*, in *Concilium: An International Review of Theology*, 143 (1981): 52.
26. Thomas McGovern, 'John Paul II on the Millennium and God as Father', in *Homiletic and Pastoral Review*, Volume 99, Number 7 (April 1999): 9.
27. Wilhelm D Bousset, *Jesu Predigt in ihrem Gegensatz zum Judentum: Ein religionsgeschichtlicher Vergleich* (Göttingen: Vandenhoeck and Ruprecht, 1892).
28. See especially Rudolf Bultmann, *Primitive Christianity in Its Contemporary Setting*, translated by RH Fuller (New York: Meridian, 1956).
29. See especially Joachim Jeremias, *The Prayers of Jesus* (Naperville: Allenson, 1967).
30. WE Nunnally, 'The Fatherhood of God at Qumran' (PhD dissertation Hebrew Union College, 1992), 235.
31. GW Bromiley, 'God', *ISBE, op cit*, 2:501; Evert J Blekkink, *The Fatherhood of God: Considered from Six Inter-Related Standpoints* (Grand Rapids, MI: Eerdmans, 1942), 32.
32. JDW Watts, 'God the Father', *ISBE, op cit*, 2:510. See also, Edward J Young, *The Book of Isaiah: The English Text, with Introduction, Exposition and Notes*, Chapters 40 through 66, NICOT (Grand Rapids: Eerdmans, 1972), 3:488.

God of the New Testament must be contrasted to the 'ruling master' God of the Old Testament.[33]

On the other hand, in the search for the origins of the New Testament position, contrary positions have sometimes been overstated and only muddied the waters. 'The Fatherhood of God is a characteristically Jewish doctrine, found in equal abundance in the Old Testament and in rabbinic literature.'[34] This view is supported by Marianne Meye Thompson, who states that the portraits of God as Father in the Old and New Testaments are marked more by continuity than by discontinuity.[35] It is also consistent with the findings of Nunnally in his review of unpublished prayers, psalms, wisdom literature, and legal testaments from Qumran, which he compares with the early Jewish midrashic and liturgical texts.[36]

As this brief survey of Christian history indicates, biblical texts have been sidelined, either in favor of Greco-Roman paradigms or of anthropocentric concerns. Unfortunately, 'there has long been a certain traditional resistance among many western Europeans to any close links between Semitic and Indo-European material',[37] especially since the renaissance, resulting in Greek philosophical ideas being read back into biblical understandings of God. However, if biblical studies are to be credible, they must take account of the abundance of material that has been found in the period since Christian prejudices has become firmly fixed in favor of Greco-Latin traditions. The literature of the Ancient Near East is especially useful in informing us of much older paradigms, without which no modern exegesis or paradigm can be complete.

Ideas from the Ancient Near East

Sumer

The Sumerians are the first people in recorded history to develop ethical, religious, social, political, and philosophical ideas.[38] The study of the fatherhood of

---

33. For example, see Romans 8:15, where Paul compares the 'spirit of servitude and fear' with the 'spirit of adoption' as sons. *Cf* G Ernest Wright, 'The Terminology of Old Testament Religion and Its Significance', *Journal of Near Eastern Studies* 1 (January-October 1942): 404.
34. Frederick John Foakes-Jackson and Kirsopp Lake, *The Beginnings of Christianity*, Part I, *The Acts of the Apostles* (London: MacMillan, 1942), 1:401.
35. Marianne Meye Thompson, *The Promise of the Father: Jesus and God in the New Testament* (Louisville, KY: Westminster John Knox, 2000), 19.
36. WE Nunnally, 'The Fatherhood of God', 238–239. In this seminal work, Nunnally examines both published and unpublished Qumranic material, and shows quite conclusively that the Judaism of that era enjoyed a personal relationship with the Father God.
37. Stephanie Dalley, 'Gilgamesh in the Arabian Nights', in *Gilgamesh: A Reader*, ed. John Maier (Wauconda, IL: Bolchazy-Carducci, 1997), 216. When Dalley refers to 'Indo-European material' she means the classics from the Greco-Roman period.
38. Sumer covers the southern half of modern Iraq, from the region of Baghdad to the Persian Gulf.

the gods must therefore commence with them. It is from the sacred stories of Sumer that we obtain the first glimpses of Ancient Near Eastern cosmogony: the account of the origin of their universe, an introduction to their gods, and the genesis of humanity.[39] Their doctrines become the 'basic creed and dogma of much of the ancient Near East', but nowhere are they systematised.[40]

In Sumerian cosmogony, the primeval sea-goddess Nammu is 'the mother who gave birth to heaven and earth'. Nothing is said of her origin or birth. Perhaps the Sumerians conceive of the primeval ocean as having existed eternally. But at some stage she gives birth to the cosmic mountain, consisting of the entwined gods An and Ki, a united heaven and earth, who in turn produce the air-god, Enlil. He subsequently separates his entwined parents: his father An carrying off heaven; Enlil carrying off his mother, Ki, the earth. The union of Enlil and mother earth sets the stage for the organisation of the universe—the creation of man, animals, and plants, and the establishment of civilisation.[41]

It with Enlil that the real significance of the fatherhood of the gods in Sumerian thought becomes plain. Nammu, the primeval ocean, precedes any father-god, and An is extolled for his virility and wisdom. It is only when Enlil breaks up the cozy arrangement between his enmeshed parents that there is a positive and perpetuating progress in the creation of earth and its cultures. No wonder he is considered 'by far the most important deity' of the Sumerian pantheon.[42]

Enlil is called the 'bull that overwhelms',[43] a powerful metaphor highlighting his fertility. He is the god responsible for planning and maintaining the most productive functions of the cosmos, ensuring prosperity for all. As 'father of the gods', he adjudicates in the highest court available to gods and humans, and upholds

---

The reigion is later known as Sumer and Akkad, and later still as Babylonia. It may have originally been inhabited by colonists who had been an oppressed economic or religious minority, not unlike the first Europeans to settle in America. Their freedom of worship may have led to their religious creativity and expression, and later to their political organisation. See Samuel Noah Kramer, *The Sacred Marriage Rite: Aspects of Faith, Myth, and Ritual in Ancient Sumer* (Bloomington, IN: Indiana University Press, 1969), 3; Kramer, *From the Poetry of Sumer: Creation, Glorification, Adoration* (Berkeley, CA: University of California Press, 1979), 51, 52; Kramer, *History Begins at Sumer: Thirty-nine Firsts in Man's Recorded History* (Philadelphia, PA: University of Philadelphia Press, 1981), xix.

39. Samuel Noah Kramer, *Sumerian Mythology: A Study of Spiritual and Literary Achievement in the Third Millennium BC* (Philadelphia: University of Philadelphia Press, 1972), 30.
40. Idem, *The Sumerians: Their History, Culture, and Character* (Chicago, IL: University of Chicago Press, 1963), 145.
41. Kramer, *History Begins at Sumer*, op cit, 82, 83; Kramer, *Sumerian Mythology*, op cit, 39-41.
42. Kramer, *History Begins at Sumer*, 88.
43. Zimmern KL II.1-6, in Stephen Langdon, *Sumerian Liturgies and Psalms*, Publications of the Babylonian Section, no. 4, The University of Pennsylvania Museum (Philadelphia, PA: University of Pennsylvania, 1919), 10:292.

divine laws that 'like heaven cannot be overturned' nor 'shattered'.[44] As father of kings, he gives earthly monarchs sovereignty, prospering their reigns and subduing their enemies.[45]

Enlil's brother Enki is another important deity, also a father god, but less powerful. He gives fecundity to land, ewe, cow, goat, and field.[46] However, his greatest significance is as divine lawgiver. Being the recipient of the divine laws or *me*'s from the hand of Enlil,[47] he upholds and maintains the created realms; promotes social structure, law, and order; and causes urban and rural realms to flourish. He is also the patron of artisans, whose work continues the creative processes of the gods.

Nanna the moon god is called 'father' in the context of the judgments he brings upon the city of Ur. This action is so out of character that the temple poet questions his sanity, that he cries out repeatedly, 'How has your heart led you on!' and, 'How now can you exist!'.[48]

The fatherhood of Utu, the sun, is presented in a more positive light. He is appreciated as the father of humanity, particularly of the wanderer, the homeless, and the orphan.[49]

Apart from the main pantheon, there are lesser deities, regarded as personal gods for the people of Sumer. The personal god intercedes for the human supplicant in the assembly of the gods.[50] He engenders, provides, protects, and claims personal obedience.[51] The relationship is perpetuated through the generations by god and goddess incarnate in human parents. The personal god of the father passes from the body of the father to the son from generation to generation, hence the term 'god of the fathers'.[52] This is a comfortable arrangement, in light of the Sumerian view of parents generally: 'the father is respected', and 'the mother is feared'.[53]

So the Sumerians primarily see the fatherhood of their gods as procreative, and secondarily as the source of wisdom. The divine laws dispensed by the father-god ensure human progress and prosperity, reconciliation and sovereignty.

---

44. 'Hymn to Enlil', in Kramer, *History Begins at Sumer, op cit*, 91.
45. *Ibid*, 89.
46. 'Enki and the World Order', in Kramer, *The Sumerians, op cit*, 174.
47. *Ibid*, 175.
48. 'Lamentation Over the Destruction of Ur', in Kramer, *The Sumerians, op cit*, 143.
49. BM 23631.29–34, in Kramer, *Poetry of Sumer, op cit*, 96.
50. Kramer, *The Sumerians*, 126, 127.
51. Thorkild Jacobsen, *The Treasures of Darkness: A History of Mesopotamian Religion* (New Haven, MA: Yale University Press, 1976), 158.
52. *Ibid*, 159.
53. Kramer, *Poetry of Sumer, op cit*, 68.

Babylon

Babylon comes from the same geographic region as Sumer. The Babylonians speak a different language, but borrow copiously from Sumerian theology and culture, adapting them to their own purposes.[54] Sumerian influence is evident in the pantheons of the three main extant Babylonian literary works—the *Gilgamesh Epic*,[55] the *Atrahasis Epic*,[56] and the *Enuma Eliš*,[57] but the Babylonian Marduk and Ishtar are ascendant.

The language of fatherhood is especially used with reference to the god presiding over the heavenly council. Anšar presides in the *Enuma Eliš* and Enlil in the *Myth of Zu*. Marduk addresses Anšar as father and father-creator (Volume II. 112), for creatorship and the maintenance of the cosmic order through judgment are roles of the father-god. When Marduk summons the full assembly of the gods, he speaks of them collectively as 'my fathers' (*ilani abê-a*). He uses a similar expression when challenging Tiamat (*ilani abê-e-a*) to lend credibility and legitimacy to his demands. When he defeats Tiamat and the gods rejoice together, he is promoted to head of the pantheon and addressed as 'the creator of the gods of his fathers' (*ba-an ilani abê-šu*). The link between the motifs of creator and judge is thus reinforced and a cyclical element added to the picture. By virtue of his position, the head of the pantheon is both creator-judge and father.

---

54. Within a few decades, Akkad, a previously insignificant town near the city of Babylon, becomes the fear and envy of nations as far-flung as the highlands of Anatolia to the north, the Mediterranean to the west, and the Indus Valley to the east. Although the economic and military activity of its dynasty lasts only from ca 2310 – 2160 BC, its cultural and linguistic influence dominate the whole of Mesopotamia and much of the Near East for two and a half millennia. The kings of Akkad represent the ideal monarchy, and their statue appear in the sanctuaries of the great urban centers. Joan Goodnick Westenholz, *Legends of the Kings of Akkade: The Texts* (Winona Lake, IN: Eisenbrauns, 1997), 1.
55. The latest and best-known version dates to the end of the Middle Babylonian period, about 1000 BC. It is written on twelve tablets in Akkadian, the main Semitic language of Assyria and Babylonia. With earlier versions extant up to 1100 years earlier, it is possible to document its evolution over that time. Jeffrey H Tigay, *The Evolution of the Gilgamesh Epic* (Philadelphia, PA: University of Pennsylvania Press, 1982).
56. The most complete edition was copied during the reign of Ammi-saduqa, great-great-grandson of Hammurabi (ca 1600 BC), although most extant copies date to ca. 700 – 650 BC. WG Lambert and AR Millard, *Atrahasis: The Babylonian Story of the Flood* (Oxford: Clarendon, 1969), 5.
57. It is commonly refereed to *The Babylonian Epic of Creation* or as *When on High*, after the opening words in translation. It is seven tablets long and is composed around 1200 BC, apparently for the purpose of legitimising Marduk's ascendency over the earlier established pantheon. S Langdon, *The Babylonian Epic of Creation: Restored from the Recently Recovered Tablets of Aššur, Transcription, Translation and Commentary* (Oxford: Clarendon, 1923); Alexander Heidel, *The Babylonian Genesis: The Story of Creation* (Chicago, IL: University of Chicago Press, 1942).

Egypt

Gods proliferate in the scattered Egyptian religio-political centers, especially Heliopolis, Memphis, and Thebes. Each center has its own theology, and approximately 740 different gods are mentioned by the time of Tuthmosis III (1504 – 1450 BC).[58]

The Heliopolitans believe Atum rises from the chaotic primordial watery abyss, dispels the darkness, and fathers children, even before completing the created realms. He thus becomes known as the 'universal father of gods'. He also becomes the father of humanity, but only because the human race arrives unexpectedly through the tears of anxious grief he sheds as he loses sight of his children playing in the watery abyss.

The relationship between the gods and humanity is never very positive. There is a revolt and only Ra's sense of justice averts human annihilation. The gods escape to their own realm, and Ra abdicates his earthlykingdom, which end up in the care of the pharaohs,[59] who claim that the gods are their fathers. The pharaohs then maintain the order of creation and civil order, using elaborate public ceremonies and rituals to prevent the re-emergence of primeval chaos. The common people thus enjoy peace and prosperity through the hands of the pharaohs.

Funerary texts enrich our understanding of the father-god motif by describing the individual roles of the gods. Ra is the most important father-god, for he provides not only barley, spelt, bread, and beer for this life;[60] he also provides for the afterlife. He sets the ladder for the resurrected soul to ascend into the sky,[61] sends his messengers to ensure it arrives safely,[62] and becomes the focus of attention as the resurrected king enters the heavenly realm.

Geb is called 'father' because of his role in putting all the bones back together, restoring intestines and eyes,[63] and providing a helping hand on the journey through the sky.[64] He affectionately welcomes the resurrected king into the heav-

---

58. Veronica Ions, *Egyptian Mythology* (New York: Peter Bedrick, 1983), 34.
59. Ra first hands rulership of the earth over to Thoth (the moon), who restores light to the world. James B Pritchard, *Ancient Near Eastern Texts: Relating to the Old Testament* (Princeton, NJ: Princeton University Press, 1969), 8. However, power is passed from demigod to demigod, until it eventually ends up with the pharaohs. Pascal Vernus, *The Gods of Ancient Egypt*, translated by JM Todd (New York, NY: John Braziller, 1998), 83.
60. Ut.205.121a, in *The Ancient Egyptian Pyramid Texts*, translated by by Raymond O Faulkner (Oxford: Clarendon, 1969), 37.
61. Ut.271.390, in *ibid*, 791.
62. Ut.214.136, in *ibid*, 41.
63. Ut 14.9c, Ut15, Pyramid Text of Pepi II, in EA Wallis Budge, *Osiris and the Egyptian Religion of Resurrection: Illustrated After Drawings from Egyptian Papyri and Monuments* (London: PL Warner, 1911, reprint, New York: University Books, 1961), 2:314.
64. Ut 485A.1030, in Faulkner, *Pyramid Texts*, 172.

enly realm and places him at the head of the other resurrected beings.[65] He facilitates the acceptance of the newcomer by the other gods, naming the resurrected pharaoh as his rightful heir in whom he is satisfied,[66] and transferring his honour to his son, the king.[67]

In Memphan theology, the son is idealised as protector and preserver of the father-deity, and is even called the 'Saviour of his father'.[68] The mother figure also obtains more rights and privileges for her son through tricking the aged father.[69]

For the Thebans, Atum is the sustainer of those left behind at a pharaoh's death,[70] and the one who makes living eternally possible.[71] Ra is still affirmed as the 'father of the Fathers of all the gods', whose substance is unknown.[72] But he is also the focus of joy for the 'common folks, the source of 'sweetness' and 'love', and the reason for all existence.[73] In earlier dynasties only the pharaohs seem to have access to the gods.[74]

As in Memphis, the ruling pharaoh in Thebes is linked with the father-god, who ensures a long and stable reign.[75] As in Heliopolis, Ra provides a ladder between the two worlds for the resurrected soul.[76] Father Geb is again a key player, providing the guarantee of resurrection for a dead pharaoh,[77] keeping magic-stealing crocodiles out of the gods' domain,[78] and ensuring no coup or foreign attack succeeds as power passes from father to son.[79] Father Osiris has a key role in the resurrection, since it is his prerogative to preserve the flesh of the deceased.[80] Horus is extolled for rescuing his father.[81]

---

65. Ut 373.655–656, in *ibid*, 123, 124.
66. Ut 127.80a, in Samuel AB Mercer, *The Pyramid Texts: In Translation and Commentary* (New York: Longmans Green, 1952), 44; Ut 3.3a, in *ibid*, 20.
67. Ut.592.1615–1619, in Faulkner, *Pyramid Texts*, 243.
68. J Gwyn Griffiths, *Plutarch's de Iside et Osiride: Edited with an Introduction Translation and Commentary* (Cambridge: University of Wales Press, 1970), 344–345.
69. *Ancient Near Eastern Texts*, 12–13.
70. Spell 72.S3, in Thomas George Allen, *The Book of the Dead or, Going Forth by Day: Ideas of the Ancient Egyptian Concerning the Hereafter as Expressed in Their Own Terms*, The Oriental Institute of the University of Chicago, Studies in Ancient Oriental Civilisation 37 (Chicago, IL: University of Chicago Press, 1974), 65.
71. Spell 170.S3, in *ibid*, 178.
72. Spell 15A4.2-3, in *ibid*, 19.
73. Spell 15B2.1-2, in *ibid*, 21.
74. Vernus, *Gods of Ancient Egypt*, 97.
75. Spell 175*b*.S3, in Allen, *Book of the Dead*, 184.
76. Spell 153.S7, in *ibid*, 152.
77. Spell 69a.S2-S4, in *ibid*, 63.
78. Spell 31*b*.S, in *ibid*, 41.
79. Spell 47.S3, in *ibid*, 51.
80. Spell 155.S1, in *ibid*, 153, 154; Spell 181*d*.S.1, in *ibid*, 194.
81. Spell 78.S16, in *ibid*, 69.

In all these instances, it is difficult to determine the exact nature of the relationship between gods and humans in general. Most of the spells and utterances seem to be quite manipulative, ensuring the success of the human supplicant in the afterlife. Even the joyous ceremonies may primarily be tools to guarantee present peace and prosperity and future security. Certainly, the relationship of the masses to Ra must be colored by the early human attempts to rebel, despite the later attempts to sweeten the bond between them.

The relationship between pharaoh and the father-god is clearer. There is a fusion of their identities, with the father-god deferring to his pharaoh-son. Such preferential treatment certainly reinforces the notion that the masses did not really count for much.

This much is certain. The Egyptian gods are called 'father' in the context of the generation of other gods, the world, and everything in it. They are also called 'father' in relation to the pharaohs, and in relation to assisting souls in the afterlife into the presence of Ra. Thus it is in the context of creation and resurrection that their fatherhood is made evident. But as for the exact nature that this relationship assumed, we must reserve judgment.

Ugarit

Our understanding of second-millennium BCE Canaanite mythology has been 'significantly enhanced' through what has been touted as the most important archaeological discovery of the early twentieth century: the library of a chief priest of the Storm-god in the ancient city of Ugarit.[82] The 'family tree' of the Canaanite pantheon is hard to establish, since the simple use of the designation 'father' is insufficient to establish filial relationship.[83] El does not physically conceive all

---

82. John W Miller, 'God as Father in the Bible and the Father Image in Several Contemporary Ancient Near Eastern Myths: A Comparison', in *SR* 14 (1985): 349. As a vassal state in the Hittite empire, Ugarit falls 'squarely within the Hittite sphere of influence'. Cyrus H Gordon, *Ugaritic Literature: A Comprehensive Translation of the Poetic and Prose Texts* (Rome: Pontifical Biblical Institute, 1949), ix. The library tablets date between 1400 and 1200 BCE, at the height of Ugarit's international trade. *Ibid*, ix, x. They are written in a previously unknown language using a cuneiform script, deciphered soon after their discovery due to the relative simplicity of the characters. Johannes C de Moor, *An Anthology of Religious Texts from Ugarit* (Leiden: EJ Brill, 1987), vii, viii. The significance of Ugaritic religious literature lies in its strategic position between the Hittite nation and Israel, forming a possible ideological bridge between them. The inhabitants of Ugarit distance themselves from the Canaanites, but their culture is largely Canaanite, allowing data from there to give 'a fairly accurate view of the Canaanite pantheon'. Jonathan N Tubb, *Canaanites: Peoples of the Past* (London: British Museum, 1998), 73.
83. The genealogy of the gods is difficult to determine because of who calls whom father. E Theodore Mullen, Jr, *The Divine Council in Canaanite and Early Hebrew Literature* (Chico, CA: Scholars, 1980), 16–17, 19–22; Conrad E L'Hereux, *Rank Among the Canaanite Gods: El, Ba'al, and the Repha'im*, Harvard Semitic Monographs 21 (Missoula, MO: Scholars Press, 1979), 12–14; N Wyatt, 'The Titles of the Ugaritic Storm God', *UF* 24 (1992): 406.

the gods—he crafts some out of clay—yet he is still called 'father of the gods'. Other clues are needed to develop an understanding of the nature and quality of fatherhood among the Canaanite gods. One source may be the narrative poems with their chronicling of human-divine relationships. In researching these, I have found that El is the only god in the Ugaritic pantheon spoken of as 'father' in relation to both gods and humanity.

In both the Kirta and Aqhat epics, the 'father of man' provides progeny for his earthly subjects and sufficient resources to maintain them. El as father-god is moved with pity for his earthly son Kirta, and orders circumstances so that Kirta sires a number of children, including Aqhat. 'To be *the* parents in the cosmic scheme was to be the highest authority.'[84]

El is not only the clansman-protector of Kirta, but as 'the king' and 'father of years' exercises dominion over all humanity. On the other hand, he becomes inebriated at a feast and needs to be carried home. His daughter 'Anat sometimes outwits him and he cowers at her wilting words. He shows his ineptitude when he accedes to Yamm and Nahar's demand for Baal to be taken from the assembly of gods. When Mot (death) swallows Baal, El hopelessly mourns in the dust and covers his loins with sackcloth. Ball must be rescued by his sister, 'Anat.

Divine fatherhood is sometimes understood in terms of harshness and vindictiveness. Here it seems pliant in the hands of demanding children. On the other hand, this myth may be an example of the transition of power from an older to a younger god, and El's delay before manifesting his divine prerogative may be a father's deliberate and measured response to the premature demands of his children.

The Ancient Near East in Summary

In summary, the fatherhood of the gods has wide scope across the Ancient Near East. It is evident in the dynamic activity of creation, in the maintenance of civil and divine order, in the accountability of gods and men in judgment, in the provision of hope for the future, and finally in resurrection from the dead. The way humans relate to the gods is largely positive. The kings do seem to have some advantage. However, there is insufficient data to compare the levels of devotion shown by kings and commoners to their father-gods.

We now turn to the Hebrew concept of God's fatherhood to see whether there has been significant borrowing or a new paradigm that is perhaps even a polemic against them.

---

84. Lowell K Handy, *Among the Host of Heaven: The Syro-Palestinian Pantheon as Bureaucracy* (Winona Lake, IN: Eisenbrauns, 1994), 79.

An Old Testament Theology of God as Father

In contrast to Ancient Near Eastern myths, the Old Testament creation accounts do not picture creation as the result of gods being engaged in sexual activity. The origins of humanity in the Sumero-Akkadian and Egyptian accounts are manipulative and accidental. In the Old Testament, God shows forethought, design, dignity, blessing, provision, and satisfied approval (Gen 1), and then He stoops first to form Adam then to construct Eve (Gen 2).

The Old Testament linking of God's fatherhood to creation means that He is recognised as Father of all creation for all time, so no one people has exclusive rights to Him. There is neither time nor place where He is unable to be Father to his children. The gods of the Ancient Near East are impotent, remote, inaccessible, self-indulgent, and bitter. But the God of the Old Testament is always there for His children, and nothing, from either the natural or supernatural realm, is able to separate Him from them (Deut 32:31–38).

There are eighteen references in seventeen verses of the Hebrew Scriptures that explicitly call God 'father'.[85] Five of these refer to God as the father of David and his dynasty,[86] eleven to Him being the father of his people,[87] and twice His love is compared to the love of a father for his child.[88] Although they range across the breadth of the canon, there are strong thematic and linguistic parallels that may be observed common among them.

The subject of God's fatherhood is not an afterthought in Hebrew Scripture, evidenced by the prominent positions given to the passages that contain them. Note that what follows are the superlative descriptions which some commentators give to many of the biblical Father-God passages. Albright opines that the Song of Moses is one of the most impressive religious poems in the entire Hebrew Scriptures.[89] Kruse suggests that there is hardly any prophecy in the Old Testament that has had so many repercussions in biblical literature as the oracle Nathan gave to king David.[90] Gordon thinks that 2 Samuel 7 is not only an ideological summit of 'Deuteronomistic history', but also of the Old Testament as a whole.[91] Dahood

---

85. This includes only verses that call God Father (ba' 'ab), and does not include references where the relationship is implied, or described in different terms, as in the "son" texts (for example 'You are my son' Psalm 2:6; Exodus 4:22–23; Hos 11:1; etc.). This has been an arbitrary decision of delimitation—the 'son' texts would make a separate study in themselves.
86. 2 Samuel 7:14; 1 Chronicles 17:13; 22:10; 28:6; Psalm 89:27[26].
87. Deuteronomy 32:6; 1 Chronicles 29:10; Psa 68:6[5]; Isaiah 63:16 (x2); 64:8; Jeremiah 3:4, 19; 31:9; Malachi 1:6; 2:10.lm
88. Psalm 103:13; Proverbs 3:12.
89. WF Albright, 'Some Remarks on the Song of Moses in Deuteronomy 32', in *Essays in Honour of Millar Burrows*, ed. Martin Noth (Leiden: Brill, 1959), 339.
90. Heinz Kruse, 'David's Covenant', in *Vetus Testamentum*, 35 (1985): 139.
91. Robert P Gordon, *1 & 2 Samuel: A Commentary* (Exeter: Paternoster, 1986), 235. See also AA

observes says that Psalm 68 is widely admitted as textually and exegetically the most difficult and obscure of the psalms.[92] Weiser notes that Psalm 103 is 'one of the finest blossoms on the tree of biblical faith',[93] while McConville reports that Jer 31:9 is said to be 'among the most poignant' in the book of Jeremiah,[94] and Kaiser calls Malachi 2:10-16 'one of the most important and one of the most difficult pericopes in the book of Malachi'.[95] Added to these, 1 Chronicles 17 comes as a climax to the book to which the genealogical foundation leads.

God's fatherhood is introduced (at least to public religious life) in a public assembly called to 'proclaim the name of the Lord' (Deut 32:3); a phrase echoing the answer given when Moses asked God to show His face (Exod 33:18-20). In the resulting theophany, God gave specific characteristics to describe Himself (34:5-7). These descriptions would later appear in the Song of Moses, and in other Father-God passages (especially Ps 103) with the following keywords or thoughts: $r^e\mu um$ (motherly yearning); $\mu enun$ (grace); $'erek$ (slow to anger—also refers to [eagle] pinions!); $\mu esed$ (faithfulness), and $'emet$ (truth), forgiving iniquity and transgression and sin, not clearing the guilty, but visiting the iniquity of the parents upon the children to the third and the fourth generation. The word for 'yearning' (from the root $r\mu m$) is especially interesting in that it includes qualities that, humanly speaking, belong to the mother.

Significant because it is the first extended portrayal of God as Father, the linguistic backdrop to the Song of Moses is painted in the subtle color of creation theology. It commences with calling heaven and earth to attention, an echo of the ten times in creation when God spoke, and a theme seen in other Father-God passages.[96] Creation themes become a backdrop for the Father-God panorama. Exodus and the covenant dominate the foreground. A contrast is drawn between the Father-God of covenant faithfulness, who initiated (at creation) and established (during the exodus) a relationship with His people, and the people who are described as 'foolish' and 'unwise' (Deut 32:6) for their ingratitude and rejection, and their insistence in worshiping 'worthless idols' (v. 21). There is a tension between the fickleness of humanity and the abiding faithfulness of God that is witnessed

---

Anderson, *2 Samuel*, Word Bible Commentary, edited by John D Watts (Dallas: Word, 1989), 11:112.

92. Mitchel Dahood, *Psalms II: 51-100*, Anchor Bible (Garden City, NY: Doubleday, 1968), 17:133.
93. Artur Weiser, *The Psalms: A Commentary*, Old Testament Library, translated by H Hartnell, edited by Peter Ackroyd *et al* (Philadelphia: Westminster Press), 657.
94. Walter Brueggemann, *To Pluck Up, to Tear Down: A Commentary on the Book of Jeremiah 1-25*, International Theological Commentary, edited by Fredrick Carlson Holgrem and George AF Knight (Grand Rapids: Eerdmans, 1988), 43.
95. Walter C Kaiser Jr, 'Divorce in Malachi 2:10-16', in *Criswell Theological Review* 2 (1987): 73.
96. Echoed by the use of certain keywords in the Nathan-vision corpus (*bnh* [build], *kun* [establish], heaven and earth (1Chr 29:11), plus Psalm 68:8; Psalm 89:6-19[5-18]; Proverbs 3:19-20; Isaiah 64:8-9; and Malachi 2:10.

right up to the time of Malachi. However, although reference to God's fatherhood in the Song of Moses is cast in the context of a Hittite suzerainty treaty, the alliance described is more in terms of relational closeness than legal bonds. God deals with the situation as a father, gently, but firmly, guiding His errant children, not as a conquering king wiping out all opposition.

God's fatherhood is quite unlike the father-gods of the ANE in at least one important regard: Nowhere in the biblical account is there a hint of humans becoming gods, unlike the pharaohs, for example, who became gods on their ascension to the throne. There are a number of places that spell out at length the principle that 'once a human always a human'. This is seen in the lengths taken to outline Solomon's genealogy. God would raise up a 'son', not by his own procreative powers, (as seen in the sexual procreative acts of the ANE father-gods,) but through David's act of procreation (2 Sam 7:14). Solomon, then, became a son by 'adoption', or in other words, his relationship with God is a spiritual, not physical one, yet profoundly affecting every area of the new king's life. This forms the pattern for the Father-son relationship with all his children.

The Father nurtures his children to the place where they may live life responsibly and accountably, like a young eagle that must learn to fly (Deut 32:11). He nurtures by building and establishing a name (2 Sam 7:9) and a dynasty (verse 16) for David, and a throne for Solomon (v 13). He assures their long-term viability (1 Chr 17:14), sometimes seen in re-establishing His scattered people (Jer 31:7 9). He promises to 'plant' His people so that they may have a place free from the oppression of wicked men (2 Sam 7:10), and where they may maintain their social/political stability (1 Chr 22:12-13). David is confident in asking God to establish the hearts of His people toward the Father to ensure continuing loyalty (1 Chr 29:18-19), but if they fail God assures them that their sins have been removed to the remotest extremes (Ps 103:11-12), and that He forgives sin and heals their sickness (verse 3).

The theme of the Father-God judging is made prominent in the passages dealt with in Psalms and Proverbs. In Psalm 68 He ascends to His throne (verse 19[18]) from where He deals out the just deserts to the oppressors of his people (verses 2-3[1-2]; 13[12]; 15-19[14-18]; 24[23]; 31[30]); He shows himself triumphant over the forces of evil, and to the mind of someone from the ANE, the forces of the underworld (Ps 68:3[2]); and He restores the prosperity of his people (verses 4-13[3-12]; 20[19]; 23[22]; 36[35]).

The Father-God's judicial acts take place from the throne of His sanctuary in Heaven, which is described in terms of righteousness, justice, mercy and truth (Ps 89:15[14]), and it is established for those who keep His covenant (Ps 103:19). This means He not only deals with oppressors of His people, but with their rebellion against the divine order as well. He declares that He will punish His sons if they forsake His laws and judgments, statutes and commandments (verses 31-33[30-

32]). The idea of God rebuking his children is explained in terms of showing them favour (Prov 3:11–12), to prevent their ultimate self-destruction. The 'son' is admonished neither to forget the father's commands (verse 1) nor to despise the discipline of the Lord, because God lovingly corrects His children. As the potter', He is given the right to continue to mold and shape human destiny to bring out the best work of art from the lump of 'clay' (Isa 64:8).

This system of accountability, is backed up by God's memory,[97] which serves not merely of to bringing His children to account, but rather functions as a guarantee for covenant continuity and stability. He remembers, 'we are dust' (Ps 103:14), and He remembers the Exodus (Isa 64:11) when humans forget. This becomes a long-term reality check, effective in situations such as when 'unfaithful Judah', (Jer 3:4–5) used her pious pretense of loyalty to manipulate God's bounty, while at the same time pursuing the hunt for lovers, and covering her 'promiscuity' with the hypocrisy of her religious professions.

Therefore, God's fatherhood is not something forced upon the unwilling. The 'child' of God was given the right of veto. The prospect of divine discipline remained for the one choosing to turn aside, should s/he opt to reject the *chuqim* (statutes) and *mišpatim* (judgments) that God had given to Moses. Initially these decrees were given as a token of parental love (Prov 3:12), and the bond between humanity and God was made sure by virtue of God's faithfulness, (*chesed*) even if there were times when the human part of the agreement broke down. It is clear that the human is free to break away from the arrangement, even though a number of Bible writers outline both the warnings and the results of pursuing such a course (for example Ps 89:47-51[46–50]).

After repeated attempts of breaking free of the Father's yearnings for them, the people repeatedly end up in hopeless despair, rendering the fatherhood of God even more poignant to them. The 'not-yet' stance of Isaiah means that sometimes the Father may appear frustratingly silent, when He should, at least to human eyes, be down here rattling a few mountains (Isa 63:19[64:1]). Perhaps the reason He does not is because He has a more gentle approach. He leads the most vulnerable, along the most accessible and gentle roads (Jer 31:9), like a father with a fumbling child, at a pace that may make the Bible writers impatient.

However, what counts in the end is the exuberance expressed by the people for their Father-God, shining above their despair. Psalm 68 expresses a hymn of praise for the Father who has jurisdiction over every realm, and old and young celebrate together in the streets (Jer 31:13). What is pictured here is a relationship that at times shows incredible intimacy, experienced on an individual level, and celebrated corporately, between the Father-God and his people. Even though many of the passages in this study are based on the Davidic covenant, it appears

---

97. God 'remembers" in Psalm103:14; Isaiah 64:11; Jeremiah 2:2; and 31:20.

the common people took this personally, and applied its benefits to themselves. They saw God as their Father, and trusted in his care for them.

Even though the human race may have deserted every covenant that God has made with them, He still remains their father because He created them in the first place. He can never cease to be their father[98]. The implication of His *chesed* (faithfulness) continuing into eternity (*leôlam*), is that the Father-God restores the realm of creation, people and land, to its pristine condition in His last act of victory (Jer 31:10-14). Above all, His parenting style may be best described in terms of the two closely related synonyms *rchm* (pity, the yearning of a mother) and *ahb* (love).

This is the Father the Hebrew Scriptures describe.

---

98 However, in the ANE this relationship could be broken after a duly appointed public ceremony, in which the father said, 'you are not my son.' See Moshe Weinfeld, 'Ancient Near Eastern Patterns in Prophetic Literature,' *Vetus Testamentum* 27 (1977): 188. There is no record of God saying this in Scripture.

Subject Index

Adventists, Seventh-day, 8, 11, 13, 21, 81, 82, 85, 86, 117, 119, 120, 121, 123, 125, 126, 128, 129, 132, 134, 135, 138, 143, 153, 154, 155, 156, 157, 158, 159, 160, 161, 163, 164, 166, 167, 190, 193, 196, 197, 222, 227, 232, 234, 235, 236, 237, 239, 240, 243, 247, 248, 251, 252, 254, 256, 257, 263, 264, 271, 272.
Atonement, 21, 132, 180, 191, 276, 277.
Biblicism, 232.
Communication, 39, 40, 43, 69, 94, 138, 167, 169, 199.
Contextualization, 168.
Culture, 18, 19, 20, 21, 23, 83, 85, 86, 88, 90, 91, 92, 93, 94, 95, 100, 103, 107, 108, 109, 110, 117, 118, 123, 126, 128, 157, 161, 163, 165, 168, 169, 101, 204, 229, 236, 237, 280, 282, 285.
Day of Atonement, 78, 149, 181, 193.
Deism, 229, 232, 236, 237.
Enlightenment, 6, 52, 96, 97, 108, 230, 236, 269, 276.
Eschatology, 73, 240.
Escahaton, the, 151, 277.
Excommunication, 216.
Fundamentalism, 18, 82, 85, 109, 234.
Gift of prophecy, 134, 156, 201, 203, 211, 212, 213, 214, 215, 216, 217, 218, 219, 220.
Great controversy, the, 86, 119, 122, 124, 125, 129, 136, 137, 148, 149, 171, 175, 178, 179, 180, 184, 186, 189, 190, 191, 240, 241, 242, 244, 251, 252.
Historicism, 81, 111, 190, 228, 229, 236, 255-274.
Inspiration, 20, 23, 33, 53, 57, 63, 86, 103, 113, 119, 120. 123, 124, 127, 129, 133, 134, 138, 172, 173, 183, 196, 199f, 218, 221, 222, 223, 227, 239, 241, 242, 251, 252, 254, 262, 277
Judgment, invetigative, 53, 185, 191, 195, 262.
Lifestyle, 140, 155–171.
Literary context, 14, 21, 32, 33, 34, 37, 41, 56, 160f.
Most Holy, 173, 181, 184.
Prophets & prophecy, 33, 46, 47, 48, 52, 54, 57, 58, 60, 62, 63, 89, 122, 130, 138, 161, 172, 174, 176, 179, 183, 184, 189, 191, 198, 200, 201, 202, 203, 205, 206, 207, 208, 209, 201, 211, 212, 213, 214, 215, 216, 218, 220, 221, 251, 264, 268.
Rationalism, 237.
Revelation, v, 8, 14, 15, 18, 20, 22, 23, 29, 30, 31, 34, 35, 38, 39, 41, 43, 44, 48, 61, 79, 78, 81, 90, 119, 124, 129, 195, 196, 200, 202, 212, 213, 215, 220, 231, 257, 258, 259, 260, 262, 264, 268, 272.
Book of, 122, 171, 172, 173, 176, 177,

179, 180, 181, 182, 183, 184, 185, 186, 187, 188, 189, 190, 191, 192, 194, 201, 203, 221, 233, 241, 242, 247, 248, 249, 251, 253, 257, 265, 266, 267.

Sabbath, 7, 11, 62, 131, 132, 136, 137, 154, 193, 232, 233. 234.

Sanctuary, 61, 78, 130, 131, 132, 133, 162, 173, 178, 179, 180, 181, 184, 191, 223, 230, 236, 262, 279.

Satan, 71, 77, 92, 93, 128, 136, 149, 165, 214, 239-254.

Second Coming, the, 81, 148, 149, 151, 182, 184, 229, 256, 271, 272, 274.

Sex, 56, 84, 92, 98, 100, 102, 103, 104,3, 104, 106, 110, 154, 158, 162, 163, 287, 289.

Ten Commandments, the, 11, 163, 177, 185.

Valuegenesis, 156.

Worship, 24, 48, 100, 125, 174, 182, 183, 193, 207, 210, 211, 218, 220, 221, 242, 276, 280, 288.

Author Index

Aland, Kurt, 32,
Albright, William, 287.
Allacuria, Ignacio, 277.
Allen, Leslie C, 244.
Allen, Thomas George, 284.
Allison, Dale C, 142.
Alpert, Rebecca, 99, 102.
Alter, Robert, 112.
Anderson, JN, 222.
Anderson, AA, 288.
Andreasen, Niels-Erik, 7.
Arasola, Kai J, 81, 228, 229, 236, 261, 262.
Archer, Gleason L, 7, 54.
Arius, 275.
Armstrong, Karen, 82.
Arnold, BT, 250.
Athanasius, 275.
Augustine, 144, 150, 275, 278.
Aune, David, 217, 219, 221, 249,.
Bailey, Randall, 100, 103.
Baker, DW, 250.
Balentine, George, 59.
Barclay, John MG, 71,
Barclay, William, 204,
Barnett, Paul, 70, 78.
Barr, David L, 33
Barr, James, 95, 104, 110,
Barr, Robert R, 277
Barrett, CK, 201,
Barthes, Roland, 96, 97.
Bartholomew, Craig, 4, 14.

Barton, John, 25, 86, 110, 113,
Basinger, David, 22
Bass, Alan, 40.
Battles, FL, 20,
Bauckham, Richard J, 31, 249, 250.
Beale, GK, 29, 30, 31, 33, 34, 35, 36, 37, 38, 39, 40, 41, 42, 43, 44, 48, 53, 249,
Behm, J, 77.
Belleville, Linda, 70, 71, 75.
Bentzen, A, 63.
Berger, Kathleen Stassen, 84, 85.
Bertoluci, Josc, 243, 244, 245.
Beveridge, Henry, 276.
Black, Matthew, 142.
Blackman, Cyril E, 9.
Bliss, Sylvester, 228, 229.
Block, Daniel, 244, 245, 246.
Booth, Walter M, 252.
Bornkamm, Günther, 70, 77.
Bouman, Herbert JA, 276.
Bousset, Wilhelm D, 278.
Bousset, Wilhelm, 278.
Bowden, John, 51.
Boyd, Gregory A, 240, 241, 245, 246, 247, 250, 251, 253.
Boyd, Gregory, 240, 241, 245, 246, 247, 250, 251, 253,
Bradford, Grame S, 126, 220.
Bratcher, Robert G, 32.
Bray, Gerald, 6.
Brett, Mark G, 103, 105.

Bricmont, Jean, 109.
Bromiley, GW, 278.
Brooten, JR, 276.
Bruce, FF, 75.
Brueggemann, Walter, 95, 107, 108, 109, 288.
Brunt, John C, 12, 13.
Budge, EA Wallis, 283
Bull & Lockhart, 162, 223, 230, 236.
Bull, Malcolm, 236.
Bultmann, Rudolph, 278.
Butler, Jonathan M, 231.
Böcher, Otto, 32.
Caird, GB, 204.
Callen, Barry L, 21, 22.
Calvin, John, 18, 141, 144, 237, 276.
Cappadocian fathers, 275.
Carroll, Robert, 110. 11.
Carson, DA, 12, 70, 71, 75, 88, 216.
Cartledge, Samuel A, 258.
Chamberlain, Michael, 124.
Charles, RH, 30.
Chisolm, Robert B, Jr, 109.
Clines, David JA, 97.
Coleman, Richard J, 9.
Collins, Yarbro, 33.
Conrad, Edgar W, 4, 5, 9, 13, 14, 15.
Conradi, LR, 131.
Constantine, 6, 7.
Coon, Roger, 127.
Cottrell, Raymond F, 138, 262.
Countryman, William, 102.
Craig, Bryan, 85.
Crane, Marilyn C, 117.
Cranfield, 202, 218, 219.
Cranfield, CB, 202, 218, 219.
Crawford, Thomas J, 276, 277.
Crawford, Thomas J, 276, 277.
Cronge, G, 108.
Crosby, Tim, 199.
Crosier, Owen, 130, 132.
Dahood, Mitchel, 287, 288.

Dalley, Stephanie, 279.
Daly, Mary, 280.
Damsteegt, P Gerard, 238.
Daniels, AG, 197, 198, 222.
Davidson, Richard, 44, 51, 61, 135, 235, 236, 241, 244.
Davies, WD, 142.
Davis, Delmer I, 163.
Davis, Marian, 129.
de Klerk, WA, 106.
de Moor, Johannes C, 285.
de Tocqueville, Alexis, 277.
de Valla, Lorenzo, 6, 7.
Dederen, Raoul, 123, 241, 257,
Delitzsch, Franz, 63.
Denney, James, 8.
Derrida, Jacques, 39, 43, 95, 96, 104.
Descartes, René, 111.
deSilva, David A, 70.
Dimant, Divorah, 31.
Dockery, DS, 9.
Dodd. CH, 35, 42, 47, 57, 142, 143.
Donaldson, Laura, 100, 101, 102, 103, 106.
Douglass, Herbert E, 122.
Driver, SR, 11.
Dube, Musa, 101, 103.
Duguid, Ian, 243, 245, 246.
Durham, John I, 69.
Edson, Hiram, 132.
Efird, James A, 30.
Eichrodt, Walter, 244.
Ellis, E Earle, 53, 73, 76.
Epiphanes, Antiochus IV, 7.
Erickson, Millard, 21, 246.
Ericson, Norman R, 41.
Faber, George Stanley, 230, 229.
Fackre, Gabriel, 23.
Faulkner, Raymond O, 283, 284.
Fee, Gordon D, 17, 248.
Fekkes, Jan, 31.
Ferret, Rick, 124.

Fiorenza, Elizabeth Schlüsser, 33, 40.
Fishburn, Janet Forsythe, 276.
Fitzmyer, Joseph A,
Floris, Joachim of, 259.
Foakes-Jackson, Frederick John30. 68.
Foerster, Werner, 32.
Forbes, Chris, 213, 214.
Foucault, Michel, 97, 100, 104, 108, 109, 110.
Fowler, James, 125,
Fowler, John M, 240.
France, RT, 11.
Franzmann, Majella, 14, 15.
Fraser, Gary, 126.
Freed, Anne, 229, 230.
Freed, Anne, 229, 230.
Freedman, DN, 48, 70.
Freud, Sigmund, 277, 278.
Froom, Leroy L, 229, 258, 259, 261, 269, 270, 274.
Fuller, Daniel P, 8, 241, 250.
Fuller, RH, 278,
Furnish, Victor P, 70, 77.
Garrett, Duane A, 9.
Geisler, Norman L, 22.
Georgi, Dieter, 68, 71, 76.
Gergen, KJ, 23.
Gesenius, William, 55.
Gilgamesh, 279, 282.
Gill, John, 229.
Gill, John, 229.
Gillespie, Thomas W, 217, 220.
Gillespie, TW, 217, 220.
Gilmour, S MacLean, 70.
Gladden, Washington, 276.
Gladson, Jerry, 7.
Goldingay, John, 83.
Goldstone, S Ross, 119.
Gordon, Colin, 108.
Gordon, Cyrus H, 285.
Gordon, Robert, 287
Graybill, Ronald D

Green, Joel B, 32, 248.
Green, Michael, 200, 213.
Green, Rayna, 100.
Green, WS, 68
Greene, Thomas, 34.
Grenz, Stanley J, 246.
Groenewald, EP, 106.
Grudem, Wayne, 216, 217, 218, 246,
Gutierrez, Gustavo, 85.
Guy, Fritz, 127, 130, 252.
Halkes, Catherina,
Halkes, Catherina, 278.
Haloviak, Bert
Hamerton-Kelly, Robert
Hammurabi
Hanson. Anthony T
Harder, Frederick
Hasel, Gerhard F, 7, 9, 21, 83, 129, 235, 255, 257, 263, 266, 267, 268.
Hauser, Robert
Hays, Richard, 32, 38, 67, 68, 69, 71, 75, 76, 78,
Hayward, James L, 203.
Heidegger, Martin, 40.
Heidel, Alexander, 282.
Heinz Kruse, Heinz, 287.
Helyer, Larry R, 250.
Hempel, J, 48.
Henrdix, Truman, 113.
Herodotus, 204.
Herr, Larry G, 54.
Hillyer, Norman, 53.
Himes, Joshua V, 227.
Hirsch, ED, 36, 37, 40,41, 42.
Hittite, 285, 289,
Holbrook, Frank, 61, 78, 187, 196, 241, 257, 264, 266.
Holgrem, Carlson, 288.
Holladay, Carl H, 71.
Hollander, John, 34.
Hooker, Morna D, 68, 70.
Hornsby, Teresa J, 14, 15.

House, Paul R, 3.
Hoyt, Fred, 124,125.
Hubbard, Robert L, Jr, 102.
Huss, John, 124, 125.
Hyde, Gordon M, 82, 138, 235, 236,
Hyde, Gordon, 82, 235, 236
Haacker, Klaus, 32.
Instone-Brewer, David, 53.
Jacobsen, Thorkild, 281.
Jasper, David, 113.
Jefferson, Thomas, 100.
Jeremias, Joachim, 142, 143, 278,
Jeremias, Joachim, 142, 143, 278.
Jervell, Jacob Stephan, 75.
Johnson, Alan F, 249.
Johnson, Cedric B, 87,
Johnston, Robert M, 142.
Jones-Haldemann, Madelyn, 165.
Jones, AT, 197,
Jones, AT, 197, 198.
Jones, Katherine, 277.
Jones, Katherine, 277.
Jones, Peter, 275.
Jones, Peter, 273.
Josephus, Flavius, 62.
Jülicher, Adolf, 142.
Kaiser, Walter, 48, 51, 59, 60, 206, 288,
Kaste, Omar, 277.
Kaufman, Philip, 48.
Keener, Craig S, 142, 249.
Keil, CF, 63.
Kellogg, JH, 126, 197, 198.
Kertelge, K, 75.
Kidner, Derek, 62, 63.
Kimball, Robert, 110.
Kingsbury, Jack D, 71.
Kissinger, Warren S, 142.
Kitzberger, Ingrid Rosa, 84.
Kline, Meredith G, 10.
Knight, George AF, 288
Knight, George R, 228, 230, 237, 240, 252,

Knowles, GWS, 278.
Koch, Timothy, 98.
Kohlberg, Lawrence, 125.
Koranteng-Pipim, Samuel, 264.
Kraft, Heinrich, 30.
Kramer, Samuel Noah, 280, 281.
Krentz, Edgar, 6.
Kritzman, LD, 108, 112.
Krodel, Gerhard, 33.
Kruse, Heinz, 287.
Kümmel, Werner G, 70.
L›Hereux, Conrad E, 285.
Lacey, HC, 222, 223.
Ladd, George Eldon, 8.
Lake, Kirsopp, 279.
Lambrecht, J, 30.
Land, Gary, 161, 198.
Langdon, Stephen, 280, 282.
Larkin, William J, Jr, 19.
LaRondelle, Hans K, 63, 249, 255, 267.
Lattey, Cuthbert, 48.
Lawson, Ronald, 121.
Lehmann, Helmut T, 141.
Lesher, Richard, 266.
Lestringant, Pierre, 29.
Leupold, HC, 62, 63,
Lewis, CS, 15.
Lincoln, Andrew, 214.
Lindsey, Duane F, 62.
Lippmann, Walter, 276.
Litch, Josiah, 189, 190, 191.
Livingstone, EA, 82.
Luther, Martin, 141, 155, 276.
Lyotard, Jean-François, 95, 96, 97, 99, 108.
Maier, John, 279.
Manners, Bruce, 128.
Marshall, I Howard, 35, 53.
Martin, Ralph P, 75.
Mayes ,ADH, 12.
McAdams, Donald R, 124, 252.
McArthur, Harvey K, 142.

McCasland, S Vernon, 54, 65, 66.
McGinn, Bernard, 253.
McGovern, Thomas, 278.
McIver, Robert K, 8, 247.
McMahon, Don S, 125, 126.
McNamara, Martin, 30.
McNeill, JT, 20.
Mede, Joseph, 229.
Mede, Jospeh, 229.
Mercer, AB Samuel, 284.
Miller, James E, 110, 128, 213.
Miller, William, 227–237.
Milton, John, 123, 251.
Moltmann, Jürgen, 278.
Montgomery, James A, 30.
Moodie, T Dunbar, 105.
Moore, Michael S, 114.
Morgan, Douglas, 122.
Morgan, Robert, 25, 86, 113,
Morris, Leon, 200.
Moskala, Jiri, 47.
Motyer, Alec, 246.
Moule, Charles FD, 67, 77.
Mounce, Robert H, 249.
Mounce, William D, 248.
Moyise, Steve, 33–48.
Mulder, Martin Jan, 31.
Mullen, E Theodore, Jr, 285.
Mussies, G, 30.
Myers, Ched, 97.
Naden, Roy C, 249.
Neufeld, Don F, 131, 236, 261.
Neusner, Jacob, 68.
Newton, Thomas, 228, 229.
Nichol, Francis D, 75, 127, 128, 132, 137, 182, 183, 184, 185, 190, 193, 200, 249, 261, 262.
Nicole, Roger, 32.
Niebuhr, H Richard, 20.
Nielsen, Kirsten, 43.
Ninow, Friedbert, 58.
Noll, Stephen F, 247.

Nolland, John, 248.
Numbers, Ronald L, 231.
Nunnally, WE, 278, 279.
Oliver, Barry D, 84, 138, 125.
Olson, AV,
Olson, Robert W, 129, 135, 174, 190.
Oosterwal, Gottfried, 165.
Origen, 141, 144, 275, 276, 277, 278.
Osbourne, Grant R, 9.
Patrick, Arthur, 118, 121, 125, 126, 128, 236, 237, 252, 257.
Paulien, Jon, 31, 32, 187, 188, 192, 197, 249, 258, 263, 267.
Payne, J Barton, 54.
Peerman, Ernest Leslie, 33.
Pfandl, Gerhard, 125, 263.
Philo, 32,
Pinnock, Clark H, 15, 21, 22, 23, 87, 258.
Pippin, Tina, 33.
Plato, 275, 278.
Plimer, Ian, 18.
Pochler, Rolf J, 129, 130.
Poirier, Tim, 146.
Porter, JR, 48,
Porter, Stanley E, 48.
Porton, Gary G, 68.
Prescott, WW, 120, 129, 131, 198, 222, 223.
Prescott, WW, 198, 120, 129, 131, 222, 223.
Prigent, Pierre, 30, 33.
Pritchard, James B, 283.
Provence, Thomas E, 76.
Pryce, Bertrand C, 61.
Qumran, 32, 52, 65, 278, 279.
Rasmussen, Steen, 237.
Reid, George W, 264.
Reumann, John, 4.
Reventlow, Hennig Graf, 51.
Rice, George E, 12, 266.
Rice, Richard, 21, 82, 240, 252, 253,

254, 266.
Ricoeur, Paul, 44,
Robertson, AT, 201.
Robinson, H Wheeler, 48,
Roennfeldt, Ray CW, 22.
Rogerson, JW, 48,
Roloff, Jürgen, 33.
Rowe, David, 230, 231.
Ruiz, Jean-Pierre, 31.
Said, Edward, 99.
Sailhamer, John, 58.
Sakenfield, Katharine Doob, 84.
Schantz, Borge, 92.
Schnackenberg, Rudolf, 142.
Schurz, Carl, 138.
Schwartz, Richard, 130.
Schweizer, E, 77.
Selbie, William, 275, 276.
Shaull, R, 85.
Sheridan, Alan, 108, 110.
Shigley, Gordon, 128.
Shotter, John, 23.
Sire, James, 256,
Smith, D Moody, Jr,
Smith, Marion, 30.
Smith, S Marion, 57,
Smith, Uriah, 128, 132, 190,
Sobrino, Jon, 277.
Southard, N, 228,.
Southard, N, 228.
Spitz, LW Jr, 276.
Spivak, Gayatri Chakravorty, 40.
Spong, John Shelby, 18, 98.
Stagg, F, 33.
Standish, Colin, 120,
Standish, Russell, 126.
Stefanovic, Ranko, 249, 255, 258, 265, 267.
Stein, Robert H, 12, 142, 143.
Stewart-Sykes, Alistar
Stewart-Sykes, Alistar, 220, 221.
Stierlin, Henri, 29.

Stockhausen, Carol K, 72.
Stone, Ken, 98, 102.
Storr, George, 144.
Strand, Kenneth A, 265, 266.
Strong, Augustus, 150.
Stuart, Douglas, 17.
Stummer, F, 48.
Sugirtharajah, RS, 101, 103.
Sumer, 200, 279, 280 281, 282, 287.
Sumney, Jerry L, 71.
Sundberg, Walter, 4.
Swete, Henry B, 30, 33.
Tabachovitz, David, 30.
Tasker, RVG, 33.
Taylor, John B, 244, 246.
Taylor, Mark, 98, 108,
Tenney, Merrill C, 32.
Terry, Milton S, 54.
Tertullian, 150.
The Midnight Cry, 149, 227, 228.
Thiele, David H, 9, 256.
Thompson, Alden, 8, 19, 20, 23, 53, 119, 127, 129, 138, 165, 241, 242.
Thompson, Leonard, 31, 41,
Thompson, Marianne M, 279.
Thompson, Marianne Meye, 279.
Tigay, Jeffrey H, 282.
Timm, Alberto R, 227.
Tobey, Ronald C, 4.
Tolbert, MA, 100.
Torrey, Charles C,
Trench, Richard Trenevix, 30.
Trenchard, Warren C, 54.
Trudinger, L Paul, 30.
Tucker, Gene M, 48.
Turner, Max, 217.
Turner, Steven, 95.
Valentine, Gilbert M, 120.
Van Dolson, Leo, 23, 264, 241.
van Unnik, WC, 67, 76.
Vance, Laura L, 232.
Vanhoozer, KJ, 36, 40, 88.

Vanhoye, A, 30, 33.
Vanni, Ugo, 30.
Veltman, Fred, 123, 146, 147.
Vernus, Pascal, 283, 284.
Vogelgesang, Jeffrey Marhsall, 31.
Volz, P, 48
Waggoner, JH, 232, 233.
Weiser, Arthur, 288.
West, Gerald, 24.
Westenholz, Joan Goodnick, 282.
Wheeler, Gerald, 200.
Whidden, Woodrow W, 133.
White, Ellen, 12, 18, 53, 86, 90, 115, 117–139, 141–151, 153–169, 171–196, 197–224. 233, 234, 239, 240, 251, 252, 255, 260, 264, 266, 267, 269, 272, 273.
White, Willie, 197, 198.
Whybray, RN, 4.
Wieland, Robert J, 123.
Wirth, WG, 222.
Witherington III, Ben, 70, 212, 218, 220.
Wolfgramm, Robert, 124.
Wright, Charles HH, 277
Wright, Christopher JH, 246
Wright, G Ernest, 279
Wright, NT, 14, 36, 49, 68.
Wyatt, Musa, 285.
Yaron, Kalmon, 244.
Yost, Donald, 222.
Young, Norman H, 78, 85.
Zimmerli, Walther, 244.

Scriptural Index

Book	Chapter and Verse	Page
Genesis	1-3	244
	1-2	287
	1	242
	1:26-28	64
	3	241, 242
	6:1-8	128
	6:1-4	245, 250
	11	106
	15:7, 10	89, 90
	16:7-13	64
	18:1, 2, 33	64
	18:1, 8	82
	24:43	56
	29:15 ff	166
	31:11-13	64
	32:24, 30	64
	37, 39-50	24
	38	19-20, 166
	48:15-16	64
Exodus	1:15-2:10	46
	2:8	56
	3:2-7	64
	3:15	166
	4:22-23	46, 47, 287
	7:10-12	92
	14:10-31	46
	15	34
	20	11
	21:10	19
	21:17	19
	24:18	46
	33:18-20	288
	34	69, 70, 71, 74
	34:5-7	288
	34:28-35	46
Leviticus	18	103
	23:11	62
Numbers	6	60
	14:33-34	46
	23:22	58
	24:8, 14, 17	58
Deuteronomy		7
	4:8	19
	5	11
	6-8	58
	12:3	100
	13:1-5	206-207
	18:10-12	104
	23:3-6	103
	23:3	19
	25:5-10	166
	28:15-68	47
	32:3	288
	32:6	287-288
	32:8	106
	32:11	289
	32:21	288
	32:31-38	287
	34:26	19
Judges	3:14	103
	13:4-5	60
	13:17-22	64
Ruth		105-107, 114
	1:4, 14	99-103
	1:16-17	102
	3:15	112
	4:1-6	102
	4:9-10	112
	4:11	59
1 Samuel	18:16	166
	17:43	105
	18	105
	28:7-25	92

2 Samuel	6:12-14	166		80:17	64
	7:9	289		82	245
	7:10	289		85:10	113
	7:13	289		89:6-19	288
	7:14	287		89:15	289
	7:16	289		89:27 (26)	287
	8:2	100		89:47-51	290
	12:26-31	100		97:7	64
	13:1-22	106		102:25-27	
1 Kings	11:1-11	106		103:3	289
2 Kings	1-2	102		103:11-12	289
	1:2-8	99		103:13	287-288
	2:23-25	99		103:14	290
	4:27	206		103:19	289
	11	10		103:31-33	289-290
	14:25	62		109:8	64
	18:3-6	208		110:64	
	20:1-7	207		149:3	166
	24:18-25:30	201		150:3-5	166
1 Chronicles			Proverbs	3:1	290
	15:20	56		3:11-12	290
	17:1-4	206		3:12	287
	17:13	287-288		3:19-20	288
	17:14	289		4:18	260
	21:1	241		18:2	112
	22:10	287		30:5-6	113
	22:12-13	289		30:19	56
	28:6	287	Ecclesiastes		
	29:10	287		7:27-29	172
	29:11	288	Song of Solomon		
	29:18-19	289		1:1	113
Esther	3:13	112		1:3	56
Job	1-2	92-93		6:8	56
	1:2	241	Isaiah	7-12	61
Psalms	2	63		7:1-16	54-47
	2:6	287		8:1, 8, 18, 22	56
	8:3-8	64		8:1-4	57
	22	62-65		9:1-7	57
	22:1-11	114		9:5-6	63
	35:9	64		11:1-9	57
	40:6-8	64		11:1-5	63
	41:9	64		11:1	61
	46:2(1)	56		13:1-14:23	242
	68	289, 290		13:16	59
	68:6(5)	287-288		14:4	245
	68:8	288		14:12-15	242-247, 251, 253
	68:18	64			
	68:26(25)			24:21-22	245
	69:4	64		27:1	246
	74:14	246			

	53	245		28:12-19	242-47, 251, 253
	55:8-9	198		29:2-3	245
	63:16	287		34:23	63
	63:19	290		37:24	63
	64:8	287, 290	Daniel		7
	64:8-9	288		7:9-10	184
	64:11	290		7:13, 14	64
Jeremiah	2:2	290		7:13	174
	3:4	287		8-9	255-256, 266
	3:4-5	290		8	260
	3:19	287		8:11-13	266
	6:13-14	209		8:13	130
	14:14	104		8:14	260
	17:16	85		9:26	64
	18:7-10	207		9:27	266
	20:7-9	203		11	266
	23:5	63		11:31	266
	25:11, 12	60		11:45	64
	26:16-19	207		12:8-13	185
	28:9	206	Hosea	1-3	14, 15
	28:10-11	206		2:8-15	46
	29:3	198		3:5	63
	29:10	60		6:1-3	61
	30-33	60		7:11	61
	30:8-9	60		8:8	61
	31:7-9	289		11:1-7	44-46
	31:7-8	59		11:1	57-59, 287
	31:9	287-288, 290	Joel	2:28-32	174
	31:10-14	290	Amos	9:11	63
	31:15	59, 60	Jonah	1:17	61
	31:20	290		2	61, 62
	31:31-34	59	Micah	3:12	208
	33:14-15, 17	60		5:2	208
	36:4-6	201	Habbakuk	2:1-4	149
	40:1	59	Zechariah	3:1-2	341
	42:7	206		8:3	63
	51:64	201	Haggai	2:1-9	46
Ezekiel	9	176-177	Malachi	1:6	287
	9:2	177		2:10	287-288
	9:3	177		2:10-16	288
	9:11	177	Matthew	1:1-17	10
	12:21-25, 27-28	149		1:5	106
	12:24	104		1:18-25	46
	14:6	209		1:23	54-47
	17:12	245		2:1-12	204
	18:30	209		2:14-18	44-48
	19:9	245		2:15	57-59
	27	244		2:18	59-60
	27:33	245		2:23	60, 61
	28:2	245		3	58

	3:13-17	46		3:33	192
	4:1-11	240		4:16-20	39
	4:1-2	47		6:27	192
	4:5	46		7:17	22
	7:12	199		8:44	242, 247, 253
	7:15-23	210		8:58	64
	7:24-27	210		9:1-6	204
	8:20	47		9:6-12	204
	9:6	174		10:35	19
	9:18	12		11:49-52	213
	11:13	205		14:9	90
	11:20-30	182		15:25	64
	12:40	61, 62		16:12-15	211
	13:3, 34	80		16:13	24
	13:18-23, 36-43	142		17:15-18	167
	14:13-21	46		19:24	62
	17:1-8	46		19:28	47
	19:25	87		20:31	10
	22:41-46	64		21:25	10
	23:23	168	Acts	1:20	64
	24	91, 149, 266-267		1:21-22	215
	24:29	189, 204		2:16-21	174, 215
	24:42-51	182		2:17-18	211
	25:1-11	145-151		2:17-21	213
	27:34	64		4:12	18
	27:35	62		4:25	63
	27:35, 36	47		9:10	213
	27:39	62		10:17	203, 205
	27:43	62, 64		10:29	205
	27:66	192		10:34-35	203
Mark	1:32-34	240		11:27	214
	4:29, 31	47		11:28	215, 219
	5:22, 23, 25	12		13:1	214
	7:32-33	204		13:11	215
	8:22-23	204		15:28	219
	15:29	62		15:29	166
	15:34	62		15:32	215
Luke	1:46-55	213		17:10-11	114
	1:67-79	213		17:16-34	198
	2:25-35	213		17:26	106
	3:11-14	205		17:28	199
	8:40-42, 49	12		19:1-5	205
	9:31	47, 59		19:19	92
	10:17-18	247-248, 253		20:22	219
	16:19-31	21		20:23	215
	21:25	189		21	219
	21:33-36	182		21:10-11	202, 215, 220
	23:34	62		21:10-14	219
	23:35	64		21:30-33	202, 220
John	2:17	64		28:25-28	215

Scriptural Index

Romans		
1:1-7	200	
4:11	192	
12:6	201-202, 218	
15:3	64	
15:28	192	
16:16	165	
16:27	200	

1 Corinthians		
4:21	214	
8	24	
9:1	215	
9:2	192	
9:22-23	167	
10:1-2	58	
11:2-16	24	
11:23	214	
12-14	82	
12:3	210, 219	
12:10	217-219	
12:28	212	
12:29	211-213, 215	
13:4-7	219	
13:9-12	203	
13:9, 12	49	
14:1	211, 213	
14:3	213, 214, 219	
14:5	216	
14:11	215	
14:4, 31	210	
14:15	214	
14:29	216-219	
14:30,32	213	
14:36-38	212-213	
14:37	220	
15:4	62	
15:13-19, 29-32	10	
15:20, 23	62	
15:33	199	
15:51-55	220	
16:20	165	

2 Corinthians		
1:3-11	72	
1:12-2:4	72	
1:22	192	
1:23	72	
2:1	72	
2:5-11	72	
2:16	73	
3	67-78	
4:2, 3	76, 77	
4:7-12	72	
4:7	73, 204	
4:16-18	73	
5:1, 4	73	
5:7	49, 73	
5:12	73	
5:16-21	74	
10:10	72	
11:21b-30	72	
11:20	72	
11:23	105	
12:8-10	72	
13:12	165	

Galatians		
1:1	215	
1:11-12	215	
3:6-14	49	
3:24	131	
5:19	103	

Ephesians		
1:13	192-193	
2:20	212, 214	
3:5	212	
4:11-14	216	
4:8	64	
4:11	212	
4:12	93	
4:19	103	
4:30	192-192	
5:14	214	
5:19	214	
6:11-12	240	
6:12-16	93	

Philippians		
2:6-11	214	

Colossians		
1:15-20	214	
1:23	270	
2:18-23	172	
2:21	172, 174	

1 Thessalonians		
5:19-22	216-218	
5:20	214, 216	
5:26	166	

2 Thessalonians		
general	267	

1 Timothy		
1:20	214	
2:8, 11-15	84	
3:6	247-248, 251, 253	

	3:16-17	81-82	5:6-7	184
	3:16	214	5:7	173, 185
2 Timothy			5:8-14	173
	2:15	88	5:9	192
	2:19	192-193	5:9-10	185
	3:15-17	18, 198	5:9-14	183
	4:13	199	5:11	183
Titus	2:7-8	82	6:1-8	187
Hebrews	1:1-2	78, 89-90	6:1, 3, 5, 7, 9, 12	192
	1:2	11	6:8-11	186
	1:6	24	6:10, 12-13	188
	2:6-9	64	6:13	204
	2:12	62	6:14	189
	4:12-13	19	6:12-17	182
	5:5-11	64	7	176-177
	6:19-20	132	7:1-3	184, 188, 195
	7:11-27	64	7:9-17	182
	8:2	132	8:1	192
	9:24	132	8:1-4	186
	10:19-22	132	8:3-4	181
	10:5-9	64	8:3-5	189, 191-192
1 Peter	1:10-11	203, 205	8:5	177-179, 180
	1:25	18, 19	8:7-9:21	189
	2:9-10	211	9:4	189, 192-194
	5:8	240	9:15	191
	5:14	166	10:4	192
2 Peter	1:10	194	10:7	195, 196
	1:21	18	11:7	194
	1:19	260	11:13-18	122
	2:4	247, 249, 251, 253	11:17-18	189
			11:18	195
	3:2	215	11:19	180-181
	3:11-12	210	12:4	247-249, 251, 253
1 John	3:8	240	12:7-9	247-248, 253
	4:1-3	210	12:9	241, 249
2 John	9	82	12:10-13	248
Jude	3	216	12:11	185
	6	247, 249, 251, 253	13	175, 266
			13:13	268
Revelation			13:18	34
	1:4	30	15:3-4	33
	1:6	185, 212	16:17	177
	2:14	221	17:9	34
	2:20-23	221	19:10	203
	4-5	173, 183	20:3	192
	4-6	179	22:10	192
	4:5	180	22:11	177, 179
	5	181-185		
	5,1-2	192		
	5:5	192		

Lightning Source UK Ltd.
Milton Keynes UK
UKHW012247240122
397636UK00001B/112